THE PANIC OF 1893

The Untold Story of Washington State's First Depression

D1617238

BRUCE A. RAMSEY

Caxton Press

For Annie, Morgan and Helen

First Printing June 2018

The Panic of 1893
The Untold Story of Washington State's First Depression

ISBN# 978-087004-621-6
First Edition

Library of Congress Control Number: 2018946181
CIP Information available at http://lccn.loc.gov

Cover and book design by Jocelyn Robertson

Printed in the United States of America

CAXTON PRESS
Caldwell, Idaho
200736

Capitalist and laborer will look back upon 1893 as a year of blackness and despair. There were months when even the most courageous heart quailed, when men accustomed to dealing with hard situations lost faith in themselves... May such a year never, never come again.

—*Tacoma News,* Jan. 1, 1894

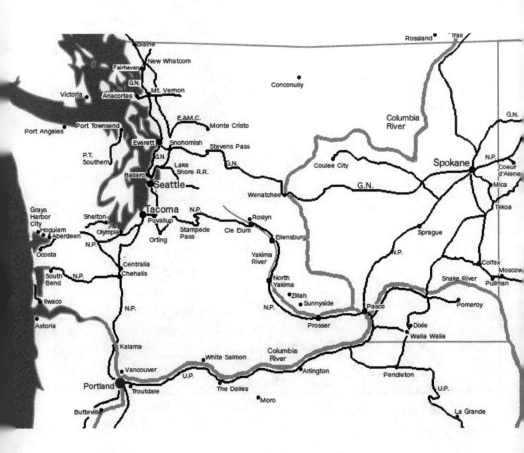

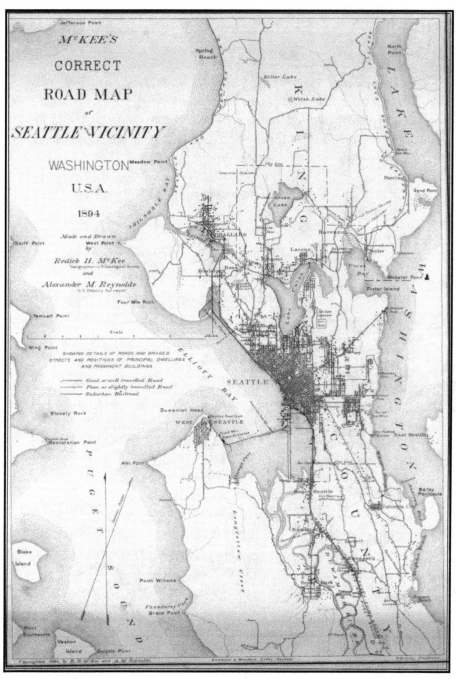

Seattle. *Courtesy of Kroll Map. Co., Seattle*

TABLE OF CONTENTS

Spokane, 1895. *Teakle Collection, Northwest Room, Spokane Public Library*

Tacoma, 1892. *Tacoma Public Library Image G17-1-074*

ACKNOWLEDGEMENTS

R esearch for this book took three years, principally in the Suzzallo Library at the University of Washington and the Tacoma Public Library's Northwest Room. Help also came from the professional staff of public libraries in Bellingham, Mount Vernon, Everett, Snohomish, Seattle, Aberdeen, Raymond, Vancouver, White Salmon, Ellensburg, Yakima, and Spokane; special collections at the University of Washington, Washington State University, and Whitman College; and from volunteers of historical societies at Okanogan, Vancouver, Bingen, South Bend, and Port Townsend. I had the help of the staff at Seattle city archives, Washington State Archives in Bellingham, Olympia, Ellensburg, and Cheney, the Seattle branch of the National Archives and National Archives at College Park, Maryland.

Special thanks to Lorraine McConaghy of Seattle's Museum of History and Industry for getting me started, to Pam McGaffin for advice, to Nettie Stanton, Mel Conner, Mark Funk and Morgan Ramsey for commenting on drafts, and to my wife, Anne, a former Citibanker, who edited the text with a toughness that rivals the best of newspaper editors.

—Bruce Ramsey

INTRODUCTION

Visiting Port Townsend in the 1920s, Oregon writer Stewart Holbrook found himself in a ghost town. It was "a fantastic sight, almost eerie. It was as if some movie outfit had erected not just a street of storefronts, but a whole city, block after block of sound buildings, complete with signs, and had then gone on to other things elsewhere, leaving the stupendous 'set' to the elements. One immense building of five stories stood up, scarred and soiled, like some late Victorian Acropolis, its scores of windows made sightless by boards..."

Port Townsend is now a National Historic District. Its 125-year-old buildings are a parade of red brick fossils, the wreckage of a commercial dream that died in a great depression people no longer know.

In 1931, when bread lines were forming for the depression they do know, Garet Garrett of the *Saturday Evening Post* observed that the men in the queues "may be hungry, but they are comfortably clothed." He recalled the depression of his youth, seeing "men in rags, with tied-on shoes, shivering with cold."

It began with the Panic of 1893. Wall Street crashed. Banks failed. Factories closed. Railroads fell into bankruptcy. Wheat sold for the lowest price in a hundred years. Money became so scarce that some communities made their own. Property owners had no cash to pay school taxes, and school districts had to pay teachers in IOUs. Cities and counties defaulted on their bonds.

Men and women were put to the test.

"Rich men sawed wood, picked blackberries and dug clams for a livelihood. Women with diamonds and valuable deeds resorted to kitchen labor to keep the larder replenished," wrote Herbert Hunt in *Tacoma: Its History and Its Builders* (1916). "Men who had ridden in carriages walked, though the empty streetcars, rattling in their poverty, would carry them for five cents."

A new political force, the People's Party, spread in the West and promised to free the people from the grasp of distant moneylenders. Workers rebelled against pay cuts. Tramps roved the land. Self-styled "armies" of workless men seized trains.

"The country was in the throes of hysteria," Hunt wrote. "Hatred soured every community. Those who had been rich, and especially the bankers, were held responsible for the cataclysm, and were threatened with personal violence."

Most of this drama has been forgotten. Libraries have shelves of books about pioneers and homesteaders, railroad builders, cowboys and bank robbers. The pioneers of the 19th century wrote accounts of drought and flood, ice and snow, wild animals and resistance from Native Americans. Their accounts tend to skim over the depression of 1890s in a paragraph.

This book aims to fill that void. It tells the story of the state of Washington in the depression of 1893-1897.

Most of this story is from the newspapers. I know newspapers; my 37-year career was mostly in Seattle newspapers as a reporter and columnist on the business and editorial pages, and as a reviewer of history books. To research this book, I spent three years reading old newspapers and selecting the best of what I found. A good news story has a freshness missing from academic work. A good editorial reveals the beliefs, prejudices, sentiments and practices of the time. To quote it directly, to listen to the logic and cadences of a newspaper editorial, is to immerse oneself in another time.

I have also used contemporary court cases, personal papers, and the correspondence between national-bank receivers and the comptroller's office in Washington, D.C. Among secondary sources, I have tended to favor the older over the newer. My aim has been to present the 1890s as people experienced them and wrote about them, mostly in chronological order.[1]

The economists list the depression of the 1890s as the second worst in U.S. history. It comes in second to the 1930s because in percentage terms, output and employment did not fall as far. But in the 1890s, Americans had less wealth to begin with. In absolute terms, the point to which the conditions of life fell was lower in the 1890s, and the suffering deeper. Also, unlike the 1930s, the depression of the 1890s came on suddenly, within weeks of the stock market crash, in a series of shocking collapses.

In the 1890s, America was on the gold standard. Gold was an international currency that made the economic world of the 1890s more globalized than it would be for another century.

The trigger that set off the Panic of 1893 was a payments crisis caused by foreign investors selling U.S. investments and taking gold out of America. This prompted a massive rush to sell assets and collect debts. The deeper cause of the panic was excessive risk-taking, poor banking practices and overuse of debt, which in the American West flowed from the illusions of men opening a new land. Trust in institutions, once lost, took a long time to regain.

American popular culture remembers the 1930s because it is more recent, and for a political reason. The 1930s brought about a revolution in government. The federal government undertook to take care of the people—through control of farmers, regulation of financial markets, a managed paper-money system, make-work programs, welfare, unemployment insurance and old-age pensions. It undertook to jump-start private investment, first with domestic spending, then with war spending. The "great" depression is part of the growing-up story of the modern state.

The 1890s was the time of *laissez-faire*. The federal government took no responsibility for unemployment, or even tried to measure it. It did not pump up spending or the money supply. It did not bail out manufacturers or banks. It did not give destitute people food, shelter, or medicine, though in Washington state local authorities did. The story of the 1890s can be viewed as a case study of what happens when the government doesn't do what it did in the 1930s.

Business recovered, and somewhat sooner than in the 1930s. Trade was one of the ways out: unlike the 1930s, in the 1890s Congress cut tariffs. For Washington state, the opportunity was in trade with Asia. Investors from Europe had triggered the depression and customers in Asia aided the recovery from it.

Recovery was still prolonged and painful. The Americans of the 1890s accepted losses and suffering people would not today.

Both the 1890s and the 1930s brought on a swirl of social and political ideas utterly unlike that of normal times. In the 1930s, the radical attractions were socialism and communism; in the 1890s it was Populism. From today's view it is easy to see Populism as left-progressive, which in part it was. But in its glorification of the farmer, its resentment of immigrants, and its hostility toward lenders and debt, it was conservative, even reactionary. If this account is not too favorable to the Populists, neither were the people of the 1890s once the depression began to fade.

The Populists blamed the gold standard for causing the depression. A battle was fought over whether the dollar should be backed by gold, by silver, by both of them at the same time—bimetallism—or merely by law; and whether America should act in the matter alone. When it came to it, America did act alone: it chose to keep the gold standard. Unlike some other decisions in U.S. history, which were made by powerful men, the monetary question was settled by a vote of the people. That election, in 1896, was the most momentous contest since the Civil War.

"Think of it," wrote the *Seattle Times* in 1895. "Fourteen millions of voters are studying an abstract and extremely difficult problem in finance, with the view of acting upon it. There never was anything like this before in the history of the world."

It was a rich debate, but the political unrest unnerved investors and prolonged the depression.

The depressions of the 1890s and the 1930s each had its march on Washington, D.C., demanding relief. The one in 1894—Coxey's Army—was the first, and more clearly associated with a set of political ideas than was the Bonus March of 1932. Each depression also had its labor battles. The big one of the 1890s, the Pullman strike of 1894, covered the entire American West, and was one of the great disasters of labor history.

These events were felt deeply in the state of Washington. Coxey's Army began in Ohio, but it recruited more men on the West Coast. When the Pullman strike shut down the Northern Pacific Railroad, it hammered the city at the western end of the line, Tacoma.

The 1930s are remembered for bank failures—partly because of the movie, *It's a Wonderful Life*—but in Washington a higher proportion of banks failed in the 1890s. Much of this book is about bank failures—which ones failed, when, why, and what happened to the bank officers and the depositors. There was no deposit insurance. Bank failures immediately shrank the amount of money in a community. Capital contracted and business shut down. Bank panics were the shockwaves that plunged town after town into a stunned quietude.

In the 1890s, national banks were lightly regulated from Washington, D.C., and inspected by federal bank examiners once a year. Washington state had no regulator to inspect state banks, savings banks, and private banks. In any case, the inspections were not enough. All kinds of banks failed in large numbers, revealing the inexperience, hubris, recklessness, and self-dealing of bankers. Failed banks were handed to government-appointed receivers, who liquidated the assets in a collapsed market.

Bank failures were not spread evenly. In Seattle eight banks eventually failed; in Tacoma, 12 did. There was a similar difference regarding municipal debt. Tacoma and Seattle both had a high level of debt, and both were shut out of the bond market for years. Tacoma's debt was relatively greater, and the choices it made regarding it were different.

The decisions made by company men and public officials, voters collectively and individuals on their own account, all mattered. An economy is not a mechanism. It is people. People created the Panic, and they got themselves out of it—eventually.

In researching the main story, others came to light. This account also answers such questions as the origin of irrigation in the Yakima Valley, and of the Lake Washington Canal; how Labor Day got started, how Washington's dairy and apple industries began, and why Seattle and not Tacoma is largest city on Puget Sound. Things happen for reasons, and it is the task of history, to say what they are.[2]

People ask me whether I will draw lessons for today from the experience of the 1890s. There are some, but that is not the main purpose of this book. It is *about* the 1890s. The people who lived through those times learned from them, and it influenced what they did in the 1930s, and it influences us today. Washington's economy today has a character, particularly in its orientation toward international trade, shaped 120 years ago.

It was a different time. The Civil War had ended 30 years before. The Wild West had come to an end and the gold rush to the Yukon was ramping up. On the waterfront, steamships were beginning to push aside sailing ships. There were as yet no airplanes or automobiles but people were using bicycles and electric streetcars. Telephones were new; during 1893 the first line was opened connecting Seattle, Portland, and Spokane. The media of the day was the daily newspaper, the primary source for this book.

Washington was a new state, barely four years old. Its 1890 population, 357,232, was less than one-twentieth of today's. Civilization was thinner and the land wilder. In Seattle, a man could go duck hunting on Lake Union. Law, too, was new and uncertain; bankers could lend to themselves in ways that later generations would define as embezzlement. Men could avoid legal punishment by fleeing the state, though if their crime was violent and personal enough, and they were in a rural area, they might be lynched.

Children grew up sooner. In the King County schools around Seattle, half the pupils in the sixth grade dropped out by the end of the seventh, and only one in four made it to graduation. Youth went to work earlier, married earlier, and started families—big families—earlier. A man might be a bank president at 30, starting a new business in a new land.

Males made up 62 percent of the state population and conducted most business and public affairs. Women worked in subordinate positions in enterprises and at home. Unlike women of an earlier era, women of the 1890s could own property and conduct business. They would not have the full vote until 1910 but in the stories of the 1890s you can sense the issue ripening. Already in the 1890s women could vote in school elections, which sometimes involved wider issues of religious discrimination or public finance.

Almost one-quarter of the population was foreign-born. The *Spokane Chronicle* reassured its readers that most of them were from Northern Europe. "Even including the 4,000 Chinamen," it said, less than 3 percent of the people came from countries "experts have

10

branded 'undesirable'." Racism was ubiquitous. At the bottom of the social order were the Native Americans, mainly a rural people. Among urban people the Chinese suffered most. To the extent they were defended in the press it was usually by pro-business voices that wanted trade with Asia.

The 1890s was a world of physical risks. People died of tuberculosis, typhoid, and scarlet fever as well as heart attack and stroke. People were maimed or killed regularly in accidents involving horses and wagons, railroads, streetcars, electric wires, boats, swimming, logs, farm equipment, guns, and wood-burning stoves. On one day in June 1893, the *Seattle Telegraph* reported four industrial injuries: a shingle worker with his thumb torn off, a lumber worker with the tip of a finger cut off, another with his thumb and finger cut off, and a miner with his leg crushed between two ore cars. In August 1893, the *Spokane Chronicle* carried the story of the death of George Maxwell, 29, a lumber-mill worker called to splice a loose belt. "His cotton blouse was unbuttoned and blew open as he ran across the basement and stooped down to pass under an iron shaft that whirls about 225 times a minute," the paper reported. "The loose corner of the blouse caught on a coupling." Co-workers heard a cry of terror and "a terrible noise of pounding on the floor."

In such a harsh world, people took economic risk in stride. Civil War veterans (Union soldiers only) had old-age pensions, but almost no one else did. Governments were smaller, and apart from the railroads, there were few big corporations. More people were farmers or otherwise self-employed. Men were expected to make their own way, and mostly they did. They had a pioneer spirit, opening up a new state and seizing once-in-a-lifetime opportunities. *The Panic of 1893* describes the backwash of a fabulous boom in which men and women took extraordinary risks.

The 1890s was a moralized time. Here is an example: In 1893, an Oregon man was reported tramping across country with his six-year-old son and eight-year-old daughter. A newspaper editorial writer of today might think such a man a poor father, but would never "blame the victim" in print. He would name the social forces that had put the man in that position, and condemn the state for failing to help him. Back then, people assumed that a man was responsible for the position he was in. The Pacific Northwest's principal newspaper, the Portland *Oregonian*, squarely blamed the father—and also the absent mother, who was "such a poor judge of men" as to choose him for a husband.

The beliefs of the 1890s resonate in their words. When a businessman couldn't pay his bills, he was "embarrassed," a word that has a moral flavor lacking in "cash-flow problem." We speak of an "economy" as a mechanism that can be adjusted by regulators and central bankers. To the people of the 1890s, economic movements were like the weather. To them, "economy" meant careful spending; the term "*the* economy" was not used at all. They might say, "business conditions" or simply, "times." The word "unemployed" was used, but the more common word was "idle." To be unemployed is passive; one is employed *by* someone. "Idle" has no such implication. What does an idle man need? Today we would say he needs a job. Back then they would say he needs *work*.

"Homeless," today's word, suggests a problem to be solved by the provision of homes. I noted "homeless" used in 1893 to describe people whose houses had been wrecked by a storm and in 1894 for children, but it was rarely used to describe men who had no money for a roof over their heads. Such men were "paupers" who were "penniless" and "destitute." A person wandering the country and riding in boxcars was a "vagabond," a "hobo" or a "tramp;" if he was begging in town he was a "vagrant." Help for the penniless was called "charity" and "alms," though most of the time it was not intended for the "shiftless." In the 1890s there was no embarrassment about such words, which today are rarely used.

For us, "depression" is a word that has been set aside as altogether too harsh, and even its softer cousin, "recession," stings the ears. But 120 years ago, the word "recession" hadn't been invented. "Depression" was the genteel word. The common term was "hard times."[3]

ILLUSIONS (1889-1893)

It is July 4, 1893. Independence Day festivities in Seattle begin with a roar from the *USS Monterey's* 12-inch guns. The *Monterey* is a larger version of the *Monitor*, the Civil War ironclad. The *Monterey's* deck is supposed to be only 2.3 feet above the water line, but it is riding a foot higher this day because the armor on the barbettes and its two turrets is made of wood, standing in for the steel armor not yet installed.

Viewed materially, Seattle's grand Fourth of July celebration is a false front, like the *Monterey's* wooden armor. In the summer of 1893, America's commercial life is in agony. Ventures are failing and men are losing work. In the midst of a business crisis a prudent people would not drain away their capital on fireworks and flags—but the people of Seattle are not entirely prudent. The profit is spiritual.

It is a time of demonstrative patriotism. The Civil War veterans are growing old and sentimental. Immigrants, many of them from Southern Europe and even Asia, are moving in, and a feeling rises that the American identity needs new steel.

To the crowd, a Protestant reverend offers a benediction, a judge intones the Declaration of Independence, and a senator expounds on the meaning of America. A band plays patriotic marches. Sailors dressed in white and blue take on longshoremen in a tug of war. Soldiers parade, followed by a troop of cavalry and men on bicycles. Teams of horses pull commercial floats. Seattle's proud business houses are hung with red-white-and-blue bunting, streamers, and flags.

At Pioneer Square, men have erected a pavilion of wood and brick decorated with woven cedar baskets. Called the Industrial Palace, it exhibits local coal, lumber, shingles, iron ore, hops, preserved fish, live oysters, and even tobacco. On its side, strings of incandescent bulbs form an image of a locomotive that glows as night falls. One man's name is spelled in red lights: *"J.J. Hill."*

U.S. NAVY OFFICIAL PHOTOGRAPH

USS Monterey. *Wikipedia*

James Jerome Hill has just brought the Great Northern Railway over Stevens Pass. It is a new kind of American transcontinental: a business road, built with private capital, much of it from London, with no cash subsidy or land grants from the U.S. government. Hill's engineers have calculated grades and curves with the aim of keeping the cost per mile below that of their subsidized competitors, the Union Pacific and the Northern Pacific. Hill also hasn't overloaded his road with debt.

Hill's road has made Seattle its Pacific terminus. Already, three nearby cities are endpoints of transcontinental lines: Vancouver, B.C., of the Canadian Pacific; Portland, of the Union Pacific; and Tacoma, of the Northern Pacific. Tacoma is Seattle's closest rival. Its salt-water harbor, the *Tacoma Ledger* boasts, is deep and wide enough for "ships of any size now made, or ever likely to be made" and has "absolute immunity from storms." Seattle has a harbor much the same, and with the Great Northern, says the *Seattle Telegraph*, the Queen City "will have an equal chance in the race for commercial ascendancy."

Hill intends not just to take some of the region's commerce, but to expand it. His rate to haul fir lumber east to St. Paul is 40 cents per 100 pounds—less than half the old Northern Pacific rate, which was too high to move common lumber. Historian Clarence Bagley will write that the 40-cent rate is "two-fifths of a cent per ton-mile, the lowest rate ever given in the world under anything like the same conditions."

James J. Hill. *Seattle Post-Intelligencer,* *11-15-97*

The 40-cent rate opens up the Midwest to the sawmills of Washington. Says the *Aberdeen Herald,* "It makes it possible for every sawmill now built, or that may be built, along the line of any of these roads to run at full capacity all the year round at a profit."

This statement is no illusion. James Hill and his railroad will be crucial for Washington and particularly for Seattle in the coming hard times and the resurgence that follows. But on July 4, 1893, Hill and his 300 guests are not in Seattle to see his name in lights. There has been a panic on Wall Street. The visions of growth—the true ones and the false ones—have faded.[4]

Recalling the period before the hard times, the *Seattle Post-Intelligencer* will later write, "For six years this enormous inflation went on. In frantic rivalry, courthouses, city halls, streetcar lines, waterworks, electric lighting plants were rushed up; the building and purchase too often being fostered by contractors and engineered by councils whose members had secured their election for the purpose of putting through just such plans. Debts had no terror, bonds scarcely a limit. The future was recklessly drawn upon."

The growth has been fabulous, with little inkling of the disaster ahead.

15

Seattle was incorporated in 1865, and by 1880 was still a village barely larger than Walla Walla. By 1890 it is among America's top 100 cities, having grown in the 1880s third-fastest among them, by more than 1,000 percent. By 1893 the Polk city-directory company estimates Seattle's population at 62,960, largest in the state and two-thirds the size of Portland, the region's predominant city. Seattle's wooden downtown, destroyed by fire in 1889, has been rebuilt in brick and stone. The "Queen City" has room to grow: mudflats to the south to be filled in for railroad yards and a hill to the north to be sluiced into Elliott Bay.

Seattle has the asset of position. It is on the eastern shore of Puget Sound, where the railroads will come. It has a large deep-water bay protected from storms and a deep and unobstructed channel to the ocean. It is also centrally located on the Sound, making it the natural center for a "mosquito fleet" of ferries. It is directly west of Snoqualmie Pass in the Cascades.

Seattle has something else: "the Seattle spirit." Half a century later, Stewart Holbrook will say: "Seattle is *the* metropolis of the Northwest. It did not become so simply because of favorable location... Seattle outdistanced all its rivals largely because of the single-mindedness of a large majority of its citizens..."

Incorporated in 1875, a decade after Seattle, Tacoma was the first of the two to have a transcontinental railroad. By 1893 the "City of Destiny" has been the terminus of the Northern Pacific for six years. Like Seattle, Tacoma sits on the shore of an inland sea. It is the only city on the Sound with regular steamship service to South America, Australia, and Asia, exporting wheat, lumber, coal, refined metals, and canned salmon and importing tea, sugar, and silk.

Tacoma's population has exploded even faster than Seattle's, making it the *second*-fastest growing (after Duluth) among the top 100 American cities. By 1893 Tacoma's population has swollen to 52,329—63 percent male, half foreign-born, many of them single men who, according to a Tacoma Chamber of Commerce report, are "almost wholly strangers to one another," and have been "separated from the restraining influences of old and familiar associations." By 1893 Tacoma has had two years of quieter growth, but it remains a challenger to Seattle for dominance on the Sound.

With an eye to a big future, Tacoma is building a three-story Pierce County courthouse and jail and a five-story city hall, with high ceilings, classic columns and a 190-foot clock tower. An Oregon observer calls Tacoma's city hall "the most magnificent north of San Francisco." Investors are putting up commercial buildings. The city is buying out the water works and electric company—a decision that will backfire, but seems right at the time. It is about to lay down fir-block pavement to replace the broken wooden planking on Pacific Avenue.

Two years later the *Ledger* will admit that Tacoma got ahead of itself: "A city hall and a courthouse were built when we did not really need them, [and] streets were opened and improved far ahead of the demand for them." The *Ledger* will regret that Tacoma burned through its credit to buy these things. But when cities bid for supremacy, this is what they do. "We can no longer be ignored," proclaims the *Tacoma News* in 1893. "We have become Seattle's greatest rival, the one city in the Northwest she has to fear."

This is as close as Tacoma will get to overtaking Seattle. Tacoma's response to the Panic will not be as strong as Seattle's.

East of the mountains, the pioneer town of Walla Walla has been eclipsed by another newcomer: Spokane. Incorporated in 1881, Spokane swells in the 1880s in the silver rush to Idaho's Coeur d'Alene country. Unlike the Puget Sound cities, Spokane is a town that in the territory *tributary* to it—a word much used in the 1890s—has no rival. Spokane is on the main line of the Great Northern *and* the Northern Pacific and also spurs of the Union Pacific and the Canadian Pacific. Eastern Washington's principal city is building an "Inland Empire" reaching into northern Idaho and southern British Columbia.

Spokane also has the 130-foot waterfall of the Spokane River. The city's hydropower has already made it one of the best-lighted towns in the West, and barely 5 percent of the potential is used.

Like Seattle, Spokane's wooden downtown was destroyed in 1889 by fire. It has also been rebuilt; in 1892, investors pour more than $1 million into new buildings, borrowing heavily to do so. "The array of fine hotels, office buildings, banks, factories, etc., now seen on all the principal streets, astonishes the visitor," writes an Easterner. "These buildings are of stone, granite or brick, many of them six, seven and more stories high." Most of this work is in anticipation. "Miles of streets in the suburbs have been graded and sidewalked, that are scarcely ever used," the *Chronicle* will admit in the coming hard times. "Double as many bridges have been constructed as needed for public convenience; treble as many officers and employees as were necessary for the conduct of public business."[5]

Not every town with big dreams is still hopeful.

In the spring of 1889 men from St. Paul lay out a city for more than 10,000 on the northern shore of Grays Harbor, three miles west of Hoquiam. They bill it as an international port, the Pacific terminus of the railroad that will connect to the Northern Pacific at Centralia.

On a map it seems logical that the great port of the Pacific Northwest should be on the ocean, not hidden behind the Olympic Peninsula on Puget Sound. Grays Harbor is, however, not as deep as Puget Sound, and the largest ships of the 1890s have trouble entering it. In addition, the site chosen for Grays Harbor City is separated from the navigable channel by a large mud flat. No problem: In July 1889 the promoters begin selling lots, $500 and up, and with the buyers' money they build a mile-and-a-quarter-long wharf. Some of the town site promotions during this period are scams from the start. At Grays Harbor City, the promoters believe their own illusions.

The railroad that is supposed to connect Grays Harbor City never comes. Its builder, George Washington Hunt, pushes his roadbed one-third the way from Centralia and runs out of cash. In February 1891, when he is in New York trying to sell bonds, the Northern Pacific attaches his property over a $140,000 debt and sinks him. Hunt's bonds don't sell. His project collapses. The Northern Pacific comes to Grays Harbor but not to Grays Harbor City. The town's 250 residents move out.

"There are upwards of 100 buildings there, but they are all deserted," says a report in the *Oregonian*. "Some of the deserted buildings are handsome structures, one business block having cost upwards of $20,000. The halls and rooms of this block have the appearance of being left while the occupants had just stepped out to lunch, while as a matter of fact the place has been abandoned for upwards of a year."[6]

Most of the boomtowns are still alive. For the people in them, the first years of statehood have been a time of wonder.

In May 1890, real-estate men entrusted with money from England come to South Bend, a rain-drenched village of 876 souls that will incorporate as a town four months later. The investors pay $80,000 for a 90-acre tongue of low-lying land directly across the Willapa River from the town. Years later, the *South Bend Journal* will call this "about the biggest deal ever consummated in the history of the South Bend real estate boom." The Northern Pacific is building a rail line to South Bend, though unfortunately not to the investors' side of the river. Says a real estate ad in the *Tacoma News*: "The railroad from South Bend to Chehalis... will soon be extended easterly through the Cowlitz Pass to North Yakima. With this line completed, South Bend has a shorter and more direct route from the seaboard to the East by sixty hours and three hundred miles, than has Tacoma or Seattle."

South Bend, says the ad, has "the only deep water harbor between San Francisco and the Straits of Fuca," and "is undoubtedly destined to be the Great Seaport of the Northwest."

Envisioning South Bend as the "Baltimore of the Pacific," investors erect a grand inn, the 87-room Willapa Hotel, three stories high with a central tower 85 feet tall, overlooking the Willapa River. It was supposed to cost $25,000, but the investors decide to line the lobby with eastern oak. They bring in German craftsmen to carve an ornate mantel. The hotel costs them more than $100,000.

Actually, South Bend's natural harbor, Willapa Bay, has just been renamed. Its old name was Shoalwater Bay, for its shallow water and mud flats. It is not a good place for a port.

On Puget Sound, Port Townsend, incorporated in 1851, does have a fine harbor for sailing ships. It is only one day's sail from the Pacific and its bottom is not too deep for anchors. (Seattle's and Tacoma's harbors are deep.) Port Townsend also has the U.S. Customs House, so that all of Puget Sound's ships in foreign trade must stop there. The *Townsend Leader* declares its city "the natural and undisputed headquarters of all shipping on Puget Sound." But if Port Townsend is to "aspire to commercial importance and industrial greatness," which the *Leader* says it does, it needs to be connected to the railroads coming from the East—and for that, Port Townsend has been built on the wrong side of Puget Sound.

In 1890, the Oregon Improvement Co., an offshoot of the Northern Pacific, sets out to build a railroad from Port Townsend to a connection south of Olympia. In anticipation of Port Townsend as a major seaport, landowners sell town lots at high prices and sink the money into brick buildings along Water Street and fine houses on the hill. "Everyone here was making money. Everyone here was happy," *Leader* editor J. Will Lyons will recall a few years later. "All felt certain that prosperity had come to stay"—but the railroad will never be completed.

Across Puget Sound on the northern side of Fidalgo Island, the new town of Anacortes is on the *right* side of Puget Sound. It already has a rail connection, but boosters dream of it having its own crossing of the Cascades, up the Skagit River, and out through the Methow Valley. The town convinces itself it has the best location of all the Sound cities. Anacortes is "destined by nature," declares the *Anacortes Progress,* "to be a great and important city."

From August 1889 to April 1890, Anacortes is transformed from a wilderness into an excitement of 10 hotels, 20 lodging houses, 21 saloons, and 40 land-sales offices. People are living in 72 "dwellings"—a word artfully selected to include shacks—and 83 tents. Anacortes is "a town crystallized," waxes the editor, "just like that wonder of nature, the mineral from a solution."

Values of town lots float up, up, up, like cinders above a fire. Then they fall. The speculators flee. The people who stay behind build real houses, and the four-story, brick-and-stone Hotel Anacortes. In 1891 they incorporate their town. They issue municipal debt. Investors build a 13-mile electric streetcar line.

Twenty miles south of the Canadian border on Bellingham Bay, Fairhaven, incorporated in 1890, follows a similar trajectory. Anticipating the arrival of the Great Northern, it attracts 8,000 boomers, many from California and the East—men, recalls one writer half a decade later, "letting their money go with open hands."

Everett Nail Works. *Seattle Post-Intelligencer, 8-16-96*

Investors put up factories, sawmills and a fine hotel expecting "that in five years more their city would be a metropolis." The Great Northern comes, but Fairhaven is not its terminus. The boom dies.

Puget Sound's newest city, Everett, is incorporated in 1893. It begins life with the grandest inheritance. Along with the usual lumber and shingle mills, it is born with a shipyard, a nail mill, a paper mill, and a smelter, built with money from oil tycoon John D. Rockefeller. The intention, says Henry Hewitt Jr., president of the Everett Land Co., is to offer manufacturers a city, unlike Seattle or Tacoma, "free from heavy municipal debt." Located right where James J. Hill's railroad is destined to hit tidewater, Everett stakes out a claim as the Great Northern's Pacific terminus. Visiting there in the summer of 1892, when brick buildings costing $350,000 are being built, lumberman Cyrus Walker writes a business associate (with some exaggeration) that the Everett Land Co. is "laying out a town large enough for a million people."[7]

In 1892, more railroad tracks are laid in Washington—421 miles of main line—than in any other state. By January 1893, the Great Northern's roadbed is completed. In the next two years, railroad building in Washington will shrink by 98 percent.

Excesses are everywhere. "There was a wave of immigration, a buoyant, speculative, adventuresome feeling," recalls New Whatcom's *Reveille*. "Everybody was credulous." Says the *Seattle Telegraph*, "Everybody's head was full of all manner of exaggerated notions about everything." In his 1916 history of Tacoma, Herbert Hunt remembers 1889-90 as a time of "beauteous expectation" and "fatal ecstasy."

"Bonds were issued recklessly," recalls the *Tacoma News*. "Mortgages flowed like a river."

"During our boom days," says the *Reveille*, "we were looking forward to railroads, mills, mines, roads, opened farms, planked streets, electric lights, streetcars, water works, sewers, and the comforts of civilization." Now, the paper says, "We have all these things."

But not paid for. The new towns have been built on credit, most of it from the East, some of it from across the Atlantic, lured to the frontier by 10-percent interest rates. Local men have bought bank stocks and land with promissory notes, their I.O.U.s taken as cash. "Everything was done in a rush and without due precaution," recalls the *Spokane Chronicle*.

After the Panic, the editors of the *Oregonian* will explain the disaster this way: during the boom there has been a considerable "absorption of money, or the energy represented by money, in unproductive undertaking." When these undertakings don't pan out, "the money spent by the settlers, lent them by Eastern capitalists, their labor and their other debts for supplies will be so much lost capital, as much as if it had been thrown into the sea." Really it is people's energy that has been spent, and when they realize that their assets have shrunk but their debts have not, there follows "a season of depression, during which energy is slowly recuperated."

But this is hindsight, the explanation of a disaster the newspapers did not see coming. New Year's Day 1893 is still in a time of illusions. "The financial storms which have lowered upon the entire world for the past two years seem to have exhausted their fury," opines the *Spokane Review*. "The coming year... will certainly prove one of the most, if not the most, prosperous year that has ever passed over the head of this bright, progressive, hopeful, resourceful young city."

The *Tacoma Ledger* hails 1893 as the beginning "of such progress as no state or city has ever before known."

The signal is about to turn from yellow to red.[8]

PANIC (1893)

The match that lights the fires of panic is a rush to exchange paper money for gold.

In 1893, the United States has been on a gold standard for 14 years. One-third of U.S. currency, by value, is gold coin, chiefly $5, $10, and $20 gold pieces. On the Pacific Coast, "paper circulates but little," writes the *Seattle Press-Times*. "Silver is the coin which is in the pockets of the people and the tills of the stores, while gold, as a general rule, remains largely in the banks." In the East, people use several kinds of paper money: Gold Certificates, Silver Certificates, United States Notes and National Currency. Only Gold Certificates are explicitly exchangeable into gold, but all are declared to be worth the value printed on them. To maintain the people's confidence that they can have gold if they want it, the Treasury aims to keep at least $100 million of it on hand.

Since the beginning of the gold era, the U.S. Mint has been coining silver dollars. In 1890, to further placate Western silver-mining interests, Congress passes the Sherman Silver Purchase Act. It directs the Treasury to buy most of U.S. silver output with a new kind of paper money called Treasury Notes. The new law creates $50 million in paper money each year. Foreign investors are uneasy; they worry that the Americans are printing too much paper relative to gold. When Republican President Benjamin Harrison signed the bill in 1890, the Treasury's gold reserve was at a comfortable $190 million. By March 1893, when Grover Cleveland is inaugurated, it has dwindled to $101 million. The first Democratic president since the Civil War begins his second (non-consecutive) term with a gold-payments crisis.

To stop the excessive issues of Treasury Notes, bankers call for the repeal of the Sherman Silver Purchase Act, so that the Treasury will have to stop buying silver. Silver plunges. In the Coeur d'Alene district of northern Idaho, the big Bunker Hill and Sullivan silver-lead mine shuts down. Two small Idaho banks fail on April 7, 1893: the Coeur d'Alene Bank, in Wallace, and the Bank of Wardner.

Bank failures are also happening in Australia. On April 7, 1893, the *Spokane Chronicle* reports the failure of the Commercial Bank of Australia, which has branches in London, Edinburgh, and Glasgow. British capital has financed an Australian real-estate boom, and the boom has collapsed.

Under the common currency of gold, a crisis in one country is felt by all. The Australian crash raises the demand for gold to pay old debts. Money is diverted from new commitments. Investor psychology shifts.

On April 19 the *Spokane Chronicle* reports a "run" of depositors demanding their money at a savings bank in Michigan. The bank beats the run by invoking the emergency power of savings banks to make depositors wait three months. The exercise of this power is another nick in the edifice of confidence, especially when the Michigan savings bank fails anyway, eight days later.

On April 21, the *Chronicle* prints a column by Wall Street prognosticator Henry Clews. The established stocks of the day are the railroad shares; Wall Street, Clews says, is worrying about the newfangled stocks called the industrial trusts, which are highly leveraged. Wall Street also worries about the bank failures in Australia and the recent break in the price of wheat, which is sold abroad and brings gold into the country. Clews writes, "There is a sort of uncontrollable confusion of cause and effect, which begets indefinite apprehensions."

The apprehensions take a few days to define themselves.

On April 22, the Treasury's gold reserve sinks below $100 million. Nothing happens. President Cleveland says there is no crisis. The government will pay its debts in gold, and there is nothing to worry about. A week goes by and newspapers write about other things.

On April 30, the government of Australia's most populous colony, Victoria, closes the banks there for five days. In Chicago, President Cleveland visits the World's Fair. In Moscow, Idaho, the largest grain dealer in the region goes bust because of the plunge in the price of wheat. The head of the company is William Mc-Connell, Idaho's governor, who is minding neither his store nor his state. He is off in Ogden, Utah, getting elected chairman of the Trans-Mississippi Congress, a group of Western states.[9]

On May 4, 1893, Wall Street panics. The *Chronicle* writes: "Crowds gathered around the trading posts of the active stocks, swung their arms, and yelled themselves hoarse in an attempt to sell. Brokers' messengers ran as if Satan was after them."

The panic is deepest in the industrial trusts, as Henry Clews foresaw. At the vortex is National Cordage, a New Jersey-based rope-and-twine trust set up to mimic John D. Rockefeller's Standard Oil Trust. Over the years, Rockefeller has bought out small oil refineries, closed them and built bigger, more efficient ones; he has laid pipeline, which is more efficient than carrying oil in wagons; he has secured freight rebates from railroads and set up national distribution of kerosene in standard blue cans. By doing these things, he is able to make himself the richest man in America while *lowering* the price of kerosene. It is an inspired formula—in petroleum. It does not work in rope and twine.

Using borrowed money, Cordage buys up rival producers, paying higher and higher prices to gain a 90 percent U.S. market share. This is about what Rockefeller has in his industry, but Cordage cannot lower costs the way Rockefeller did in oil. It cannot raise prices because its former rivals will get back in the rope and twine business, which they are doing anyway. By early 1893, Cordage is borrowing money to keep rope and twine off the market.

After the stock exchange closes May 4, Cordage files for receivership, turning itself over to a court-appointed bankruptcy trustee. Its action throws into doubt cartels in sugar, linseed oil, and whiskey. Distrust of trusts spreads through Wall Street. On May 5, traders panic again. The market plunges, pauses, bounds partway back, and then stabilizes, stunned.

In the Evergreen State, editorial pages dismiss the distant market crash as a flurry. "Flurry" is their special word for making the momentous seem small. The *Seattle Post-Intelligencer* waits more than a week to have an opinion on the market, and then writes, "The so-called 'panic' in Wall Street really amounted to nothing but the pricking of a number of inflated industrial bubbles." The *Tacoma News* calls it a "financial breeze." The *Tacoma Ledger* writes, "The real business world is little affected by it."

Whether the editors believe this, it is what they have to say. Washington's newspaper editors cannot be "calamity howlers." Even to advise readers to stop spending on luxuries—excellent advice at this moment—would infuriate local merchants who have bought advertising that keeps the newspaper in business.

On May 8, the Chemical National Bank of Chicago, which has a highly visible branch at the World's Fair, goes down. "The failure had no effect in financial circles," the *Spokane Chronicle* declares. Two days later comes the closure in Chicago of the Columbia National Bank, which the *Chronicle* now admits has suffered "a constant run" since the Chemical failed. The Capital National Bank of Indianapolis, which had a deposit at the Chemical, also fails. By week's end the sickness has rippled outward to small towns in the Midwest. In California, the Bank of Santa Clara County fails after the cashier dies and funds go missing.

On May 13, a hard run—a crowd of depositors outside the doors—hits the Plankinton Bank of Milwaukee, which holds large loans to a furniture retailer that failed. An iron box holding $500,000 in gold is rushed from Chicago on a special train and moved through Milwaukee on a wagon guarded by men with Winchester rifles. A shout goes up from 300 depositors when it arrives. The newspapers report that the Plankinton Bank is saved. Two weeks later it fails.

On May 14, the *Seattle Telegraph's* editorial is titled, "There Is No Panic." "The only serious failures have been in Australia," it says.

Newspapers report the closures of a steel producer in Pennsylvania, a coffee broker in New York, a chain of grain elevators in Nebraska, a boot and shoe wholesaler in Chicago, and rolling mills in Duluth. Then the stories stop, as if a publisher said, "Enough."[10]

Other stories, foreboding ones, get into print. The body of Herman Schaffner is found floating in Lake Michigan. He is the largest dealer in commercial paper in the Midwest and his bank's failure sets off runs all over Chicago. His death is a page-one story.

Another page-one story is about Samuel A. Wheelwright, a former mayor of Tacoma. Wheelwright is an old Democrat, who as mayor once allowed Tacoma to be an "open town" with saloons, gambling dens, and brothels. Wheelwright even lectured Tacomans on forgiveness, castigating the honorable women who "spurned the soiled doves of society." Writes the *Tacoma Ledger*, "He began to lose friends from that day, and as a matter of course to drink and go downhill."

Out of office, Wheelwright pursues a dream: that when people from his home state visit the 1893 World's Fair in Chicago, they stay at a Washington club, run by him. He signs up 300 members, taking fees of $3 for women and $5 for men.

On May 1, 1893, the World's Fair opens. Chicago has no Washington club. Wheelwright has spent the money and has no prospect of repaying it. On May 14, he is found dead with a bottle of chloroform in his rented room. The coroner calls it an accident; two weeks later the newspapers report it as a suicide.

In Tacoma comes another suicide. John P. Fyrk, 35, is an immigrant Swede. He and his Scottish wife, Matilda, have three young children. Since arriving from Minneapolis two years before, John Fyrk has been working as a carpenter at the St. Paul & Tacoma Lumber mill, the city's largest. Laid off with $50 in pay, he goes shopping with Matilda. Each buys a $5 pair of shoes. Then he goes to a saloon, indulges all night, and staggers home in the morning with only 35 cents in his pockets. He insists that the barkeeper has taken his money. He goes back and demands it, and the bartender tells him to get lost. Fyrk looks for work and can find none. He is morose. He wakes up at 5 a.m. on May 27, tells Matilda he is going out to feed the chickens, and instead goes to the back of the saloon, stands on a barrel and hangs himself.

The *Ledger's* reporter describes Matilda Fyrk with a frankness that would today be forbidden. She is middle-aged, he says, and has "the dull, careworn appearance of a neglected wife, upon whom the cares of motherhood and wifehood fell heavily." She tells the reporter she knew John was in that saloon, frittering away the family money. "I was afraid to go in," she says. "I wish I could have, for I

Merchants Bank Building. *Tacoma Public Library Image TPL-1000*

feel sure that I could have saved some of that money, perhaps not all of it, but some anyhow." She is destitute. She takes her children to live with the one friend she has, Thea Foss, who lives with her husband Andrew in a boathouse on Commencement Bay.

Fyrk will be forgotten. Thea Foss will become the most famous woman in Puget Sound maritime history.

In Moscow, Idaho, Michael Leitch of Pullman, Washington, is overdue on a $1,995 loan from the Moscow National Bank. On June 19, he comes in to see bank president Robert S. Browne—the 31-year-old son-in-law of Idaho's governor. Leitch is agitated; he sits across from Browne's desk, gets up, walks around, and sits again. He says someone has stolen his hat and cane, and is sore about it. He asks Browne if the bank will take his real estate in lieu of the cash, a request he has made several times before, and Browne again says no. Leitch gets up, paces the office, and walks behind Browne, which makes the bank president nervous. Leitch finally says he can pay July 1, when a certain man pays him. Browne says that will be fine, though Leitch has made such promises before. Leitch leaves Browne's office, but on the banking floor turns back, signaling to Browne for one more word. At a teller's cage, Leitch asks Browne for an extra $100 on the loan. Browne says no. Leitch flares up: *"What?"* Browne repeats: No more.

Leitch pulls a Colt .44 and fires at Browne's head. The bullet strikes the metal grate of the teller's cage and caroms off. A fragment strikes Browne's neck. His uncle—the governor's brother—snatches the revolver from Leitch and holds him at gunpoint. Waiting for the police to arrive, Leitch rails at the injustice of Robert S. Browne and the Moscow National Bank.

Outside, word spreads that Browne has been murdered. The people respect him, and until they learn he is safe they talk of lynching the man who shot him. Later they will change their opinion of the man who shot at their town banker. [11]

The urge to pull money from the banks is subterranean. For most of May, it goes unreported. In Washington it surfaces first near Tacoma in Pierce County.

On May 25, the three-year-old Bank of Puyallup closes. Its president, Willis Boatman, 67, is one of the Puyallup Valley's pioneers, having come over the Oregon Trail in 1852 with his wife Mary Ann in a wagon drawn by oxen. The Boatmans have reared seven children and grown wealthy by raising hops. Willis Boatman will later claim in a lawsuit, "I don't know anything about banking." He has left management to Samuel Dusinberre, who is secretary of the Washington Bankers Association. When the Panic begins, Dusinberre, 32, refuses Boatman's request for a $10,000 loan, but Dusinberre and his wife Agnes take out one for $997 on the day the bank closes. In the next five years Dusinberre will be the only Washington banker to go to prison.

On May 31, comes a much bigger failure. The *Tacoma Ledger* breaks the news in an editorial. "Doubt has been expressed of the solvency of the Merchants National Bank of this city," it says. The Merchants National is Tacoma's oldest bank, founded in 1880 as the Bank of New Tacoma. In 1883, Walter J. Thompson, then 30, bought the bank and reorganized it under a national charter. He has been president of it for most of the years since. Thompson is a civic pillar, a former territorial legislator, a real estate developer and a founder of the Tacoma Chamber of Commerce. He is a benefactor of the Tacoma's public library and public schools. He is a Unitarian and supporter of woman suffrage. "He entertained many prominent men," recalls historian Herbert Hunt, "and his home was a gathering place for the intellectuals."

He runs a rotten bank.

For 10 days the Merchants National has faced "unusual or quiet demands," the *Ledger* says. "So far it has met them all, and will continue to meet them." The editorial states flatly that the Merchants National has been "carefully examined" and "found to be entirely solvent."

Newspapers will use this tone of assurance again and again. Just *who* has examined the bank and found it entirely solvent? It is a national bank, so unlike Washington's state-chartered banks in the 1890s, it is subject to bank examiners. Has it been examined recently? The editorial does not say. Nor does the *Ledger* impart some useful knowledge about the man who has just replaced Thompson as the bank's president: Nelson Bennett. He is known as the developer of the city of Fairhaven on Bellingham Bay and for having supervised the construction of the Northern Pacific's tunnel at Stampede Pass. He is also owner of the *Tacoma Ledger*. Bennett has a duty to his bank, and he is corrupting his newspaper to perform it. Newspapers will one day avoid such conflicts of interest, but not in 1893.

Bennett has been the bank's president since a late-night meeting of the board May 21. As part of his appointment, Bennett buys the bank's building in a transaction that brings a quick $79,500. The other Tacoma banks, which have advanced the cash through their Clearing House Association, provide another $33,000 in return for promissory notes. In a May 31 statement to the press, Tacoma's bankers promise to protect the Merchants National's depositors.

However, the Merchants National owes $74,733 to the Chase National Bank of New York. The Chase has called the loan twice earlier in May, and on May 31 it calls it again. Weakened by withdrawals, the Merchants National cannot pay.

On May 31, the day the *Ledger's* "entirely solvent" editorial appears, the Merchants National closes half an hour after opening. It is the first national bank in Washington to fail in the Panic of 1893. The newspapers report that the bank has *suspended*, a term that implies payments may be resumed. They assure readers that depositors will be paid in full: *Just be patient.* In the next four years newspapers will say this again and again. In fact, the Merchants National will

Nelson Bennett. *Tacoma Public Library Image C72349*

never reopen. The depositors will get only 18 cents on the dollar, and not for a long time.

All that is in the future. At the moment the *suspension* of the Merchants National needs to be explained. The *Ledger* blames "vicious and idle gossip" by sidewalk "croakers" on Pacific Avenue, and the calling of the loan by the bankers in New York.

Tacoma's other daily, the *News*, asks why the other Tacoma banks haven't saved the Merchants National, as they said they would. Oh no, the Clearing House man says, we promised to protect the *depositors*. Not Chase. In the event, neither is protected. By making a promise and breaking it, the Clearing House undermines all the banks in Tacoma.

Speaking from New York, the president of Chase denies that his bank forced the closure. But in legal papers, Chase will admit that it called the loan twice earlier in May.

The Chase's president puts the blame on the reckless West-

Anthony Cannon. *Matthews, Northrup & Co., Buffalo, 1890*

erners. "Like most Western banks in rapidly growing and so-called boom towns, they were doubtless loaded up with local paper, more than they could carry in a tight market," he says in a prepared statement. "Doubtless" is the key word: it tips us off that Chase's president doesn't know for sure; he has no examiner's report to rely on.

The *Ledger* takes his statement as an insult. The New York banker has made "a vicious reflection on all our banks," Bennett's paper says. In a headline, it labels Chase's president "An Enemy of the West."

The *News* offers a different explanation: the Merchants National's stylish brick building, the one Bennett bought at the last minute, ate up too much of the bank's capital. Started in 1890, it is the finest bank building in Tacoma: six stories, its banking hall faced in Mexican mahogany with marble trim. Its vault is two stories high, with an upper compartment reachable by an iron stairway. A bank officer tells the *Ledger* that if the bank had not spent its money on the building, "We would have been much better off."

After losing the Merchants National, the Tacoma newspapers proclaim victory. "The Anxiety Is Ended," headlines the story in the *Ledger*. "Tacoma has passed through the most serious crisis in her history," says the rival *News* in an editorial entitled, "The Sun Comes Out." A few days later, the *News* editors say, "If people would stop talking bad times, there would be none, but if we can't close the mouths of these croakers, let us set up an opposition shout that will drown out their voices."

This the newspapers proceed to do. There has been, however, a "flurry" east of the mountains.[12]

In Spokane, one of the three city founders is Anthony M. Cannon, a man of intense eyes and flowing white beard. He was born in 1837 to the family of a staunch Illinois abolitionist. Scantily educated, Cannon left home at 20 to find his fortune in the West. He came to Portland, where he met and married Jennie Clarke, a widow with five children. She was a working woman, teaching Chinese immigrants to use Singer sewing machines. In 1878, Anthony and Jennie, their friend John J. Browne and his wife, and two Chinese servants rode on horseback to Spokane Falls, a place with a useful waterfall, a sawmill, and several families in shacks. The mill owner, James Glover, had surveyed a site for a city that existed entirely in his imagination. He sold Cannon and Browne a half-interest in it for a promise to pay $3,200—a promise they kept by selling town lots to new residents. Fifteen years later, the place by the waterfall has boomed into the dominant city in Eastern Washington. Cannon, Browne, and Glover are each president of a bank.

In the boom year 1890, Cannon is said to be the richest man in Eastern Washington, worth $2-4 million. He has interests in the Spokane Falls Water Power Co., a streetcar line, an auditorium, and a cemetery. He owns the *Spokane Review* newspaper and the city's oldest bank, the Bank of Spokane Falls. For pioneers to have such conglomerate (and conflicting) interests is not unusual. These are men who built cities from nothing. Few are trained as bankers; certainly Cannon was not. They have become bankers because they could, because they were expected to, and because their other projects, and their friends' projects, require money.

In the Panic of 1893, the banks of these pioneer entrepreneurs are some of the first to fail.

Cannon has left many of his bank's decisions in the hands of the cashier, his stepdaughter's husband. In Cannon's obituary, it will be said that the son-in-law had "questionable judgment." In hindsight, Cannon's judgment is also not good, not least for his choice of cashier. There is more. For his bank, Cannon has just finished building a miniature Corinthian temple of black marble imported from Vermont. He has also sunk the bank's money into a coal mine in the Cascades. He is president of a venture to build a 24-mile portage railroad around the Columbia River rapids at The Dalles. He has an interest in a venture to salvage steel rails from a ship that sank off of Grays Harbor. Years later, Glover will write of Cannon, "I think he overestimated his abilities sometimes. There was nothing he would not tackle. This attitude on his part was largely responsible, I believe, for the fact that he lost all his money."

Cannon has borrowed to the hilt. When credit tightens, he sends his agent to New York to pledge his frontier assets for more loans. The New Yorkers refuse. Cannon asks for help from the other Spokane banks who have just made him head of the new clearing house. "After an examination of his affairs," writes historian Nelson Durham, "this was denied." On the morning of June 5, 1893, Cannon's Bank of Spokane Falls stays closed.

The news creates a sensation. When such an institution goes down, "with A.M. Cannon and his supposed enormous wealth at its back," writes the *Walla Walla Statesman,* "it is indeed time to be extremely cautious."

Runs hit all the banks in Spokane. The next morning the Washington National Bank, of which Cannon is vice president and principal stockholder, stays closed, as does Washington Savings Bank, its affiliate. At 2 p.m. the Citizens National Bank goes down.

Four banks have failed in Spokane in two days. Cannon's *Spokane Review* says "the fatal mistake" was the decision of the other bankers not to support his Bank of Spokane Falls. The public, it says, "had lost faith in everybody and everything."

The rival *Spokane Chronicle* will soon be cheerleading its readers, playing the same role as the papers in Tacoma. But its first reaction is grim. Its editors are scared.

"A great calamity hangs over the city, such a calamity as seldom comes to a civilized people," they write. "The good sense that has always characterized the good people of Spokane seems to have been forgotten. Each man has forgotten his neighbor and in the general confusion has forgotten himself."

"The banks of Spokane are solvent," the *Chronicle* insists. "They have abundant resources to meet every obligation. No one who has money entrusted to their care can lose one cent of it." The *Chronicle* appeals to its readers' social conscience, reminding them that banks provide the lubrication that keeps people at work. It beseeches its readers to return their cash: "Do not bury it, do not hide it in your closet, but let it be used as a blessing for your neighbor as well as yourself... Unless this money is put back into circulation quickly, whether any more banks shall close their doors or not, Spokane will be prostrated for years."

Spokane will make it through. Cannon will not.

For depositors, the Bank of Spokane Falls is a total loss.[13]

Ben Snipes. *Kittitas County Historical Museum*

Fear spreads.

Two decades later, writer Hugh Fraser will describe the Panic of 1893 in *Seven Years on the Pacific Slope*: "The spirit, already weakened by excess, was released from reason entirely, and the cowardly terror which we called panic seized us for its own."

On June 7, 1893, a run begins in the Central Washington town of Roslyn, home of the state's biggest coal mine. The target is the branch of Ben E. Snipes & Co., the oldest bank in Kittitas County.

In the 1860s and 1870s Ben Snipes was the cattle king of Central Washington. In 1886, the year the Northern Pacific arrived in Ellensburg, he became the town's first banker.

Snipes's bank has been cursed by bad luck. On July 4, 1889, Ellensburg's business district burns, destroying his brand-new stone building. He rebuilds it. Then, on September 4, 1892, five bandits ride up on horses and hold up his branch in Roslyn, brandishing Colt .45s. They smack the cashier on the head with his own gun, shoot the assistant cashier in the hip and ride off with $5,000. The *Tacoma Ledger* says, "It was one of the most daring pieces of work yet recorded in the history of bank robbery."

A posse searches for the robbers. It can't find them. Snipes offers a reward and money for an extra prosecutor. Three men are captured, two are tried and one is convicted. They are the wrong men. A woman betrays the actual robbers, the McCarty gang of Baker County, Oregon. Two men are captured; they escape from the Ellensburg jail and are seized by armed citizens. The two are tried and the jury deadlocks. Prosecutors have no money for a second trial and let the robbers go free.

Two weeks after this botch of justice a run hits the Roslyn bank. It does more economic damage than the robbery: it kills the bank. On June 9, 1893, the offices of Ben E. Snipes & Co. at Roslyn and Ellensburg remain closed.

A few days later, Snipes faces a meeting of depositors. He does not want a receiver—a court-appointed trustee—to come in and liquidate his bank. He assures the depositors he will reopen it. He will try to do this within 30 days, and every depositor will be paid in full with interest. As security, he offers them a deed of trust on his personal real estate. The depositors pass a resolution that, "having unbounded confidence in the honesty and integrity of Benjamin E. Snipes, we hereby express sympathy for him in his embarrassment" and do not need the deed of trust.

"Snipes' Bank Secure," proclaims the headline in the *Tacoma Ledger*. The headline is false. The bank is not secure. Though its balance sheet will show nearly two dollars in assets for every dollar in claims, the assets are in cattle, buildings, town lots, and IOUs, none of them as good as cash. Depositors will not see a cent for seven years.

The first wave of bank runs continues across the state, hitting the new towns built on credit. On June 13 the state-chartered Bank of Everett, oldest of the town's seven banks—a year and a half old—closes. The weekly *Everett Herald* does not cover the event as news, having told its readers five days before, "Affairs in Everett are in a good, healthy condition from a business and financial standpoint, according to all reports from the banks."

Assurances of this sort begin to backfire. On June 14, Walter Granger, general agent of the Northern Pacific, Yakima & Kittitas Irrigation Co.—the largest irrigation project in the state—is with his pregnant wife and infant child on the dusty streets of Zillah, in the Yakima Valley. An employee comes up with one of the company's postdated "time checks" in hand. He demands cash. The check is payable July 31, a month and a half later.

The man's anxiety is understandable. Banks are dropping like overripe apples, and by July 31 there might be no bank to honor his check. "As the fellow was partly drunk," writes Granger to his boss, "I tried to pacify him by explaining the check was perfectly good... but that it was impossible for me to pay it sooner." Granger's assurance fails. After he turns away to attend to his child, the man pastes him with "a terrific blow under the eye, cutting open the flesh to the bone," Granger writes. It is a taste of the anger people feel when given promises in place of money.

Bank failures continue. On June 22, the First National Bank of Whatcom closes. The next day New Whatcom's Columbia National Bank also closes.

The outraged editor at the *Bellingham Bay Express* blames the failures in New Whatcom on the "calamity howlers," the "irresponsible wind-bag element" that knows nothing of banking, that gabs on the street corner, abusing its freedom of speech. The paper declares that spreading bank-killing rumors is a criminal act and offers the suggestion that "some banker should fill his traducer with lead."

In New York, the interest rate on "call money"—short-term borrowing that acts as a safety net between banks—spikes in late June 1893 at 74 percent. Usually it is in the single digits. The extreme tightness of credit brings down banks all over the country by making it hard for them to raise cash to pay depositors. On June 26, the First National Bank of Port Angeles closes. On July 3, the state-chartered Bank of Sumas closes, and on July 5, the Puget Sound National Bank of Everett closes. This time the *Everett Herald* notices: it prints the story in three sentences, the last of which is, "There has been no run on the bank."[14]

As the first wave of failures abates and call money temporarily falls back to 12 percent, the newspapers congratulate their towns. "Tacoma has passed through the most serious crisis in her history and has proved herself buoyant," the *News* says. Tacoma is not done with the crisis and the mood on the street is not buoyant. A California man writes the *Tacoma Ledger*, "I have never heard so much discontent and cry-out of hard times amongst business men as in this city."

The *Chronicle* says, "Thanks, friends, thanks," to Pacific Coast bankers who shipped Spokane banks several hundred-thousand dollars of emergency cash. Tacoma banks have received $500,000 in gold coin and the Bellingham Bay banks $140,000. But the movement of coin is not a good sign. By law, national banks are required to keep 15 percent of their deposits in reserve, of which three-fifths can be earning interest in other, big-city banks. Beginning in the last week of May, banks all over the West have been pulling their reserves out of New York, because they need the cash; and the New York banks are calling in loans they have out because *they* need the cash.

For most businesses, loans are not available on any terms. Enterprises that need credit are in immediate crisis. The financial system is in shock. Not until 20 years later will America have a central bank to provide emergency credit. In New York, the banks are unable to settle accounts and begin writing each other IOUs they call clearing house certificates.

In 1893, the federal government does have responsibility for the national currency. On June 30, President Cleveland says he will call Congress into session August 7 to repeal the Sherman Silver Purchase Act, which has undermined world confidence that the United States will stay on the gold standard. Congress will act slowly and will not settle the issue until November. Meanwhile, the Panic continues and more businesses fail.

In mid-July comes the second wave of runs. The July 17 closure of the Bank of Anacortes is little noticed outside of Skagit County, and the stockholders' vote July 18 to close the Hoquiam National Bank makes hardly a ripple statewide. But the failure in Denver of 12 banks after massive runs July 17 to 19 makes front-page news across the state of Washington.

On July 21, the Traders Bank of Tacoma closes, setting off a city-wide run that three days later knocks out the Tacoma National Bank, the city's largest. "The feeling among the working class of depositors is very bitter and many rumors are rife upon the curb," says the *Seattle Telegraph*. The *Tacoma News* sends a reporter to listen to the "calamity howlers" and "croakers" on Pacific Avenue, and quotes one saying, "I would like to see every bank in the city go under."

"—these banks!" says another man. "I don't owe them anything, and I would be just as well off if they were all broke as I am now."

Tacoma's savings banks require 30-day or 60-day notice for withdrawals—a privilege commercial banks don't have. To reassure depositors, banks stack gold coins in their windows.

On July 26, Wall Street panics again. Call money in New York surges back to 72 percent and is not available at all for banks with less than stellar credit. The First National Bank of Spokane and the Spokane Savings Bank go down. The next day in Portland, the Oregon National Bank closes. Its owner, George B. Markle, controls the Ellensburg National Bank in Central Washington, and that bank closes, too.

On July 27, the stockholders of the Washington National Bank of Tacoma vote to liquidate the bank.

On July 29, the Puget Sound Loan, Trust & Banking Co. of New Whatcom closes, and on July 31 comes what historian Lotte Roth will call "the real calamity": the last bank standing in New Whatcom, the Bellingham Bay National Bank, closes. The *Reveille* angrily reports that a man has been taking bets around town that the B.B. National would go down. That man, the editor says, "ought to be put in the Bay sewn up in a sack with a stone in it. He would be good to poison dogfish with, that fellow."[15]

The Panic of 1893 is the most serious financial crisis of the 30 year-old national-bank system. Through October 1893, 158 national banks suspend. The state with the most suspensions, 16, is Colorado; the second, with 14, is Washington. In Colorado most of the suspended banks reopen; in Washington, most do not. Eleven of the Evergreen State's unregulated banks also suspend.

Bank customers nationwide are stuffing money in deposit boxes and burying it in cans. In August there is a famine of cash. "Paper notes seem to have disappeared," says the *Oregonian*. The

New York banks relieve the famine by selling assets to buyers abroad, bringing back gold from Europe. In August the Treasury's reserve rises above $100 million for the first time since April. By September the currency shortage subsides.

The bank failures taper off. From August through November 1893, banks close their doors in Colfax, Port Townsend, Auburn, and the Okanogan County mining camp of Conconully.

The financial storm of 1893 has left towns strewn with invisible wreckage. People have lost their savings and bankers have lost the public's trust. In a few places the wipeout is complete, with no banks left for merchants to conduct business. At Port Angeles people use checks on the closed First National as money until Danish immigrant Gregers Lauridsen creates tokens and scrip. At New Whatcom, Charles Cissna, 33, owner of a store called The Fair, prints scrip in denominations from 5 cents to $5, inscribed with the words, "In Trade. Due the Bearer and Payable Only in Merchandise." He issues $15,000 of it, all of which is at risk of becoming waste paper if his store fails. It does not fail. His private currency will circulate in Whatcom County for the rest of the decade.[16]

The wreckage from the Panic is not just of banks, but in the lives of people. An example: At the bottom of Seattle's Beacon Hill just above the railroad tracks, Charlotte Fetting, 81, lives with her unemployed son Ernest, 35, in an unpainted shack.

The Fettings are misers. They are living in want, yet Ernest has $1,000 in the People's Savings Bank. In July 1893, when the Panic makes him distrustful of banks, he withdraws his money in $20 gold pieces and stashes them in his shack. He lends a friend $300 and gives his mother $10. He spends $10, 1 percent of his hoard.

On September 4, 1893, brother-in-law James King comes from Tacoma and treats Ernest to a night out downtown. They return at 1 a.m. to find Charlotte dead on the cabin's floor, her hands bound, and her head bloodied by blows from a stove lid. The $10 gold piece is still in her pocket, but the hidden money—$680 in gold—is gone. Two months later King is found dead, floating in Puget Sound. An associate of King's is tried for Charlotte Fetting's murder but is not convicted.

The newspapers note that the woman's murder started with her son pulling his $1,000 out of the bank. The *Seattle Telegraph* wags its editorial finger: "The murder was a direct consequence of the senseless scare about the stability of our banks."

Another story: In December 1893, a man is found talking gibberish in a darkened Seattle hotel room. He is Newell Sturdevant, about 45, who until recently operated a fruit and confection shop in Tacoma. His mind, says the *Seattle Telegraph*, "is believed to have been wrecked by the failure of a bank in that city." It is the Merchants National, in which Sturdevant had a deposit of $256.

Fetting distrusted the banks and Sturdevant trusted them. It didn't matter. Both suffered losses. Over that summer and fall, 30 banks fail in Washington, making victims of thousands. The Panic of 1893 has been a stampede beyond stopping by anyone in it.[17]

SHUTDOWN (1893)

In the last days of July 1893, the South Bend Chamber of Commerce throws a dance the local paper says will be "the grandest affair of the kind ever held in Southwestern Washington." The *USS Monterey*, the ironclad whose guns boomed on the Fourth of July at Seattle, moors in the shallow waters of Willapa Bay. People come to South Bend on foot, by horseback, in boats, wagons, and on the new Northern Pacific line from Chehalis for rides out to the warship. Back in town, the new Willapa Hotel is opened up, lighted with electricity from top to bottom, and decorated inside with evergreen boughs and flowers. Tables are set up with sandwiches, lemonade, coffee, cake, and ice cream. Ten officers from the Monterey attend, dancing with the women well past midnight.

The Willapa Hotel has been built in anticipation of a city that will never be. The hotel will never open for business. It will be boarded up for more than 25 years and torn down for scrap, one of many casualties of the Panic of 1893.[18]

Fear and distrust are coursing through Washington enterprises—the lumber mills and mines, wheat farms and shipping lines, newspapers and governments, and even the utopian colonies.

Begin with the railroads. If banks are the nation's financial arteries, railroads are its commercial arteries. In the 1890s they are the only practical means of transport across the continent and are vital to the towns of the new West.

In 1893, weakness surfaces at the Seattle, Lake Shore & Eastern Railroad, commonly called the Lake Shore—the railroad that a century later will become the Burke-Gilman Trail. Promoted by Thomas Burke, Daniel Gilman, and other champions of Seattle, its mission was originally to build around the northern end of Lake Washington and over Snoqualmie Pass, giving Seattle a connection to the East. The main line gets as far as the foot of the Cascades,

The Willapa Hotel. *Pacific County Historical Society*

a branch goes north to connect with the Canadian Pacific, and a disconnected segment is built west from Spokane. In 1890, Eastern investors, who have no loyalty to Seattle, sell control of the Lake Shore to the Northern Pacific.

By early 1893, the Northern Pacific is in default on its payments to the Lake Shore stockholders. On March 24, 1893, six weeks before the crash on Wall Street, the stockholders put the Lake Shore into receivership.

The immediate loser is a venture on the east side of Lake Washington, where the Great Western Iron & Steel Co. is planning a steel mill. The plan is to use iron ore from a mine near Snoqualmie Pass with local limestone and coal to make steel rails. In honor of the venture's English leader, Peter Kirk, a new town is to be named Kirkland. The plan requires the Lake Shore to lay tracks to the iron mine. The Lake Shore stops expanding and Peter Kirk's project dies.

On August 15, 1893, the Northern Pacific falls into receivership, unable to pay the interest on its bonds. The *Seattle Press-Times* says the Northern Pacific's problem is "the enormous load of indebtedness heaped upon the railroad by reckless and profligate management in its earliest history." In addition, much of its main line needs to be rebuilt in order to compete with the Great Northern. Northern Pacific Vice President James Williams blames business conditions. He says, "The depression prevailing over the whole country has been exceptionally severe in the younger states, so that general business along the main and branch lines has been practically at a standstill."

During the boom, the railroads were extending prosperity simply by building. Now the building stops. Weakness seeps through the railroads' territory. Speculative ventures die, men are laid off and towns along the line turn quiet.

The third transcontinental serving Washington is the Union Pacific. It is the northern trunk of the original golden-spike transcontinental, created and subsidized by Congress. From its Pacific Northwest terminus at Portland it goes to southern Idaho and east to Omaha, Nebraska. A branch runs to Spokane. On October 13, 1893, the Union Pacific asks for a receiver.

The 1890s are often recalled as the era of no federal involvement in business. In some ways that is true, but railroad receivers are appointed by federal judges. By the end of 1893, roads with one-quarter of the nation's railroad mileage are under supervision of the federal courts and the government's receivers generally keep them running. A receiver can lay-off or cut the pay of workers and suspend payment of debt, and they do all of these things.

The Great Northern, which is not in receivership, also cuts pay starting in August 1893. At Spokane, its section hands are cut from $1.50 a day to $1.25. They strike and they lose.[19]

By 1893, lumber has been produced on Puget Sound for 40 years. Pioneers have built "cargo mills" at tidewater to put lumber on sailing ships. When the Northern Pacific comes, lumbermen build mills that can also serve trains. The first such mill is St. Paul & Tacoma Lumber on Tacoma's Commencement Bay.

At first, only specialty lumber is worth shipping east. The new mills develop a market in heavy bridge timbers, Douglas fir flooring and car stock, the 8-foot boards used to build railcars. But these cargoes are not enough to fill the trains moving East, and most of the cars return empty.

For years the Western red cedar, *Thuja plicata*, has been wasted. "Cedar logs were regarded as almost useless," writes the *Everett Herald*. "Loggers would throw them out of the booms to float unused down into the Sound." Then someone notices that in the temperate jungles of Western Washington, cedar shingles last a long time. Like the California redwood, red cedar contains an oil that resists rot.

A new industry rises. In 1890 and 1891, red cedar shingles are carried on the Northern Pacific to Illinois and Iowa, where they sweep aside the shingles of white pine. On Puget Sound, shingle mills spring up like horsetails. Land is cheap, cedar is cheaper, and credit is easy at banks. Shingles sell at prices fixed by the Washington and Oregon Shingle Manufacturers Association—prices high enough to pay the Northern Pacific's freight rates.

In 1892, 127 shingle mills, most of them small, are opened in Washington. Output more than doubles, to 1.8 billion little slabs of wood. But there is a problem. The newcomers in the industry—former doctors, lawyers, insurance men and real estate men—glut the market.

In April 1893, the shingle association suspends the price list. Pricing is a free-for-all. The *Lumberman* says this is being done "in the hope of bringing the price cutters to their senses." It does not work.

In May, mill owners talk of selling shingles to a pool, which would hold them off the market until it could sell at the association price. The mill owners would pledge their unsold shingles for cash at the bank. The mill owners like the plan, but their bankers do not. They don't want shingles.

The mill owners vote at a meeting to close all mills for 30 days. A minority objects. Some shingle men have contracts to fill. Others can't afford to stop working. The small mills don't want to be pushed around by the big mills. The mill men cannot enforce the agreement. Shingle prices fall further. From May to August 1893, shingle shipments on the Northern Pacific drop 83 percent.[20]

Wages fall in tandem with prices.

On July 1, 1893, shingle mill owners agree to cut wages 10 to 25 percent. At Ballard, the three-year-old West Coast Shingle Weavers' Union refuses to take cuts. Given the hazard to life and limb, especially to fingers, the union says the old pay was "none too much for the work performed."

L to R: sawyer at two-block machine, filer, knee-bolter and cut-off man at Smith Bros. shingle mill, Arlington, Washington, 1899. *L.E. Smith, author's collection*

Most of the mills close. The state's largest producer the previous year, the C.D. Stimson Co. of Ballard, restarts July 18 by offering jobs at 10 percent below union scale. The men refuse and Stimson hires nonunion men. John W. Dorman, Stimson's manager, says to the *Seattle Press-Times*: "There seems to be plenty of 'green' men who will work if the union men will leave them alone."

Seattle Cedar Lumber, the state's sixth largest producer, also cuts pay and hires non-union men when its union crew walks out. "We are not fighting union men," says mill manager Alexander Mc-Ewan. "We will employ every one of them who will work at our prices." He says, "We cannot afford to pay the wages the union men want. Our reduction of 10 per cent in wages is small in comparison with the reduction in the price of shingles." He is right about that.

Union spokesman Truman Ingalls says, "All the shingle mills on the Sound are watching our actions... If these mills are successful in gutting our wages, a cut will be inaugurated by all the mills on the Sound." And he is right about that. It is what happens.

Ballard's union men are mostly peaceful. They nail a misshapen slab to a telephone pole and label it the "scab labor" shingle, their prediction that the mills cannot run without their skill. They are wrong; Stimson and Seattle Cedar have some problems and buyers in the Midwest reject some shipments as poorly cut—maybe because they are and maybe because the buyers don't need shingles—but the mills stay open. A month later comes another round of wage cuts. By late August, Stimson and Seattle Cedar are the only shingle mills in Ballard still operating.

In October 1893, the West Coast Shingle Weavers Union agrees to wage cuts of 15 to 20 percent. Other mills restart. In Whatcom County, mills survive by paying workers in mill scrip—I.O.U.s. payable when the shingle buyers remit payment. The newspapers hail this as a way to keep the mills open but the workers resent having to sell their scrip at a discount. They want real money.[21]

The miners of the Pacific Northwest are strong men, many of them immigrants, and the keepers of a zealous unionism. But in 1893, they are in no mood to fight.

The region's big fight was in 1892, in the silver mines of northern Idaho. It ended in a union defeat. A lockout led to violence and the calling in of federal troops. Seventeen union men were sent to prison.

The year before that, in 1891, the Oregon Improvement Co. locked out the white miners' union, the Knights of Labor, at the Franklin and Newcastle coal mines east of Seattle. The employer's aim was to roll back the 15 percent pay increase of 1890, to keep the right to hire and fire workers, and to require workers to buy at the company store. To break the union, the company brought in 600 black miners from Missouri, Illinois, Kentucky, and Tennessee under armed guard, and armed the new men with carbines. There was a gun battle and two miners were killed. Governor Elisha Ferry sent in five companies of National Guard. The union was broken. Workers signed pledges not to strike again and took a 25 percent cut in pay.

In 1893, the Knights still represent the white miners at the Gilman coal mine in King County near Issaquah. In July, the owners announce a 15 percent wage cut. They cut the cost of rent and board in the company town by the same percentage. The union calls a strike and on the first day nearly half the miners cross the line. The strike collapses. In 1893, there is no drop in coal production in Washington.

Miners do win one point: At Franklin, says the *Tacoma News,* former Tacoma policeman Charles Todd is head of the mine owners' police. He also owns the saloon. Todd's job is "to herd the newly imported negro miners," and "for over two years he has been the terror and physical owner of the town of Franklin." While in his saloon in November 1893, Todd slaps and insults a black miner who orders a drink. The miner is a head shorter and 60 pounds lighter than Todd, but he jumps the big boss, belts him to the floor, beats him unmercifully and begins taking "bites of flesh from his ears, nose and cheeks." His fellow miners stand and watch, grinning. "For months," says the *News*, "they had been waiting for revenge on Todd, and at last it had come."[22]

Like miners, sailors have been carriers of a zealous and sometimes violent unionism.

In July 1893, the *Tacoma Ledger* reports the trial of two union sailors for striking a non-union sailor "across the base of the nose and over the eyes with a bar of iron." Each attacker is sentenced to a year in the Pierce County jail.

In Port Townsend, union and non-union sailors coexist uneasily for months, each group in its favored Water Street taproom. On August 11, 1893, union men beat up a non-union man who goes in the wrong tavern. The union men send one of theirs to the non-union house. He is ejected. His union brothers come to his aid and the non-union men fire their guns. James Connors, a union sailor, is wounded.

In the coastwise trade, the Sailors' Union of the Pacific has set a scale of $40 a month. In September 1893, the Ship Owners' Association demands a cut to $35, a wage many are already paying. The union refuses.

On September 23, 1893, dynamite explodes at a boardinghouse for non-union sailors in San Francisco. The blast blows men out of their beds and across the street, killing five and mangling others. The union denies responsibility and offers a $1,000 reward for the bomber. Three men, former union members, are arrested. One will eventually be tried and acquitted, but the union has been at war with non-union men for years, and the newspapers assume it is guilty. "This country has no use for organizations that breed murderers," declares the New Whatcom *Reveille*.

The union's power is broken. In mid-October a wire story from San Francisco says the Sailors' Union now "recognizes the impossibility of maintaining any standard of wages or of compelling ship owners to patronize its office in this port... It is the hope of the union's officers that after the present depression is over the union will again be able to resume its old place."

On Puget Sound, the coal ship *Ivanhoe* cuts wages on the San Francisco run to $30 a month. The captain offers work to twelve union men, and eight accept. The other four go to the union and get no help. They return to accept the captain's offer but he has hired non-union men and refuses to discharge them.

Soon wages fall to $25 a month and eventually even lower.[23]

Daily newspapers are hit hard in the crash. In June 1893, Tacoma's afternoon daily, the *News,* is sold by the sheriff to William McIntyre, one of the owners, and editor Frank Lane loses his one-third stake. In October, the *Seattle Press-Times* is put into receivership after it defaults on a $20,000 loan. The *Tacoma News,* the *Spokane Chronicle*, and the *Spokane Review* all shrink from eight pages to four.

In August, the *Tacoma Ledger* asks those of its 200 employees earning more than $15 a week to take a 20 percent cut. All agree except a dozen compositors, represented by the International Typographical Union. They earn a minimum of $4.50 per 8-hour day and refuse to drop to $3.60.

In a letter to the union, manager Clinton Snowden argues that many businesses have had to cut expenses and that the *Ledger* must also. The union says it cannot because it must show solidarity with members at other papers.

Snowden replies, "I answer that your first interest, and mine, is the employment which pays us." Neither workers nor owners caused the hard times or can make them go away. "It is therefore imperative," Snowden writes, "that we adjust ourselves to them as best we may."

The union refuses.

On November 20, 1893, the *Ledger* discharges the union compositors and calls in twelve non-union men from California, most of them from the *Los Angeles Times*. Four turn around en route when they discover they are replacing union men. The eight others are met by police at the Tacoma depot and escorted to the *Ledger*.

The *Seattle Post-Intelligencer* has a page-one story under a headline it would never use a century later: "Rats for the Tacoma Ledger." The "rats" are the eight replacements. The *Ledger*, it says, "will be the only rat daily paper in the state of Washington."

The *Ledger's* pressmen refuse to work with "rats," and quit. On November 21, the *Ledger* temporarily shrinks to a one-page handbill. In it Snowden uses an argument from fairness to justify the lockout—that the compositors and pressmen are the only workers refusing the cut and therefore "were willing that the other men, who were living as they were, by the same business, should bear all the burden..."

On December 1, *Ledger* owner Nelson Bennett uses a racial argument to show his concern for white labor. As a contractor for the Northern Pacific, he says, "I put white men at work at $2 and gradually raised their wages to $2.50, although there was no time when I could not have employed Chinamen at 80 cents." But Bennett says he cannot pay what the compositors demand.

In their statement, the compositors argue that the 20-percent cut would leave them with daily pay lower than their counterparts in Seattle or "anywhere else in the entire country," and that it is unacceptable for local men to be replaced by out-of-town replacements. "These imported workmen belong to a class of social outcasts known as 'rats' or 'scabs,' " they say, calling the replacements "outcasts and characterless individuals, who live nowhere, who have surrendered what manhood they ever possessed to become what they are—the supple tools of tyrannical and mercenary men."

On November 23, the *Ledger's* union compositors, pressmen and some reporters and editors start a new paper, the *Tacoma Morning Union*, with money from the International Typographical Union and printing from the union-shop *Tacoma News*. In its first issue, the *Union* has news stories, display ads, and an editorial announcing that it is "ready to do business on a business basis." It does so, setting out an editorial line that is pro-union and always with the aim of taking readers and advertisers from the *Ledger*.

The *Union* reports that Bennett has set aside $150,000 to defend the *Ledger*. The *Union* publicly advises him that there are better uses for his money. It is right about that: Bennett will eventually sell the *Ledger*, leaving editor Snowden, under different owners, battling it out with the *Union* until mid-1897. The *Ledger* will be forced into receivership; the new owners will settle with the typographers' union and force Snowden and his "rat" pressmen out. Four years hence, the *Tacoma Union* will die, having won the battle for which it was created.[24]

The Panic hits local government hard.

By 1893, cities and counties in Washington have borrowed heavily for streets, sewers, water, and power. The town that gets in the most trouble with this is Tacoma. In 1893, pioneer Tacoma entrepreneur Charles Wright offers to sell the Tacoma Light & Water Co.'s waterworks and power plant to the city for $1,750,000. Wright, often called "the father of Tacoma," is in his final years, and has retired to Philadelphia. The *Post-Intelligencer* repeatedly warns that he has priced his waterworks $1 million too high. It accuses him of buying off Tacoma's politicians and its two daily newspapers to put over a "water swindle." On April 11, 1893, Tacoma ignores the Seattle paper and votes yes on $2,150,000 in bonds. This will pay for Wright's waterworks and power plant. It will also provide the city with $330,000 in working capital and $100,000 for a bridge to the tide flats. Tacoma's debt now reaches its constitutional limit.

In Seattle, voters approve $975,000 in sewer and warrant-funding bonds. Seattle offers its 5-percent, 20-year bonds for sale in June 1893. In the midst of the Panic there are no takers. In October, a Wall Street firm agrees to take some of Seattle's bonds at 94 cents on the dollar—a sweet deal, an Eastern newspaper says, available only because Seattle has avoided deficit spending and has had no bank failures. (It will have its first failure in December.)

Tacoma has had deficit spending *and* bank failures. It bypasses the bond market by paying Wright all of its 5-percent, 20-year bonds, taking Wright's cash for the amount in excess of the assets he's turning over. The *Post-Intelligencer* is right about the waterworks deal. It is a swindle, and it will bring Tacoma years of grief.

Seattle and Tacoma are now loaded with debt, and no longer able to raise money in New York. These are the last bonds either city will issue for half a decade. The two cities will enter the hard times with heavy interest obligations, but they will think and act on these obligations differently.

In the summer and fall of 1893, most cities, counties, and school districts are reduced to funding capital projects, if any, in warrants—I.O.U.s that accrue interest and have no fixed maturity dates. The Spokane School Board pays for a school in 8-percent warrants that come in $1, $2, $5, and $10 denominations for the contractor to pay his workers. The *Chronicle* says the warrants are to be "made of the best linen paper, with the amount of the warrant stamped in colors on its face."

The panic squeezes local authorities. By September 1893, 61 percent of Spokane's city funds are in suspended banks. Tacoma schools are paying teachers partly in 8-percent warrants, which trade at a 5-to-10 percent discount. Whatcom County defaults on its bonds.

Public spending falls. To save money, Seattle heats some schools with wood rather than coal. Its teachers lose 20 days of sick pay and the three schools with vice principals let them go. Ballard puts off the opening of school to October 16. Tacoma and Everett lay off police, and Seattle and Spokane cut police pay.

Small towns, some of which have only recently installed electric arc lamps in the streets, shut them off. In August, the Ballard City Council votes to shut off its street lights; it debates firing the night watchman but relents because the man will be needed even more in the dark. In September, Montesano shuts down the city light plant *and* fires the night watchman. In South Bend, which is paying 45 percent of its tax revenues for street lights, voters fail by 3 votes to approve a buyout of the Willapa Harbor Electric Co. In October, South Bend replaces its electric street lights with kerosene lamps. South Bend is in deep trouble, and two years later it will cut the pay of city officials to $1 a year.

Sailing ships loading grain at Tacoma. *Tacoma Daily Ledger, 7-28-95*

In November 1893, after Ballard's voters reject a bond measure, it stops paying city officials. By then, Mayor Arthur E. Pretty is working in a shingle mill.

Sometimes the cuts don't stick. When King County limits justices of the peace to the amount of fees they collect, they sue and win a ruling—from a judge, of course—that they must be paid their full salaries. Spokane's Republican mayor, Edward Powell, whose pay is set in the city charter, refuses to take less. "I do not think that the city is an object of charity," he says.

In Spokane County, the *Chronicle* finds one public employee untouched by cuts. Dogcatcher Jerry Ogle is paid by the dog: 50 cents a day for the dogs he keeps and 50 cents for each dog put down. Ogle brags to the reporter that he can make $3,000 a year. Two months later his job ends and he has made only $300. He opens the cages and lets the last 14 dogs run free.[25]

By the 1890s wheat has become the principal cash crop in Eastern Washington. In the hills of the Palouse, which have deep soil, farmers sow and harvest with horse-drawn machines. They pack the wheat in jute sacks and take the sacks by wagon to rail stops where they are loaded into boxcars. At Portland and Tacoma, men unload the sacks and pack them into wooden ships that sail for Liverpool and Antwerp.

If the harvest is good and the price high, a farmer can pay for much of his land with one year's crop. The value of his land will go up and he can borrow more at the bank. But he pays a fixed transportation charge and if the price of wheat falls, the loss is his.

In 1892, farmers suffer a low harvest *and* a low price. Then comes the tightening of credit. At the Walla Walla Savings Bank, deposits fall to the lowest in several years. On May 27, 1893, on the eve of the bank panic, manager William Stine writes a commercial banker in Portland: "Never in all my experience has money been so tight and close as now. We are not advancing a dollar to anyone nor do we intend to until our farmer friends must absolutely have some money with which to garner the next harvest."

The wheat crop in the fields looks fabulous. "The moisture now in the ground exceeds anything ever known here at this time of year," Stine writes. "If we can weather this financial storm [in] 60 days we will be entirely out of the woods." The price of wheat is even lower than the year before, but Walla Walla Savings is not about to lend money to farmers to hold back their crop. "The very day that wheat is ready for market," Stine vows, "that day they will have to sell... be the price what it may."

In June, the price of wheat at Walla Walla falls more. In 1892, it was 57 cents a bushel and people complained; by early August 1893 it falls to 40 cents.

"From Pendleton to Walla Walla, the wheat is the finest I ever saw," a farm-machinery man tells the *Spokane Chronicle* in August. But in the second week of September it begins to rain. The dust turns to mud, the harvest stops, and farmers wait for the sun to save the wheat they have cut but not stacked.

It rains. In Walla Walla it rains 1.87 inches in three days. Writes the *Chronicle*, October 9: "It beat down standing grain, drenched the half-finished stacks and soaked the scattered sheaves left by the binders until the grain swelled and sprouted."

On October 18 the *Chronicle* writes, "All along the line of the

Palouse railway are soaked and steaming stacks of grain. When the sunshine came last Wednesday the farmers hastened to take off the tops of the stacks and scatter the sheaves to dry. Sunday evening the grain and straw were dry and firm, ready for the stackers. Monday morning the rain was pouring down as if it had never rested, drenching the uncovered stacks and beating the scattered sheaves into the mud."

Grain in burlap bags is soaked through and starts to sprout. Roads are impassable.

For a few days in late October the sky clears. Then it snows. The unharvested stalks, weakened by the rains, break under the weight.

From September through November 1893, the Washington Agricultural College at Pullman—the school that will become Washington State University—measures precipitation of 10.5 inches. Palouse farmers save more than half their crop, but much of it can be used only for animal feed. The farmers have few animals. A Colfax merchant says to the *Chronicle*, "Many of our farmers keep but one cow, and pay no attention to poultry, and never think of raising a hog or two for their winter's meat." Now they rush to buy pigs and chickens.

Outside of the Palouse, the damage to the wheat crop is less. Over the winter, Tacoma will still export a healthy 4 million bushels of wheat—but at low prices. Perhaps a million bushels remain on the farm, cut and stacked but not worth the cost of threshing and transport.

Farmers have been buying groceries on credit and paying when the harvest came in. After the ruined harvest of 1893, signs go up in the stores: "Cash Only." Food prices fall. Says the *Seattle Post-Intelligencer*, "One can now purchase groceries at about Eastern prices, freight added, in all the Palouse towns"—if one has the cash.

Most Palouse farmers keep their land. Those who lose it, says a *Seattle P-I* story several years later, are mostly "the farmers of large areas who had staked their entire capital and credit upon a single year, holding land under heavy mortgage and farm implements unpaid-for."

The year 1893 is a disaster not only for growers but the banks that finance them. Stine's hope that the Walla Walla Savings Bank will be "entirely out of the woods" is not realized. On December 9, 1893, the bank goes under.[26]

Another casualty of the Panic of 1893 is an experiment in socialism located on the northern shore of the Olympic Peninsula. In the two decades following the publication of Edward Bellamy's utopian novel, *Looking Backward* (1888), several such experiments are started in Washington. These are economic ventures as much as displays of belief.

This one, the Puget Sound Co-operative Colony, is next to the non-socialist village of Port Angeles. Colony members have built a sawmill, a brickyard, and a hotel. All the property is owned by the colony, to avoid what founder George Venable Smith calls "the monstrous impiety of the pretended personal ownership of land." All work is paid in scrip accepted at the colony store. The scrip is measured in hours rather than dollars on the theory that every person's hours are of equal worth.

As a business model this is not a success. It is impossible to get everyone to work for the common good. Writes historian Charles LeWarne, "There was always opportunity just outside the colony for the malcontents, the rebels, the disenchanted, the drifters, the personally ambitious and for the physically crowded out." By 1893, the colony has degenerated into a business venture riven by factionalism and burdened with debt.

In November 1893, dissident trustees file suit in Clallam County Superior Court against the colony's president, Thomas Maloney, asking the court to appoint a receiver to take the assets from his control.

On the evening of December 2, 1893, three days before the question of receivership is to be heard in court, a steamer arrives at the Port Angeles wharf. It has been chartered at Seattle by wholesalers who want to take back the goods for which they have not been paid. Men step onto the dock and the ship moves out. A sign goes up at the colony store: "Closed for Stock-Taking." Windows are covered. A suspicious trustee asks President Maloney: What's up? The answer: Inventory taking. Normal before a lawsuit.

Inside the store, men are packing goods in boxes. At midnight the steamer quietly returns to the dock and offloads horses and a wagon. Within minutes boxes begin moving to the dock. The dissident trustees rush to an attorney's house, roust him out of bed, and he rushes to the judge's house and rousts *him* out of bed. The judge writes an injunction stopping it all, but by the time the trustees have it in hand, the steamer has slipped into the night along with the wagon, the horses, and the inventory of the Puget Sound Co-operative Colony store.

The *Tacoma Union* says, "Perhaps there never has been such a case on Puget Sound, wherein plans laid beforehand were so fully carried out, so expeditiously executed, and a stock of merchandise valued at nearly $10,000 so suddenly removed."

Soon after, the court appoints a receiver. The socialist experiment at Port Angeles is ended, swept away in the troubles of the capitalist world around it.[27]

BLAME (1893)

In his statement to the special session of Congress that begins August 7, 1893, President Cleveland blames the Panic on the Sherman Silver Purchase Act. By forcing the Treasury to buy the nation's output of silver with newly printed dollars, the law forces a continuous increase of the money supply without adding to the stock of gold thereby putting a strain on the gold standard. Investors, especially foreigners, worry that the Treasury will run out of gold and have been demanding gold instead of paper. To restore confidence, Cleveland says, the United States must convince the world that it will continue to pay in gold, "the money universally recognized by all civilized countries."

Many newspapers in the Evergreen State are skeptical of the president's explanation, which is also Wall Street's explanation. The *Seattle Telegraph*, a gold-Democrat paper, argues that the collapse had broader causes than a U.S. currency law. A worldwide boom ended in late 1890 with Argentina's default on gold loans from Baring Brothers of London. A panic has hit Australia. The building of the American rail network, which has kept a huge workforce busy, is about done. "There were business crises before the Sherman law was ever thought of," the *Telegraph* says, "and there will be others after it is forgotten." The *Telegraph* agrees, however, that the Sherman law should be repealed.

The *Spokane Chronicle* is the most prominent silver-Democrat paper in the state. It reluctantly supports the silver-purchase law, which has the Treasury buying silver at the world market price—about 70 cents—though this policy is not what the *Chronicle* really wants. It wants a law ordering the Treasury to buy all the silver the world offers at the fixed price of $1.29 and provide silver at that price to everyone who offers silver certificates. The policy is called *free silver*. It amounts to a silver standard at $1.29 an ounce, the official price of silver before the Civil War.

President Grover Cleveland. *Tacoma Daily News, 6-27-96*

In the 1890s the United States has *free gold*. Since 1879 people have been free to sell the Treasury their gold at $20.67 an ounce and buy gold at that price (plus the cost of minting) with gold certificates. Most of the silver men call themselves "bimetallists," meaning that they want free silver *and* free gold, a gold standard and a silver standard at the same time, with 16 ounces of silver equal to one ounce of gold. The ratio is from history. In the 1790s, 15.5 to 1 was the ratio in the market, and was written into law; in 1834 this was changed to 16 to 1 to reflect changes in the market. But with silver trading in 1893 at 70 cents in the world market, the gold-silver ratio is 30-to-1. Can America unilaterally make 16-to-1 work, as if the world market did not exist?

The state's leading Republican paper, the *Seattle Post-Intelligencer,* answers that question with mathematical assurance: 16-to-1 cannot work. And surely the *P-I* is right about this. America is connected to the world economy. If the Treasury offers to buy the world's silver at $1.29 and pays in dollars that can be exchanged for gold at $20.67, the world will bring it silver and take out gold until the gold is gone. The U.S. dollar will become a silver currency like the Mexican peso. The *Post-Intelligencer* runs more than 85 editorials from June through October explaining this and demanding the repeal of the Sherman Silver Purchase Act, a measure that falls short of free silver but that helped bring on the Panic.

In Seattle, the chamber of commerce urges repeal of the act, as do leaders of 17 banks. In Tacoma, a small meeting of its chamber of commerce approves a resolution urging repeal, but with an amendment by Nelson Bennett of the *Ledger* to protect silver producers, presumably with a tariff. The next day's *Tacoma News* declares the chamber's position insane and the chamber meets again and votes for straight repeal.

Congress passes the repeal bill, and on November 1, 1893, President Cleveland kills the Sherman Silver Purchase Act. "At last the silver incubus has been lifted from the markets," writes Wall Street savant Henry Clews, who expects "a general revival of business." The *Spokane Chronicle,* which denies the existence of a silver incubus, takes hope in that people like Clews believe in it. Just as "faith in what is known as Christian Science often operates upon sick people who believe in it," the *Chronicle* argues, the faith of gold bugs like Henry Clews may bring a revival of confidence.

It doesn't. It is too late.[28]

The deeper cause of the hard times lies in the excesses that preceded them. In Tacoma, the Reverend Leavitt Hallock of the First Congregational Church makes the front page of the *News* with a Sunday sermon comparing the wild men of the West with the wise men of the East. "The first thing which the East seems to say... is 'go slow,' " the reverend declares. "She has saved more and spent less. She has kept the margin for a rainy day, and you have put it all in and all you could borrow, and that's the difference, and that's the reason why it pinches harder." The second thing, he says, the East would say to the West is, "be honest." He mentions the peddling of town lots to buyers who have never seen them.

On three separate days, the *News* rises in defense of its readers by attacking the minister's sermon. The editors tacitly admit that much of the Reverend Hallock's charge is true. "Honesty is about as common in the West as in the East," they say. "We lack certain refinements in dishonesty and are perhaps more frankly dishonest when we are so, but that is to be expected in a country that is filled with men of courage who lack hypocrisy." As for the charge that Westerners are improvident debtors, they say, "If his style of man had been the Tacoma pioneer there would have been no buildings here today but sawmills, no industries but the digging of clams, no shipping but the Siwash canoes."

In Washington, D.C., the voice critical of Western excess is

Comptroller James Eckels.
Seattle Post-Intelligencer, 9-4-96

that of the comptroller of the currency, James Eckels. He is the federal regulator of the national banks and plays a huge role in the banking crisis nationwide. His pronouncements are page-one news. In a speech in New York, Eckels denounces the "speculators in the extreme West and portions of the South" who have staked out "waste places" for new towns. "Disaster has befallen upon speculative institutions and boom cities of Washington, Oregon, California, Colorado, Kansas, and Missouri, which have in turn injured the solvent ones," Eckels says, "but the states of New England and the East and those of the Northwest have thus far escaped, and will, because the foundation upon which they are built is rock, not sand." (By "Northwest," he means the Great Lakes states, not the "extreme West.")

It is noticed immediately that Eckels named Washington first.

The *Spokane Review* condemns Eckels' statement as a "gratuitous insult... positively indecent, unpatriotic, ungenerous, narrow, spiteful, contemptible" by a man who knows little of the West. Indeed, Eckels is not from the West; before being picked for high office he was a lawyer in Ottawa, Illinois, a small town near Chicago. He made friends with Grover Cleveland in 1879, while at law school in Albany, New York, and he was given the comptroller job because Cleveland trusted him. In fact, Eckels is the first currency comptroller with no experience in banking. At 35, he looks so young that hotel employees have mistaken him for a messenger boy. He takes the job seriously, though, and soon knows a good deal more than newspaper editorial writers about the condition of the national banks, because the bank examiners and receivers throughout the country report to him.

Bank examiner Charles Clary writes to Eckels in October 1893 about the Port Townsend National: "This bank was viciously managed when it was first opened. The president, who lived away from the town, neglected his duty... The cashier and resident directors made improper loans to themselves and to their schemes without proper security..."

Clary also examines the wreckage of the First National Bank of Whatcom. It has been "wickedly mismanaged," he writes. The receiver, George Blanchard, complains about cashier Charles Atkins, who is effectively the chief executive officer. Atkins, he says, is involved in land development on the side. He has lent money to himself and his wife in excess of the federal loan limit—10 percent of bank capital—with "no security whatever."

Examiner Thomas Jennings writes to Eckels in August 1893 regarding the First National Bank of Spokane—the bank headed by pioneer sawmill owner James Glover—that probably no law was broken. But, the examiner says, "the lending of almost the entire capital of the bank to practically one person upon insufficient or no security at all, and the failure of the books of the Association to show the true condition of its affairs, are to my mind *morally* incriminating."

Receiver Robert Wingate, who takes over the remains of the Merchants National Bank of Tacoma, writes Eckels in February 1894, concerning the self-dealing of its former president, Walter J. Thompson: "He seems to have considerable misconception of the purposes for which banks are established." Thompson has also employed his brother-in-law and former Tacoma mayor, Henry Drum, as cashier.

The most sweeping indictment of Washington's pioneer bankers is an anonymous missive typed on telegraph-office paper and sent to Eckels: "The recent collapse of banking institutions in the Puget Sound section of the State of Washington," it says, "has been no surprise to those who have visited the district in question and observed the manner in which everybody has been doing business." The writer describes "the town-site folly" in which promoters platted New Dungeness, Gig Harbor, Port Angeles, Port Madison, Port Gardner, Fairhaven, Sehome, New Whatcom, Ballard, Edmonds, Mukilteo, Lowell, Everett, Stanwood, and Anacortes.

"In the county of Whatcom, cities have been platted for nearly forty miles of shoreline," the unnamed man writes. "No sane man will insist that either at the present or any other time in the remote future will there be any necessity or support for a continuous city from Blaine on the British Columbia line around to Port Angeles on the Olympic Peninsula." Even more striking, he writes, is the booming of Grays Harbor, a remote inlet south of the "almost unexplored" Olympic Peninsula. It has "a fair harbor for vessels" and might support "one small but lively city," but instead has eight town sites, including Grays Harbor City, a town site already reclaimed by the owls and raccoons.

Around Puget Sound and Grays Harbor, the anonymous writer concludes, "enough unproductive and worthless town lots are being carried to bankrupt a state four times as populous as Washington." Thousands of those lots are held as loan security by banks that lent recklessly, without due diligence and foresight.

Sitting in Washington, D.C., Eckels has been given a thoroughly unfavorable picture of banking in the "extreme West."[29]

A century later, investor Warren Buffett will say, "Only when the tide goes out do you discover who's been swimming naked." In 1893 the retraction of credit exposes financial crimes all across the country.

In the 1890s, graft is called "boodle," and public officials who take bribes or dip their hands into the till are called "boodlers."

Before the Panic, Puget Sound's big boodler was Winfield Scott Parker, the marshal and tax collector of Fairhaven. "Parker was congenial and popular," recalls a writer a few years later. "His liberality in spending money and his capacity for the absorption of good whiskey, as well as smoking to the point of inveteracy, added to his popularity among the crowd of Californians and Eastern people who were letting their money go with open hands." At Thanksgiving, 1891, Parker pockets $15,000 and flees to Argentina, and is absent when the Panic hits.

The squeeze of 1893 brings out a bevy of boodlers. In Seattle the city treasurer, Adolph Krug, is discovered to have boodled $124,000. The *Tacoma Ledger* prints a list of Krug's loans, saying that he has made the city's funds available to "gamblers, capitalists, dive-keepers, newspaper owners, bankers and almost anyone who wanted money," including $1,500 to Seattle's mayor. Krug flees the city, but is nabbed at St. Paul in a citizen's arrest. He is convicted and sentenced to seven years in prison.

In New Whatcom, city treasurer Philip Isensee is accused of boodling $68,000. He flees, is collared at Yale, British Columbia, and brought back to be tried for embezzlement. In his defense, he claims he doesn't know where the money went and suggests it may have been stolen, but not by him. He says he doesn't know how much he has paid out because he writes checks without filling out the stubs. He has had only a vague idea of how much the city has in the bank. He admits that he once discovered $800 in city warrants under his desk when he moved it. In short, says the New Whatcom *Reveille*, the city treasurer's defense is that he is a paragon of "incompetency and stupidity." The jury finds him guilty and sentences him to four years in prison.

Two years hence, Clallam County Treasurer Messena J. Clump, 36, will be arrested for embezzling $4,000 while in office in 1893. Confined by sheriff's deputies at Port Angeles, he will escape at night, be rowed out to a waiting boat and spirited to Tatoosh Island, a windswept rock off the northwest point of the Olympic Peninsula. Months later, disguised by new side whiskers and a false name, he will be arrested working as a mower on a farm near Boise, Idaho. He will be brought back to Port Angeles for trial, convicted and sentenced to six years in prison.

Some of the arguments in boodlers' trials are odd. In Spokane, when councilman Peter Graham is sacked in 1893 for accepting boodle from a sewer contractor, he argues in court that taking a bribe is not against the law—and is acquitted.

Financial crime also plagues private business. At the collapsed Washington Farmers' Insurance Co., Spokane, promissory notes for $21,000 are taken by insiders who say the company owes them. Manager James Hopkins is convicted of embezzlement and sent to prison. Farmers counting on $2.1 million in fire coverage are left to fight with creditors over $8 in cash and assets claimed to be worth $5,000.

A handful of bankers go beyond recklessness into the realm of undisputed criminality. In Buckley, Pierce County, Samuel Herman Hart, 47, and Frank A. Dinsmore, 23, have been running the Buckley State Bank, which is not really a state bank because it was never incorporated. For a year and a half they take deposits from hop growers and lumbermen and make pawnshop-type loans on items easily sold, sometimes with interest as high as 5 percent a month. Hart joins the Masonic Lodge; he ingratiates himself with local Democrats, and in November 1892 is their nominee for Pierce County treasurer. He loses. On November 18, 1893, Hart and Dinsmore fill their pockets with the remaining cash, torch the business records and vamoose.

The Buckley bank is left $30,000 short. The press reports all sorts of rumors: that the men are Mormons or Jews; that they have taken a boat to China or Japan, and that Hart has been having "intimate relations with a woman" who is not his wife. The other-woman story is a red herring planted by detectives in order to persuade Nellie Hart, who is left behind, to turn against her husband. She does. Through her help, detectives nab Hart at his family home in Baltimore and announce that he is really Louis L. Kann, a bunco artist of infamy, and that "Dinsmore" is his son. From Olympia, Governor John McGraw sends a man to Baltimore with an order of extradition, but Kann's lawyer beats the order in federal appeals court and he and his son remain free.

On Whidbey Island, the tiny Island County Bank at Coupeville closes November 30, 1893, with only $7 in its cash drawer. Its manager and cashier, Englishman Thomas S. Beals, Jr., 27, has left town, supposedly to raise cash for the bank. Beals is found in Tacoma partying in Opera Alley—the red-light district—in the company of a "soiled dove" named Gertie Willis. The *Tacoma Ledger* reports that Beals rented a whole whorehouse and that one such bacchanalia cost $600 in wine alone. In an interview with the *Tacoma Union*, Beals denies that he rented the whole house; he insists that he went to the bordellos one at a time. He denies the figure for wine, saying that he spent only $800 or $900 all together, and that he is not responsible for the $5,000 missing from the bank. Beals has a last romp with Gertie Willis and flees on the eve of his trial for embezzlement. In September 1894, the *Townsend Daily Leader* guesses Beals is "either in Mexico or China."

At Puyallup, cashier Samuel Dusinberre of the Bank of Puyallup, who so courageously denies a $10,000 loan to the bank's president, has already "lent" $31,000 to his family and friends. He is enticed into a business venture, the venture is failing, and he "lends" himself $10,000 to save it. When the bank fails, Dusinberre's peculations are discovered, and he pleads guilty to grand larceny. He is sentenced to three years in the state penitentiary at Walla Walla.

A few people who lose their money respond with threats of violence. At the Bank of Puyallup, President Willis Boatman receives a letter vowing to shoot him on sight if depositors are not paid. "I care nothing for my life and have lived as long as I want to," the anonymous writer says. "If you can make a pauper of me while you root around in your luxuries, I will rid the country of one of the robbers."

A Puyallup tinsmith is fingered for making that threat and is put on trial for it, but the judge dismisses the case for lack of evidence.

In June 1893, the people of Moscow, Idaho, were ready to lynch borrower Mike Leitch for shooting their bank president. In December, a jury finds Leitch guilty of "assault with intent to do great bodily harm," but not of attempted murder, and he is sentenced to only two years in the Idaho penitentiary. The *Pullman Herald* reports, "An effort is already being made to secure his pardon, and a petition to that effect is being circulated." The ostensible reason to pardon him is that he is not in strong health, but it is notable that in a time of rampant financial crime and bank failures, people have become much more willing to excuse a man who shoots a banker.[30]

In the backwash of the Panic, blame falls on the men who have mismanaged banks, businesses, and government treasuries. Though the crisis was set off by a stampede of foreign investors, the underlying problem has been the excessive risk-taking, the bad investments, and the poor management by individuals. And as the hard times continue, there will be more decisions and more blame to go around.

The flip side of blame is credit. Even among the despised class of bankers, some attempt to save their institutions by sound decisions and concerted effort, and some succeed.

The banks that make it through the Panic and hard times of the 1890s will become some of Washington's principal institutions of the 20th century. These include, in Walla Walla, the Baker-Boyer National (now the state's oldest bank); in Spokane, the Old National; in Tacoma, Puget Sound Savings, which will become Puget Sound National; in Seattle, Dexter Horton & Co. and the Seattle National, which will become Seattle-First National; the National Bank of Commerce, which will become Rainier National; People's Savings, which will become Peoples National; and the Washington National Building and Loan Investment Association, which will become Washington Mutual. All of these institutions suffer; deposits at the National Bank of Commerce of Seattle fall 59 percent in the last nine months of 1893, but the bank stays open.

Port Angeles, Port Townsend, New Whatcom, Anacortes, Everett, Ellensburg, Spokane, and Tacoma are hit hard by the bank closures, but Seattle is not. Crows the *Post-Intelligencer* of July 20, 1893, less than two months into the Panic, "There has not been a single failure of any description among the banks or business houses of Seattle."

Several reasons are offered. Seattle is one of the state's older cities, and more people have put down roots there. Unlike Spokane, it is not reliant on silver. Unlike Everett, its real estate is not under the thumb of a single land company. Unlike Tacoma, its waterfront is not controlled by a railroad.

Seattle also has such bankers as Jacob Furth, the Bohemian-born Jew who founded Puget Sound National Bank of Seattle. On the eve of the Panic of 1893, Furth becomes president of the Puget Sound National as well as the People's Savings. At the height of the Panic the Puget Sound National's directors vote to call in the bank's loans. Furth objects; the businessmen of Seattle are his friends, and he has promised them the bank's support. He demands and gets 10 days' delay, and uses the time to raise money in New York. He doubles the capital of the Puget Sound National and avoids calling in the loans. His strategy works. The Puget Sound National will emerge from the hard times of the 1890s with the largest book of loans of any national bank in Washington.

In Tacoma, Chester Thorne raises $200,000 to save the National Bank of Commerce of Tacoma and later comes to the rescue of Fidelity Trust. But in the summer of 1893 it is the solidarity of Seattle bankers that makes news. In

Jacob Furth. *Seattle Post-Intelligencer,* 1-3-97

The Quarterly Journal of Economics for January 1894, Albert Clark Stevens writes: "At Seattle, Washington, banks met, and resolved early during the depression that 'they would stand by each other through thick and thin.' "

Says the *Seattle Press-Times*: "It has been asserted that an ironclad agreement has been entered into between all the mercantile, manufacturing and banking interests to assist each other." No such treaty exists, the *Press-Times* says, but Seattle's commercial men have acted "as though there were."

A story circulates of how Seattle did this. In August 1893, the *Yakima Herald* writes: "No jealousies, such as are said to have precipitated the first Spokane failures, were permitted to exist. The lawyers were pledged not to enforce outside collections, and the banks engaged every strong box of the safety deposit companies. Then they were ready for business. If a depositor took his account from a bank, every other bank was immediately notified by telephone and not one of them would open an account with him or accept his deposit. Application at the safe depositories showed that there was no chance for him there, and the only course left for him was to return his money to the original bank," which would accept the money only as a time deposit.

On August 9 the *Tacoma News* runs an interview with an anonymous Seattle banker. Seattle's secret is not that its banks are stronger financially, the man says, but that the city's businessmen have "been able to keep the people under control." Employees who pull out their savings are told they will be fired and blacklisted. Depositors who pull out their savings are paid in gold, and banks refuse to exchange the gold for high-denomination banknotes that are easier to conceal. Says the banker, "The banks control the safe deposit business of this city. Therefore we make it rather disagreeable for the timid depositors who have withdrawn their money. It is almost impossible to rent a safe deposit box in this city today."

In November 1893, the *Oregonian* reports that banks have shrunk their book of loans by only $100,000 in Seattle, and at least $500,000 in Tacoma, Spokane, and Portland. Much of Seattle's success, the *Oregonian* says, is by banks lending to each other and by tapping stockholders for new capital.

Seattle has strengthened its name. In September. a Philadelphia manufacturer of bottles visits Tacoma with an eye to opening the first glass manufactory in the Pacific Northwest. A plant could be built in Tacoma, the man tells the *Ledger.* But he complains of "a lack of unity" there, while people in Seattle, he says, "stand together very much more than the Tacoma people." No doubt these comments pain the *Ledger*, but it prints them.[31]

THE CAUSTIC (1893)

The newspapers' initial reaction to the onset of hard times is that they will be short. On June 13, 1893, the *Spokane Chronicle* suggests, "Better times will dawn before the close of the present year—perhaps before the close of the summer." Four days later the *Tacoma Ledger* notes the reduction in railroad rates and asks, "Have Good Times Arrived?"

Given the answer to be no, the problem arises of how to cope. The *Ledger* invites readers to write about, "How to be happy though poor," and prints a page of replies. They are mostly homilies—"If you can't get what you want, like what you can get." Still, it is a kind of preparation.

In September 1893, a letter arrives in Tacoma for Amaryllis Thompson, the wife of former president Walter J. Thompson of the Merchants National Bank. The writer, Ada Boynton, is a fellow Unitarian; she lives in Everett but knows the Thompsons from when she and her husband, a newspaper editor, lived in Tacoma. She is caring for seven children, three from his first marriage and four of their own. Now come the hard times. She asks that the Thompsons take her 17 year-old stepdaughter, Marnie, as a servant for $5 a month, payable either in cash or in Mrs. Thompson's old clothes. (Mrs. Thompson's response is not recorded.) Ada Boynton had hoped to send Marnie to "the state Normal"—teachers' college—but she writes, "I must send my girl to work." The girl had shown talent playing the neighbor's piano, but the neighbor has sold the piano and Marnie no longer plays. Her stepmother is heartbroken. She writes, "Sometimes I am very wicked—bitter against God."

Facing hard times, people are mostly on their own. "No relief seems to be in sight, so we must prepare to sustain ourselves," writes the *Ellensburgh Capital* in an editorial entitled, "Our Darkest Hour." "It is now the duty of businessmen to stand together and by each other," the paper writes. "Money is very scarce and hard to get, and we must all exercise patience and charity." The editorial warns collectors of debts that it is "useless in nearly all cases to crowd people, and the less there is done of it the better."

In "Advice to Unemployed," the *Tacoma Ledger* advises men out of work to stop bellyaching, keep up their courage, and not be choosy about work. "If men are unable to get employment there are still many things they can do," the paper says. "The winter's supply of wood can be cut, chopped and stacked; those who have gardens can look after them; needed but delayed repairs to the house can be made..."

The *Seattle Telegraph* observes that people in 'collapsed boom' towns seem to be waiting for some distant corporation to come and puff up the value of their land. The *Telegraph's* advice: "Get out and work. If you have only a town lot, work that for all it is worth. In this climate much can be done with very little." Says the *Walla Walla Statesman*: "There is altogether too much talk about 'hard times'... Keep your mouth shut, saw wood and say nothing."

Almost everyone in Washington is a newcomer and in the hard-hit cities the newspapers worry that their readers will move back east. "Hard times are migratory times," says the *Spokane Review* in an appeal to readers not to go. Says the *Ledger*, "Workingmen who think times are dull will find them no better by going east."

And if people are out of work for a while, the *Ledger* argues, "They can live here as cheaply, if not more cheaply, than anywhere else." On the Tacoma docks, halibut sells for 1 or 2 cents a pound. "As a last resort," says the *Everett Herald*, "we have the 'old settler's meal' provided 'when the tide is out' on Puget Sound."

The newspapers return often to the thought that adversity is good medicine. The *Seattle Telegraph* suggests that never again will factory workers "be caught by depression with their pockets so empty." The *Spokane Review* is thinking of speculators. "Hard times," it says, are reminders that "the earth is not intended for an idler's paradise," and that men cannot build a life by selling each other town lots. Hard times "wreck many a fond illusion, but they are a caustic which burns to purify."[32]

In August 1893, anarchist Emma Goldman tells a gathering of jobless in New York that if they want bread they should take it—

and she is arrested for inciting to riot. In Chicago the unemployed march to the mayor's office and demand work, and a mob of Italians throw stones at police. In Colorado, Governor Davis H. Waite calls for his followers to fight Wall Street with "argument and the ballot," but warns that if the "money power" uses force, his supporters will do the same. "It is better, infinitely better," he declares, "that blood should flow to the horses' bridles than our national liberties should be destroyed." For saying this, Waite's enemies dub him "Bloody Bridles."

In Denver, city, county, and charitable groups struggle to feed and shelter idle men, many from the silver mines. A murder occurs about a week after Denver's bank runs. The apparent murderer, an Italian saloonkeeper, is taken from jail by a mob of 10,000 men who batter their way in with a ram. They string up the man to a tree, riddle him with bullets, and drag his corpse through the streets.

"Denver Is Alarmed," is the headline in the *Seattle Post-Intelligencer* on July 28. Given the "immense crowd of idle workingmen," the story says, "there is a dread in the minds of many citizens that a riot of enormous size, having for its purpose the looting of the city, may break out at any time. The banks of the city have called upon United States troops at Fort Logan, of which there are 700, to be ready to protect their institutions."

Denver officials close down a tent camp and pass out hundreds of train tickets for idle men to leave town. "Before leaving, the crowds entered stores and asked for food," the wire story says. "No threats were made, but they got what they wanted."

The *Seattle Telegraph* warns that mass idleness may breed riot and rebellion. "It is always possible to call out the troops and use the argument of the ball cartridge upon the men," it says. "But what can be done with the women and children?"

Argues the *Telegraph*: "The wealth of the country must come to the rescue." It means private wealth: "The rich man may ask: 'Am I my brother's keeper?' He may say with truth that he has made what he has by his business skill, his thrift, his industry. But mere words will prove a poor bulwark against the assault which may come at almost any day against property rights and existing social institutions."

All this is a push to do more.[33]

In 1893, Americans do not expect the federal government to provide work just to keep people employed. For president, they have elected a Democrat, Grover Cleveland, who said in his 1893 inaugural, "While the people should patriotically and cheerfully support their government, its functions do not include the support of the people."

Governments do provide work by building things. In 1893, building things is a popular idea, particularly at the local level. In 1893, the Everett Land Co. offers to sell the new municipality its water works, electric works, and street railway, at a loss, and spend the money to build a jetty. The *Everett Herald* is for it. On Oct. 12, it notes that men in Everett are idle. "The city needs to have them employed," it says. "Trade needs it. Every interest demands that such a legitimate method of relief should be adopted, and without delay." There is a further reason: "We cannot afford to have people go away from the city to find employment."

Everett's city government is barely five months old. It has little money and no credit history. It puts municipal ownership to a vote and men turn it down.

In Tacoma, protesters urge the city to pave Pacific Avenue using day labor rather than contractors' crews, to pay the men in cash and not warrants, to work them no more than 8 hours a day—this is the era of 10-hour days—and to rotate the crews weekly. The *Ledger* denounces these proposals. It reminds readers that spending on the idle is paid for by those still working. "It is of far more importance to the city and its people that those who are now employed and their employers shall be protected and kept going than that those who are unemployed should be given work," it argues. "It is not the unemployed who build cities."

The next day the *Ledger* softens. "No doubt there are some worthy cases, perhaps in the aggregate considerable numbers, who are tied at home by large families or perhaps invalid relatives," it says. "Such could be looked after, and when possible employment provided. But to say that this city must provide work for all who are unemployed, under the conditions suggested last Saturday, will bring every mendicant in the West here and... tax every legitimate enterprise out of existence."

In fact, Tacoma is buying its water works and extending sewers. Late in 1893, Tacoma's mayor tells the New York *Review of Reviews* that sewer work has employed 300 men and the contractor replacing the wooden planking on Pacific Avenue employs another 200. Public jobs are reserved for heads of families and men who have lived in Tacoma for at least six months. Crews are rotated so that no man works more than two weeks per month. Seattle does the same, using sewer work to employ 600 men by mid-winter, rotating crews every 15 days to spread the work.

In Seattle, the school board votes to discharge all unmarried janitors, reserving the jobs for men with wives to support. Janitor J.D. Lonsway asks for time to find a wife, and is told it is not possible. He is discharged. Some districts refuse to employ married women as teachers because they are presumed to have husbands to support them.

Spokane almost comes to riot over public contracting. After voters approve a bond measure to take over the waterworks and lay pipe up the Spokane River, a property owner gets a court order blocking the work. Hundreds of angry idle men gather in the snowy street to denounce the rich. They talk fancifully of blowing up the *Spokane Review* building. Then they rush to the shuttered Bank of Spokane Falls and call for its owner, Anthony Cannon, who is also president of the water company.

Cannon comes. "I was told that you wanted to see me, and I came to you," he tells the angry crowd. "I was told that you wanted to hang me or something, but I came. I, too, am a laboring man and have worked constantly in this city for nearly seventeen years, until my constitution is broken. During those years the enterprises in which I have been interested have paid out $1,750,000 for labor alone. I always have been a friend of labor and always intend to be."

Cannon says he will talk to the man who brought the lawsuit. The crowd is mollified. It disperses, and the next day it is announced that the lawsuit will be withdrawn. The man who filed it is too scared to go through with it.

The work on the Spokane waterworks begins in 1894. On January 24 there are 1,262 applicants for no more than 350 jobs.[34]

Indian hop pickers on the Seattle waterfront. *Arthur H. Lee, Seattle Post-Intelligencer,* *8-25-97*

Among whites is an assumption that they have a bumping privilege to take non-white jobs. This is expressed in the newspapers, and there is no debate about it.

Racial privilege is asserted in the harvest of hops, the major crop west of the Cascades. "This year the hop picking should be given to and done by white men and not by Indians, at least so long as white men want the work," writes the *Reveille* of New Whatcom. "It is bad policy for white men in need of work to allow Mr. Siwash to loaf most of the year, producing nothing, and then come off his perch when there is work to be done which white capital and industry has created."

The hop harvest—and it is a big one in 1893—begins in early September. It requires thousands of pickers. In previous years they were mostly Native American women and children who are willing to pick when the ground is muddy and the vines wet. The Native Americans come to the fields around Puyallup from as far away as Cape Flattery, Vancouver Island, the British Columbia coast, and southeastern Alaska, their canoes speckling Puget Sound on the way to Tacoma. They also pick in the new irrigated hop fields in the Yakima Valley.

In 1893, the *Tacoma Ledger* arranges for group rates—$6.50 round-trip—for white pickers to go to Yakima on the Northern Pacific. Not all who sign up are unemployed. The *Ledger* headlines its story, "A Six Weeks' Picnic," and its reporter finds young office workers who imagine it as a paid camp-out. Many will come back early, complaining of 12-hour days in the hot sun.

Whites are also recruited to pick in the hop fields of Pierce County. In September 1893, the *Ledger* quotes a U.S. immigration inspector at Orting. "There are hundreds of these white people in the valley, and the growers are showing the proper spirit in giving them work," the official says. Most of the Native Americans are turned away.

Not all of them. At H. Paulson's farm southeast of Sumner, a group of white men stake out hop boxes before dawn. The hired Quileute pickers arrive and are held at gunpoint. With the help of the administrator of Pierce County's poor farm—the closest representative of the government—Paulson convinces the whites to back off.

"What are we to do?" says one of the white workers to the *Tacoma News*. "We are starving. Have had nothing to eat for three days except some potatoes and salt." Perhaps so, but they do not attempt to push out workers of their own race. Nor does the *News* quote the opinions of the Quileutes.[35]

The other workers cast aside are Asians. In Kent, King County, a committee of white pickers warns hop growers that they will not condone the employment of Japanese, many of which, the *Ledger* says, "have sneaked over the boundary from British Columbia" and have offered to pick at less pay per box. "All growers save one promised to obey," writes the paper.

The *Seattle Press-Times* lays the bumping privilege on the line: "In a few cases the selfish growers have encouraged Chinese and Japanese labor, but from the recent experiences of growers in Oregon and California it will not be safe for these small-souled individuals to carry out their cheap labor ideas too far, as the temper of the many thousand good men out of employment is not of a character, with want staring in the faces of their wives and children, to allow

CHINESE SMUGGLERS IN THE GRIP OF THE LAW.

A Tacoma perspective. *Tacoma Daily Ledger, 9-19-97*

Mongolians or Japs to usurp what by all rights of Christian civilization belongs to them."

Compared with Asians, African Americans are less numerous in Washington and, outside the coal mines, they do not often compete directly with whites. To the whites, the Chinese are a foreign race with a foreign language, a foreign religion, foreign hairstyles—pigtails—and a foreign vice, the use of opium. Chinese work hard, and are willing to work for less than the whites.

By 1893, anti-Chinese feeling among whites is still strong, though it has peaked. In 1885 and 1886, white mobs expelled the Chinese from Whatcom County, from Tacoma, and many from Seattle, and in 1890, from Hoquiam and Aberdeen.

At the federal level, anti-Chinese sentiment is codified in the Geary Act of 1892. The new law requires all Chinese, and only Chinese, to obtain federal identification cards or be deported.

President Cleveland has little enthusiasm for the Geary Act, which was signed into law by President Harrison. Cleveland's secretary of state worries about reprisals against American missionaries in China, and in the president's name publicly asks Oregon Governor Sylvester Pennoyer to protect the rights of Chinese in his state. Pennoyer, who has left the Democrats for the People's Party, is notoriously anti-Chinese. He replies, publicly: "I will tend to my business. Let the president attend to his." In the state of Washington, newspapers denounce Pennoyer for his insolence but not his racism.

In May 1893, the U.S. Supreme Court rules the Geary Act constitutional. The federal government, however, seems unwilling to enforce it.

The racial bumping privilege now asserts itself. On Sept. 4, 1893, in Butteville, Oregon, 56 Chinese who had been contracted to pick hops are driven out of the fields by a mob of whites who had been assured of work by Portland employment agents.

On September 20, 11 Chinese pickers are run off of a farm north of Yakima by what the *Yakima Herald* calls "about 40 hobos who have been working promiscuously about several different fields, in all of which they have endeavored to create trouble." Five other Chinese pickers hide in the fields until the hobos go away. The story is written in sympathy with the hop farmer, who has employed "Chinamen because he was unable to obtain other help."

A week later white pickers in the Yakima hop fields strike for $1.50 a box. They have driven out the Chinese pickers, who were hired as strikebreakers for $1.23. The police vow to protect the Chinese.

At La Grande, Oregon, on Sept. 24, 1893, a mob of 200 forms after the saloons close at midnight and attacks the Chinese quarter, stealing goods, setting fires, and running the Chinese out of town. The mob reaches the house of the local missionary, where 30 of the town's Chinese seek refuge. The missionary, the Reverend L.G. Trumbull, is not there, but his wife is, along with her daughter. Says the wire story datelined La Grande, "When the mob demanded their delivery, she appeared with a Winchester and announced that the first man to enter the house would be shot. The mob dispersed." Most of La Grande's Chinese take the train for Portland.

Fourteen whites from La Grande are indicted for their actions that night. None is found guilty.

In Washington the Chinese pull back from the boomtowns and concentrate in the Chinatowns of the older cities—Seattle, Port Townsend, and Walla Walla—and also Spokane.

The Chinese have many enemies in the daily press. The

labor-backed *Tacoma Union* calls them "filthy, lecherous parasites." Even in relatively tolerant Seattle, the *Telegraph* bares its racial fangs: It argues that ejecting the Chinese is part of the greater Darwinian struggle. "It does not look right, but it seems inevitable," the *Telegraph* says. "The red men could not live in contact with the white men. The white men cannot live in contact with the Mongolian. The fittest must survive. It is cruel, but it is natural."

Seattle's leading paper, the *Post-Intelligencer*, is quiet during the anti-Chinese campaign in late 1893. In May 1894, it observes that there has been no similar campaign against cheap labor from Europe. The focus, the *P-I* says, "seems to be more of a matter of race hate and prejudice than it is of the interests of labor."[36]

People are kinder to individuals, at least to those of their own race. In Tacoma, after unemployed plasterer Charles Patnud leaves his wife and three young children penniless and owing five months' rent, the wife tries to survive by taking in washing. She is owed $1.50, the customer doesn't pay and her children have nothing to eat. Neighbors send over boxes of groceries, the county commissioner pays a visit, and it becomes a page-one story in the *Tacoma News*.

In December 1893, the *Ledger* runs a letter from a Tacoma principal asking for donations of clothes and especially shoes. "We have children who are too poorly clad to come to school comfortably," the principal says. The paper also publishes a notice asking teachers what items their pupils need. It calls upon readers to help, and they do.

The *Ledger* sends out a social worker to the "nigger tract," a shantytown built on land of unclear title west of downtown Tacoma. The social worker finds that people have food but need clothes and fuel to keep warm.

A few families are driven to desperation. On November 13, 1893, three children—identified as Sophia, 14, May, 8, and Mike, 3—knock on a Seattle door that belongs to the home of the police matron. They are arrested for begging. They say their family name is Julian, they live in Everett and they have five brothers and sisters. They say their father has left to find work and their mother has been taking in laundry to pay the rent. They say their mother put them on the steamer this morning to beg in Seattle.

They are not punished. The *Telegraph's* reporter notes that the driver of the patrol wagon buys them a bag of doughnuts and cakes, and that someone has given Sophia a silver dollar. But they are not allowed to beg in Seattle. The police escort them to the steamer and send them back to Everett.

In Seattle, an elderly couple, both sick, is taken to Providence Hospital. "The man was a saw filer until he became too old to work, and they now live in a shanty," reports the *Post-Intelligencer*. "They are destitute." The hospital has twelve charity cases. The city government has been paying the bills of those from the city, and Mayor James Ronald orders this to stop. The city attorney advises him that under state law the county should pay.

Washington's four-year-old constitution has a clause forbidding any county, city, or town from giving money or loaning its credit to a private party "except for the necessary support of the poor and infirm." Fred Gasch, King County commissioner, takes this to mean that any county, city, or town *may* support the poor and infirm, and that Seattle and King County should share the load. The county can take care of people from outside the city at the county poor farm, where it has a physician. But he says, "The county has no physician in town."

Dr. F.S. Palmer, Seattle's public health officer, suggests the county hire one. Commissioner Gasch replies, "We expect to take care of persons who are properly county charges and no more."

In September 1893, John Murphy, jobless and drunk, hits a man in a Seattle bar. The man follows him outside and strikes him on the head with a railroad coupling pin, leaving him bloodied on the ground. Police send Murphy to Providence Hospital where Sister Superior Mary Eugene says they will care for him but would like to see the trouble between the city and county settled. The *Post-Intelligencer's* story is entitled, "May Die of Red Tape."

Murphy does not die, nor does the dispute. In November 1893, another charity case makes the news. John Holm, a penniless man, has broken his leg. Health officer Palmer is adamant that the city is "called upon to treat only prisoners and smallpox cases" and should not pay for the broken leg. Dr. S.J. Holmes, president of the Seattle Board of Health, says, "This thing will end in the courts. Someone will die in the streets, both city and county refusing to tender aid. Then the point of responsibility will be settled."

A year later Seattle and King County still lack a written agreement. In his annual report for 1894, health officer Palmer writes that unofficially, the city is paying the hospital bills of penniless accident victims who live in the city, "until such time as they can be transferred to the county hospital." He allows that the arrangement is not ideal, but claims that the actual care provided to paupers in Seattle has never been better.[37]

In the winter of 1893-94, the survival of many able-bodied men and women will require aid.

In the rural areas, help, if any, is from a neighbor. Rarely is this mentioned in a newspaper, though the following year, the *Spokane Chronicle* mentions the family of sheep shearer William Margelin. He has left and his family is destitute. Says the *Chronicle*, "Neighbors hurried to their assistance and all is well today."

In small towns, shopkeepers sell on credit to longtime customers. Writing in 1897, the *Snohomish Tribune* says, "During the past three or four years they have carried on their books a good many people who otherwise would have been unable to live."

In the cities, aid is organized. These are early days in the profession of social work and of non-profit organizations, and an opportunity for them to grow.

To some, this is not a welcome thought. In November 1893, the *Oregonian* recalls the first generation of settlers. "People then knew that they had to take care of themselves and didn't think of piling up in the towns and asking for charity." The paper reluctantly admits things have changed.

In September 1893, the *Seattle Telegraph* editorializes in support of the New York *World's* bold method of distributing bread, by which it gives away 1,000 loaves in two hours: "The only credentials which the applicant need present is that he is hungry," the *Telegraph* says. "The *World's* idea is the rational one that few people will take the trouble to call at the depository and get a loaf of bread if they do not really need it, and that if a few impostors avail themselves of the charity the trifling imposition is nothing in comparison with the good accomplished."

A century later this will be called a food bank. It is not common in the 1890s. The thought then is that for a housewife to feed a tramp at the back door may be an act of kindness, but that it also promotes beggary. In the *Review of Reviews* for January 1894, Congregational pastor Washington Gladden argues that the millions out of work are in that condition for different reasons. Some were hardworking and self-reliant but not thrifty; others were thrifty but unwisely put their savings in land and houses. Still others are "chronic paupers"—drunks, drifters and derelicts. "The treatment accorded to the one class," writes Gladden, "ought to differ radically from that bestowed upon the other." Gladden is no reactionary; he is a progressive, a leading light in the Social Gospel movement.

The progressives' answer to the problem of charity is to turn it over to professionals who know how to make these distinctions. In 1893, the Protestant churches of Tacoma form the Associated Bureau of Charities to coordinate efforts and keep a central registry of people helped. Its manager, Baptist Reverend Barnabus MacLafferty, argues that giving charity without judging the recipient is a selfish act, done to make the giver feel good. It is an evasion of genuine responsibility for others. "Indiscriminate giving is totally demoralizing," he tells the *Tacoma News*. "It demoralizes both giver and recipient."

The traditional view—to help the poor directly—is expressed by the Reverend Wallace Nutting of Seattle's First Congregational Church. "People ought not to be sent on their way to some charitable bureau provided you can furnish them with food or lodging," he tells parishioners. "It is better to make a mistake in that way than to let them, for whom Christ died, go away empty."

In the 1890s, the progressive view gains ground. Reporting to the *Review of Reviews*, Seattle mayor Ronald writes that members of the city's Bureau of Charities are "efficiently weeding out chronic pauperism." Partly they do this by requiring work. For example, the Salvation Army has a wood yard on city land where men may cut wood for pay and buy a meal for five cents. Tacoma's Associated

Bureau of Charities requires that meals be provided only to those who have sawn wood for one hour. At its annual meeting in January 1894, the Tacoma group says its wood-sawing requirement has cut the number of men wanting aid.

The *Tacoma Union* thinks this regime too harsh. It tells the story of a man too weak from hunger to cut wood. "He was taken into a neighboring restaurant and given a fifteen-cent meal," the *Union* says. "So rapidly did the viands pass down the throat of the starving wretch that another fifteen-cent meal was placed before him, which he also ate..." The *Union* argues that such men should be fed before being put to work.

In Spokane, where county councilmen have been giving out grocery credit to individuals, an investigation finds that much of it has been going for pickles, jellies, spices, and "fancy butter." Councilmen vote to hire Dora Cannon, niece of banker Anthony Cannon, at $75 a month to dispense flour, beans, coffee, and meat in a professional way. "The name and address of every person receiving aid from Mrs. Cannon's storehouse is registered, with their nativity, age, occupation, number in the family and amount of supplies received," the *Spokane Chronicle* reports. "This list is carefully compared whenever possible with the lists of charity organizations to see who is receiving double aid. Besides this, when any work can be had which the man or woman receiving aid can do they are notified and expected to do the work." During the last week of November, the dispensary serves 131 people.

Spokane's city and county governments also pay much of the costs of the People's Tabernacle, which occupies a four-story building on Sprague Street. From October 1893 to April 1894, it doles out salt pork, beans, molasses, flour, firewood, and soap, and to the homeless, it offers a place to stay for two days. In mid-November 1893, the *Chronicle* finds 35 men "out of work, dead broke and in various stages of dilapidation," occupying the cots, with a few having to sleep on the floor. By late November, 70 men are sleeping there. "Lieutenant" Tom Lavery, who has a city salary for running the Tabernacle, says: "We take everyone that comes, take care of him and get him work if possible." Often it is farm work, and in winter, clearing snow from the railroad tracks.

THE CAUSTIC

Lavery wants people to know he's tough. "A woman was in yesterday," he tells the *Spokane Review*. "She was alone in the world, without furniture or food, and wanted a supply of wood and eatables. I offered her a place out of the city where she could have good wages and a home, but she spurned the offer and said she didn't have to do any one's dirty work. Her name is on the black list."

Dora Cannon and Tom Lavery get most of the ink in Spokane's newspapers but their help goes to fewer than half the town's down-and-outers. In January 1894, the *Review* reports that 200 men are sleeping at the All Nations Saloon, 80 each at the Horseshoe and Shamrock saloons, 70 at the Vega and at saloons elsewhere. Saloons already provide free lunches; these places expand the service to free suppers and a place to sleep, drinks not included. The taprooms have no cots; down-and-outers have to sleep on couches, chairs, and the floor. But the saloons are warm, soup is free, and nobody demands work.[38]

ADRIFT (1893-1894)

The private and individual response to destitution spans the spectrum. A few men—almost always men—respond to ill fortune by killing themselves.

Already mentioned is the hanging suicide of carpenter John Fyrk in Tacoma in May 1893. In August, C.P. Moore, a clothing salesman staying at Tacoma's Grand Pacific Hotel, takes a lethal dose of morphine; the *Ledger* says he "owed several bills around town and, having no money to square up his debts, felt miserable." In September, Carroll Dean, 18, rows away from the shore in Ballard, finds a secluded spot, and shoots himself. He leaves a note saying he did not have work. And in October, a ruined merchant in Vancouver, Washington, George P. Sears, 58, takes a fatal dose of laudanum.

Strangest is the story of James Wheatley, a former railroad brakeman about 30 years old. Wheatley (or Whatley or Wheatly, depending on who's telling the story) arrives in Seattle in November 1893 from Palmer, South Dakota, and rents a room at the Queen City Hotel on South Second Avenue. After a week he is out of money and cannot pay his hotel bill. He downs an ounce of carbolic acid—a disinfectant made of coal tar—which shocks him so hard he bites a chunk out of the tumbler. He rushes out of the hotel into Closson & Kelly's drugstore, pleading: "I'm burning up." The druggist gives him a drink of almond oil, followed with a mixture of almond oil and lime water. The concoction does not save Wheatley, who expires in agony on the drugstore floor.

The story's meaning is debatable. The *Tacoma Union* reports it as an economic story, of a man "out of work and utterly despondent." The *Seattle Post-Intelligencer* and the *Tacoma Ledger* quote the man's suicide note, which says, "The reason I want to do away with myself is because I have an idea to kill someone—I do not care who it is." To them, it is a story of insanity.

Suicides increase during the hard times of the 1890s, though the rate is still only about half that of a century later. A man might go to bed hungry, but if he looks for help, he can find it—if he is willing to accept the indignity of alms. Only a handful of men would rather die than do this.[39]

It is a common belief that hard times bring crime, but the experience of the 1890s is mostly the opposite. A police detective tells the *Tacoma News* that most crimes are related to drink, which in hard times, fewer can afford. In 1893, in Spokane, arrests drop 41 percent.

Still some crimes reflect the hard times, and the newspapers pick that up. In Seattle, an unemployed restaurant worker named James Dolan makes the papers when he smashes a bank's plate glass window with his hickory cane—he has a lame leg—and waits to be arrested. To the judge he pleads guilty and says, "I was out of money, could get no work and had nothing to eat. I am no man to beg; I would not steal; I had to do something. I have been hungry for three days." The superintendent at the private Bureau of Charities sees his story in the *P-I*, offers him work, and the judge suspends his sentence.

The Seattle papers print a story that in Tacoma a man walks out of a grocery with a sack of flour, saying he cannot pay and his family is starving, and that the cop who arrests him pays the man's bill. The *Ledger* sends a reporter to verify this by interviewing patrolmen, and they deny it. The paper accuses the Seattle press of printing lies to make Tacoma look bad—to look so poor that men are stealing to eat—though from another perspective, the story makes Tacoma's police look good.

At Port Townsend, Hattie Stratton's frequent trips to Victoria arouse the suspicion of the U.S. Customs agent on the steamer. He follows her to an opium dealer in Victoria's Chinatown. On August 30, 1893, with the steamer back in U.S. waters, he confronts her. She is holding 18 five-tael cans, recorded as 9 pounds, of Chinese opium, secreted in custom-made leggings that hang by suspenders under her long skirts.

The story of the "petticoat smuggler" splashes onto front pages. Though Hattie Stratton is smuggling narcotics for a Chinese syndicate and gives a false name when arrested, the *Seattle P-I* reports

that in Port Angeles the "universal sympathy is with the smuggler."
She is a sympathetic figure to middle-class readers, a 21-year-old
white woman "of exceptionally fine character, whom the tongue of
scandal has never touched," says the Port Angeles *Democrat-Leader.*
Her excuse for dope-running has special meaning in Port Angeles,
where dozens of residents have squatted on the Government Reserve—land set aside during the Civil War for a military base but
never used—and have just been told they can have titles at a nominal cost. Hattie Stratton says she needs the money in order to pay
the fees on her claim and that of her father, a Civil War veteran who
is old and in ill-health. As if to underline her need for money, as soon
as she is free on bail she goes with her sister to Puyallup to pick hops.

Hattie Stratton pleads guilty. Her sentence is deferred, and
on April 6, 1894, at the request of the judge and district attorney,
President Cleveland grants her a full pardon.

The pardon is for the crime of smuggling, not violating the
drug laws. In 1893, opium is not illegal; federal officers will sell her
opium at public auction, mainly to Chinese buyers. Officers seize
the opium because she is evading the $12 per pound import duty.
In November 1893, Treasury agent A.K. Tingle will report that at
Puget Sound ports, no opium "has ever been entered for duty." At
$12 duty, all opium is smuggled. He recommends the tax be lowered
to $4 if the government wants any revenue from it. The following
year Congress lowers it to $6 and legal importation begins, though
opium will continue to be smuggled to evade the tax.[40]

In the public spaces, a person who is idle and without a place
to stay—particularly if he begs—risks arrest for vagrancy. The law
defines a vagrant as a person without visible means of support while
able to work. Decades later, courts will strike this down as criminaliz-
ing poverty. That is not its purpose. Its purpose is to rid the community of those who refuse to work. Says the *Oregonian*, "If [a man] will
not work, when he is fed, somebody must have worked for him; he is
consuming the fruit of some other person's toil. This is the injustice
the tramp law steps in to correct." The community depends upon
the ethic of self-reliance, which allows for what the *Oregonian* calls an
"honest, proud-spirited poverty that scorns alms."

The *Tacoma Ledger*, which supports this view, argues that men known to be diligent workers need never be idle "because employment is certain to seek them." Recognizing that self-reliance is even more deeply rooted in East Asian cultures—but without irritating its readers by saying so—the *Spokane Chronicle* writes in 1894: "Nobody in Spokane ever saw a Chinaman begging bread or arrested for vagrancy."

Still, men once busy are idle now. Reports the *Chronicle* in October 1893: "Patrick Call, a young Irish miner, was arrested yesterday by Officer Owens for begging on the street. He was convicted of vagrancy, but Judge [Eugene] Miller said there were worse men at large and gave him the lowest possible fine, $2 and costs."

Here is the *Post-Intelligencer* in November 1893: "Thomas Brown and Thomas Burns, vagrants, were sentenced yesterday by Judge [Joseph] Glasgow, in the municipal court, to 30 days each in jail. The judge immediately suspended sentence for two hours in order to give them a chance to get out of town." Suspended sentences are common; in Tacoma municipal court, of the 137 persons found guilty of vagrancy in the first 11 months of 1893, three-quarters are given a suspended sentence and allowed to leave town. Only if they are picked up again will they serve time, typically a month.

In *The Road* (1907), Jack London describes serving a month in prison in 1894 at Niagara Falls, New York, for vagrancy. By his account he does nothing to deserve this. But he suffers this only once, and he vagabonds across the continent and back.

In the depression of the 1890s, the vagrancy law raises troubling questions. In November 1893, the *Post-Intelligencer* argues, "In these hard times, when hundreds of honest men willing to work for their bread cannot get anything to do, it is an inhuman and unlawful act to arrest a man as a vagrant who is idle because nobody has any work for him to do."

The duty of every man, the *P-I* says in November 1893, is "the individual practice of philanthropy within the circle of his own absolute knowledge," by judging who is worthwhile and who is not. A year earlier, the paper had argued that that "private individualism" was preferable to "paternalism." Now the paper has changed its tune. "Individual philanthropy," it says, "is not enough in these times. The real efficient, charitable work must be represented by both *individualism* and *paternalism*."

The paternalism it advocates is a free employment bureau. Seattle sets one up in April 1894 over the objection of private employment agents, who typically charge $2 per head.[41]

Living poor doesn't take much in the 1890s. A single man, working in the mill, may build a shack of scrap lumber. If he loses his job, he can keep his shack; he wasn't paying rent anyway. "Such a thing as ground rent is unknown except on business streets," writes James Cooper Wheeler in "Shack Life on Puget Sound."

Wheeler visits an inlet near Tacoma where men have built shacks on rafts. Many in these homemade houseboats are living off fish, clams, berries, and what food they can share. Their life, he writes, "is a peculiarly independent and happy one, and entirely satisfying to the unambitious man."

An idle man can always hit the road—in desperation, in resignation, or as a lark. Among the wide spaces of the West in the time before the automobile, "the road" means the railroad, riding without paying. It is a dangerous way to travel; a tramp can fall or be thrown off. On June 3, 1893, the *Post-Intelligencer* runs a story about a young tramp who plunged from a passenger train and died: "It was said that trainmen shoved the tramp off the train, but Conductor Maloney says this is wholly untrue."

Vagabonds mostly ride in boxcars or on a "blind baggage," the platform of a baggage car with no door at the end, facing another car with no door at the end. In *The Road*, Jack London has a chapter on an escapade in 1894 in which, at age 18, he outwitted two brakemen trying to chase him off three blind baggages. The more dangerous place is underneath the cars on the brake beam. In June 1894, the *Spokane Review* has this report from Yakima: "Thomas White, who was riding on a brake beam, lost his hold, presumably by falling asleep. He was very badly injured, both legs being crushed below the knees and one hand was taken off at the wrist. He was brought here and taken to the hospital, where he died in a short time."

Proper opinion holds tramps in low esteem. But not all vagabonds are tramps. A tramp, says the *Oregonian*, is "a vicious compound of beggar and thief, who is not only out of work, but propos-

Illustration (obviously staged) of "riding the rods" from the 1907 Macmillan edition of Jack London's *The Road*.

es to remain so." In April 1893, the *Ellensburgh Capital* runs a story about a man who fell off a freight train, lost both his legs and died. The reporter explains that the man, F.M. Williams, 22, "was not a tramp, as he had $24.05 in his pockets."

In October 1893, the *Spokane Review* carries the story of Nicholas Andrews, 40, whose right foot is crushed while attempting to steal a ride. It identifies him as a blacksmith from Bay City, Michigan, not a tramp.

In August 1893, the *Yakima Herald* writes of J.O Stevens and wife, who "walked the entire distance from Tacoma to this place in search of work." Definitely not tramps.

The distinction is not always clear. Some men of the road will work but not work hard. Some will work hard but also steal. Some will promise to work and not show up.

The first chapter in *The Road* has Jack London at a kitchen door in Reno, Nevada, hungry and begging food from a man eating a meat pie. In response to London, the man says, "I don't believe you want to work. You wouldn't work if you had the chance."

"Try me," says London. The man offers him work the next morning moving bricks and a meal *after* that. London promises to do the work, but asks for food now. The man refuses. "I know your kind," he says, neatly placing London in the category of a tramp telling a lie in order to fill his belly.

The man has judged London correctly. To the reader London admits he has no intention of doing the work; he intends to get out of town that night on a blind baggage. But he has made the reader think about what it would be like to be hungry and have to wheedle a meat pie out of a cynical man.

A common response to a backdoor beggar is to give him work, then food. "The women often asked the men to split a little wood," writes Marie Hamel Royer in *The Saxon Story* (1982), an account of immigrants in Whatcom County. "Even though some men were tough-looking customers, unshaven and dispirited, they were never turned away hungry."[42]

In a world with little free public food, people tend to be generous with their private food—if they do not feel used. But in the summer of 1893, several communities along the Northern Pacific Railroad in Washington reach a tipping point. In August 1893, the *Yakima Herald* reports an influx of hobos followed by petty thefts: "Fruit was stolen from the orchards, choice trees were stripped of their luscious burdens; meats were stolen from the family larder; saddles from the farmer's stables; chickens from convenient roosts; honey from tempting hives..."

This note from the *Ellensburgh Capital*, one week later: "An unusual number of strange men have been in town for several days past, and coincident with their advent a number of burglaries have been committed."

At Cle Elum, a Northern Pacific brakeman catches a tramp stealing overcoats from a caboose. Following a new town ordinance, authorities give the thief the choice of jail or a quarter-mile dash while flayed by the brakeman wielding a blacksnake whip. The man chooses to run, and the *Tacoma News* reports him struck on the "head, back, shoulders and legs, with great vigor."

Tramps are typically filthy, and when they find themselves in the new Tacoma jail, they are required to shower. When the *Ledger* praises this policy, the *People's Advocate*, a Populist paper in Chehalis, takes the *Ledger* to task: "Many of those men are American citizens, who through wrong laws of our government are thrown into the condition they are now in." The *Ledger*, it says, should be "taking the laborer's part" rather than siding with the cops.

The *Ledger*, which has just had a fight with its own labor, does not accept the *Advocate's* criticism. The showers at the city jail are for *tramps*. "Why the *Advocate* should thus mix up laboring men with tramps is past finding out," the *Ledger* writes, "since a tramp resembles nothing so remotely as a man who works."[43]

Washington newspapers offer occasional reports of vagabonding as adventure. One such tale is "Red's Eastern Trip," in the *Seattle Post-Intelligencer* of November 6, 1893. John Gleason, a 16-year-old newsboy nicknamed Red, tells the story of his trip to the Chicago World's Fair. He says he and Jimmy Egan left Seattle in July with nothing but pocket change, riding a boxcar to Portland. They ride east to La Grande, Oregon, where Jimmy is nabbed by a man seeking a reward. Red continues on, but is taken at Cheyenne, Wyoming, escapes and rides a brake beam to Denver.

"I stayed a week in Denver an' was eaten pie all the time, robbin' a baker's wagon and sellin' papers," he says. He rides to Chicago, "part of the time on the blind baggage and the rest of the time on deck, that's on top of the cars... When I first got to Chicago I had $5 I had made on the way, and I put up four bits to go into the World's Fair grounds and stayed there a week. I slept in a dry goods box and stole lunches from baskets... When I got broke I sold papers at the 63rd Street entrance.

"I stayed in Chicago three weeks and got drunk there. You can get drunk for 10 cents there; why, you can get pretty much near a gallon of beer for 10 cents.

"Coming home I struck the Calhoun Opera Company and came through to Portland with 'em. I shined their shoes with a shoebox outfit I stole at Denver and stole away in a scenery car. The fellow that had me in the car lost his job for it at Portland. They got on to me at Pendleton, but I rode the blind baggage to Portland."

Red says he arrived home with 45 cents in his pocket.

In December the *P-I* prints the story of Red's friend Jimmy Egan, who confirms Red's story through La Grande but says Red made it no farther than Denver, where he posted a letter. Egan says *he* saw the Chicago fair, having escaped from the people who were trying to send him home.

The *Oregonian* also has a piece about Jimmy Egan, who it says is 14 and the son of John J. Egan, night editor of the *Seattle Telegraph*. The *Oregonian* quotes an account of Egan in the *Chicago Dispatch*, which corroborates his story.

A century later there is no way to know how much of either boy's story is true. But the trains of the 1890s, with their sliding-door boxcars, blind baggages and brake beams, make free travel possible for wayward youth and unemployed men. (Today's trains are not so accommodating.) Note also the tone in which these stories are told. The attitude toward youth and risk in the 1890s is different from today's. See it also in this story from the *Seattle Press-Times* in September 1893:

"The police had a visit yesterday morning from two youthful tramps. They were Carl Ridderbjilke, an 11-year-old from Victoria, and the other was Albert White, a youth of 12 from Tacoma. The boy with the unpronounceable name was born in Japan of Swedish parents. His father, now divorced, is in the east and his mother is in the insane asylum in Victoria. Ridderbjilke has been left to take care of himself and he seemed perfectly capable of doing so. White is also a self-governed youth though his parents have a home for him in Tacoma.

"The two lads had been partners in Victoria and had come to Seattle on the *City of Kingston*. They were bound for New Whatcom and said they expected to walk. After resting a few hours at headquarters, they continued on their way, rejoicing."

In the next day's paper is a statement from White's mother—in Victoria, not Tacoma—who says the boys ran away to pick hops. Writes the *Press-Times'* reporter, "They have gone on their way rejoicing, and will probably pick hops all right. They evidently are able to take care of themselves..."

These are 11- and 12-year-old boys who have run away from home and crossed an international frontier without a parent's permission. Because they appear to be doing fine, the newspaper declares they are free to go. [44]

WEALERS (1894)

In the midst of the Panic of 1893, the American Bi-Metallic League holds a convention in Chicago. People call it the Silver Congress. It includes everyone who is anyone in the world of money agitation, including Nebraska Congressman William Jennings Bryan, 33. The conventioneers are welcomed by Chicago's mayor, Carter Henry Harrison. A few months later, Harrison will be assassinated by a frustrated jobseeker, but on this night he is in full form. "Some of you may be rather wild," he tells the crowd. "It is said that you are silver lunatics. I look down upon you, and I am rather glad to welcome such lunatics. It is 'crazy men' that march the world forward..." For the next few days, speakers address the crowd as "fellow lunatics."

The tone is set. Two moonbeams cross here for the first time. One is Carl Browne, a big, tall, loud man with long, graying hair and beard. He wears a showman's cowboy suit with leather fringe and buttons of Mexican silver half-dollars. Around his neck is a string of amber beads. He calls this "the garb of the frontiersman," which he is not. He has worn this suit hawking patent medicines on the streets of Los Angeles. Browne is a Theosophist. He believes in reincarnation of the spirit—and also in the plentiful creation of money for the American people.

Years later, a journalist will recall the second man: "He wears spectacles. Above a thin, down-growing mustache the face is that of a man of ideas and action; the lower features, especially the mouth, denote a shy, secretive, sentimental, credulous man of mystical preoccupations." He is Jacob Coxey, 39, of Massillon, Ohio. Coxey is a former member of the Greenback Party and current supporter of the People's Party. He owns a 15-acre sandstone quarry that employs 50 workers.

Coxey and Browne talk. When the Silver Congress ends, Browne returns to the streets of Chicago, where he stands atop a barrel in his amber beads and fringed suit to harangue the crowds at Lake Front Park. Browne immerses himself in the ferment, feeling the energy of the people as they repeatedly march on city hall and demand that Mayor Harrison provide bread and work.

Back home, Coxey has a thought of how Congress might rescue idle men. In January 1894, he asks Browne to come and hear it. America's roads are bad, Coxey says, especially in the West. Men can be put to work building better ones. To pay for this, Congress can print $500 million, an amount larger than the annual federal budget, in "legal tenders"—greenbacks—and lend them to the states at zero interest. Coxey has long been a paper-money man; he has named his son Legal Tender.

Coxey's plan needs a push, and Browne has an idea about that. Perhaps he remembers a news story out of St. Louis the previous August about a proposal to march on Washington, D.C., with 50,000 unemployed men. Browne proposes just such a march.

Coxey and Browne define their movement as a crusade for Christian principles on Earth. Coxey's religion is not about an afterlife; to a reporter he says, "Let's have heaven here and now." His crusade will set out on Easter Sunday 1894, almost a year after the Panic began. His banner will say, *Peace on Earth, Good Will to Men, but Death to Interest-Bearing Bonds*. It will call itself the Army of the Commonweal in Christ. The newspapers will call its members commonwealers and then, for headlines, "wealers." They will call the movement Coxey's Army.

"Army" is an inspired word. Never mind that the men are unarmed and are setting out to lobby, not fight. In a nation that remembers the Civil War, the word "army" has a meaning, and comes with other words that have meanings. Armies have *recruits*. They sleep in *barracks*, and in the open air they *bivouac*. They eat *rations*. They are led by *commanders* and *generals*. Above all, they *march*. All these words will be used in press accounts, and even discounted by quotation marks they will give Coxey's walk to Washington, D.C., an aura of revolution.[45]

An unbidden thing happens. Coxey inspires others. He has started a national movement. His "armies" become the national media story of the 1890s depression.

In Washington state, the newspapers first take notice in mid-March, when a Coxey imitator, Lewis Fry, recruits an "army" in Los Angeles. Fry's demands are similar to Coxey's: that the government issue $1 billion in paper money to create work for idle citizens— he specifies *citizens*—and that immigration be stopped. The press laughs at his talk of going to Washington, D.C., but Fry is for real. His is the first of the "industrial armies" to move. He starts out March 17, 1894, with 300 men.

J.S. Coxey. *Seattle Post-Intelligencer, 8-3-95*

On March 25, Coxey starts out from Massillon, Ohio, with 122 men. It is a wisp of the thousands he predicted, but 43 newsmen are there to make a story of it, and they do their work. The next day papers across the country run a wire story that says: "Men who had been inclined to laugh at the army as a visionary enterprise admit that there is much seriousness behind it."

Other "armies" form: typographer Charles Kelley's group out of San Francisco, stonemason Solomon Shreffler's group out of Portland, and so on. The press warms to it. The story offers readers a daily adventure: Will the "industrials" brave the freezing rain and snow? Most do. Will the people feed them? Many do, especially in the poorer towns. From California, Fry's men jump freight trains and ride all the way to Texas, where the Southern Pacific Railroad leaves them stuck in the desert. Will they die? No; the governor of Texas intercedes for them and they move on. At Oakland, Kelley's men are surrounded by California militia with a Gatling gun. Authorities then provide them with a train of boxcars to get them out of town.

Washington state's editorial pages are cool to Coxey's "petition in boots." The *Aberdeen Herald*, a Democratic weekly, is warmer than most when it says that men out of work, restless and broke, "have the same right of petition that the rich have." It says the commonwealers "are not to be treated with contempt, neither with fear."

They elicit both. The fear is of what will happen when the "army" arrives in Washington, D.C., destitute and demanding. The *Tacoma Union*, recently purchased by Republican Civil War cavalryman William Visscher, writes: "The only way that such a mob could get inside the capitol grounds would be by violence... which would be instantly quelled by the military."

The contempt is expressed in the label "tramps," which sticks easily to jobless men riding in boxcars, living on charity and not looking for work. Men who *are* looking for work, says the *Oregonian*, "go quietly in search of employment, each for himself, and do not pretend to hunt for employment in 'armies' with brass bands." It adds, "Nobody is going to hire an army."

To the *Oregonian*, the Coxeyites are the "anti-work army;" to the *Townsend Leader*, the "industriless industrials." The *Spokane Chronicle* calls them a "battalion of bums;" the *Everett Times*, "an army of tramps;" the *Tacoma Ledger*, "a horde of loafers;" and the *Seattle Post-Intelligencer*, "a band of organized vagrants," most of whom "would not saw wood to pay for breakfast." Even Jack London, who travels in Iowa with Kelley's Army and sympathizes with them, remembers them in *The Road* as "hobos."

Editorial writers also object to the terms "industrial armies" and "industrials." The Republican *Everett Herald* writes: "There is something in the word 'industrial' that has been applied to them, or appropriated by them, which is calculated to give a false impression." They are, the *Herald* says, "idlers, vagabonds and tramps who are not seeking work at fair wages but are trying to get the government to support them."

More charitably, the *Seattle Telegraph* allows that most of the Coxeyites would be willing to work, and suggests that cities might find work for them. But it disturbs Seattle's Democratic paper that the "industrials" think they are in a position "to choose their work and prescribe their wages." And the editors have a deeper thought. "There is something about this movement which is hard to define," they say. "For centuries the footsteps of our race have ever been toward the West... The Anglo-Saxon race has hitherto gained its triumphs through individual self-reliance. It is something new that from points all along the Pacific Coast between Canada and Mexico, organized troops of men have set their faces towards the East to seek from the government what their fathers would have scorned to receive from the hands of the state."

Puyallup hop grower, Ezra Meeker, 63, recalls his fellow pioneers. *They* never thought anyone owed them jobs. "They employed themselves," he writes to the *Ledger*. "Men beg now. They didn't do so then."

Still, says the *Tacoma News*, the Coxey armies have made their mark. "A hundred years and more from now," the *News* says, "school boys and girls will read of the nineteenth century crusade so unlike any that have preceded it."

Years later, there will be other marches on Washington, D.C. This is the first.[46]

By the end of March 1894, Coxey forces are being organized in Tacoma and Seattle.

In Seattle, the organizer is an unemployed surveyor named Henry Shepard, who has done day work on the Seattle sewers. Shepard is a short man with a mustache and side-whiskers, and, says the *Telegraph*, "does not impress one as being a great general." He will not last long, but he gets things moving. On April 18, several hundred of his "Northwestern Industrial Army" parade through downtown Seattle. Horses pull a float bedecked with flags and the slogan, "Gold at a Premium, Humanity at a Discount." Another float offers back-to-back portraits of Lady Liberty and George Washington.

Tacoma's organizer is the man who stands out. In an age when young men wear bushy mustaches and old men wear beards, he is clean-shaven. He is Frank T. Cantwell, 24, and everyone calls him "Jumbo." Six feet tall, he has the body of a prizefighter and enormous hands.

He does not drink, which gives him power over those who do. A correspondent of the *Tacoma News* describes him as a natural politician, always willing to help and win people's friendship. "Jumbo Cantwell had more friends in Tacoma than anyone imagined," the correspondent will write years later. "Men weak in character and stubborn in nature were glad to do his bidding. He early influenced just that class of men who want to obey someone—provided that someone is of their own kind, understanding their vices, though superior in some of their low tastes."

Jumbo becomes a public figure in Tacoma as the bouncer at Harry Morgan's dance hall on Pacific Avenue. After Morgan's death, he makes a play for the widow, Charlotte, a striking blonde who dresses in black. She is no pushover; in January 1893, she applies for police protection against him, at one point pulling a gun on him. But he wins her over, and within the year she marries him.

In 1893, Jumbo comes to trial for assaulting Detective Edward Flannigan. At trial, Jumbo's attorney accuses police of bribery and false arrests, prompting the spectators to jeer at the cops. It is a typical Jumbo ploy: attack, never defend. The *Post-Intelligencer* reports: "The jury was out only a few minutes, and acquitted 'Jumbo.'"

Jumbo is not a man to be intimidated.

While organizing the Coxey forces in Tacoma in April 1894, Jumbo speaks for almost two hours to a packed house at Tacoma's National Theater, mixing humor, profanity, and populism. "There is something magnetic about him," says the *News*. Says the *Union*, "His language is not very Emersonian, but he does know how to talk to the commonwealers."

Jumbo tells the *News*, "I ain't goin' to Washington to get a $2-a-day job. I don't want work. I ain't ready to go to work, but there's thousands of men who want work, and they have to have it to keep from starving." He insists that his men are not hobos. A *News* reporter interviews commonwealers and finds sawmill and shingle mill workers, loggers, railroad workers, miners, a sailor, a teamster, a printer, a baker, a boilermaker, a blacksmith, a horseshoer, a chainman, a cigar maker, and a clam digger—but no tramps. A reporter from the *Ledger* asserts that a quarter of them are tramps, and that many of the workers are using the march on Washington to get home to families along the way.

On April 19, Jumbo parades 300 men through downtown Tacoma, four abreast. Their demands: government jobs for all idle citizens, no immigration for 10 years and a law preventing non-citizens from owning land. Editor Visscher of the *Tacoma Union* returns to work from a bout of sickness and is converted. He announces that Coxeyism is "the beginning of a movement that is going to right the wrongs of the people."

Jumbo Cantwell and Henry Shepard agree to join forces at Puyallup. On April 25, Shepard's Seattle men begin the trek to Puyallup by marching down Second Avenue past a wall of onlookers. "Most remarkable," reports the *Post-Intelligencer*, is "the sympathy extended to the commander, officers, rank and file by the thousands of peo-

"Jumbo" Cantwell. *Tacoma Daily News,* 7-11-94

ple." At one point someone shouts, "Three cheers for Commander Shepard!" The parade's leader bows left and right, doffing his hat. The *Telegraph*, for all its doubts about the movement's means and ends, says, "God bless them."

On April 28, Jumbo leads 600 men out of Tacoma toward Puyallup. Accompanied by his St. Bernard dog, he strides down Pacific Avenue in the rain, wearing a broad-brimmed hat and a Mackintosh over a navy blue coat with brass buttons. Behind him a man carries a big 44-star flag donated by the Grand Army of the Republic, the fraternity of northern Civil War veterans.

For Seattle and Tacoma, well-wishing is easy. The commonwealers are leaving. The burden of supporting them is passed on to other towns, and there is some guilt about that. At Seattle's Plymouth Congregational Church, the Reverend Wallace Nutting gives a farewell sermon to a full house that includes Henry Shepard. Reminding the crowd of their Christian duty to support the poor, Nutting finds no virtue in "the unbrotherly dumping of human folly or anger or poverty upon the East."

Shepard's and Jumbo's men join forces at Puyallup, where the 1,200 to 1,500 commonwealers expect to be fed by a population of less than 1,000. Teams of men go house to house, knocking on doors in the morning, asking the women to prepare food to be picked up at 4 p.m. The men are under orders not to threaten, and they don't need to. They are intimidating as it is.

On May 2, 1894, the town officials and people of Puyallup petition Republican Governor John McGraw to come and help them. He comes and is told the commonwealers want a train. He tells a mass meeting of commonwealers he cannot get them a train, and furthermore that it is a mistake for so many penniless men to converge on Washington, D.C., to demand work. "It is wholly wrong," he says. "No possible good can come of it." He tells them to send a delegation and for the rest of them to go home.[47]

The commonwealers have come to Puyallup because it is on the main line of the Northern Pacific, which runs over Stampede Pass through Ellensburg, Yakima, Pasco, and Spokane. Jumbo goes to the Northern Pacific and tries to hire a train of boxcars to carry the men East. The railroad is in receivership and under control of the federal courts. It declines. It will not carry men as cargo. The Great Northern is even less helpful: It has been shut down by a strike.

In other places, Coxey "armies" are stealing trains. In the early hours of April 24, an "army" led by teamster William Hogan at Butte, Montana, steals a Northern Pacific engine and coal cars and heads east with 300 men. A train of U.S. marshals catches up to it at Billings, where the commonwealers are being feted as heroes. When the marshals rush the stolen engine, commonwealers and locals close in on them, pelting them with rocks and clubs. The marshals fire, killing two Billings men, and then flee. The commonwealers switch out the coal cars for boxcars and steam off. Shortly before midnight on April 25, at about the time Shepard's men are bedding down in their first camp on the road to Puyallup, Hogan and his men are captured by 500 Army infantrymen at Forsyth, Montana, on the orders of President Cleveland. Hogan's men put up no fight. They have had the train for 60 hours and have traveled 326 miles.

From Portland, the "army" led by Solomon Shreffler makes it to Troutdale, 15 miles east, where it is served by an injunction from federal Judge Charles Bellinger not to trespass on railroad property.

The men ignore it. On April 28, 1894, they commandeer an engine, hook it up to some boxcars, load up 500 men and head east through the Columbia Gorge, American flags flying. Already, Multnomah County Sheriff Penumbra Kelly has asked Oregon's Populist governor, Sylvester Pennoyer, for state troops and has been denied, and U.S. Marshal H.C. Grady has wired U.S. Attorney General Richard Olney for assistance of the Army. Olney delivers. After traveling eight hours and 120 miles,

Governor John McGraw. *Seattle Post-Intelligencer, 1-6-95*

Shreffler and his men are stopped at Arlington, Oregon, by 122 soldiers of the Fourth Cavalry from Walla Walla. Shreffler's men are sent back to Portland, where a mass demonstration supports them. Shreffler and other leaders are jailed but released when they apologize to Judge Bellinger for ignoring his injunction. One historian says: "The court showed no great desire really to punish the men, and followed a cautious policy, perhaps considering the widespread public sympathy."

Jumbo Cantwell seizes the moment. The Northern Pacific, he tells his men, is "in the hands of the United States... Well, who is the United States, but the people? And you—*you* are the people. And if we, the people, vote to take that which is ours, there ain't marshals enough in the country to prevent us."

Unfortunately for him, by April 30 there are 70 deputy U.S. marshals at Puyallup. "I'll fool them guys," Jumbo boasts. "We're goin' to ride."

As a group, the deputy marshals cannot allow a horde of "industrials" to steal a train, but with a freeloader here and there, an individual marshal will look the other way. Sensing this, Jumbo splits his "army" into squads.

At 7 p.m. on May 3, the first of Jumbo's squads stops a Northern Pacific freight train between Alderton and Orting, just out of Puyallup. The men swarm on. At the coal camp of Palmer, 25 miles from Orting, six deputy marshals sidetrack the train. Their job done, the deputies bed down in the station, leaving the common-wealers outside. When it rains, the commonwealers pound on the doors and the deputies let them in. "Before morning," writes the *Post-Intelligencer*, "marshals and commonwealers were trying to sleep side by side, some on the floor and some on the benches." In the morning, 117 of Jumbo's commonwealers leave Palmer, the *Ledger* writes, "weary and footsore," walking toward Stampede Pass.

The remaining Tacoma men dribble out of Puyallup, walk-ing up the line past small towns— "all Coxey towns, especially Buck-ley," the *Telegraph* says—not trying to steal trains, but only to ride. They climb on top of the cars and onto the blind baggages. Some prepare squares of wood, their "tickets," to serve as seats under the cars on the brake beams. It's a dangerous ride, and one man tells the *Ledger*: "It fills your whiskers with sand and your eyes with cinders." But it is out of the rain, which is better than sitting on top of the cars.

The trains stop at the entrance of the 1.86-mile Stampede Tunnel, and freeloaders are made to walk over the pass on switch-backs in the deep snow. On the other side they ride again. They are wet and cold, but they are moving east.[48]

Because Henry Shepard does not accept Jumbo's tactics, the Seattle men depose him and elect attorney Edward J. Jeffries, who does. The Seattle commonwealers begin the journey over the Cas-cades in small groups, stealing rides on trains.

In Ellensburg, the *Capital* estimates that by May 6, some 200 "wealers" are in the Central Washington town. Jumbo comes through and "prevails upon" the Chinese owners of a restaurant to use it as a commissary; likewise, a baker allows the men to bake all the bread they need. Farmers bring in wagons of potatoes, and two butchers each donate a quarter of beef. Coxey sympathizers give with enthusiasm and others without it—but they give. Soon the Ellensburg commissary is feeding 250 men a day with beef stew, bread, and beans.

Over the course of 10 days, 1,200 to 1,500 Washington

wealers sluice through Ellensburg. "As a body they conducted themselves in a very orderly and lawful manner," the *Capital* says after they leave. "As it is, we are well rid of them, and we may comfort ourselves with the thought that it might have been worse."

Some men take reckless chances. At Cle Elum, 60 men pile into a gondola car and coast the 28 miles to Ellensburg. They arrive in one piece, but another group comes to grief after leaving Ellensburg on the Yakima River in a flat-bottomed boat. It is spring—high water—and in the Yakima Canyon their boat swirls in an eddy, strikes a log and capsizes. Four men are drowned, four reach shore, and eleven others are marooned on a log in mid-stream. The men on the log are rescued by rigging a pulley to a tall tree, the last man after shivering for nine hours.

At Yakima (then called North Yakima) on May 9, the wealers abandon Jumbo's small-group strategy and seize a string of boxcars. This breaks the unwritten truce with the deputies, and the two groups immediately have a standoff. After several hours, the engineer backs up the train to separate it from the crowd, and townspeople shout to the wealers to set the brakes. They do, and deputies start shoving the wealers off the boxcars in an effort to reach the brakes. Several wealers are injured.

One of the deputies later says to the *Tacoma News*: "The citizens began to throw stones and clubs at the deputies and shouted: 'Shoot them! Cut them! Kill them!' The commonwealers were excited before, but when they received this encouragement they began to throw stones and then the fight commenced in earnest."

The *Yakima Herald* writes: "One of the marshals was getting the worst of the encounter and pulled his gun and fired. Immediately a number of revolvers were brought into play and eight or ten shots fired." Other witnesses say an onlooker fired first.

Deputy marshal John Jolly, a "sporting man" recruited from a gambling den, is shot in the gut. Jolly says a fellow marshal shot him by mistake—a charge the other man denies. The slug, a .45, is the caliber of the deputies' sidearms. Jolly's wound is reported as likely fatal, but he will recover and return to his life of drink and cards.

The deputies arrest 157 commonwealers, lock them into

two boxcars without water or toilets and transport them overnight to Spokane. At the depot there, hundreds of demonstrators, under Jumbo's orders not to riot, jeer at the marshals guarding the train. The men in the boxcars, still without water, carve air holes with pocket knives. After an hour, four passenger cars are attached to the train, it pulls out, and away from the city the wealers are transferred to coaches and given food and water. The train takes them back to Seattle.

In Seattle, Coxeyites recognize six deputy marshals eating breakfast at a restaurant. They raise an alarm. A crowd gathers; when the marshals come out, hundreds of men follow them down the street cursing, and a few shouting, "Hang them!" The deputies duck into a building and escape out the back.

Fearing an attempt to storm the jail, federal Judge Cornelius Hanford orders five companies of infantry from the Army barracks at Vancouver. They arrive in Seattle and the peace is kept.

The commonwealers arrested at Yakima are tried in groups for violating the court order not to interfere with railroad property. Hanford sentences some of them to 60 days at McNeil Island penitentiary. Of the "industrials," he says: "They were not delegated by the community to force their views upon the government."

As they are led to the city dock in manacles, the convicted men break into a song, the chorus of which goes:
Come along, march along
　　while the air is pure and balmy.
And every mother's son
　　will march to Washington,
　　and join General Coxey's Army.

East of Spokane, hundreds of commonwealers cross into Idaho.[49]

From Ohio, after slogging through rain and mud for more than a month, on May 1, 1894, Coxey's Army arrives at the Capitol in Washington, D.C. Coxey is riding in a buggy with his wife and two-year-old son, Legal Tender. Coxey's crusade partner, Carl Browne, rides a horse as 600 commonwealers walk. To avoid a line of police, Coxey slips through the shrubbery and mounts the Capitol steps to speak. He is immediately arrested for trespassing. Some newspapers say he had it coming because he was warned—which he was. Others condemn the government for arresting the head of a nationwide political movement for "walking on the grass." Coxey is taken to police court, is convicted, and spends a brief time in jail. Afterward he testifies before a committee of Congress.

Coxey has made a noise, but his movement dies. Historian Carlos Schwantes writes: "The wholesale imprisonment of Coxeyites in the West during May and June, far more than the May 1 debacle on the Capitol steps, drained all life from the petition in boots." The harassment amounts to "psychological warfare," Schwantes writes, and it works.

For a few more days the newspapers are full of stories of Coxey "armies." More trains are stolen. At Troy, Montana, commonwealers steal and ride a Great Northern train nearly 40 miles before workers tear up tracks to derail it. Then the stories trail off. After a little more than two months, perhaps half of Washington state's "industrials" make it to the nation's capital. Jumbo Cantwell is a man of poor character; he leaves Spokane on a passenger train without his wife, Charlotte, but in the company of a winsome 17-year-old, Hilda Steen, who returns to her alarmed parents a few days later. Jumbo parades in the capital on July 4 with some of his men, but by then the press has lost interest. The *Tacoma Ledger* scoffs: "His rise was like that of the rocket, one of the 2-cent sort, and he came down like the stick."

In mid-July, Charlotte Cantwell, called by the *Washington Post* "Mrs. Jumbo," arrives in Washington, D.C., leading 200 men. By then, her husband is gone. Two of his men, returning to Tacoma, say he pocketed $3,000 of Commonweal money and "skipped to South America," though this is never confirmed. Charlotte sticks by the men and earns their gratitude. A year later in Tacoma, Jumbo is nowhere to be found when she loses 320 acres of land from non-payment of a $5,000 mortgage.

The Seattle men's leader, Edward Jeffries, takes them to Duluth, Minnesota, by jumping trains. They traverse the Great Lakes to Cleveland by boat, then "hobo it" to the national capital. Interviewed on his way home in September, he will tell the *Spokane Chron-*

icle that the trip to Washington, D.C. was "an educational campaign, meant to sow discontent as we went along." In that, he says, his men were successful because they made lots of political converts along the way.

Historians will celebrate Coxey's Army as the first "march on Washington." Coxey's dream of federal road-building is remembered as a precursor of the public works programs of the New Deal. But his men's aim is to influence the Congress of 1894—and Congress ignores them. On its original terms, the movement is a failure.

It is also a warning. The American people will put up with only so much hard times.[50]

STRIKERS (1894)

The first half of 1894 is a time of suspicion, insolence and adventure. "The unrest prevailing in the nation," says the *Seattle Telegraph*, "...permeates all classes. It is undefined and undefinable." Solid citizens, ordinarily sure of the world around them, "face the future with a feeling of blank dismay."

In Moscow, Idaho, farmers form the Freeman's Protective Silver Federation, organizing in secret. Its main purpose is to resist the foreclosure of mortgages, either by intimidating mortgage holders or would-be bidders at foreclosure sales. Opponents dub it "The Shotgun League."

In Seattle, Coxey supporters enroll 350 to 400 men in a "Patriot Army," which begins military drills on Saturday mornings. Its leader, Seattle councilman J. Eugene Jordan, denounces "the destruction of half our national currency and national values, dictated by British influence" and accuses the government of "aggravating and badgering the millions of half-starved labor-seeking citizens, tempting them to violence rather than mollifying them in their distress."

In Baker County, Oregon, whites attack Chinese miners and railroad men. Whites organize the Home Protective Association and tell the Chinese they must leave town in 60 days. Washington newspapers bubble with stories about Chinese crossing illegally from British Columbia and the attempts to catch and deport them. "So far we have wisely kept out the Chinaman, who is un-American in all things," declares the *Tacoma Ledger*.

A group founded in Iowa called the American Protective Association claims that "subjection" to the Church of Rome "is incompatible with citizenship" in the United States. West of the Cascades, the A.P.A. organizes chapters in Tacoma, Seattle, Olympia, Port Angeles, Everett, Forks, Fremont, Puyallup, and Orting. The group says it is "against the employment of the subject of any un-American ecclesiastical power"—i.e., Catholics— "as officers or teachers of public schools." In Orting, Pierce County, the A.P.A. backs one of two candidates for director of public schools, and the man wins; in Ballard, the group backs a challenger to the city treasurer, a Catholic, and wins. In Tacoma, the A.P.A. successfully lobbies the city council not to contract with the Catholic and Episcopalian hospitals to care for the poor.

In Seattle, the Reverend Robert E. Dunlap of the First Christian Church draws crowds by denouncing the Roman Catholic Church 13 Sundays in a row. In Seattle, the A.P.A. declares that Martina Johnson, a teacher at the Denny School, is guilty of "gross vulgarity in the schoolroom and contempt for just authority and free government." To document the woman's vulgarity, the A.P.A. calls a teenage girl, who testifies that Johnson has called pupils "fools," "dunces," and "blockheads." Seattle's newspapers rise to the teacher's defense, accusing the A.P.A. of picking on her only because she is Catholic. The school board backs off. The A.P.A. is stymied in Seattle—though a year and a half later it will win three seats on the Seattle School Board.

In Tacoma, Vicar General Peter F. Hylebos of St. Leo's Catholic Church says, "The influence of the A.P.A. is driving Catholics out of office in this city, and if it is continued, it will ruin the city. Four Catholics were let out of office yesterday, presumably because they were Catholics." One is Tacoma's fire chief, Henry Lillis, who is accused of drunkenness.

In Eastern Washington, the state has its first lynchings in three years. It is of two white men: George F. Parker, who is on trial for fatally shooting a man while committing a burglary, and Ed Hill, who fatally stabbed a man in a brawl but is sentenced to only one year for assault. In the early hours of June 2, 1894, masked men drag Parker and Hill from their cells at the Whitman County Courthouse at Colfax. Parker takes it silently, but the *Spokane Chronicle* reports that Hill's screams can be heard a quarter of a mile away. The *Chronicle* honors the lynchers' rope with the headline, "Hemp Wins."

Most newspapers make no connection between the lynchings and the climate of agitation, but the *Seattle Telegraph* does. It notes that the lynchings were not done in the heat of anger over the crimes, which were committed months before. They were done out of distrust of the institutions of justice. "We are not altogether surprised at this," the paper says. "During the last twelve months the institutions of the country have been steadily assaulted, not with criticism, which is always both permissible and beneficial, but with calumny and abuse. A pestilential influence has been at work inciting people to believe that the laws are mere waste paper, the administration of the law mere tools and the people little else than slaves."[51]

Into this ferment comes the American Railway Union, led by Eugene V. Debs, former secretary-treasurer of the Brotherhood of Locomotive Firemen. Debs believes the railroad brotherhoods— craft unions of the firemen, trainmen, car men and engineers—are weak because they are divided. He and 50 others meet in Chicago in June 1893 to create an industrial union to represent all railroad workers (though in June 1894 they vote in convention to deny membership to blacks). In the winter of 1893-94, the American Railway Union sets up locals at Seattle, Tacoma, Spokane, and across the West.

The union's first victory is in court, where it challenges the receiver of the Union Pacific Railroad, who has cut workers' wages and banned strikes. In April 1894, the court rolls back the wage cuts and allows workers the right to strike.

Two weeks later the Great Northern announces a 10 percent pay cut. This is on top of a 15-to-20 percent cut in August 1893 and 6 percent early in 1894. These cuts are comparable to others in industry, and the old brotherhoods reluctantly agree to them. The American Railway Union does not, and on April 13, 1894, it calls the workers out. They go, and within a few days all Great Northern trains west of Minot, South Dakota, are stopped.

The state of Washington has never been through a strike like this. The *Post-Intelligencer* doesn't like it, but it declares the right to strike "cannot be questioned" as long as strikers commit no violence or intimidation. The *Seattle Telegraph* disagrees. On April 16, it argues that a railroad is "*de facto,* if not legally, a public institution," and that "neither owners nor employees ought to be allowed to close it down." The *Telegraph* is also bothered that the strike was called

Eugene Debs. *Clip Art*

by one man, Eugene Debs. "Every year the number of persons who subordinate their individual judgment to that of some council or the head of some organization is becoming larger," the *Telegraph* says. "These organizations all claim to be purely voluntary, and so they are in one sense. No man is in the abstract compelled to join them, but in many cases he is forced to do so."

When Debs meets Great Northern President James J. Hill on April 25, 1894, Hill asks him: How am I to know that you, and not the brotherhoods, represent the workers? Debs's reply: Because your trains are stopped. Hill suggests the workers have a vote. Debs says no.

A few days later, businessmen from St. Paul and Minneapolis appeal to Hill and Debs to accept a board of arbitration. They agree. The head of the board is Charles Pillsbury, whose flour mills along the Great Northern have had to shut down. The arbitrators side with the union. They order the disputed pay cuts canceled and three quarters of the previous cuts rescinded, with union men, except those guilty of malicious conduct, allowed to return to their jobs. After 18 days, the strike ends with a union victory.[52]

Another struggle begins in Chicago at the Pullman Palace Car Co., whose president, George Pullman, pioneered the railroad sleeper car 30 years before. Pullman sells sleeper cars and also leases them to railroads, with Pullman employees to run them. To keep these employees socially separate from customers, it hires only black men as Pullman porters, and by the 1890s is the nation's largest employer of African Americans. It is not these men who strike, but the white workers who assemble the cars.

Hard times have shriveled the demand for new Pullman sleeper cars. Employment in the car plant shrinks from 5,800 in May 1893 to 2,000 in November. In April 1894, the total bounds back to 4,200 by winning outside work, but at a cost: Pullman has bid low to get the work, and his workers will have to take pay cuts averaging 28 percent starting May 1. "This company cannot control the selling price of cars and it cannot pay more for making them than it can contract to sell them for," Pullman says.

Similar cuts are being made all across America for just such reasons. But there is always a question of how much. An amount financially right may feel morally wrong. Men will fight to keep what they have and if they agree to sacrifice they will want to see that the man asking them is sacrificing as much. But because his business of leasing sleeper cars to railroads is still profitable, Pullman makes no cut in the dividend to stockholders. Nor does he cut the pay of car-shop superintendents and foremen, who, he says, are not so easily replaced as workers.

There is another matter. On the shores of Lake Calumet, south of Chicago, Pullman has built a model village for his employees. It has two-story brick row houses with basements, gas, water, and sewer service. It has tree-lined streets, a park, a membership library ($3 a year), and a fire department. By early 1893, the town of Pullman has 12,500 residents, most of them foreign-born. Five-sixths of the houses are rentals.

By May 1894, landlords in surrounding towns have been cutting rents in an effort to keep tenants. Pullman refuses to cut rents. His workers don't have to live in his village, he says. To him, wages and rents are separate issues. To the strikers they are connected. The local Methodist minister says he knows a Pullman worker who rents four rooms for $14.50 a month and is left with 76 cents a day for his family to live on. Ordinary people may know little of finance, but they understand this. A socialist cartoon shows a fat boss labeled "Pullman" squeezing a worker in a screw press between slabs labeled "Low Wages" and "High Rent." The cartoon hits a mark.

On May 11, 1894, the Pullman workers, who are non-union, begin a wildcat strike, demanding a rollback of the wage cuts. Pullman makes no effort to replace them. He shuts down the plant.[53]

THE CONDITION OF THE LABORING MAN AT PULLMAN.—

Labor is in a state of unrest. In response to pay cuts of 10, 20, or 30 percent, workers across the country are throwing down their tools. Most intransigent are the Eastern European immigrants who have dirty jobs, volatile temperaments, and little reverence for American law. In Detroit, 400 Poles demand that the city pay $1.50 a day for ditch-digging work at Grosse Pointe. With stones and shovels, they attack a non-union crew working for less. When the sheriff and deputies attempt to protect the men, a Pole knocks out the sheriff with a shovel and the deputies kill two of the Poles. During a strike in the soft-coal country around Connellsville, Pennsylvania, Hungarian workers at the H.C. Frick Coke Co. shoot the chief engineer in the head and crush his skull with stones.

At Roslyn, Washington, the Northern Pacific Coal Co. (not owned by the railroad) has been charging railroads $1.75 a ton for coal and paying workers $1 a ton to mine it. Sales are slow; the company has been running the mines two days a week at a loss. In May 1894, it reaches a deal with the Union Pacific. It will supply coal at $1 a ton, replacing coal from Wyoming. Roslyn's miners will have to accept a 20 percent cut, to 80 cents per ton, but the company says it is a good deal because they will have double the hours of work, and work year-round. The miners go out on strike.

In the Coeur d'Alene Mountains, workers at the Bunker Hill and Sullivan silver-lead mine revive their old demand that car men and shovelers earn the miner's wage of $3.50 a day. The company says no. Silver has fallen to 62 cents an ounce, and $3 is all the car men and shovelers, union or non-union, are going to get. The union backs down.

In June 1894, comes a new effort. At the mining camp of Gem, Idaho, the miners' union blacklists 30 men, including superintendents and shift bosses. On July 3, about 35 union men, hiding their faces with handkerchiefs and gunnysack masks, ride through the streets of Gem. Two of them barge into the blacksmith shop of John Kneebone, who testified against the union two years before. He is unarmed; he jumps out of a window and runs. He is shot in the back and dies instantly. The masked men then take the Gem's general manager, who has told blacklisted men to ignore the threats against them, and three others. The captives are hustled to the Montana border and made to swear an oath never to return.

The *Chronicle* calls for "immediate action on the part of the authorities to protect life and property in the Coeur d'Alenes." The *Spokesman-Review* (the *Review's* new name, beginning June 29) takes a more strident anti-union line. It blames the violence on "agitators" from Butte and calls for the imposition of martial law, so that the murderers can be "arrested, tried and hanged."

There is no martial law nor, for a few days, much of any law in Idaho's silver district.[54]

In mid-June 1894, Eugene Debs opens a convention of the American Railway Union. His men have beaten the Great Northern. They are feeling their oats, and they decide to take on George Pullman, though Pullman's workers are not in their union. Debs challenges Pullman to accept outside arbitration. Pullman refuses. He says his decision not to operate at a loss is final.

The American Railway Union declares that it will strike every railroad that leases Pullman sleeper cars. The brotherhoods of firemen, trainmen, car men, and engineers oppose this. They have contracts with the railroads, which have contracts with Pullman. Debs ignores them.

The railroad workers follow Debs. Beginning at noon on June 27, 1894, the American Railway Union shuts down most of the Western transcontinental trains, including the Southern Pacific, the Santa Fe, the Union Pacific, and Northern Pacific. The Great Northern and the Canadian Pacific, which have their own sleeping cars, remain open.

This is an odd strike: a walkout by men who have no grievance against their employers. George Pullman has locked out his shop employees in Chicago, and that, says the *Ledger*, is a matter about which, in Tacoma, "nobody knows or cares." Not one man in Washington is a party to it. Nor is the bankrupt Northern Pacific a party to it. Says the *Post-Intelligencer*: "This American Railway Union, under the leadership of Debs, takes a period of extreme depression and forces a strike when there is a vast amount of labor seeking employment; it throws out of employment thousands of men who would receive no benefit even if it won, and who are sacrificed in a quarrel that is none of their business."

The fight transcends Pullman. Supporters attach romantic notions to it. The Snohomish *Eye* calls it "a decisive contest between manhood and money." To Debs, it is a struggle for "labor's right to exist." Really it is about the American Railway Union's right to wield the kind of power Debs is asserting. The America of 1894 has no airlines and no nationwide web of paved roads. To cross the continent, the alternative to the railroad is the horse-drawn wagon on a dirt track. The press, the public, and the government are not ready to accept that a man to whom they have delegated no authority—and *this* man, Eugene V. Debs—shall have the power to shut down half the railroads in the country, and by implication all of them, for such a reason as this, or for any reason. Debs and his union, says the *Oregonian*, are "a threat to every man carrying on business."

Half a century later, Congress will define "sympathy" strikes as secondary boycotts and make them illegal. But in the 1890s there is no such law. There is, however, a federal law forbidding interference with the U.S. Mail, which the strike has done. On that authority, Attorney General Richard Olney gets a court injunction forbidding union leaders from supporting the railroad strike. When they ignore it, President Cleveland orders federal marshals and troops into Chicago. Illinois Governor Peter Altgeld, who a year earlier pardoned three labor radicals imprisoned for the Haymarket bombing, objects to the president's action. Cleveland ignores him.

KING DEBS.

Labor's 'king' athwart the arteries of commerce. *Harper's Weekly,* 7-14-94

Union men are enraged. Feeling that the state of Illinois is on their side, men, women, and children take to the rail yards, surround federal marshals and jeer at them. Words turn to acts. The crowd rocks boxcars back and forth, pushes them over and sets them on fire—hundreds of them. Chicago descends into chaos.[55]

In Western Washington, the shutdown of the Northern Pacific main line has the greatest effect on Tacoma. Several million shingles pile up, waiting for shipment east, and mills start shutting down. No trains go through the Stampede Tunnel, though the railroad does carry passengers to Seattle and Portland with non-union crews.

On July 1, 1894, a crowd of 500 at the Northern Pacific depot in Tacoma confronts deputy U.S. marshals guarding the cars. The marshals put up a rope to keep the crowd back, and the crowd ignores it, surging in. The *Ledger* reports that a "tough looking individual" repeatedly shoves deputy Gus Rinick back, cursing and taunting him. Rinick pulls out a revolver and says, "Back, or I'll blow your brains out." The crowd boos and curses Rinick, who is struck with a rock. A shout goes out:

"Put up your gun or you'll get another rock." Rinick puts up his gun and the moment passes.

On July 5, three non-union men coming off work from the Northern Pacific's Tacoma roundhouse are jumped by a group of

35 to 40 men. James McFarland, 50, is hit in the head with a rock that leaves a gash eight inches long. Thomas J. Vivian, 46, is struck across the face with a board that cuts his chin and face and almost takes off the lower part of his right ear. J. McClelland is struck below the ear, knocked to the ground and kicked in the face.

On July 6, Alexander B. Todd, the non-union engineer for the Northern Pacific train from Portland, leaves the Tacoma depot carrying a revolver, just in case. He is followed up Pacific Avenue by a group of 50 to 60 men wearing white ribbons, the strikers' badge. At 13th Street, one of them clubs him to the pavement with a black-snake—a weighted leather bag. They kick Todd in the body and face. Finally he is able to pull out his revolver, get off two wild shots and escape into a building.

The anti-union *Ledger* reports that Todd is "unmercifully beaten." The pro-union *Union* reports the beating, but says: "No bones were broken and he is not seriously injured." It adds: "The strikers and their friends justify the deed by saying, 'He is an old railroad man and is thoroughly aware of the chances he was taking when he consented to take the place of another railroader.' " The *News*, also pro-union, deplores the beating of Todd but says strikers didn't do it. "The strikers and their honest sympathizers deplore all resorts to violence," the *News* assures its readers.

On July 3, the first Northern Pacific train east leaves from Tacoma. It carries the division general manager and 69 deputy marshals armed with revolvers and Winchester rifles. The train is met with protests at Ellensburg, Sprague, and Pasco, where six derailed cars block the track. At 5 p.m. on July 5, it rolls into the Spokane depot, met by a crowd of men, women, and boys. Most are not railroad men; the handful later arrested includes a shoemaker, a baker, a bus driver, and an elevator operator. The crowd is defined by its political opinions and sense of adventure.

The marshals dismount and form a cordon, letting the passengers leave. The crowd remembers the marshals at this spot two months before, with the commonwealers imprisoned in boxcars. It jeers and does not disband.

Over several hours the crowd swells to more than 2,000. Around 9 p.m., word spreads that the train is about to proceed east.

The crowd rushes for the roundhouse. Police string up a rope and tell the crowd to stay behind it. Men cut the rope. They push a refrigerator car and two engines onto the main track and derail them at open switches, blocking the main line. Boys climb onto the derailed engines and ring the bells. The crowd hoots.

Local police begin herding the crowd back. It yields, but when police are joined by the hated deputy marshals, the mood darkens. A stone flies. Within moments the air is thick with them, and three marshals are hit, one of them on the head. A deputy fires his Winchester into the air. More stones fly, and more deputies fire into the air—except one, whose bullet strikes the forearm of carpenter Erick Carlson, 43, a block away.

It takes a few minutes before the crowd realizes a man has been shot. Then it roars.

"Kill the deputies!"

"Drag out the murdering hounds!"

"Hang them!"

"Clean 'em out!"

"Lynch 'em!"

The crowd is still intimidated by the armed deputies. "Had a determined man taken charge of the mob and rushed upon the deputies he could have found followers and the loss of life would have been great," the *Chronicle* says.

At this point Spokane police chief Peter Mertz stands up and announces that he will replace the deputies with police and members of the American Railway Union. "That satisfied them," writes the *Chronicle*.[56]

Other acts of defiance occur. On July 7, all but one of the 60-man Company G of the Washington National Guard, which has been training near Olympia, refuses to ride home to Spokane on a non-union train. They reach this decision, the *Post-Intelligencer* reports, after "some of the fathers who had sons in the troop declared that they would disown their boys if they rode with non-union crews." The young men's superior, Lieutenant Colonel Michael McCarthy, brands this a mutiny and has them disarmed and put under guard. His superior, Brigadier General A.P. Curry, lines them up and appeals to their consciences. He asks them if they are loyal to the flag and to the state of Washington. All 60 say they are. Are they ready to follow orders, and even to shoot to kill, should it be necessary? They say they are. He gives them back their rifles and they ride on the non-union train.

On the way home, at one station the train is shot at, and at another it passes a row of effigies hanging from a telegraph pole, each labeled, "scab." At Sprague, the guardsmen stop to repair a small trestle burned by strikers and to take coal. There they face a mob that hurls stones at them for more than an hour.

At the depot in Spokane, the men face a display intended to insult them: a row of baby carriages.

The *Spokesman-Review* gives Company G a one-sentence editorial: "It's Company N.G., now." No Good, apparently. A court of inquiry later declares that Curry was wrong to give them back their weapons. Governor John McGraw orders 35 members of Company G discharged.

As the chaos begins to subside, some union men turn to sabotage. In Idaho's silver district on July 7, an explosion shakes the mining camp of Wardner. A dynamite stick has been hurled at the Bunker Hill and Sullivan's power plant, which compresses air for the mine. The dynamite hits a stump which limits the damage. The rest of the day, men roll boulders down the mountainside toward the mine works. The *Spokane Chronicle* reports: "Huge boulders, heavy masses of slag and big logs have been bounding down the slope all day, crushing everything before them in their half-mile run."

On July 10, strikers on the Northern Pacific wrap rags on the beams of a 1,400-foot long, 80-foot-high trestle west of the Stampede Tunnel, soak them in engine oil and set them afire. They also burn the road's bridge over the Yakima River at Thorp. The same day, someone sabotages a switch in Tacoma and derails the passenger train from Portland, flipping the engine and tender on their sides. In California, at Sacramento, strikers also derail a train, killing the engineer and three others. In Tacoma no one is hurt.

The Cleveland administration declares the Union Pacific and the Northern Pacific roads of military significance. The Army imposes order in Chicago and Sacramento. Army units arrive in

Tacoma, Seattle, Spokane, the Coeur d'Alene mining camps, and all along the Northern Pacific. The Army has fewer than 28,000 men nationwide; its troop movements during the protests and strikes of 1894 are its largest since the Civil War.

Sensing that he is losing the fight, Debs calls for help from the American Federation of Labor. It declines. From Chicago the head of the once-powerful Knights of Labor, James R. Sovereign, orders a nationwide general strike. His locals ignore him. In Pullman, Washington, a town named for George Pullman, the Freeman's Protective Silver Federation announces a boycott of the Northern Pacific and every Spokane merchant that deals with it. The effort fizzles out. The railroad strike slowly dies. In mid-August, the employees at the Pullman shops in Chicago accept the wage cut.

Debs is arrested. He will be convicted of violating the injunction against interfering with interstate commerce and the U.S. Mail, and sent to prison for six months. In Seattle, federal Judge Cornelius Hanford—the Hanford Site is named for him—sentences two Spokane rioters to seven months in prison. At the July 30 sentencing, Hanford says Spokane has had too many "strange spectacles" of lawlessness in the past four years. The city is unlikely to attract the new money and new blood it needs, he says, "until the courts have demonstrated their power to preserve peace and protect property and protect individuals."

Fifteen men who struck the bankrupt Seattle, Lake Shore & Eastern Railroad ask Hanford to order the receiver to reinstate them. The men have been denied their old jobs. They say they are innocent; when they went out, they were only obeying the order of their union. They have not harmed the railroad's property.

Hanford says no. In the 1890s, to strike is to quit one's job. These men quit, and other men had "the courage necessary," the judge says, to take their places at a hazardous time. "For no offense other than doing honest work," Hanford says, the strikebreakers "have been jeered at and abused by crowds of people subservient to, or in sympathy with, Debs; the cabs in which they ride show the scars made by stones and missiles hurled at their heads. To deprive them of their situations at this time would be an injustice to them." The strikers, he says, "are receiving fair treatment by being placed upon the waiting list."

Under its federal receiver, the Northern Pacific invites all strikers to apply for work, provided they have not been "agitators" and that they renounce Debs's union. The railroad does not dismiss the strikebreakers.

The *Oregonian* praises the new men on the trains for showing a spirit "rarely seen among the average run of easy-moving and good-natured railway men." Newspapers, however, report a surge of accidents by the "green" men. In Tacoma a green switchman loses his thumb and three fingers while coupling cars. In Aberdeen, a green switchman falls between two cars and loses his foot. In Seattle, a green engineer runs a yard engine onto the main line and slams into an inbound coal train. The coal train's engineer and fireman jump for their lives—fortunately for them, not on the side where the tender, which flips over, would have crushed them.

On July 29, a green engineer on a westbound Northern Pacific freight train loses control and crashes into an eastbound passenger train at South Prairie in Pierce County. The passengers are unharmed, but the crash pins the new fireman, Harry Clement, between engine and tender for two hours, killing him. A tramp who had been stealing a ride between the passenger train's two engines is smashed into an unrecognizable mess. The negligent engineer, says the *Tacoma Union*, "jumped from his engine and took to the woods."

In retaliation for pro-strike newspaper coverage in Tacoma, the Northern Pacific cancels contracts to provide service to the *News* and the *Union*.[57]

At Roslyn, the coal miners have been on strike for more than two months. The company sets a deadline of July 21 to accept the 20 percent pay cut. It threatens to import black strikebreakers, which it did five years before. The miners, most of them white, ignore the deadline. Two days later the state organizer for the United Mine Workers tells them the collapse of the Pullman strike has made their position worse. It may be wise to fight another day. They ignore him, too.

"Negroes for Roslyn" is the page-one story in the *Seattle P I* of July 27. In it, a company man says many of the miners on strike "are ready to go to work, but they have been threatened with being killed and blown up with dynamite if they returned to work." He says that when the black miners arrive, the company will have plenty of work for the existing miners as well, except the ringleaders. "We know who the men are," he says, and they "will never be allowed in the mines again."

The strike leaders denounce this as a "sandy"—a bluff. It is not. On August 25, 1894, a day the *Kittitas County Courier and Roslyn News* labels "Black Saturday," 200 African American miners arrive with their families and are given work. By this time most of the white miners who struck have signed contracts at the new rates. Their union is dissolved.

The American Railway Union will also die. Forty years later, during the New Deal, labor historian O.D. Boyle will recall Debs's nationwide strike on behalf of the Pullman workers as "a debacle unequalled in the history of railroad labor."[58]

The strikes of the summer of 1894 are not mainly about workers bettering their wages and hours. They are a lashing-out in anger, a grasp for power, an attempt at retribution. Like the Coxey armies, they do not achieve their aims.

After such a summer, it would seem doubtful that workers and employers would join in a common festival, but they do. On September 3, 1894, America has its first national celebration of Labor Day. The holiday, begun by East Coast unions, has been celebrated in Seattle since 1888. "Originally," the *P-I* says, the picnics and parades were held "by a few labor organizations, but finally by common occurrence of public opinion in the propriety of it." By 1894, Labor Day has been made a state holiday in Oregon, but not in Washington.

On June 28, 1894, a few days before ordering federal troops into Chicago to crush the American Railway Union strike, President Cleveland offers an olive branch to workers. He signs a bill marking the first Monday in September a federal holiday.

In Tacoma, the *Ledger* grumbles that it ought to be called "*Organized* Labor Day," because politicians set it up to please the unions. Most people, the *Ledger* says, "will go about their business as usual because it is not meant for them and they do not want it."

125

The *Ledger* is mistaken. The public embraces Labor Day. The festivities come with political speeches, but mostly it is a celebration of local work and industry. In Spokane, the city decks itself out in flags and bunting, and holds a parade. The bricklayers' union has a float of masons at work, pulled by a team of horses. Grocer John F. Adams displays men roasting coffee, making candy, and baking bread. The Washington Mill Co. offers a brass band atop a huge saw log. The city offers the mayor, city officials, and firemen with fire-fighting gear. Says the *Chronicle*: "Nearly every trade, business house and labor organization was represented, and the procession was over an hour passing a given point."

After the speeches come sporting contests. The big events are bicycle races, a new thing in the 1890s. There is also the tug of war between the bricklayers and the building laborers; a sack race and a blindfolded men's wheelbarrow race; a married women's foot race and an unmarried ladies' foot race, both in long skirts; a men's race and a *union* men's race. And there are prizes. The winner of the 50-pound dumb-bell throw is awarded a $20 gold piece. The winner of the ladies' shooting contest wins a fall hat and the winner of the fat man's race is awarded a box of cigars.

A few weeks later, the African-American miners of Roslyn celebrate Emancipation Day. The white miners have had to take a pay cut but the black miners have new work at the same wage rate as the whites. Happy in a new land, they barbecue two oxen, two hogs, and a dozen sheep, listening to stirring oratory on what the *Tacoma Ledger* calls "The Progress of the Colored Race."[59]

POPS (1894)

In May 1894, with Coxey's Army defeated, *The Eye* of Snohomish advises its supporters to "remain at home and reorganize for a march on the ballot box." *The Eye* is aligned with the People's Party, formed in Omaha in 1891. The party's adherents are called Populists or, by the headline writers of unfriendly papers, "Pops."

The Pops are not stylish; at a time when stylish men have a mustache but no chin whiskers, the stereotypical Pop has a full beard.

The Pops are the party of the left. "No Compromise with the Gold Bug Plutocracy," shouts an 1893 headline in the New Whatcom *Champion*, a Populist journal. The Pops are against Wall Street, the banks and the rich, who they accuse of rigging the system to subjugate the poor. What professors of political economy see as market forces—supply and demand—the Pops see as manipulation and control. When a publication for investors says men of the East will not invest in the West until people there stop agitating for a silver standard, a Populist editor replies: "This is a threat direct and pointed, and will no doubt prove true to the extent that the money power is able to subjugate the people."

Modern writers tend to treat the Pops kindly, as the forerunners of today's progressives. Early in the New Deal, historian Charles Beard will call them "the progenitors of most 'new' thoughts in current politics." But the Pops have an unlovely side: ignorance, zealotry, nativism, and racism. They demonize opponents as agents of a dark and conspiratorial power. Their opponents do not overlook these things. Says the *Cosmopolis Enterprise*: "There are exceptions, but the average Populist is a narrow-minded, poorly informed person, with a tendency to be a bigot."

On the eve of the November 1894 elections, William Visscher, author, poet, and ex-editor of the *Tacoma Union*, leaves the Republicans for the Pops. "For years our currency and this govern-

127

A Republican jab at Populist fusion with Democrats, 1896. *Los Angeles Times, Aug. 20, 1896*

ment have been ruled by the Rothschilds, by Lombard Street," he tells a People's Party meeting. "Lombard Street rules Wall Street, and Wall Street rules us."

Visscher doesn't descend to anti-Semitism, but some do. *The Eye* calls 1894 Republican Senate hopeful (and future senator) Levi Ankeny "the millionaire Jew banker." And Mary E. Hobart, the New Whatcom firebrand the *Tacoma Ledger* calls "the priestess of the Populists," sells copies of a book she says tells the secrets of "the hook-nosed Jews, the Rothschilds," who own the world's money.

The Populists have several such bibles. One is Sarah E.V. Emery's *Seven Financial Conspiracies Which Have Enslaved the American People* (1894). Another is William Hope Harvey's *Coin's Financial School* (1894). The Pops also have papers and pamphlets. "Week after week a flood of literature, full of ideas which are called incendiary, and perhaps justly so, goes out into every corner of the land," writes the *Seattle Times*. "The people are reading it and are growing restless, perhaps beyond control."

The Populist story reaches back to 1873, when Congress re-enacted the gold standard, to take effect in 1879. Many Americans wanted the paper-money regime of the Civil War to continue. They formed the Greenback Party, which ran a candidate for president in 1880. Their story of how and why the bankers won went into the books read by the Populists. It is a tale of rich and poor, good and evil, chicanery and crime.

Like the Greenback Party of 15 years earlier, the People's Party advocates unbacked paper money— "legal tenders." The Pops want the government to double the currency in circulation to $50 per person. They loathe moneylenders and usury. At Blaine, What-com County, where the Populists sweep the elections of December 1893 by a vote of four to one, the city council votes to cancel all un-sold city bonds, and on February 20, 1894, Mayor George Westcott follows through publicly by setting the bonds on fire.

As the anti-corporate party, the Pops would put the railroads, telegraphs, irrigation canals, and grain trade in the hands of the government. They are vague on how to do this without incurring debt. The *Spokane Chronicle*, a silver-Democrat paper, accuses them of a "tendency toward state socialism" but not "in any definite, intelli-gible and scientific form." That is about right.

The People's Party platform of 1892 says the power of gov-ernment "should be expanded as rapidly and as far as the good sense of an intelligent people and the teachings of experience shall justi-fy, to the end that oppression, injustice and poverty shall eventually cease..." The Pops are not for a 20th century welfare state—in the 1890s no one is—but they do call for government to provide work. On January 17, 1894, before Coxey is heard of, Judge Frank T. Reid speaks for the People's Party to a crowd of 1,800 in Tacoma. He calls for government to "employ at once all unemployed men in the United States in the construction of great public works"—roads, or the proposed canal across Nicaragua—and be paid in legal tenders. Another Populist idea is that the government should build irrigation ditches to reclaim federal land, with workers paid partly in "irriga-tion scrip" to be redeemed when the irrigated land is sold.

"Legal Tender" Greenback

The Pops have their own cadre of papers: the New Whatcom *Champion*, the Vancouver *Register*, the Seattle *People's Call*, the *Tacoma Sun*, the Snohomish *Eye*, and the Ellensburg *Dawn*. Judging from the copies that survive, these dish up more doctrine than news.

To the Republican press, the "Pops" are the party of the free lunch. Says the *Daily Reveille*: "The Populists, God bless them, want free silver, light silver, rag money, free trade, subtreasury money, somebody to pay their debts, and anything to raise sheol about, without any chance of success here or hereafter, and they want the greatest inflation possible." The *Bellingham Bay Express* compares the Pops to quack doctors. The *Tacoma Union*, in its Republican phase, says Populism arises from a "disposition to obtain something for nothing, or to compel the industrious members of society to divide the fruits of the toil with the idlers and drones." Democratic papers stress the statism. The *Yakima Herald* says of the Populists: "They want an absolutely centralized popular despotism, which shall do everything for the citizen, from lending him money and warehousing his rutabagas to fixing his hours of labor and prescribing the rate of profit on his investments."

The *Telegraph*, the flagship of Seattle Democrats, defends the gold standard and opposes the Pops' idea of unbacked paper money. The *Telegraph* argues: "A dollar is a unit of value, something that we measure all other values by." "A dollar is 23.22 grains of pure gold, just as a foot is twelve inches... If the definition given to a dollar by act of Congress were done away with, a dollar in this country would simply be a name, and the government printing office might go on turning out dollar bills night and day and they would simply be spoiling so much clean paper."[60]

The 1890s is the Populists' decade, especially in the West. There the pioneers and their children, says the *Seattle Times*, "feel in an experimental mood and are willing to try almost any new thing in the way of government or social reform."

The People's Party's first showing is in the national election of 1892. Democrat Grover Cleveland unseats Republican Benjamin Harrison. People's Party nominee James B. Weaver, who had been the Greenback nominee in 1880, comes in third. The Populists carry North Dakota, Kansas, Colorado, Nevada, and Idaho. Washington goes for Harrison, but gives Weaver nearly 22 percent of the vote, two and a half times his national share. The People's Party elects four members to the lower house in Olympia.

In 1892, the People's Party elects governors in Kansas and Colorado. The governor of Oregon, Sylvester Pennoyer, elected twice as a Democrat, joins the new party. The three governors become the public face of Populism, each making page-one news in the state of Washington.

The Panic gives the People's Party momentum. In Oregon, in May 1893, the month the Panic begins, Governor Pennoyer calls for President Cleveland's impeachment for not enforcing the Geary Act against the Chinese. (Cleveland's excuse for not registering the Chinese is that Congress has appropriated no money.) In

1896 Silver Certificate: Electricity lighting the world

131

Charles Gloystein. *Seattle Post-Intelligencer,* 8-8-94

July, Pennoyer refuses to greet Vice President Adlai Stevenson in Portland, insisting he come to Salem. In October, Pennoyer refuses to go to San Francisco to attend the christening of the battleship *Oregon,* because he believes military spending is wasteful. In November, Pennoyer sets Thanksgiving a week earlier than Cleveland has, the date not being fixed by law. For all these antics Washington newspapers heckle him. The *Seattle Post-Intelligencer* calls Pennoyer "the oracle, the demigod of the bubble-and-squeak Populist party of Oregon." Many readers are disgusted, some are entertained and not a few are pleased.

In Kansas, Populist Governor Lorenzo D. Lewelling begins his term in 1893 by ordering the state militia to clear the House of Representatives in Topeka of the Republicans, who the Populists accuse of winning a majority by fraud. The Republicans barricade themselves in and Lewelling orders the militia to clean them out. The militia's commander refuses the order. Lewelling then backs down, but only after Topeka is filled with armed citizens ready for war.

In Colorado in March 1894, Populist Governor Davis Waite calls up the state militia to surround the Denver City Hall, where two appointees of the fire and police board refuse to accept dismissal. Waite also backs down, but the *Seattle P-I* says he has "come within a hair's breadth of precipitating wholesale murder in the streets of Denver."

In Washington, the People's Party spreads peacefully. In April 1893, in the first election in the new city of Everett, a Populist comes within four votes of beating the Democrat-Republican "fusion" candidate for mayor. In December 1893, Populists win the offices of mayor, marshal, treasurer, and health officer of Port Angeles, the home of the Puget Sound Co-operative Colony. The Pops have no chance in Republican Seattle, but in April 1894, while Jumbo Cantwell is recruiting his "industrial army," a Populist comes in second in a three-way race for mayor of Tacoma. In May 1894, Populist Horatio Belt beats a Republican in a two-way race and becomes mayor of Spokane.

In June 1894, the Populists have a setback. Pennoyer allows another Populist to be nominated to succeed him as governor of Oregon. Pennoyer aims for a seat in the U.S. Senate by campaigning for Populist candidates to the state legislature, which in the 1890s elects U.S. senators. He fails. Oregon voters, sick of their page-one governor, give the governor's seat and legislature to the Republicans.[61]

Sylvester Pennoyer. *Clip Art*

In mid-summer 1894, the Pops are tarred with an apparent political abduction and murder.

The man is Charles Gloystein, 37. He is a proud Republican living at Mica, Spokane County, a Populist stronghold. After Pennoyer's humiliation in June, Gloystein puts up a sign at the local crossroads, taunting his neighbors:

Coming Events Cast Their Shadows Before! Have You Heard from Oregon? Nope! 'Rah for Oregon!

Two days later an effigy of Gloystein is hung in front of the community schoolhouse. On its back a placard says:

I am Charles F. Gloystein, a Traitor to My Farm, to My Home, and to My God! Hell Is My Future Home!

Gloystein's 7-year-old boy sees the effigy the next morning

133

and runs home to tell his father.

In the local paper, a neighbor, A.C. Rubeck, denies that he hung the effigy but argues that Gloystein asked for it. Rubeck heads the local chapter of the Freeman's Protective Silver Federation.

Gloystein writes a reply blaming Rubeck. His letter is printed in the paper July 28. On the night of July 29, the sound of knocking awakens his wife, Salina. Gloystein says someone outside needs help with a wagon. He goes out and is gone. The next morning, men find his bloodied straw hat. Salina says he has been threatened with death several times and now they have got him. She is beside herself.

The community is in an uproar. For days, gangs of men scour the land for signs of a murdered man. They find nothing.

The story is page-one news across the Pacific Northwest, and the Republican papers are quick to make a lesson of it. The *Post-Intelligencer* runs four page-one stories and six editorials on it in the first month, plus 14 other items, most of them roundups of scalding opinion from other papers. The *P-I* calls Gloystein's disappearance the work of the "Populist Ku Klux Klan" and expresses the hope that it "will drive every thoughtful, decent man out of the ranks of Populism."

Republican Governor John McGraw offers a $500 reward for Gloystein's body and another $500 for his murderers.

Some Democratic papers cast doubts on the political-murder story. If Gloystein was afraid of being murdered, asks the *Colfax Advocate*, why did he go off in the night? Then again, would such a man voluntarily desert his wife and five little children?

The Populist papers label it a Republican trick. The *Ballard Searchlight* argues that "a human cur who would endeavor to stir up strife in his neighborhood by sticking up an obnoxious sign board" might also fake his own murder to make the Populists look bad. Noting the $500 posted by Governor McGraw, the *Vancouver Register* suggests: "It might be profitable for the Republican tricksters of Spokane County to now bring their man in and claim the reward."

F.F. Lischke, editor of a Populist paper in Sprague and officer of the local Freeman's Protective Silver Federation, is shaken, both by the apparent murder and his fellow Populists' denial of it. He publicly renounces his political faith for its "prejudice, ignorance, injustice, cowardice and demagoguery," and returns to being a Democrat.

The skeptics are right. Gloystein is alive. In late September, Thomas E. Delaney of Farmington walks into the office of Spokane County Sheriff Francis Pugh and says he's been working alongside Gloystein on a farm in Oregon. Sheriff Pugh leaves the next day, and on September 22 confronts Gloystein in a barn at Moro, Oregon, a few miles south of the Columbia River. Gloystein's one luxury on his $1.50-a-day pay has been a mail subscription to the *Spokane Chronicle*, so he can read about himself.

Gloystein admits to Pugh that he staged his abduction, right from the knocking that awakened Salina. He walked off into the night, planted the bloodied hat, hopped a freight train and hoboed it to Oregon. By his account there was no conspiracy. It was one Republican's trick, all right, but not from political motives. Gloystein fled because he was scared.

In several newspapers that never assumed Gloystein dead, the story of his cowardice runs on page one. "Hark, From the Tomb!" headlines the *Seattle Telegraph*. "We Told You So," says Snohomish's Populist sheet, *The Eye*. The *Post-Intelligencer*, embarrassed, buries the story on page 3.[62]

In the 1894 campaign, the Republican newspapers argue that Populism has been a disaster. In each of the Populist states, says the *Everett Herald*: "Populist rule has struck down private and public credit." The *Spokesman-Review* says the People's Party has bankrupted Kansas.

Still, Populism has an influence. In the West, Republicans tack left. At the state convention the silver Republicans of Eastern Washington and Pierce County team up against the gold Republicans of King County and push through a free-silver plank. The Democrats are for free silver, too. Of its northern neighbor the *Oregonian* complains: "On the money question, all parties in the state have gone daft."

Nationwide, in 1894, the Republicans gain 118 seats in the House, the largest swing in U.S. history. They end up with half the seats in the Senate and 68 percent in the House. The People's Party takes only 2 percent of the House seats, mostly in the South. In Kansas Governor Lewelling is defeated. In Colorado, Governor "Bloody Bridles" Waite is defeated. In Ohio, Jacob Coxey loses his bid for a seat in Congress on the People's Party line, coming in third.

In New Whatcom, the *Reveille* says the Populist triumph in only two states, Nevada and South Carolina, "shows the class of people required for the growth of Populism."

In Olympia, the Republicans take 76 percent of the seats in the Senate and 69 percent in the House. It's the Democrats, however, that have been shattered. Twenty-one Populists are elected to the lower house, leaving the Democrats with only two. The Pops' strongest showing is in the counties hardest hit by bank failures: Pierce, Spokane and next-door Lincoln, and Whatcom.

In Puyallup, the chairman of the platform committee of the Pierce County People's Party, John Rogers, produces a moderate platform that the *Tacoma Ledger* dismisses as a "blank cartridge." When Rogers and his Republican opponent for a seat in the Legislature debate before a crowd of 500, the *Ledger* declares that the Republican tore Rogers' "populistic effusions into a million atoms." But on Nov. 6, 1894, Puyallup, which six months earlier petitioned a Republican governor to remove Jumbo Cantwell's "army," elects Populist John Rogers to the state House of Representatives.

He will be the next governor of Washington.[63]

Populism worries men of business.

Early in 1895, the *Tacoma Ledger* prints a long letter from Clinton P. Ferry, who is living in the East. Ferry, 58, is one of Tacoma's founders; people call him "the Duke of Tacoma." He is worried about the public spirit in the city he helped build.

"The next two years will largely decide the question of Tacoma's superiority," Ferry writes. "The result depends largely upon the action of the people." And the people, he fears, are infected with resentment and distrust.

"Tacoma has the terminus of a great railroad," he says. "There are so many people who are not proud of that fact, who to me cursed the road when I was at Tacoma last." They still have pride when slandered by a rival city, but he says: "There is something beyond that which is necessary to build cities. You will find it in Chicago and in a place near Tacoma." He means Seattle.

A few weeks later, a *Ledger* editor, probably Clinton Snowden, chimes in. The spirit of progress "is as strong in Tacoma as in Seattle," the editorial says. "There is this difference however, between the two cities. In Seattle, when some undertaking requiring the display of public spirit is accomplished, everybody is proud of it and boasts about it, and those who have accomplished it are given full credit for it." Not so in Tacoma. "If a bank was in trouble," the editor says, "these harpies gathered about it to gloat over its downfall, and if some citizen risked or stood ready to risk his private capital to save it and its depositors, they derided and denounced him as a public enemy. If an individual made an effort... that was profitable, he was a hog, and if it was unprofitable, as most frequently happened, it served him right."

What the *Ledger* and Ferry are describing about Tacoma is Populism in its personal, emotional aspect. Populism is more than a platform. It is an attitude—a little man's attitude. The charge against Populism is that it sneers at thrift, industry, and ambition; it declares that the game is rigged and its winners crooks; and it demands to eat but will not pay.

In Washington, the movement is still on the rise.[64]

BANKERS (1893-1894)

A thought arises that the men who wrecked the banks should go to prison. Mostly they don't.

Many bankers have been negligent. At the failed Port Townsend National Bank, examiner Charles Clary writes: "The president, who lived away from the town, neglected his duty." At Tacoma's failed State Savings Bank, W.F. Reynolds is president for only 90 days before it fails. He lives in Chicago and has never visited it. At the failed First National Bank of Whatcom, the directors have not met in a year and a half.

Many bankers have been self-dealing. At the Port Townsend National, cashier W.A. Wilcox borrowed the bank's money and lost it on a fish-preserving plant. But adventure is not a crime, nor is lending to officers and directors. In the 1890s, it *is* illegal for a national bank to lend an amount greater than 10 percent of its capital to any borrower. But the law provides no punishment unless the loans are made in an illegal way, such as by forging documents or bypassing the loan process.

It is under such a provision that cashier Sam Dusinberre of the Bank of Puyallup pleads guilty to grand larceny. The Bank of Puyallup is the first bank in Washington to fail in the Panic, and from 1893 through 1897, its cashier is the only banker in Washington sent to prison.

After imprisonment in the Washington State Penitentiary for a little more than a year, Dusinberre mounts a campaign to get out. A complication arises: the warden has been caught embezzling money from the prison's sale of gunnysacks, and Dusinberre was his secretary. On December 8, 1894, the warden commits suicide. The new warden, however, vouches for Dusinberre, as does the judge who sentenced him and the attorney for the Bank of Puyallup's receiver. A Republican-to-Republican letter also arrives on his behalf from Levi P. Morton, governor of Dusinberre's home state of New

York and former vice president of the United States. On June 13, 1895, Governor John McGraw issues Dusinberre a full pardon. In 1896, Dusinberre leaves the state for a job at Westinghouse in Pittsburgh. He never works in banking again.[65]

The state's most high-profile bank case is against James K. Edmiston, 31, president of the Walla Walla Savings Bank and the Security Savings Bank of Seattle.

Edmiston is the promoter of the new town of Columbia City southeast of Seattle. His Washington Co-operative Home Co. sells building lots on the installment plan, keeping title to the lots and pledging them to Security Savings in exchange for cash. Some $26,000 of Edmiston's debt is also guaranteed by Walla Walla Savings.

In March 1893, he asks his manager in Walla Walla, William Stine, to guarantee $15,000 more. Stine is a good banker. "I cannot see any way clear to do so," Stine writes. "It looks to me as a gross prostitution of my position, unknown to the directors of this Bank and I cannot nor will I do it." By July, Stine is out, replaced by a manager who joins Edmiston in borrowing from the bank they run.

On December 9, 1893, after the disastrous wheat harvest, Walla Walla Savings goes down and takes Security Savings with it. Seattle has its first bank failure of the Panic of 1893.

The closure of Walla Walla Savings creates a sensation in Walla Walla, Washington's oldest town. Edmiston is overdrawn by $30,569. He tells creditors he can get two-thirds of it from his mother in Scotland and will raise the rest as soon as he can. But the *Seattle Post-Intelligencer* reports "a very bitter feeling among other depositors of the bank, who demand that there shall be no 'whitewashing.' "

In April 1894, Edmiston is put on trial, not at Walla Walla, because feelings there are scalding, but at Pomeroy in nearby Garfield County. The charge is embezzlement. Stine, his former manager, testifies that Edmiston forged mortgages and used bank assets to settle personal debts. The judge tells the jury to disregard this testimony.

The jury's initial vote is 9 to 3 for conviction, but after four hours it finds Edmiston not guilty. People on the train back to Walla

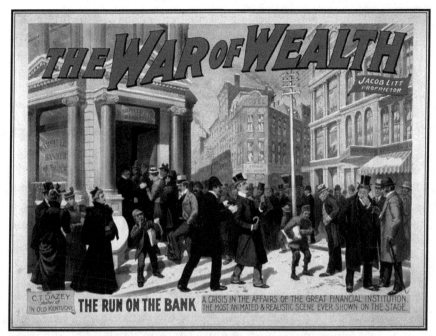

Bankers in popular culture, 1895: a Broadway show about a bank run.

Walla are outraged. At nearby Dixie, the people hang Edmiston in effigy.

At the trial, one of the witnesses against Edmiston is Walla Walla saloon proprietor Henry Tobin, who had a $4,500 deposit in Walla Walla Savings. Tobin testifies that he came to the bank on Friday, December 8, 1893, to take $1,000 out, and that Edmiston told him to wait until Monday. By then the bank was closed.

Tobin leaves the trial early when he is told his son Walter, 3, is ill with brain fever. The boy dies. On April 23, the bereaved father sees Edmiston, scot-free, in conversation on a Walla Walla street corner. Tobin's anger flares. He is carrying a .38 caliber American bulldog revolver. He levels it at Edmiston and pulls the trigger at close range. The gun misfires. Edmiston turns to run; Tobin fires and the bullet goes through Edmiston's coat. Edmiston flees, with Tobin behind him. Tobin stops for a second shot, misses again, and releases a third shot into the air by accident. He stops, shoots again, and misses.

Edmiston sees a horse and wagon, grabs the reins to commandeer it, but is blocked by its astonished owner. Tobin had given up the chase, but seeing Edmiston fussing with the horse, he gives chase again. Edmiston flees. Tobin stops, aims carefully this time, and releases a fifth shot from about 70 feet. He misses. His weapon has a short barrel, and he has not used a gun since the Civil War.

"The son of a bitch! He robbed me and now my family is sick and starving," Tobin rants. He goes home; he is arrested, taken to court that day and fined $20 for simple assault.

Edmiston is so reviled in Walla Walla that his attorney persuades the court to move the new trial to Yakima. In February 1895, he is tried there for the crime of accepting a person's deposit when he knew his bank was "in a failing condition." It is a new law, and a troubling one: it assumes that once a bank reaches a certain stage of sickness, the banker is obliged to stop taking deposits—which, of course, will kill it.

Edmiston is charged with unlawfully accepting a deposit of $40 from Mrs. C.L. Whitney on the day the bank closes. He testifies that he was expecting a shipment of cash from Portland on the noon train, and that none came. His cashier testifies that Edmiston admitted he had planned the closing in advance.

The jury is out 45 hours. The men come back weary, disgusted, and deadlocked, six to six. The *Walla Walla Statesman* is disappointed at the hung jury: "That he is guilty there is not a shadow of a doubt," it declares. It says Edmiston deserves 10 years in the penitentiary.

In June 1895, Edmiston is put on trial a third time. Walla Walla's ambitious young prosecutor, Miles Poindexter, who will later become a U.S. senator, is determined to get a conviction. He tells the Yakima jury: "We are not trying him for forgery. We are trying him for robbing Mrs. Whitney... If this defendant was acquitted here now, none of the other parties who helped rob this bank and the citizens of Walla Walla County will be brought to justice."

The judge tells the jury to "entirely disregard" Poindexter's florid accusations of robbery because Edmiston is not charged with robbery.

Like the jury in the previous trial, this jury deadlocks initially, six to six. After deliberating 24 hours, the jurors wanting acquittal agree to support conviction with a recommendation for clemency, a statement that has no legal weight. On June 8, 1895, Edmiston becomes the first man convicted under the state law forbidding the officers of a failing bank from accepting deposits. He notes that two of the jurors are Populists, and blames the verdict on them.

The judge sentences Edmiston to two years at the state penitentiary. He appeals and is released on a $2,000 bond. In December 1895, his appeal is denied and he flees the country.

Edmiston will never return to the United States. Fifteen years later he will begin sending money to the customers of his two banks who lost their deposits in 1893. On January 28, 1911, he will receive a full pardon from Washington Governor Marion Hay, who will state that Edmiston has repaid "all known living creditors."

One man will dispute that: Henry Tobin, the man who shot at Edmiston on the streets of Walla Walla. Tobin will write a complaint to Hay that he has not received a single dollar.

In April 1912, Edmiston will send Tobin $4,000, and Tobin will pen no more complaints.[66]

In most cases, the law fails to punish the negligence or wrongdoing of Washington bankers.

In Tacoma, the *Union* newspaper pushes hard for indictments of "the wreckers of the Merchants National Bank." The Merchants was the first national bank in the state to fail in the Panic. It has loans to insiders of more than $100,000 in excess of its capital, including large sums to its ex-president, Walter J. Thompson, and its vice-president, Henry Drum. Both men's loans are secured only by promissory notes.

It is "a nice piece of financiering," the *Union* says, "to loan yourself somebody else's money on security approved by yourself." The *Union* concludes: "The grand jury might look up this class of crookedness and see if there is not some law to reach it." In March 1894, a federal grand jury considers a charge of making false entries on the bank's books. The prosecutor says a conviction is doubtful, but the grand jurors indict the bank's four top officers anyway. At trial, the judge finds the case so weak that he instructs the jury to acquit, which it does without leaving the courtroom.

The usual case against bankers is not for self-dealing but for accepting deposits when the bank was failing. Under this provision, prosecutors bring charges against at least six cashiers and three bank presidents in Washington. Except for J.K. Edmiston, all are either acquitted at trial, have their cases dismissed by the judge or, in one case, charges dropped because the man has moved out of state and it's too expensive to bring him back. Looking back in 1898, the *Seattle Post-Intelligencer* notes that no banker in Washington has ever gone to prison under this law.

One more case, of a banker who shirks his responsibility to depositors and is not charged at all: James R. Morrison is president and cashier of a one-man bank, barely a year old, at Ilwaco, at the mouth of the Columbia River. He is also chairman of the Pacific County Republican Central Committee and the party's nominee for county auditor. In September 1894, he closes his bank, announces he is taking a trip to Spokane, and disappears. Behind him are complaints that he has run off with money of the Masons and the Ancient Order of United Workmen. Pacific County loses a deposit in his bank.

Of Morrison, the *South Bend Journal* writes: "There is little doubt that he is at least temporarily insane, judging from the letters addressed to his wife, in which he appears to imagine that he is in charge of the hotel at Sealand which he ran some two years ago." The letters are mailed from Sacramento. After a few weeks Morrison is reported at his sister's home in Columbus, Ohio, suffering from amnesia. Upon his return to Ilwaco, he tells a reporter that two years of his life are blank and that he "does not recollect having engaged in the banking business."

In December 1894, Morrison moves his family to California. The *South Bend Journal*, a Republican paper that supported his aborted candidacy for auditor, announces that the former banker "is slowly recovering from his strange loss of memory."[67]

Some of the closed banks may be resurrected. But which ones, and by whom?

If the man who led the bank to ruin says he can revive it, shall he be trusted? That question arises in June 1893 with the failure of Ben E. Snipes & Co. of Ellensburg. It is a state-chartered bank under the supervision of the county court. Snipes, the bank's owner, asks his depositors not to petition the court for a receiver. A new man, he says, won't know the assets. He won't *care* about the bank. He will dump the assets to get the job done and move on, and during hard times the assets will sell for pennies on the dollar and the depositors will come up short. Snipes knows what the assets are worth. He promises to pay depositors 100 cents on the dollar if they will trust him. As security, he offers them a deed of trust on his personal property, which they initially reject but later accept.

The court leaves Snipes in charge, subject to three trustees. In November 1893, he sells $100,000 of the bank's assets without asking the trustees. It is a reasonable sale and they approve it afterward, but Snipes has bypassed the trustees and broken a promise. Several depositors file a lawsuit and in December 1893, Snipes is out. The superior court appoints a receiver who takes years to sell the assets. The payout to depositors is only 9.72 cents on the dollar, the final payment coming a full decade after the failure.

The town's other bank, the Ellensburg National, closes in July 1893 because it is owned by George B. Markle of Portland, whose Oregon National Bank fails the same day. After three months, U.S. Comptroller Eckels, the regulator of all the national banks, allows Markle to reopen his Ellensburg bank, which in 1895 adopts a policy of no loans to officers or directors.

Eckels also allows the Oregon National to reopen, which it does on September 9, 1893. But most of its depositors have had to agree to a restriction on their right to withdraw funds. The problem lies with public money. On December 9, 1893, a grand jury decides that restricting Multnomah County's right to withdraw its $160,117 deposit satisfies the legal definition of embezzlement. It indicts Markle, his cashier and the county sheriff who signed the depositors' agreement. Upon his arrest, Markle closes the Oregon National and turns it over to a receiver.

No doubt the indictment of Markle feels good to the public, but this is not embezzlement. The prosecutor will lose the case, as he should. The immediate losers, however, are the failed bank's employees and depositors. After four years, the depositors, including Multnomah County, will be paid 50 cents on the dollar.[68]

When a national bank fails, Comptroller Eckels sends one of his bank examiners. Usually Eckels will also appoint a receiver to take charge of the assets and, if necessary, to liquidate them. In hard times, receiver is a plum job.

In 1893, Eckels sends examiner Lionel Stagge, 27, to a bank in The Dalles, Oregon, that closed. Stagge reopens it. He does it again with a small bank in Portland. Then Eckels sends him to the First National Bank of Spokane, a failure that will require a receiver.

In November 1893, Stagge writes Eckels that Washington's at-large Republican congressman, John L. Wilson, dropped by to ask that the receiver's job be given to his brother Henry, and after Eckels appointed someone else, Wilson dropped by again to complain. Stagge is a perceptive judge of men. "I might state here, privately, that the Hon. J.L. Wilson is a politician, in every sense of the word," he writes. "Mr. Wilson is considered here a very tricky man, and I believe he fully deserves his reputation."

Eckels is the appointee of a Democratic president, and Democrats expect him to appoint other Democrats as receivers. In Washington state his bank receivers are mostly Republicans. The Democrats make a fuss. "Comptroller Eckels says the affairs of the national banks in Oregon and Washington have given him more trouble than all the states in the Union," reports the *Post-Intelligencer.* To the *P-I,* Eckels describes the job seekers as turkey buzzards circling a carcass.

In December 1893, when the Oregon National closes a second time, several of Portland's Democratic politicians ask Eckels for the receiver's job. He ignores them and gives the job to young Lionel Stagge, moving him from examiner to receiver—the job Congressman Wilson wanted for his brother. But there are some things about Stagge of which the regulator is unaware. In January 1894, the story is leaked that in 1889, under the name A.L. Waterhouse, Stagge pleaded guilty to passing a bad check. All across the region, the newspapers trumpet that the receiver of the Oregon National Bank served a year in the Oregon State Penitentiary.

Confronted, the young bank receiver admits it. He was Waterhouse. Upon release from prison, he became Stagge.

In 1891, at 24, he married Nellie Straight, 23, of Eugene.

The daughter of a former Idaho newspaper publisher, she had been a music student at the University of Oregon, a college debater and solo singer at the 1891 commencement. Stagge did not tell her of his past.

Stagge remade himself. For two years after leaving prison, he sold ads for the *Oregonian*. On May 5, 1893, the day after the Wall Street panic, he incorporated a company to publish a monthly journal, *Pacific Banker and Investor*, with money from Nellie's father. Representing his magazine, Stagge interviewed Comptroller Eckels in Washington, D.C., impressed him, and was offered the job of bank examiner.

In less than four years, Stagge has gone from a prison cell to receiver of the largest failed bank in Oregon.

In his defense, he notes that the bad check was for only $35. But as bank examiner and receiver, he says: "I have... in my absolute possession several hundred thousand dollars. Every cent of these funds have been accounted for." As for changing his name, he says, "What else could I do?"

"I do not intend to leave Portland," Stagge says. "I will stay here, if I may, and continue in my endeavors to atone for my only offense and regain my reputation."

Though he kept her in the dark, Nellie stands by him.

Newspapers around the Pacific Northwest weigh in on the Stagge case. The *Oregonian* comes to the defense of its former salesman, who now rents an office in its building. It compares Stagge to Jean Valjean, the reformed convict in Victor Hugo's *Les Miserables*. The *Spokane Review* also supports him, saying he "ought to live down this severe misfortune" and become an example "to other young men who make a false start."

The *Tacoma News* quotes Stagge's statement about not leaving Portland. Its editorial writer finds Stagge's "if I may" particularly meaningful. "Here was a man who forged a check when poor and lonely in a city where he was a stranger," the *News* writes in sympathy. "On his trial he made no defense but pleaded guilty and served his term. He left prison with the determination that he would live down the one misdeed of his life and attain a position of usefulness and respect in the very community where his misfortune had befallen him... The plea the man makes is full of manliness."

The *Tacoma Ledger* is not so generous. It notes that Stagge has received letters of sympathy "signed by many Hebrews." But bank receiver, it says, is a position of public trust. This is "not a case in which sympathy alone should prevail," the paper argues.

Stagge offers Eckels his resignation. After several discussions with President Cleveland and receiving letters and a petition on Stagge's behalf, the comptroller seems willing to keep him. But Stagge's bondsmen begin to insist on control of his disbursements because of the forged check he once wrote. After three months, Eckels replaces Stagge with a trusted friend of President Cleveland's from Chicago.

Stagge is out of a job. But he is no Jean Valjean. The cynical *Tacoma Ledger* is right about him: he is not trustworthy. He leaves his wife and he leaves the Pacific Northwest. For the next 40 years, he will live on the East Coast as a confidence man, gulling wealthy men and women out of small amounts, often by posing as a journalist or author of vanity books. He will be convicted many times, and finally be sentenced to three years in prison.[69]

Some of the closed banks reopen. In Spokane, the Washington National Bank reopens July 6, 1893, after being closed a month. In Everett, the Puget Sound National Bank reopens October 23, 1893, with what the *Everett Herald* describes as "a large, wholesome-looking pile of gold and silver on the counter." The Tacoma National Bank reopens December 4, 1893, after its president, William Blackwell, mortgages his property and buys the bank's building for $63,000.

Reopening almost always involves depositors agreeing not to withdraw all their money. At Port Angeles, the First National Bank asks savers to accept bank scrip in 20 equal parts, at 6 percent interest, one coupon cashable each month.

There is no vote on these agreements. They are binding only on those who sign. Depositors sign in the hope that if enough do, the bank will reopen. But some depositors refuse to sign, and sometimes their truculence pays. When the Bellingham Bay National Bank reopens January 9, 1894, owners of 18 percent of the deposits, who have not signed, are immediately free to withdraw all their money.

Some plans to reopen fail. To revive the Columbia National

Bank of New Whatcom, cashier J.E. Baker asks for a $50,000 loan from a New York bank. The Columbia National's receiver, George Blanchard, tells the New York bank that the Columbia National's management was criminally careless, and the New York bank denies the loan. The Columbia National's directors are outraged. A committee of depositors petitions Comptroller Eckels to fire the receiver, saying he has "officiously intermeddled" in their bank's revival. Bank examiner Zoeth Eldredge, who has already told Eckels he has found "evidence of bad and reckless management," tells him: "The great bulk of the loans are in the hands of the directors and their relatives, not one dollar of which the receiver has been able to collect." Eckels supports his receiver and the bank stays closed. It eventually pays out 18.24 cents on the dollar.

In late 1893, Eckels vetoes the reopening of the First National Bank of Port Angeles even after its directors raise $30,000 cash in New York. The *Post-Intelligencer's* Washington, D.C., correspondent reports that Eckels is concerned that the directors or their friends still owe the bank $50,000. To Eckels' demand for more security they offer too little. Reports the *P-I*: "This finally so provoked the comptroller that he made the plain statement that in his opinion, the directors of the bank were not honest men and that he had permitted them to play horse with him long enough."

The comptroller and the directors settle their dispute, and the First National Bank of Port Angeles reopens April 26, 1894. Its reopening, says the *Port Angeles Democrat-Leader*, brings "a feeling of relief, the restoration of confidence, the air of cheerfulness, hopefulness and buoyancy..."

In Tacoma, the state-chartered Traders Bank, closed in July 1893, also reopens. Stockholder Henry Strong, president of the Eastman Kodak Co. of Rochester, N.Y., and Tacoma businessmen Henry Hewitt and George Browne raise the money to reopen the Traders on January 25, 1894. The Traders is the only bank in the state to reopen without restrictions on withdrawing deposits. Every depositor is free to withdraw all his money—and too many do. The bank lasts four months before closing a second time. The First National Bank of Port Angeles also closes again.

Of the 14 banks in Washington that fail and reopen between

1893 and 1895, some of them under other names, only one will survive the hard times: the tiny Commercial Bank of Conconully, which closes voluntarily. By the end of 1896, all the rest will be gone. Capital alone will not revive them. The banks' initial failure breeds distrust, and their limits on the right to withdraw deposits breeds more distrust. Without the public's trust, a bank cannot survive.[70]

In the 1890s, there is no deposit insurance. But all national banks, and in Washington all state banks, have double-liability stock. If a bank fails, the authority in charge can assess stockholders—*bill* them—for an amount up to the par value of their shares. This is a way to make depositors whole. It also aims to make bank officers cautious, because they are usually the biggest stockholders.

This system is used from the 1860s to the 1930s. Over that time, in the country as a whole, stockholders of dead national banks pay about half their assessments. But in the hard times of the 1890s, national-bank stockholders in Washington pay less than 30 cents on the dollar.

In the spring of 1894, stockholders of the "wickedly mismanaged" First National Bank of Whatcom are assessed for 100 percent of par value. The bank's president, the cashier, and his wife all fail to pay. At the Merchants National Bank of Tacoma receiver Robert Wingate waits six months to declare an assessment, by which time the stockholders, including the bank's president, have transferred assets out of his reach.

In Washington state most presidents and cashiers of failed banks are good neither for their loans nor their assessments. Receivers have to sell assets, raising cash from buildings and land when there is little market for either. At the Merchants National, receiver Wingate writes Eckels in June 1894: "Businessmen have barely sufficient money to run their several businesses and there is no money for the purchase of real estate. This statement of affairs is good for Spokane, Portland, Seattle and Tacoma." Except at a sacrifice price, he writes: "It is impossible to sell anything."

A few things have value. The failed First National Bank of Spokane owns the Last Chance Mine, a silver-lead property in the Coeur d'Alene Mountains. At first, receiver F. Lewis Clark undertakes to run the mine on behalf of the First National's depositors. Then he gets crafty, sells the mine to himself, and resigns as bank receiver. By doing this he makes himself one of Spokane's new millionaires. The dead bank's depositors are left with 44 cents on the dollar.

Washington has 85 bank failures in the mid-1890s, counting banks that reopen and close again as *two* failures. The principal blame can be laid to the unprofessionalism of pioneer bankers. Government offers little protection. For the national banks, supervision is inadequate, and for state and local banks it doesn't exist at all. The state law's threat to prosecute reckless bankers is toothless. The protective system of stockholder assessments—a system imposed by law—breaks down. Receivers wait until they know how much money they need, by which time stockholders fail to pay. Receivers end up selling the bank's assets into collapsed markets and coming up short. Depositors wait years for their money and usually settle for less than all of it.

The public's trust is gone.[71]

THE BOTTOM (1894)

In July 1894, Thomas Burke, whose name today is on Seattle's Burke Museum and Burke-Gilman Trail, receives a letter from an American artist in Paris.

The artist, Alexander Harrison, has a painting of sun-dappled nudes in an orchard. Called *En Arcadie*, it is the best work of the sort Harrison will ever do. He has held on to it for eight years and wants to sell it. Now, he writes, the conservator of the Musée du Luxembourg has expressed an interest in it.

"It occurred to me that as you failed to do me the great favor which you proposed doing in New York, that you might still feel inclined to do it here instead," Harrison writes. He is asking Burke to buy the painting and donate it to the museum.

"You will perhaps wonder why I do not offer to present the picture myself," Harrison writes. "Well, because this is neither the best form nor the best policy—and because I can't afford to do it. That is, if I can find my friend good enough to do it for me. So far as the price is concerned *'entre nous'* I shall of course leave that for you to decide."

Burke is the Seattle attorney for the Great Northern—the man who secured the road's right of way into the city. He is also a co-founder of the *Seattle Telegraph*, the town's gold-Democrat newspaper.

Burke writes Harrison that he cannot buy the painting.

"In 1890 I was drawn by the importunity of a friend" — promoter Daniel Gilman— "into two disastrous ventures," Burke writes. "I left the management of them to him. On my return from Europe in the spring of 1892, I found that one of the enterprises [was] on the brink of ruin; and, unless I acted promptly, would drag me down with it. As soon as I could turn myself I sold out the concern with a net loss upwards of $62,000." That was the *Telegraph*.

Their other venture is a trolley line from downtown Seat-

153

Thomas Burke, *"Men Behind the Seattle Spirit: The Argus Cartoons,"* 1906

tle to Ballard. That investment is also a loser. "I am still holding that up in the hope that the return of good times will pull it out," Burke writes. "That has already swallowed up $63,000. I am now employing every resource at my command to save this last $63,000 or at least a part of it.

"In ordinary times I could stand the loss of $125,000 but now, people who are owing me can't pay," he writes, "and I don't want to press them, for to do so might mean their ruin." The last line of the draft letter is crossed out: "The result of all this is that it is only by the most extraordinary efforts that I can meet my own pressing engagements."

To sell his holdings now, Burke writes: "would be to sacrifice everything. I think, however, the tide of business has turned, and perhaps in six months I may be in condition to render you the service in question..."

Hard times bring a constipation of obligations. Burke owes $25,000 on a loan from James J. Hill, president of the Great Northern. In October 1894 Burke sends Hill a check for the interest but writes: "I am unable to pay the principal now, owing to the impossibility of collecting what is owing me." Even a prominent businessman such as Burke cannot afford to buy an oil painting, because he is strapped. He never buys the painting.[72]

Debtors everywhere are asking for more time. At Morse Hardware Co. in New Whatcom, handwritten notes from local farmers and tradesmen tell a similar story.

From West Ferndale, Silas Cole writes in January 1894: "It is impossible for me to pay any bills just at present. It is close scratching to get my bread. The bank has my money." From Lynden, A. Williams offers a horse to erase $100 in debt. From Sumas, H.C. Paden writes, enclosing $10. He says he can't pay his whole bill until several men pay him, and that he has been "carrying these men since June."

He adds, "I never saw such hard times in my life."

In March 1894, New Whatcom ship owner and lumber exporter Edwin Langdon writes Morse Hardware that he can't pay because his remittance from Chile is late.

In April 1894, S.H. Hutchcroft of Seattle writes: "We intend to pay you one hundred cents on the dollar... I hope you will not feel it is necessary to put our account into a judgment, as it will just put more costs and will not settle the matter any sooner. Enclosed please find money order for $25.00 and as soon as we can will send you some more."

In May 1894, Charles Cline of Lynden writes Morse Hardware that he has received several letters asking that he pay the $20 he owes and hasn't answered them. "I have been ashamed to write," he confesses, "because I have not been able to raise the money."

In June 1894, H.P. Branin, who runs a general store in Custer, writes that he can pay nothing. "I cannot get a dollar from anyone," he says. "Business is dead."[73]

Real estate is especially dead. Rents fall, and in the once-booming new towns they fall almost to nothing.

Henry Baker of Walla Walla is attending to his real estate, the Baker Estate's properties at Fairhaven, where the corner room in the bank building is rented to confectioner Aaron Grube. Already in December 1892, Grube asked for a reduction in rent on account of hard times. In June 1893, when the Panic hits, Baker agrees to cut the rent to $25 a month for three months only, "provided there are no repairs called for by you during that time." By the end of August 1893, Baker instructs his agent to offer Grube $20 a month "in order to hold him." On the day after Christmas 1893, Baker cuts Grube's rent to $15—payable in advance.

In late 1893, Baker tenant I.N. Orchard, a real estate man, demands that the rent on a lesser room with a bank vault be lowered from $10 a month to $7. He threatens to move out, and Baker tries to reason with him. "The rents have already been reduced nearly 50 percent the last year on that room," Baker writes. "You have one of the best locations for your business in the City and you cannot afford to be moving about for any small rent like that."

The two men are dickering over one silver dime per day.

By mid-1894 Grube and Orchard are both gone. Baker's rental agent then asks to occupy the corner room—at zero rent. Baker offers the less-valuable bank-vault room at zero rent. In 1895, when the rental agent is pressed for rent on the corner room, he offers to pay with a town lot. Baker counters with $5 a month but if the agent can rent the bank-vault room, he can have the corner room for $2.50 in cash. Two years earlier, the rent was $25. It has fallen 90 percent.

Real estate is dead everywhere. In Tacoma, the *Union* runs a column saying the city has more than 400 empty stores.[74]

In March 1894, the Mason Mortgage Co. of Tacoma falls into receivership. Its owner, Allen C. Mason, has been one of Tacoma's most successful men. Arriving from Illinois virtually penniless, in less than four years he has made a fortune opening up new additions to Tacoma, putting in streetcar lines and helping buyers with mortgages. He has sold the mortgages to Eastern investors under his guarantee that the mortgages will be paid. At bankruptcy, his $2 million in guarantees are backed by just $25 in cash.

Other businesses fall into receivership in 1894: the Seattle Coal & Iron Co., owner of the Gilman coal mine; the Seattle Terminal Railway & Elevator Co., serving the Seattle waterfront; the Washington & Columbia River Railroad, George Washington Hunt's system connecting Walla Walla and Pendleton; the Shelton Southwestern Railroad Co., a logging road; the Point Defiance, Tacoma & Edison Railway in Tacoma; the Diamond Palace jewelry store in downtown Seattle, whose owner skips town; the Tacoma Grocery Co.; the Puget Sound Shingle Co. and the Pacific Coast Lumber Co. in Tacoma; the Tacoma Railway & Motor Co. streetcar lines in Tacoma, and the Grant Street Lines in Seattle.

A creditor asks that a receiver be appointed for the Seattle Dry Dock & Shipbuilding Co., but Judge Cornelius Hanford declines, ruling that owner Robert Moran is able to save his company. The judge is correct in his assessment. Moran will emerge from the hard times as the city's most prominent shipbuilder.

In the mid-1890s, America has no national bankruptcy law.

Insolvent national banks and interstate railroads are under the authority of the federal comptroller and the federal courts, respectively, but most businesses that are "embarrassed" are at the mercy of state court judges.

In mid-1894, Tacoma attorney Charles Sumner Fogg argues in a paper to the Washington State Bar Association that the receivership system has been pushed too far beyond its origin in the chancery courts of England: "The appointment of a receiver to take possession of property is a harsh and extraordinary remedy, and ought to be invoked only in cases where it is absolutely necessary to attain the ends of justice." Instead, he writes, "it has come to be an almost everyday infliction in ordinary cases." Under Washington law, he says, "the appointment of a receiver depends upon the discretion of the judge" —an elected judge, with an incentive to please the voters.

The result, he writes, is not good. "We have in Washington at this time a great army of receivers... receivers for banks; receivers for corporations; receivers for partnerships; receivers for property of all kinds and in all conditions," so that "the property and business of the debtor is seized and taken from the owner's control, his business broken up and destroyed without any adequate remedy for the wrong thus inflicted."[75]

To keep working during hard times, people accept less. In February 1894, the *Spokane Review* reports that David Strothers has underbid nine other funeral directors for the contract to bury Spokane County's paupers. The previous contract was $5 a body. Strothers bids 90 cents.

The *Review's* reporter wonders why a man would bury a corpse for 90 cents when the law makes him dig a grave six feet deep. A fellow undertaker explains it. "A man may die here unknown and unidentified and be buried at the expense of the county, and have well-to-do relatives in the East," he says. The relatives "find it out in the course of time, and who is in a better position to get the job of another funeral, with a possible chance at embalming the body for shipment east?"

Everywhere fixed prices fall. For several years, a cartel of meatpackers has controlled the wholesale price of beef west of the

Cascades. In the months after the Panic the cartel shatters and the price falls. A similar combine has controlled the retail price of flour in Spokane, setting it at 90 cents for a 50-pound sack. In January 1894, the price drops to 75 cents, then to 65 cents. The Centennial Mills Co. announces it is installing new machinery to double its capacity to produce flour and lower its cost per pound.

In February 1894, the price of bread to Spokane's restaurants, which had been 28 loaves for a dollar, falls to 36 loaves, then 40. Price-cutting by a white restaurant man incites a price war with Japanese restaurant men. The price of the house dinner at a dozen white-owned restaurants falls from 15 cents to 10 cents. The *Spokane Review* reports: "The fare includes beefsteak, pork chop, cutlets and all sorts of stews, with two eggs thrown in. Potatoes are plentiful and bread is as free to the customer as air."

A year ago, says a white restaurant man, his overhead costs— rent, fuel, lights, wages—worked out to 8 cents a meal, and he served 300 meals a day. He has cut his overhead to 1½ cents a meal, partly by serving 1,000 meals a day. "We feed hundreds who put their last dime on the counter," he says. "Many of them got the money by begging. It is comparatively easy to beg a dime."

In Shelton, Mason County, where the two barbers have been charging 15 cents for a shave, a third barber comes to town and offers shaves for a dime. In Tacoma's Opera Alley, a prostitute tells a reporter from the *News* that her competitors—some 500 of them in Tacoma—have been charging less also, and that she "did likewise."[76]

Years later, economists will assign mid-1894 as the bottom of the depression. "Trade and business are prostrated," writes the *Tacoma Ledger* in July. "No new enterprises are begun." However, this is not altogether true. As the Chinese say: "In every crisis is opportunity." Enterprises *are* begun, and they begin to offset part of the general shrinkage.

The obvious opportunity is in foodstuffs. The *Oregonian* writes: "We have been building towns, extending railroads, putting in streetcar lines, looking out for water powers and timber, and speculating in lands, and have done too little in production of fruits, cereals, butter and pork."

Start with butter. The *Oregonian* recalls that in the early days: "The old pioneer had his herds of cattle, but seldom a drop of milk in the house. He hadn't time, it was too much bother, and milk and butter were unnecessary anyway." People said the Northwest was not butter country; their taste for butter was met by shipping in butter from Iowa, on ice. In 1893, creamery butter is retailing at the Cow Butter Stores at 30 cents a pound. This is an hour's pay, or more, for a skilled laborer, and three times the price of good beef. Butter will fall a year later to 25 and sometimes 20 cents, which is still expensive. Those who cannot afford it buy "butterine" —oleomargarine—made from beef fat. It is also shipped in by rail.

In March 1894, the *Chronicle* notes that since Spokane brought in 20 carloads of butter the year before, there must be money to be made in "a properly managed dairy."

In 1892, there are two creameries—milk processors—in Washington. By August 1894, there are 20, including ones in Whatcom County, the Skagit Valley, Snohomish, Elma, Vancouver, Thorp, Ellensburg, Yakima, and Cheney, together taking 30 percent of the market. A year later there will be 52 creameries taking 70 percent of the market.

In the winter after the Panic, wheat farmers buy pigs and chickens to transform their unsold grain into ham, bacon, fryers, and fresh eggs. These, too, have been imported from the Midwest. At Pullman, a new instructor at the Washington Agricultural College, William J. Spillman, sets to work calculating how many pounds of wheat it takes to create one pound of pork. He also begins crossbreeding strains of wheat, a project for which he and the college will become famous.

New products need packaging. In April 1894, the Pacific Box & Basket Co. opens a plant in Tacoma to make butter tubs—the first on the Pacific Coast—as well as wooden baskets and fruit boxes. In August, a venture is announced to make beer bottles and glass jars in Tacoma to replace glassware shipped from the East. Late in the year, a San Francisco company says it will ship beer to Tacoma and open a plant to bottle it there.

Other new ventures aim at selling more products outside the region. One is fresh fish. Early in 1894, George H. Hackett, a Mas-

The whaleback City of Everett. *Everett Public Library*

sachusetts manufacturer of refrigerated boxcars, makes a trial shipment of fresh salmon and smelt from Everett to Boston. For the four-day trip, he uses chemical refrigeration, which keeps the fish at 30 degrees. For shorter shipments, salmon are packed on ice. Fruit also gets a push. In September 1894, a spokesman for H.F. Herrin & Co., Spokane, says: "Until this season there never was a carload of Eastern Washington fruit shipped to the East. Already this year one firm alone has forwarded 45 straight carloads." The big hope is peaches, which sell in Minneapolis at 75 cents a box. Snake River growers report, however, that the highest profit per acre is from apples. The *Spokane Chronicle* crows: "Washington is going to be the greatest apple state in the union."

It will be. This is when it begins.

In May 1894, C & C Milling Co., Spokane, loads 34 cars of flour for shipment to China, via the port of Tacoma. The *Chronicle* says Spokane's three flour mills have a capacity of 3,000 barrels a day, an amount that can be "doubled or trebled every year for at least ten years" before the region runs short of wheat.

Lumber mills begin returning to work, though at painfully low prices. In August 1894, after the Pullman strike ends, hundreds of cars of shingles move east from Puget Sound, filling several months of orders. In September, the Fremont Mill Co. in Seattle gets an order from Minnesota for railroad timbers and 1 million board feet of lumber from China. At Port Angeles, the Red Cedar Shingle & Lumber Co. sets to work on 3 million board feet of railroad ties and timbers for Hawaii. The islands are not yet a U.S. possession; this is an export shipment, Port Angeles's first. In October, a Tacoma company sends 500 red cedar doors to South Africa. Cedar doors also move east by rail. The *Puget Sound Lumberman* writes: "Only three years ago, the red cedar door trade was unknown east of the Cascade Mountains."

In mid-1894, Tacoma's businessmen offer a $25,000 subsidy for the owners of a steel rolling mill in Iowa to move it to Lakewood (then called Lake View), Pierce County. Steel men promise 75 to 90 jobs, increasing to 350 jobs as steel users set up nearby. Developers subdivide land and begin putting up houses. In April 1895, the mill begins production.

Seattle increases its wholesale business with Alaska. "About three years ago, Seattle had no trade in Alaska to speak of, all goods being purchased in Portland and San Francisco," says the *Post-Intelligencer.* Seattle has wrested away Portland's trade and now contends for San Francisco's.

On October 24, 1894, Everett has a landmark moment. The Pacific Steel Barge Co. launches the *City of Everett,* an odd-looking vessel called a whaleback. On top, its hull looks like a submarine's— rounded, so that the waves can wash over it, but with an upturned, snout-like bow. Its bottom is flat. Designer Alexander McDougall invented the whaleback for the Great Lakes; his company, the American Steel Barge Co., has been building them at Duluth, Minnesota. His Everett yard, backed by John D. Rockefeller, is his second. With the *City of Everett* he aims to spread his whaleback design to the Pacific and have it be the preferred ship design for the 20th century.

At 361 feet, the *City of Everett* is the longest ship ever launched on the Pacific Coast. For the three-year-old town of Everett, population 5,000, its christening is a huge event. Mayor Norton D. Walling declares a holiday. Business shuts down. Building owners deck out their establishments in Fourth of July bunting. A parade is held with industrial floats drawn by horses. A sawmill has a float with a 24-by-24 beam 68 feet long. The nail mill has a float with a machine ingesting steel wire and spitting out nails. A shingle mill has a float with a 10-block machine chunking out shingles, and a meat company has a wagon of hanging sides of beef. The shipyard's float displays a model of the *City of Everett* in wood, and a bakery has it done in bread. The proud *Everett Times* says: "The *City of Everett* will be a constant advertisement of the manufacturing city in which she was built."[77]

At summer's end 1894, the *Ledger* announces that business is improving—at least, "everybody says this is true." Newspapers assert that it *ought* to be true. "The crazy, cruel, suicidal strikes which paralyzed all business for several months are out of the way," says the *Blaine Journal*. The uncertainty over tariffs has ended: the Democratic Congress has cut them. "Lastly," says the *Spokane Chronicle*, "the nation has sobered up from a long debauch of over-speculation and extravagance in public and private affairs."

Recovery, however, is elusive.

In June 1894 the *Ellensburgh Capital* announces that the Middle Kittitas Irrigation District, which plans a 56-mile canal starting at Cle Elum, has sold $200,000 of bonds to a broker in Spokane. Says the *Capital*, "These are the first irrigation bonds ever sold in the state of Washington." The paper has jumped the gun; the broker in Spokane is *trying* to sell them.

In August 1894, Spokane contractor Peter Costello sets up in Ellensburg and begins hiring 300 men at $1.50 a day. "Already the business pulse is quickening," reports the *Capital*. "So many four-horse teams have not been seen in our streets since the boom days."

Costello meets his first monthly payroll out of his own pocket. For the second and third, he issues time checks, expecting the bonds will sell. They never do. No investors want them. In November 1894, the project shuts down.

The men are sore. Their "time checks" bear no interest and can be cashed only at a discount. Some of the men threaten Costello, but he has not been paid, either. They surround a meeting of the canal company directors but let them go after they promise to borrow $1,000. No money comes of this. The workers petition Governor John McGraw and nothing comes of that, either.

The mayor of Ellensburg offers the men food and, in an old blacksmith shop, shelter. Over several weeks about half of them drift away. The people of Ellensburg, who fed the "industrials" six months earlier, exhibit a tapering generosity. Pretty soon the food is a pile of dead rabbits. The men demand the rabbits be cleaned, and the Ellensburgers shake their heads. Feeding unpaid workers is not their responsibility. The idle men begin badgering passengers on the morning trains, telling them not to come to Ellensburg, where the people let you starve. Writes one Ellensburger to the *Seattle P-I:* "People are getting tired of the whole business."

On December 3, the last 30 men leave town, declaring that they will walk across the Cascades to Olympia and demand that the Legislature ban time checks. But it is winter and they soon give up.

The hard times are not over. The price of beef on the hoof has fallen to 2 cents a pound, the lowest in decades. The market for horses falls so low that in eastern Oregon some ranchers turn their animals loose.

Since 1893, the price of hops has fallen by more than half. A year earlier, pickers earned $1 a box—a day's work for an average picker—and white pickers pushed Native American pickers out of the fields. This year, the Yakima growers still pay $1, but the Puyallup growers cut the rate to 75 cents, and the 500-acre Meeker farm cuts it to 65 cents. Recalling their treatment the year before, the tribal members of Alaska and British Columbia stay home. Pickers are scarce. Insects infest the crop and some of the hops rot on the vine.

At Walla Walla, wheat falls to 19 cents a bushel, about the cost of heading it, threshing it, sacking it, and selling it. That price, the *Garfield Enterprise* says, is "almost as bad as a total loss of the crop."

Public authorities cut back. Seattle replaces its residential-area arc lamps with cheaper incandescents. New Whatcom defaults on $15,000 interest due on $477,000 of bonds. In Ballard, voters reject a property tax to keep open the public schools, and the school district cuts the 1894-95 school year to four months.

Newspapers bleed. Among the dailies, the *Tacoma News* is sold at a sheriff's sale in June 1894 and the *Walla Walla Union* is sold at a sheriff's sale in July. In August, the *Bellingham Bay Express* shuts down. In October, the *Tacoma Union*, having already converted most unpaid wages to stock, goes into receivership but keeps publishing. In December, the *Seattle Post-Intelligencer* buys the money-losing *Telegraph* for its linotype machines and customer lists, and shuts it down.

A *Telegraph* employee later recalls that for months he was paid in checks backed with no funds.

Late in 1894, the pace of bank failures quickens. Three banks fail in Spokane. At Grays Harbor, the county treasurer hears that a receiver is about to be appointed for the Aberdeen Bank, the oldest of the two banks in town. The treasurer writes a check on the bank for $3,200 and takes it to the Bank of Montesano. That bank's president, F.L. Carr, and cashier, Charles Lamb, borrow a railroad handcar and race the 11 miles to Aberdeen to collect on it. They present the county's check at 2:15 p.m., but the cashier puts them off until the bank closes at 3:00. It never reopens.

In Tacoma, the Tacoma National Bank is in trouble again. President William Blackwell, who mortgaged his family properties to reopen it, is in Philadelphia to raise another $100,000 on the bank's securities. He fails; Tacoma's name does not inspire confidence in the East. On December 3, 1894, the Tacoma National Bank closes for the second time, this time for good, its deposits having fallen in four years by 91 percent. Blackwell takes a $100-a-month job managing the Tacoma Hotel.[78]

For many, the winter of 1894-95 is a desperate time. Relief efforts are local: in Spokane, by the People's Tabernacle; and in Tacoma and Seattle, by the Associated Charities. In January 1895, King County commissioners give food and clothing aid to 4,680 men, women, and children. Reports the *Seattle P-I*: "Nearly every day there is a long train of applicants, many of whom are refused aid. Some of them appear to be able-bodied men, while others are broken down and have pinched and expressionless faces that tell a story of want and suffering more plainly than any words."

The *Tacoma Ledger* sums up 1894: "It has been a hard, cruel, cold, sterile, unproductive and unhappy year."[79]

VISIONS (1893-1897)

Just as the Puget Sound Co-operative Colony at Port Angeles is going extinct, another utopian venture begins. On property overlooking the Columbia River at White Salmon, a pioneer farmer founds the Washington Co-operative Colony. A credulous reporter at the *Spokane Chronicle* becomes the colony's herald.

The unnamed reporter's first story, on February 12, 1894, is entitled, "Land of Corn and Wine." The farmer is offering his vineyards, nursery and orchards to men and women who are industrious, honest, moral, peaceable, healthy, and have $100 in cash. Members will elect a board of directors to assign people's work. All will receive equal pay in coupons good at the cooperative store, and convertible for cash. The colony will take care of the sick and the old. Competition will be banished.

A colonist says he expects to work long hours for a few months, then settle down to an eight-hour day. Later, he says: "We can shorten the work to five or six hours and still grow wealthy."

On February 20, the *Chronicle* reports that 20 families are preparing to leave for White Salmon. "The plan of cooperation leaves each family to regulate its home life as it chooses," the story says. "Only the husband is required to work as the executive board may direct, though if the wife wishes to pay her initiation fee and devote her time to the general work of the colony, the family will be allowed double pay." Here is an offer to treat women as equals.

The man behind this, A. Harry Jewett, 48, left home at 16 and served in the Civil War in the 13th Illinois Infantry. Ten years after the war he came west with his wife, Jennie, and staked out their 160-acre homestead to create the first nursery in Washington Territory east of the Cascades. In 1891, he laid out the town of White Salmon. Jewett is an admirer of Edward Bellamy's socialist utopian novel, *Looking Backward* (1888). Jennie is also interested in social reform; she is a prohibitionist and suffragette. Early in the 20th century she will work in the movement that will win the full vote for women in Washington in 1910.

Interviewed by the *Oregonian* in March 1894, Jewett sounds every inch the practical man. "Our object is a business one, having for its object liberal returns for capital invested," he says. "The only difference between it and other co-operative associations is that in this one the shareholder will receive that proportion of the profit to which his shares of stock and the amount of labor expended entitles him. Each member will be a worker, and will follow that department of labor to which he is adapted. There will be no drones in our organization."

The Jewetts give themselves two seats on the colony's board of directors and two seats to their friends, Daniel and Marietta Hunsacker, leaving three seats for recruits. If they vote together, the two couples have control.

The *Chronicle's* reporter, who never visits the site, is promoting utopia. In May, the paper runs his story entitled, "All Are Like Brothers." The colonists, it says, are busy clearing land, grafting and transplanting trees, breaking ground and planting crops. They plan to build a sawmill and cut timber for houses. Until then, they are living in tents.

Each member is credited with a dollar a day. "Three ladies have been admitted to full membership in the colony—Mrs. Jewett, Mrs. Hunsacker and Miss Nina Woods. They, like the men, do whatever work is mapped out by the board of directors, receive their $1 a day and have a voice in the management of the colony." The other wives are doing their own housework.

In June, the *Chronicle* reports that the colonists are sawing lumber for their houses. Already three of eight planned houses are built. In July, the *Chronicle* reports that one man, a harness maker, has "gone back to the world of competition," but that two neighboring farmers are joining the colony.

Six weeks go by without a *Chronicle* story. On August 28, 1894, comes news. There has been a quarrel. The colony is breaking up. Ten families are leaving, with only the Jewetts, the Hunsackers, another couple, and single woman staying behind.

The reporter's source is letters, which don't say what the

quarrel was about. Perhaps the people in the tents wanted to build their houses but were ordered to work on the irrigation ditches.

"Only one thing is sure," the reporter writes. "Woman suffrage did it." One or two of the men, the *Chronicle's* reporter says, objected from the first to Mrs. Jewett and Mrs. Hunsacker being on the board, which would give two families control of the colony. The objectors were overruled. "About ten days ago the crisis came," the *Chronicle* man reports. "The majority of the society wanted one plan of work adopted and the majority of the board favored another. The Hunsackers and the Jewetts voted together and their plan was adopted. That settled it. Ten families seceded from the colony." Says the saddened scribe: "Another sweet dream is ended." The social experiment has lasted less than six months.

A. Harry Jewett. *Gorge Heritage Museum, Bingen*

Harry and Jennie Jewett will stay in White Salmon for the rest of their lives, farming and running a health resort. They are remembered in the name of White Salmon's main street, Jewett Boulevard.[80]

On the coast south of the Olympic Peninsula is Grays Harbor, a large bay—actually a flooded Ice Age river valley—surrounded by some of the richest timber in North America. At the head of the bay, on a navigable channel 50 feet deep, is Aberdeen. The town ships out lumber and canned salmon on sailing ships. It imagines itself a great port. What it wants is a railroad.

George Washington Hunt promised Grays Harbor City, Hoquiam and Aberdeen a railroad, but it never came. The railroad that comes, the Northern Pacific, crosses the Chehalis River just short of Aberdeen. It veers along the harbor's southern shore to a tract barely above sea level bought by Frank Deckebach and two others. They have enticed the Northern Pacific by giving it half the land in their town site, which they fancifully name Ocosta by the Sea.

In long-running newspaper ads, Ocosta proclaims itself "the only Terminus on the Pacific Ocean recognized by the Northern Pacific Railway." The site has been selected by the Northern Pacific's chief engineer, the ad says, as a place "combining all conditions of safety, wharfage, deep water unobstructed by bars and a sightly location for a city." A puff piece in the *Oregonian* says that on Grays Harbor: "Ocosta is the only place where such a city can be advantageously located."

This is smoke. *Tacoma* is the Pacific terminus of the Northern Pacific. Tacoma is on firm ground next to a deep harbor; Ocosta is on a mud flat. The *Oregonian* may call Ocosta "the most westerly point in the United States" on the national rail grid, but the place is a spongy lowland, a place where the roadbed can be washed out by a high tide. As a seaport, Ocosta needs a wharf three-quarters of a mile long to reach the navigable channel, which is unmarked and known to shift.

More smoke: In downtown Seattle a billboard is erected that says, "Invest Money in Ocosta-by-the-Sea and Double It." In the *Tacoma Ledger* an ad says: "What the Northern Pacific has done at Tacoma will be again witnessed at Ocosta."

The Ocosta town site is opened to investors May 1, 1890, in the heat of the new state's speculative fever. The promoters invite the press. George Macdonald, managing editor of the Snohomish *Eye*, will recall years later: "Ocosta, when reached, we observed to be a marsh, with raised wooden walks, to which the appearance of being lined with trees had been given by spiking evergreens, or small saplings, to the string pieces of the walks every 10 or 15 feet." The marketing does its work: The Ocosta Land Co. sells hundreds of lots, many to buyers who never go there.

The *Aberdeen Herald's* editor, F.R. Wall, scorns his town's new rival. He dubs Ocosta "the liquid settlement" and "Ocosta, in the Mud." To the *Herald's* editor: "It is not Ocosta by the sea, except at high water." After a bad storm, the *Herald* sardonically says, "The town was almost submerged, and a number of the residents came to Aberdeen for safety."

Around Ocosta, the water in wells—fresh water—rises and falls with the tides.

Still, Ocosta grows. People move in. A newspaper is started, a flour mill, a shingle and lumber mill, a hotel and a brewery. Deckebach, the town's first mayor, starts the Bank of Ocosta and gets himself elected to the Washington State Senate—its youngest member. In 1892, the Northern Pacific arrives, and Ocosta's population reaches 450.

Meanwhile, Ocosta's rival, Aberdeen, has also grown. With a population of 1,860, it is an infant itself, but it has four sawmills with an established seaborne trade. Aberdeen also has a physical advantage: it can more easily accommodate ships. The Northern Pacific decision-makers see the advantages of Aberdeen, and in September 1891, nine months before their branch line from Chehalis reaches Ocosta, they offer to add a two-mile branch into Aberdeen in exchange for free right-of-way and a $2,500 subsidy for a depot.

It is a reasonable offer. The Northern Pacific has never paid for right-of-way into a Western town. But the owner of Aberdeen's first sawmill, Arnold J. West, says the two miles of track will not benefit him, and he demands $15,000 for a right-of-way over his land. In early 1893, he relents, but by the time the city council approves the right-of-way, the Northern Pacific is almost in receivership. Its loan covenants do not allow it to build a branch line, even a short one. Aberdeen will have to build the line itself.

The materials are there, thanks partly to Spokane pioneer Anthony Cannon. Recall that at the beginning of the Panic, one of the ventures that sank his Bank of Spokane Falls was a scheme to build a 22-mile railroad around the rapids at The Dalles, Oregon. Rails for that road were shipped from England in the bark *Abercorn*. In January 1888, the *Abercorn* is repulsed by rough seas at the Columbia bar and is wrecked north of Grays Harbor. Fourteen bodies wash ashore, and only three men survive.

For four years, the wreck rests near the shore, laden with more than 5,000 steel rails originally valued at $8.40 each. In 1892,

Cannon and his partners hire men to build a trestle to the wreck, transfer the rails to a barge and pile them along the Chehalis River. Then comes the Panic, and the partners abandon their project at The Dalles and the salvaged rails. In 1894, banker William P. Book and Aberdeen lumbermen Charles R. Wilson and John M. Weatherwax buy the rails at a tax sale for 13 cents each.

The men donate the rails to build Aberdeen's branch line, keeping enough to sell later for a good profit. Three sawmill owners, including West, donate the crossties, and West and others donate the private right-of-way. The Northern Pacific agrees to furnish a construction train, fastenings, switches, and an engineer to oversee the work.

Town founder Samuel Benn donates 100 town lots, which three years before were valued at $300 each and now are offered to any man for ten days' work. Other lots are raffled off at $1 and $1.50 a ticket. The town puts on a musical, "Railroad, Railroad," admission 25 cents, each ticket a chance to win a town lot. The benefit raises $100.

In September 1894, the first crew, including mayor Clyde Weatherwax, begins grading earth. Early in 1895, the Northern Pacific brings in gravel. On April 1, 1895, the first Northern Pacific train rolls into the Aberdeen station. In the celebration, the Northern Pacific agent gives away chocolate creams to the ladies and children, and cigars to the men.

People will joke for years about the rough ride in the railroad's last two miles, because the rails are pitted with corrosion from salt water. But the salvaged rails do the job. Because the people acted rather than wait for a distant institution, Aberdeen is saved.

Ocosta is not. In June 1895, two months after the first Northern Pacific train rolls into Aberdeen, Frank Deckebach's Bank of Ocosta dies with 22 cents in its cash drawer. That September the *Ocosta Pioneer* shuts down.

In February 1896, a correspondent in Ocosta writes that all manufacturing has closed, and that families are living on clams, crab, fish, garden vegetables, and farm animals.

Late in 1896, one of the closed mills is moved to Cosmopolis.

A few years later Ocosta's three-story hotel will be barged 12 miles across the harbor to Hoquiam.

In 1908, the Northern Pacific will cut daily train service to twice a week, and in 1927 it will abandon the line. In 1932, Ocosta will disincorporate itself.

Its name lives on in the 21st century in the Ocosta School District and several schools. But of the 1890s town of Ocosta by the Sea only one house remains standing: a white Victorian with a square corner turret, built in 1892. People call it the Ocosta Castle.[81]

In eastern Snohomish County lies the biggest mining camp in Washington. Its name is from the title of Alexandre Dumas's novel, *The Count of Monte Cristo* (1844).

The ore at Monte Cristo, discovered in 1889, contains gold, silver, lead, and arsenic. To mine it, teams of men blast tunnels into mountains 5,000 to 6,000 feet above sea level. Cable-bucket tramways, one of them two miles long with a half-mile drop, carry the ore to the camp. To build the tramways, men and horses have hauled cables and cast-iron wheels up mountainsides. They have erected a mill to concentrate 500 tons of ore a day, shrinking its mass by two-thirds. From Monte Cristo a railroad moves the concentrate 50 miles to the smelter.

The smelter is at Everett. The men there work 12-hour shifts in noxious fumes. Says one critic, "Sulfur and arsenic soon line the intestines and lungs, and a man becomes what is known as 'leaded.' His circulation is poor, he gets weak, has no appetite, and if he don't stop, it means death." For this, the pay is 13½ cents an hour.

During the hard times of the 1890s the smelter is life-support for Everett. It is a new city, founded in 1891. Founders Henry Hewitt, Charles Colby, and Colgate Hoyt sited it where the Great Northern would hit tidewater, gambling that James J. Hill would make their town his Pacific terminus. They lost that gamble, but they still have the rail connection to the gold and silver of Monte Cristo.

A visitor describes Monte Cristo as a "hastily-built, jammed-together" huddle of houses at the foot of mountains. Every winter and spring, its residents fight snow several yards deep. The

Concentrator at Monte Cristo. *Seattle Post-Intelligencer, 8-6-96*

railroad clears the track with a rotary snowplow brought from the East, though when snow slides block the tracks, men must stop the train and probe for logs and rocks to protect the snowplow's blades. "I thought we had handled snow enough in Michigan to know how to get along with it," says mine president Joseph Colby in March 1894. Two months later, in May, an avalanche takes out an 80-foot tramway tower. To replace it, crews install 100-foot poles sunk 15 feet into the mountain.

The capital for the smelter, the railroad and much of Monte Cristo has come from John D. Rockefeller, America's richest man. In June 1894, the *Everett Herald* writes that Monte Cristo has absorbed more capital than "any enterprise in the state except the railroads." The paper is proud of that, taking it as an indication of the ore's value.

In August 1894, the concentrator starts up and ships its first processed ore to Everett. There it is smelted into bars of gold-silver alloy, which are loaded onto a ship for San Francisco.

In September 1894, Colgate Hoyt, trustee of Rockefeller's Monte Cristo Mining Co., comes out from New York, tours the mining camp and meets with the press. "There is an immense body of low-grade ore there that can be mined and reduced at a profit," he says. "Like all ventures of this kind, it costs a great deal to get matters in shape to handle the ores profitably. About all the preliminary work has been done, and in a short time the resulting profit will follow."

The emphasis is on the word "profit." The warning phrase is *low-grade*. At the smelter, Monte Cristo's ore is mixed with higher-grade British Columbia ore. In early 1895, Tacoma metallurgist Willis E. Everette tells the press that Monte Cristo's ore cannot be profitably smelted on its own and that Rockefeller has lost $1.5 million on his investment. The *Everett Times* calls the metallurgist a liar. "The Monte Cristo mines are yielding ore far richer than expected," it says. "Before another year the Monte Cristo mining district will be found the most valuable on the American continent."

The metallurgist is right about the ore. In an effort to make his investment pay, Rockefeller cuts out Joseph Colby and Colgate Hoyt and closes the offices in Seattle and New York. He sends deputy J.B. Crooker to Everett. Crooker invests in new Cornish rollers for the concentrator to grind the ore more finely. He focuses his efforts on the best of Rockefeller's three mines, the Pride of the Mountains.

The disaster comes in November 1897. A flood rips out the rail line in the canyon of the Stillaguamish River. A Rockefeller man announces that the railroad has never paid for itself and will not be rebuilt. All the mines of Monte Cristo have to shut down. The cynics say the announcement is a ploy, and that Rockefeller will use the disaster to squeeze out rival mine owners—which is what he does. His men reopen the railroad in 1900, now owning everything from mines to smelter. If there is any profit to be made, he will have it.

The answer comes in 1903: Monte Cristo can be operated only at a loss. Rockefeller sells the mines, the railroad and the smelter at a sacrifice price. The mines close, and within a few years the smelter does also. The railroad limps along as a tourist line, then it closes, too.

A century hence, Monte Cristo will be Western Washington's most famous ghost town, reachable only by trail.[82]

Irrigation is the great project of Central Washington. Government took over that work so early—decades before the New

Paul Schulze. *Tacoma Daily News,*
11-13-94

Deal in the 1930s—that 21st century people have forgotten that it began as a private enterprise. At the onset of the Panic of 1893, the *Tacoma Ledger* lists eight irrigation projects in Central and Eastern Washington, all of them private, aiming to bring under cultivation 283,000 acres. Most are financed with 8-percent gold bonds. The largest is the Northern Pacific, Yakima and Kittitas Irrigation Co.

In the 1880s, the Northern Pacific Railroad lays track up the Yakima Valley and is granted odd-numbered sections of federal land 20 miles on either side. The valley's soil is the deep sediment of a prehistoric lake, and the Yakima River runs through the middle of it. Already settlers have irrigated plots with a small system they call the Konnewock Ditch. In 1889, Walter Granger, who has built canals in Montana, forms the irrigation company, borrows money and secures the Northern Pacific's land for a few dollars an acre.

It's a real estate play: buy land worth next to nothing, build irrigation works costing $10 to $15 an acre, sell the land for $55 an acre, and continue billing farmers for the water. It's a risky proposition, but it advances. The railroad provides capital, and by 1891, when work on the canal begins, the railroad owns two-thirds of the irrigation company's stock. Granger is general manager, based at Zillah. The irrigation company's president is Paul Schulze, the Northern Pacific land agent at Tacoma.

Schulze has come over from Germany, where he was born into minor Prussian nobility. Journalist E.V. Smalley will remember Schulze as "a high-toned adventurer, without religion or morals" who "inspired confidence by his zeal, intelligence and audacity." With no capital of his own, Schulze attaches himself to the Northern Pacific. Smalley recalls Schulze sharing lavish dinners and fine wines with his friends at which he freely denounces his enemies with "strange oaths."

Paul Schulze "knew no superiors and few equals," writes Tacoma historian Herbert Hunt. "He was domineering, high tempered, ridiculously vain." A friend recalls Schulze as "sensitive and high-strung," peculiar in some ways but "the best friend I ever had." In its obituary, the *Yakima Herald* recalls that Schulze was one of the railroad men who bypassed the original village of Yakima and put the depot north of town. Owners were obliged to move their buildings and buy new land to put them on. They bellyache about this for years and can never forget the man who got them to do it.

Schulze is just the man to push through a canal 42 miles long. Of his many projects, from the Tacoma streetcars to the Ocosta Land Co., the Sunnyside Canal is his favorite. Before the Panic of 1893, he sends to Germany for a shipment of hop plants to test in the irrigated soil. They grow well. The irrigation project "was his hobby," recalls the *Ledger* after his downfall. "He thought of it by day and dreamed of it at night."

And he makes his project big. The Sunnyside Canal is wide and deep enough to float a small steamboat. In April 1893, when the work is two-thirds done, consulting engineer George G. Anderson of Denver tells Schulze the project is *too* big. "Though you have a canal well built as to stability and capacity, it has cost more than it should have," Anderson writes. He advises Schulze to cut the work short and sell the land already watered. This is not the advice Schulze wants to hear, and he ignores it—but construction stops anyway because he has no more money.

While Granger pays irrigation employees with post-dated checks, Schulze is trying to sell bonds in New York. Schulze is also fending off three banks to which he owes money personally, as well as the New York Life, whose Portland agent accepted his promissory note to buy a life insurance policy.

In June 1893, in the midst of the Panic, the *Yakima Herald* announces, "Big Sale of Irrigation Bonds." There is no sale of bonds. Schulze returns to Tacoma empty-handed.

In November 1893, Frank Allyn, president of the Commercial Bank of Tacoma, writes Cyrus Walker, president of the Puget Mill Co., Port Gamble, about "our friend" Schulze: "I've been see- ing Schulze about every day—he kept up pretty well during the late trying times—but he is now about as blue & discouraged as anyone I know... He has lost confidence in a hope of anything from that London agent and hardly knows where to turn."

In May 1894, Schulze travels back to New York to sell $700,000 in bonds. On June 13, Allyn writes of him: "A week ago he wired the 'sale practically closed, but require 10 days or 12 to con- clude details' ... Yesterday when I was wired, '*sale closed*—subject only to slight change in *form* of bond'... But of course no sale is ever end- ed till you get your *money*." The next day's *Yakima Herald* announces a bond sale—prematurely.

In July 1894, the *Herald* writes, "Paul Schulze is still in New York looking after the sale of the Irrigation Company's bonds. An association of capitalists have guaranteed the bonds, and the money would no doubt have been received before this but for the strike" of the American Railway Union.

In August 1894, with the railroad strike over, Allyn writes Walker again of their friend Schulze. "I saw him this a.m. He as- sures me everything is arranged satisfactorily and the money will be forthcoming within 6 weeks—he is seemingly confident, but I fail to learn that he has a written contract with his parties, and we know that (these days) even a written contract isn't always sufficient... I fear (from past experience). I profoundly hope all is well—his friends here seem generally to think so—but from what I have said, don't you think you had better come down & talk with him yourself?"

Luckless in New York, Schulze relies on the general manager of the Seattle Transfer Co., Benjamin Shaubut, who sets up an office in London to recruit investors. In September 1894, Shaubut writes: "Irrigation bonds of any kind or description are a drug here... The Yakima have been pretty well hawked around before I came over, consequently I had a very difficult time getting anybody to look at them at all." But Shaubut says he has a line on investors in Scotland, and assures Schulze: "It will be only a matter of a few days when we will close the deal."

In November 1894, the *Yakima Herald* runs a sub-headline,

"The Sunnyside Ditch Bonds are Actually Sold At Last." But they are not. In despair, Schulze twice downs a dose of chloral hydrate, a sedative, in an attempt at suicide. The chemical sickens him but does not kill him. Publicly he says nothing.

By the end of 1894, his creditors are closing in on him. The California lender that provided the final payment for the Yakima Valley land duns Schulze repeatedly. In January 1895, it loses patience and pushes the Sunnyside project into receivership. Schulze, still trying to save himself, is named one of the receivers.

He is on borrowed time. As Northern Pacific land agent, Schulze has been collecting money from buyers of the railroad's real estate and diverting it to his other enterprises, including the Sunnyside project. By early 1895, land buyers are complaining to the railroad that they have not received their title deeds. The head office senses a problem in Tacoma. It sends out investigators, and they discover a financial rat's nest.

Schulze has been contemplating suicide for years. He has told friends that he does not believe in an afterlife and that a man has a right to exit the world on his own choosing. On April 12, 1895, while his Japanese cook is out shopping, Schulze downs a final glass of champagne, writes a letter to his girlfriend, the actress Marie Wainwright, holds a .38 Smith & Wesson to his temple and blows his brains out.

Schulze's last financial act is to write a bad check, spending most of the cash on behalf of the irrigation company. He dies leaving his cook unpaid. His furniture has to be sold to pay his funeral expenses. His friend Paul Mohr, who had left Tacoma entrusting him with a collection of fine wines, discovers that all that is left is one bottle of Zinfandel.

A year later, investigators conclude that Schulze misappropriated from several companies more than $1.5 million. A relatively small part of it financed his high living. The larger part he used to pursue his dream to irrigate the Yakima Valley.[83]

Seattle's leaders have dreamed for years of a canal to connect Lake Washington to Puget Sound. Now that Washington is a state and has a voice in Congress, there comes a push for the government to build it. Other Washington towns are not happy: They fear Seattle will leave no federal harbor money for them.

"Seattle already has miles of deep-water harborage," complains the *Spokane Review*. The real reason to connect Lake Washington to Puget Sound, the *Review* asserts, is to back up Peter Kirk's project to build a steel mill and new town at Kirkland. And this, says the *Review*, amounts to "digging a ditch aimed to boom town lots belonging to a private corporation." Several papers note that the newspaper most enthusiastic about the canal, the *Post-Intelligencer*, is owned by Leigh Hunt, who has a stake in the Kirkland townsite.

The rest of the state, says the *Review*, has shown more interest in the canals of Mars.

Government engineers have a plan to build a canal that follows Lake Washington's natural outflow through Lake Union, but the plan attracts only pennies from Congress. There is, however, second project, a *south* canal. Its proponents offer to cut it through Beacon Hill and the adjacent mud flats, reaching tidewater south of downtown Seattle. It is a private project led by former territorial governor Eugene Semple.

Semple's inspiration is to imagine the moved earth reclaiming the mud flats. Just south of downtown Seattle, polluted with the city's sewage and trash, lie 1,500 acres of wasteland that can be made into clean, new land—*flat* land, which Seattle has little of. The Duwamish mud flats can be a place for industry, and for a railroad yard next to the port. The plan is simple: The canal creates the land, and the land pays for the canal. While irrigators in Eastern Washington use canals to make dry land wet, Semple will make wet land dry.

Semple's task is to convince investors that the reclaimed land will pay for the canal. In the spring of 1893, the ex-governor pushes a bill through the legislature. The new law allows a private canal company to recapture its costs from the created land plus 15 percent profit.

In the midst of hard times, Semple plows ahead. In July 1895, a year after the lowest point of the depression, the *Post-Intelligencer* prints a map of the imagined new district, showing Semple's canal, a straightened Duwamish and a new Harbor Island.

Semple says the project will cost $7 million. Through family connections, and leaning on Seattle's reputation as the city that has had few bank failures, he finds investors in St. Louis for his Lake Washington Waterway Co. One caveat: they insist that Seattle promise a $500,000 subsidy. Attracting investment with community subsidies—*private* subsidies—is a common thing in the 1890s. But to collect pledges of such a sum is quite a task during hard times.

Eugene Semple

During the spring of 1895, the *Post-Intelligencer* toots the horn for the subsidy. The canal will give Seattle "the best harbor on the Pacific Coast," the paper says—and also "will mean the spending of $7 million" to build it. By mid-May, 2,500 individuals and companies have pledged to pay the $500,000 when the canal is completed. The pledges will never be called upon, but they satisfy the St. Louis investors.

In July 1895, work begins. A dredge begins digging out the west Duwamish channel and piling up earth for Harbor Island.

This is the Seattle spirit, admirers say.

Meanwhile, the federal government continues low-budget survey and right-of-way work on the north canal. The two canals are not compatible. The north canal would lower Lake Washington, which would undercut the south canal.

In December 1894, Edward O. Graves, president of the Seattle Chamber of Commerce, is asked about the two canals. The north canal, he says, has a natural advantage "such as to commend the plan to every engineer who has seen it." But the main object of the south canal, he says, "is to secure earth which to fill up the tide flats. Every foot of land which they reclaim will be given an immediate value, whether the canal is finished or not."

The north canal will win the contest, opening June 16, 1917, to boat traffic. The south canal will be stopped years earlier, blocked

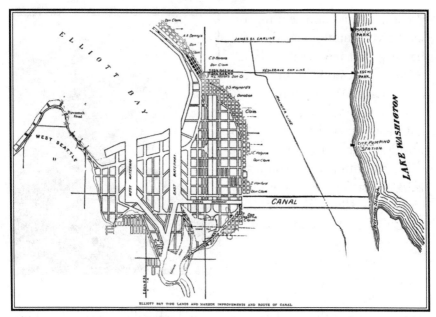

The proposed South Canal and streets on reclaimed mud flats. *Seattle Post-Intelligencer, 7-28-95*

by lawsuits and the logic of engineering. But Semple's project does its work: it keeps up hope during the hard times. It also turns the Duwamish mudflats into an industrial district of far greater economic value than a canal to Lake Washington.

A century later, all that is left of the south canal is a deep gash in the side of Beacon Hill at Columbian Way.[84]

STRUGGLE (1895)

Optimism does not come easy at the outset of 1895. Commercial values have collapsed. "The prices now ruling in every market," the *Tacoma Ledger* writes in January 1895, "are the lowest known in modern times... There can be no permanent improvement while these prices last."

In Port Angeles, Red Cedar Shingle & Lumber has not been paid for its big sale to Hawaii and falls into receivership. In Everett, American Steel Barge has no orders for more whalebacks—a dead-end design—and shuts down.

Newspapers everywhere carry notices of sheriff's sales. In Spokane, the Dutch-owned Northwestern and Pacific Hypotheek-bank forecloses on 61 building lots owned by Anthony Cannon, an action, writes historian John Fahey, "wiping out the old man's last assets in the city he had fostered." By 1896, one-quarter of Spokane's central business district will be owned by the Dutch.

The transfer of property to lenders does free it from debt. Says the *Tacoma News*, "a vast interest burden will be lifted from our shoulders." Private debt is being wiped out, one unpayable loan at a time.[85]

The public credit is under stress.

In February 1895, the U.S. Treasury's gold reserve, meant to be always above $100 million, shrivels to $44 million. Outside the Subtreasury in New York, hundreds of people wait to exchange paper money for gold. In the 1890s, this is as close as America comes to leaving the gold standard.

President Cleveland wants to sell bonds for gold, but Congress will not authorize more bonds. Citing a law passed during the Civil War, Cleveland ignores Congress and cuts a deal with financier J.P. Morgan to sell bonds for gold with the help of Baron Nathan Rothschild in London. The gold standard is saved, but on terms set

181

by Morgan and by foreigners. It's an I-told-you-so moment for the Populists and a shameful one for many Americans. The *Snohomish Tribune* says: "We don't like to have Baron Rothschild or any other foreigner talk of taking care of the American Treasury."

Local treasuries are also hurting. In Washington, state and local authorities are paying bills in warrants—interest-accruing IOUs. The issuer redeems the warrant by paying the principal and accumulated interest. Unlike bonds, warrants have no time limit. Nor do they have to be sold to willing investors. The issuer simply prints them and pays bills with them, redeeming them at its convenience.

This is no-payments, print-your-own-money financing, and politicians soon overuse it. In December 1893, Port Angeles elects three Populists and four fusionists to the city council. A year after they leave office the *Port Angeles Democrat-Leader* recalls how they burdened the town with an enormous debt by issuing "hundreds of dollars of city warrants at each succeeding meeting..."

In Everett, incorporated in 1893, the city's first-year income is about $40,000. By March 1895, Everett is carrying $72,000 in warrants. In Anacortes, by early 1894, the town government is carrying debt, mostly warrants, of $127,000, the equivalent of 25 years' of its much-shrunken budget.

Under Washington's constitution, local authority debt is limited to 1.5 percent of the assessed value of property, though a vote of the people can raise it to 5 percent. After the Panic of 1893, assessed values plunge. From 1892 to 1895, they fall in Seattle by 29 percent, in Tacoma by 39 percent and in Spokane from 1892 to 1894, by half. This automatically increases the ratio of debt to value. Communities everywhere find themselves above their debt limits, many forbidden to borrow more without a vote, and some forbidden to borrow more at all. Some issue warrants anyway.

Warrants trade in a secondary market if investors can be found to buy them. In October 1894, Seattle warrant broker Charles H. Lilly refuses to buy Clallam County warrants offered at 48 cents on the dollar, claiming that the county "has been bankrupted by Populist officials." By early 1895, the warrants of Whatcom County, a Populist stronghold, have fallen to 65 cents. In February, two of the three county commissioners—the two Pops—vote to reverse the order in which warrants are redeemed, ordering the new warrants— the ones *they* plan to issue—paid out of current revenues, leaving the old warrants to be paid only from past-due taxes. Their plan is stopped by the Washington Supreme Court.

The usual way out of warrant debt is to sell lower-interest bonds and pay off higher-interest warrants. In April 1895, a measure to sell bonds to take up $367,000 in school-district warrants is offered to Seattle voters—including women, because it is about schools. The measure has failed once to pass the 60 percent hurdle, and the Populists campaign for it to fail again. Despite a sharp drop in property-tax revenues, Seattle votes 74 percent yes.

Measures to replace warrants with bonds pass in Ballard, Everett, Port Townsend, and Vancouver. But such measures meet resistance in Pierce County, which has been above its debt limit since May 1893. In November 1894, Pierce County voters fall just short of 60 percent approval for replacing county warrants with bonds. In June 1895, the county tries again. Voters are offered six different batches of warrants to fund. The Populist-leaning judge of Pierce County Superior Court, John Stallcup, argues in the *Tacoma Union* for a "no" vote on all of them. Replacing warrants with bonds, he says, is "a scheme" of investors who have been buying warrants below par, and who are manipulating "pliant and imbecile" officials into paying full par value.

Only one of Pierce County's six measures—to cover juror fees, court costs and election expenses—reaches the 60 percent threshold. The other five fail.

A businessman returning from New York and Chicago tells the *Ledger* that investors there are alarmed by Pierce County's vote. He says Easterners will buy Seattle's street-paving bonds but not Tacoma's. Pierce County is cut off from Eastern capital. Local capital quickly takes up the slack. The Union Savings Bank & Trust Co. of Tacoma steps in and buys $44,000 of 6 percent Pierce County bonds. Two years hence the Union Savings will fail when the Tacoma warrant debt it holds is declared invalid by the Washington Supreme Court—a ruling later reversed. But for the moment, the Union Savings is Pierce County's savior.[86]

In 1895, Seattle and Tacoma get in trouble over public money deposited in banks. Seattle's trouble comes first.

In the spring, the legislature passes a law to prevent further losses of public funds. The law says a bank can take government deposits only if bondsmen guarantee payment in case the bank fails. This is deposit insurance for government customers only, and it quickly backfires.

The disaster hits the Merchants National Bank of Seattle, the city's third-oldest bank and Seattle's only national bank to fail in the 1890s. In three days, nearly one-third of the Merchants National's deposits are pulled out, not by individual depositors, but by the U.S. Treasury, King County, the City of Seattle, and Union Electric, a street-lighting company. On May 21, 1895, the Merchants National goes down.

Dr. P.B.M. Miller, president of the Seattle Board of Health and a large depositor of the Merchants National, steps forward with a plausible theory of how the run started. In a letter to Eckels, and also the *Post-Intelligencer,* Miller argues that the men with the motive to tip off public treasurers were the bondsmen who would have had to make good their losses. Miller pushes for an investigation, starting with the bank's founder and president, Angus Macintosh. He is the bondsman carrying the largest risk, $20,000, and he should know the condition of his bank. He is also the largest stockholder in the Union Electric. In 1898, Macintosh will be brought before a grand jury and questioned about this, but he will not be indicted. He will also refuse to pay the receiver's assessment of $45,000 on his bank stock, and he will get away with paying nothing.

In Tacoma, things are worse.

Beginning in 1891, city treasurer George Washington Boggs puts city funds into the Tacoma Trust & Savings Bank, which later changes its name to the Bank of Tacoma. The bank survives the Panic of 1893, but only just; individual deposits continue to drain out, leaving the city the principal depositor. When Boggs leaves office in April 1894, the city is stuck with a deposit so large that it will kill the bank to withdraw it.

In mid-1895, Tacoma's city council pushes for the city's money. Hearing of this, more private depositors take their money out, and on August 19, 1895, the Bank of Tacoma fails. The city's $228,664—80 percent of the deposits in the bank—is frozen.

After the failure, it is reported that the bank's two biggest borrowers are its president, William Burton Allen, and Tacoma's former city treasurer, George Washington Boggs. The bank lent money for real estate investments of Allen and his cashier, who has fled the state and is living by kiting checks. While acting as city treasurer, Boggs had a personal bank account that was credited with 3 percent interest on the city's deposits. This gave him an incentive to pump up the amount of the city's deposits. In addition, the bank gave Boggs an overdraft privilege to write checks on funds he didn't have.

This is finance everyone can understand: These men have been using the city's money for themselves. The public is furious. "Round them up," demands the *Tacoma Union*. "Round up the looters." Boggs and Allen are duly arrested.

Some Tacomans defend Boggs: he was *such* a generous guy. Big-hearted. Free with money. This talk makes the *News* furious. "Paul Schulze was another 'big hearted' fellow," it retorts. "He and George parted 'with their money like princes.' *Their* money, indeed."

It is illegal for a bank to pay a private person interest on public funds. Accused of this, Allen testifies that the 3 percent paid to Boggs "was a mere matter of bookkeeping." Actually, Allen says, the bank thought of it as a political contribution.

Boggs tells the court he never kept track of how much he had in his account. He just wrote checks.

More complications: from July 1893 onward, the city's deposits made by Boggs were not of cash but of questionable warrants. He was supposed to use the city's cash to redeem warrants held by the public, the oldest warrants first, paying 100 cents on the dollar plus interest, and canceling them. Instead, he used the city's cash to buy warrants out of order, from any willing seller, paying 100 cents but no interest. Instead of canceling the warrants, he stamped them "unpaid for want of funds" and sold them to the banks as deposits at the same 100 cents on the dollar. The city's debt was effectively extended. The banks stood to gain the accrued interest when the city redeemed the warrants. The Bank of Tacoma accepted the warrants. So did the Columbia National Bank, the German-American Safe Deposit & Savings Bank, and the Commercial Bank of Tacoma.

On October 15, 1895, the Columbia National and the German-American, which are next door and have common officers, sue the city. They argue that because the warrants were over the city's debt limit, and because Boggs effectively redeemed them by buying them at par, that they are no better than canceled checks. The banks say the city owes *them* money.

The next day, Boggs's successor, Treasurer J.W. McCauley, demands payment of the city's $6,300 deposit at the Commercial, its $58,369 deposit at the German-American, and part of its $112,216 deposit at the Columbia National. The Commercial is unable to come up with $6,300 in cash and immediately fails. The German-American and the Columbia National refuse to pay. The city goes to superior court and puts the German-American in receivership. On October 22, when the receiver enters its front door with the chief of police, bankers scurry out the back door with cash to hide in the Columbia National. The receiver finds only $1.10. Two days later Comptroller Eckels in Washington, D.C., orders the Columbia National closed.

Tacoma's treasurer has brought down four banks in two months.

The *Union* notes charitably that Tacoma still has eight banks left, but there is a problem. The city is $30,000 short for the interest on the $2.08 million of water and light bonds paid to Charles Wright. The interest is due December 1, 1895, and none of the eight remaining banks will give the city a loan.

Mayor Edward Orr tells a meeting of businessmen they will have to raise the money for the bond interest, else the city's credit will be ruined. Already Pierce County has shamed itself by failing to validate its warrants. Now this. The businessmen raise the money—a loan—from the gentry of Tacoma. The city's good name is saved.

Banker Allen is brought to trial in May 1896, but the jury follows the judge's instructions and finds him not guilty. Further charges are dropped in 1897. City Treasurer Boggs is convicted of embezzlement and sentenced to six years in prison.

The public has been yearning for something like this. Before the trial, the *Tacoma News* says: "If there be no law to punish him, an outraged people should take the law into their own hands and make an example of him."[87]

Take the law into their own hands. This does happen in Washington, though not to bankers. On August 11, 1895, the state has another lynching, this time at Ellensburg. The trouble starts in the Teutonia Saloon, a tavern frequented by Germans. John Buerglin, a local known as Dutch John, calls his pals over for a drink. Sam Vinson, 55, a no-account who has been staggering from taproom to taproom, asks: "Am I in it?" Dutch John replies, "No. You ain't in it. I lend you two dollars and you not pay it, you not drink *mit* me."

Vinson is insulted. He grabs a knife from the free-lunch table and goes for Dutch John. Seeing this, one of the owners comes around the bar with a wooden mallet. Enter Vinson's son Charles, 29, who once put a Chinese man in the hospital by shoving him off a Seattle streetcar. The young Vinson pulls a .44 revolver on the saloon owner. The elder Vinson, meanwhile, slices Dutch John in the gut as Dutch John clobbers him with a bottle. The other owner, Mike Kohlhepp, brandishes a pool cue and orders young Vinson to clear out of his saloon. The young man fires his .44 at Kohlhepp. Mortally wounded, Kohlhepp wrestles him to the floor. Police come and hustle father and son off to jail, while Dutch John staggers two blocks to the doctor's office, cradling his intestines.

Kohlhepp dies an hour later, Dutch John two days later. Both are good men, and their deaths inflame the town. At midnight, a mob congeals outside the Kittitas County courthouse. Tipped off, the sheriff has sent his deputy away with the key to the cell and has posted five guards. The mob overwhelms them. Illuminated by a candle, men pound on the cell's steel door with sledgehammers, crowbars, and a section of railroad rail. Young Vinson taunts them, spitting tobacco juice on them and fanning their candle out with his hat. Someone shoots into the cell, but misses. The elder Vinson, sobering up, is quiet.

Well past 1 a.m., the bolts holding the door break, and the

mob drags father and son into the street. The first thought is to string up a rope to a telephone pole, but a homeowner complains that the mob is bothering his wife. The crossbeam is too high anyway. Down the street is a poplar eight inches in diameter with two branches seven feet off the ground. This will do.

Asked for his final words, the elder Vinson wails: "My God, haven't I a friend in this crowd? I never harmed any of you." His son says: "I hate it on my mother's account. You'll be sorry for this."

The *Ellensburg Capital* describes the scene: "The hands of the men were quickly tied, ropes were put around each neck, and the old man was pulled up. When his feet were off the ground, a voice said, addressing Charles Vinson, 'Your pa's up there; go up and see him.' Then they pulled the boy up, and both men slowly choked to death, with their faces not over eight inches apart. As they hung under the low spreading limbs their feet were not two inches from the ground, and they presented a horrible sight." An angry German hits Sam Vinson twice in the head.

To the editors of the *Seattle Post-Intelligencer,* the lynching is serious, deplorable, disgraceful—and understandable. The lynching, the editors say, "is the protest of outraged justice against the long line of paltering procedure which has set one murderer after another free."

The *Yakima Herald* connects the lynching to the trials of the Snipes & Co. bank robbers two years before, when the real robbers walked free. The failure of justice taught the men of Ellensburg not to trust the courts. It also led to the failure of Ben Snipes's bank, freezing the savings of dozens of families in Kittitas County.

Washington newspapers condemn the lynching, not out of sympathy for the Vinsons—the men "got what they deserved," says the *Seattle Times*—but because lynching makes the state look bad. The *Everett Herald,* however, advises its readers not to worry about that. "Not one dollar will be kept from investment in this state because of a periodical lynching," the *Herald* says. "Vigilance committees do not assail any man's property. On the contrary, their work clears the air, and is always followed by a period of lessened activity among the criminal classes."

Five men are put on trial in Ellensburg for being in the lynch mob. Multiple witnesses put them there. All are acquitted.[88]

In the mid-1890s, the progressive idea in social work is that individual charity is wrong. Speaking to the annual meeting of Seattle's Bureau of Associated Charities, the Reverend W.H.G. Temple of the Plymouth Congregational Church recounts how he has been hounded by sniveling children and women begging with borrowed babies. "At last I have quit giving," he says. "I had to. Now when a man comes to me for help, I send him to President [David C.] Garrett's bureau or to Major Morton's woodpile" —organized charities that require the able-bodied to work.

"Free soup in winter is a terrible temptation to idle and shiftless persons," says Fred Gasch, chairman of the King County Commission, in his speech to the Associated Charities. "What influence can be worse than to see that those who beg fare better than those who work? We shall have just as many paupers as we lure into an easy life of idleness." Nonetheless, King County welfare rolls now have 800 names.

The year 1895 is notable for a new idea in social work: community gardens. A century later it will be called a p-patch. The idea comes from Detroit and is called the Pingree plan after Detroit's mayor, Hazen Pingree. In Washington, Seattle tries it first. Family men are given seeds and, if they need them, lent tools and plots of private land. Pioneer David T. Denny offers 160 acres of the old Denny farm at the south end of Lake Union. Other landowners chip in.

The average cost of seeds—for onions, carrots, turnips, lettuce, radishes, peas, beans and potatoes—is $1.44 per applicant. By September, the tillers report some success, especially with potatoes. The cost of subsidies is $203.70; the value of the food raised is 12 times as much: $2,450.

Self-help works. The plan will be judged a success and kept going through the rest of the hard times.[89]

In the midst of the strife, struggle, malfeasance, and gloom, an apparent recovery begins. Early in 1895, commodity prices begin to move up: steel, petroleum, beef, wheat, and lumber. Businesses scramble for the gains.

In March 1895, the Alaska Steamship Co., led by Captain Charles E. Peabody, enters the Alaska market with the 140-foot steamer *Willapa*. The existing carrier, the Pacific Coast Steamship Co., tries to kill the new entrant by cutting the round-trip passenger fare from $100 to $50 and, later in the year, to $10, but Alaska Steamship survives.

In April 1895, Simon Oppenheimer of Spokane raises $300,000 in the Netherlands to develop the city's water power for a flour mill, a lumber mill, and an electric utility to compete with the Washington Water Power Co. On Tacoma's tide flats, the Pacific Meat Co. begins work on a five-story meatpacking plant, the largest in the West.

In May 1895, stocks jump on Wall Street on heavy foreign buying. With Chicago wheat up 10 to 12 cents a bushel, British ship owners raise charter rates. The Northern Pacific Steamship Co., which has been carrying flour from Tacoma to Asia on three steamships, orders two more from British shipyards.

By June 1895, silver has moved up just enough to make the better mines pay at reduced wages. In northern Idaho, the Bunker Hill & Sullivan Co. reopens its big silver-lead mine without a union contract, paying $3 a day for miners and $2.50 for others.

Lumber revives. Ballard comes alive with the buzz of circular saws. A visitor describes "a forest of black chimney stacks, half buried in steam and smoke." Puget Sound's lumber exports will jump 50 percent this year, but lumber and shingle prices stay at rock-bottom. Wages do not increase.

In June 1895, the *Tacoma Ledger* announces that a recovery is underway. It is mistaken. Economists will label this period the false recovery. The trend reverses, and liquidation resumes.

In July 1895, Vancouver loses the streetcar line it has had since 1889. Land developers had put in the original system of horse-drawn cars to connect their town lots to the business district and the Portland ferry. The line has never covered its costs and a receiver shuts it down. After a year the rails will be torn up. Already in 1895, streetcar rails are being torn up in Anacortes and Port Townsend, the first going to Shelton for a logging road and the second to Montana for a mine.

In August 1895, the *Post-Intelligencer* runs a page-one story on a confrontation on a farm in the Palouse. The sheriff there has sold a 600-acre farm to the holder of the second mortgage. The new owner sends four men to lay claim to the wheat crop grown by the tenants. The owner's men camp in the fields to stop the tenants from harvesting the wheat. At dusk a crowd shows up yielding whips and quirts—or rifles and shotguns, depending on who's telling the story—and the repo men slink away. A few days later, federal Judge Cornelius Hanford, who the year before defended the rights of railroads against Coxeyites, rules that the crop belongs to the tenants who raised it, not to the new landowner.

In September 1895, the Reverend Andrew J. Hanson announces to a conference of Methodists in Seattle that lice have ruined the harvest of hops in Puyallup. It is a sign, he says, of the hand of Providence. "Thank God!" the delegates chant, affirming their enmity to beer. The *Seattle P-I's* editors reply that the powers at work are entirely natural: the hop crop is "a failure because the lice were permitted to over-run it; they were permitted to over-run it because the price is so low" that hops are not worth growing. After this discouraging year, many farmers west of the Cascades will stop growing hops.

In October 1895, the Oregon Improvement Co. falls into receivership a second and final time. The company will not build the Port Townsend Southern Railroad to Olympia, and Port Townsend will remain cut off from the national rail network. Port Townsend's power company, which has not been paid for the town's street lights, threatens to turn them off. The town's voters approve a tax levy to keep half the lights on and the rest go dark.

On November 4, 1895, "The War of Wealth," a Broadway play based on the Panic of 1893, opens in Seattle. With 200 actors and an elaborate set, the play, by Charles Turner Dazey, is the story of a run on a bank. Writes the *P-I*: "The grand climax is reached at the end of the third act... with anxious depositors crowding one another in efforts to get their money back again, while the president of the bank appeals to them for more time." In the play, an express wagon arrives with a clatter of hooves, and depositors get their money.

No wagon of cash saves the day at New Whatcom. On the same day as "The War of Wealth" opens in Seattle, New Whatcom's biggest bank, the Bellingham Bay National, fails for the second time. The failure ties up $7,000 in Whatcom County funds. In a fit of determination, county treasurer Ernest W. Purdy buys the bank's double-combination safe for $700 and declares that the county will not put any more money in banks.[90]

In December 1895, the *Tacoma News* reports that Thomas Riggs, an investor who recently moved from Washington, D.C., and leased Paul Schulze's house, has brought with him two Chinese manservants. Hiring a Chinese, says the *News*, is "a breach of the unwritten law of Tacoma." The next morning the *Seattle Post-Intelligencer* runs the page-one headline, "Tacoma Much Stirred."

A decade earlier, the white men of Tacoma ran the Chinese out of town. Except for two merchants, no Chinese has dared move to Tacoma since then. The *Tacoma News says*: "Tacoma has for many years enjoyed the enviable reputation of being the one city on the Pacific coast in which the Chinese coolie found no abiding place."

Riggs explains that white servant girls want $20 to $25 a month, "and are inefficient at that," while the Chinese are clean and do good work. The *News* accuses him of prejudice against Scandinavians.

Three leaders of the 1885 mob say they will confront Riggs and demand he discharge his servants. If he doesn't, they say, they will call a public meeting and see what happens.

The *Tacoma Union* cheers them on. Chinese, it says, would be welcomed "if they would adapt to American ways and manners, spending their earnings here instead of sending their savings and their bones back to China." The Japanese are all right. "They are a quiet, orderly people, most of them professing Christianity, and they are addicted to none of the vile and unclean habits of the laboring classes of Chinese." The Chinese man, the *Union* says, is "a slave by nature and previous condition of servitude." The *Union* suggests that every year the people of Tacoma should celebrate November 3, the day in 1885 they expelled the Chinese forever.

Without defending the Chinese, the *Ledger* defends the right

FIZZ! ✦ BANG!

THE CHINESE MUST GO, "ALLE SAMEE."

The real China-bashing. *Snohomish County Tribune. 4-6-93*

of Thomas Riggs to hire whatever household servants he wants. In reply, the *Union* concedes that under the law, "Mr. Riggs has the right to employ Chinese or baboons or trained hyenas to do his household work." Then it argues that he should bow to the sensibilities of his fellow Tacomans and fire them.

A group of pastors, the Ministerial Association of Tacoma, pleads for "the preservation of order and respect for law and for humanity." None of the dailies reports what the Chinese think.

A three-man anti-Chinese delegation knocks on Riggs's door, which is opened by a trembling servant. Riggs invites them in and hears them out. He tells them they represent no one but themselves and they have no business telling him what to do in his house. And besides, he says, he has more money invested in Washington than the three of them together.

The same three men preside over a meeting of 1,200 people, mostly working men, at Germania Hall. Tacoma Councilman Matthew P. Bulger, a leader of the Chinese expulsion a decade earlier and now chairman of the People's Party state central committee, tells the meeting that the Chinese are a "dirty, lying, contemptible, thieving, heathen" people, and that the pastors who defend them are "traitors to Jesus Christ" and to "their own flesh and blood." He dismisses Riggs as a "coupon-clipper." The crowd approves a resolution that "the Chinese coolies are not needed or wanted here and that their presence should not and will not be tolerated."

Riggs announces that he will put the question of his servants to the Tacoma Chamber of Commerce. And he does. Consulted as a judicial body, the Chamber finds in favor of Riggs and his servants. The law protects everyone, the Chamber says, "high or low, rich or poor, white or black, red or yellow." And there is a commercial interest: "Prior to June 18, 1892, when the Northern Pacific steamship *Phra Nang* entered Tacoma harbor, our foreign business was confined to shipments of wheat to Great Britain," the Chamber says. "From having absolutely no trade relations with the Orient three years ago we have sprung into prominence as a port having within three years shipped 613,000 barrels of flour to China..."

Having won in the forum of his choosing, Riggs bows to social pressure and dismisses his servants. They leave town.

In fact, Riggs does not have the support of Tacoma. In March 1896, members of the Tacoma Chamber of Commerce vote out their trade-sensitive president in favor of an anti-Chinese challenger. And in April, city voters approve by two-to-one a charter amendment that forbids the city of Tacoma from hiring Chinese "in any capacity whatsoever."

That same month in Seattle, after being approached by local Chinese merchants, the Seattle Chamber of Commerce quietly asks China's embassy in Washington, D.C., to open a consular office. For vice-consul it will recommend the head of the Quong Tuck Co., Seattle merchant Chin Gee Hee, one of the first five Chinese to be admitted as Chamber members.

Word leaks out that China might open a consulate on Puget Sound. Says the New Whatcom *Blade*: "Take it, Seattle—we don't want it."

194

"All right," replies the *Seattle Times*. The *Times* asks rhetorically whether Tacoma would even allow a Chinese diplomat inside the city limits. The *Union* replies that it would, though the city "has no Chinese residents except for a few merchants and their servants, nor will it ever have."

"Seattle is welcome to its coolies and its Chinatown," the *Union* crows. "The fact remains that Tacoma is the shipping port of Puget Sound, and always will be, whether it has Chinamen or not."

A real Chinese: Chin Gee Hee. *Seattle Post-Intelligencer, 10-29-96*

China does not open a consulate on Puget Sound.[91]

The one star that brightens all through 1895 is that of gold. For more than 20 years, prices have fallen, which means the purchasing power of gold has risen. Interest in mining it, says the *Post-Intelligencer* at mid-year, "is at fever heat and borders on a craze of the most intense character."

In London, investors boom shares in the mines of South Africa. Colorado has a gold boom at Cripple Creek. In Washington, miners flock to the gold workings near Leavenworth, the Swauk district of Kittitas County, the Methow Valley, and the Okanogan. Bigger still is the rush just across the 49th Parallel. Rossland, British Columbia, transforms from a handful of miners at the beginning of 1895 to 2,500 by mid-year. "Mines that could have been bought a year ago for a few hundred or, at most, a few thousand dollars, could not now be bought with half a million," boasts the *Spokane Chronicle*. Most miners at Rossland are Americans. They bring money back to Spokane, and it becomes the first of Washington's cities to shake off the hard times.

An even bigger gold play is at hand. Excitement about Alaska and the Yukon has been building all through the lean years. In October 1893, the *Seattle Telegraph* reports the arrival of a placer miner with $8,000 in gold dust. In August 1894, the *P-I* reports the finding of a two-pound nugget. In June 1895, the *Seattle Times* reports men offering a $50 premium for the $150 berths on the steamer *Excelsior*, which is "laden almost to the water's edge" for the long trip up the Yukon River.

To be sure, the papers describe the North as bleak, cold, and short of food. A Seattle man calls it "the most barren, Godforsaken spot the sun ever shone on." Writes a former Shelton logger from Circle City, Alaska: "In summer it keeps a man busy fighting mosquitoes and flies, and rustling for a grubstake, and in winter he must fly around lively to keep from freezing... The winter of 1893-94 the temperature was down to 77 degrees below zero..."

Nonetheless, with the hard times continuing, the U.S. Treasury hungry for gold and gold's purchasing power continuing to rise, the North beckons.[92]

ENDURANCE (1896)

By 1896, Western Washington's former boomtowns are on the ropes.

At South Bend, bank examiner William Seeley writes that there is "absolutely no market" for real estate. Since 1892, the South Bend Land Co. has paid no taxes on hundreds of unsold lots.

At Port Townsend, bank examiner A.D. Lynch writes in December 1895: "There is little or no business in this locality, and values have depreciated to a point which seems incredible. Properties which at one time sold for $25,000 have, within a few months, sold for $500 and $800. Lots which sold at from $200 to $500 are now valued at from $1 to $5 and with no buyers."

At Anacortes, Seeley writes in 1896, there are "a large number of modern store buildings offered for sale at a nominal figure, the majority of them being unoccupied." The new Hotel Anacortes is vacant, and its market value, Seeley writes, is only "what might be obtained from wreckers for the material."

At New Whatcom, residents too poor to feed their cattle and horses set them free to roam the streets. Farmers bringing in carts of produce have to fend off the hungry animals with dogs and clubs. Editor H.B. Williams of the *Reveille* is disgusted. "Sacks of flour, boxes of fruit, bags of grain, packages of groceries and crates of vegetables are all plunder," he fumes. "It is probably safe to say that no other city in the United States of the size of New Whatcom permits the nuisance of stock running at large."[93]

"Cities that were springing up as if by magic five years ago," writes James Vernon, editor of the *Everett Times,* "are today struggling to maintain their credit..."

And sometimes to wreck it. At the end of 1895, Spokane County's Populist treasurer, George Mudgett, announces that the county has cash enough to pay the $11,000 bond interest due January 1, 1896, but that as far as he is concerned, bondholders have no higher claim than warrant holders. He says he won't pay the bond-holders. The bondholders sue, and Mudgett pays.

At Port Angeles, where the people have voted in a Populist mayor and treasurer, city salaries are months behind. City Treasurer Julius E. Krueger, former secretary of the Puget Sound Co-oper-ative Colony, refuses to redeem city warrants, some of them four years old. He lets the cash pile up and gives city employees a payday. A warrant holder demands payment and is told the money has been spent. He sues the city. Judge James McClinton instructs the prose-cutor to begin criminal proceedings against Krueger. The prosecu-tor files the case and drops it.

At Port Townsend the county prosecutor sues the county treasurer, asking that the superior court invalidate Jefferson Coun-ty's $225,000 in bonds. The judge throws out the case for lack of standing, and the debt remains.

Towns whose credit is ruined are pushed to the wall. At New Whatcom, where the big land company has been behind on its taxes for years, the city slashes operating expenses in 1895 by 77 percent. Policemen, paid in warrants worth 75 cents on the dollar, are effec-tively working for 9 cents an hour. By early March 1896, council-men are meeting in the new city hall, sitting at a $150 table in $44 chairs and wearing overcoats because the city cannot afford to heat the room. The town owes $21,882 back interest on bonds that have been in default for more than a year.

At Anacortes, the combined debt of the town and school district, supposed to be no more than 3 percent of assessed value, surges toward 40 percent. The school district has defaulted on its bonds and stopped issuing warrants because, the *Anacortes American* says, "the public refused to accept them at any rate of discount." In mid-1895, voters agree to a property-tax increase to keep open three mixed-year classrooms of 40 pupils each. The city dedicates its entire general tax revenue to debt service and operates solely on license fees from saloons.

Cities everywhere cut back. At Spokane, the revenue for sup-port of the city government in 1894, 1895, and 1896 is half that of 1892. At Snohomish in March 1896, the school board runs out of money and closes the school three months early. Six teachers continue private classes, charging $2 per student per month.

At Everett in 1895, the city government cuts spending by more than half. In May 1896, the mayor, Dr. William C. Cox, warns the city council it will have to cut more "or the city will be obliged to discontinue business by the end of the year." The council lays off the janitor and the city engineer. It ends telephone service for the city clerk. It puts up for sale the fire department's horse-drawn chemical engine it purchased two years earlier.

Judge John C. Stallcup. *Tacoma Morning Union,* 12-6-96

At Vancouver, the city council orders the fire department to return to their owner the team of horses used to haul the fire engine. The men will have to use a hand-drawn hose cart.[94]

The big problem is in Tacoma, a city whose spirit, the *Ledger* says, is "deep down in the dumps."

Recall the $2.08 million in bonds Tacoma paid in 1893 to Charles Wright, most of it to buy his waterworks and electric plant. The waterworks provide only a quarter of the water Wright promised. The city sues Wright for making false promises and wins a judgment of $787,500. Wright appeals, refusing to pay. Pierce County Judge John Stallcup files a lawsuit to repudiate the bonds, arguing that the city cannot be obligated to pay for water it never got. He loses the suit but advises the city that Wright owns all the bonds, and it's OK not to pay him. The amount, $54,500, is due June 1, 1896. This is the payment following the one of December 1895, when businessmen saved Tacoma from default.

Responding to Stallcup, Tacoma's new treasurer, Republican William Sternberg, denounces the idea of bond default. "People here act, write and talk as though the city had gone to eternal destruction," he writes in an open letter, "and that there was nothing in the future for her but to struggle along as best as she could as a village buried among the stumps, and live on clams, berries and fish, laying aside the hope of ever becoming a great city..." Actually, Sternberg argues, during the hard times Tacoma has built up its lumber industry, meatpacking, metal smelting, and trade with the Orient. "Real estate is the only thing that has gone backward," he writes. "In times of great financial depression, it is the first commodity to go down and the last to come up." Meanwhile, he argues, Tacoma must make good on the promises engraved on its bonds, as has its neighbor to the north.

Seattle, writes Tacoma's treasurer, "is now proudly parading as the city who pays her debts, and is justly making capital for herself out of our misfortunes."

The *Ledger* agrees with Sternberg. It denounces "the reckless and scandalous efforts" to default on the June interest. Tacoma's two other dailies reluctantly agree. The *News* supports payment because it "sees no legal way of escaping payment and because a default in payment would work no good result." The *Union* swallows hard and allows, "It is our nauseating duty to pay the interest on the fraud-tainted water bonds..."

The businessmen who put up the money in December 1895 have first call on the city's cash. As June 1, 1896, approaches, the city repays them—and they immediately hand the cash back to the city. Tacoma meets its obligations to Wright once again.

Tacoma is still in a financial hole. Its total debt is close to 15 percent of the assessed value of its taxable property—three times the state constitution's limit on debt approved by a public vote. Tacoma has nearly $3.9 million in debt, of which $893,670 is in the face value of warrants on which interest is accumulating at 8 percent.

Interest rates on bonds are 4 to 5 percent. The city's first step out of the financial hole would be to sell bonds and use the proceeds to pay off the warrants. But this would add more than $1 million to its bond debt. Unlike the interest on warrants, which piles up and is paid only when the warrants are redeemed, the interest on bonds has to be paid every six months. In mid-1896, Tacoma does not have the cash to do this.

Interest payments are not the city's only financial problem. In the spring of 1896, city employees, who are behind warrant holders in the queue for payment, have not been paid for the previous seven months.[95]

Prices continue to fall. Business and labor try to resist this, and they cannot.

Lumber mill men are weary of running at near-zero profit. In 1895, they set up the Central Lumber Co. in San Francisco—a cartel of the principal mills of British Columbia, Washington, Oregon. and California. By colluding they aim to limit output and, the *Tacoma Ledger* says, "make the lumber business profitable."

In March 1896, the cartel puts up the price of lumber. But by then, California lumberyard men, who have been reading about the cartel in the newspapers, have piled up inventory. Demand for lumber is low. The cartel mills slow down while four mills not in the cartel operate flat out. The four renegades cut prices and scoop up what business remains.

The cartel men chafe under the output restrictions. Owners of small mills suspect the big mills of cheating. A small mill that needs to keep operating to avoid the receiver defects to the renegades and cuts prices. Others follow. By the end of 1896, the cartel the *Post-Intelligencer* calls "the most stupendous trust ever organized on the Pacific Coast" collapses.

Salmon canning, which has been employing men on the Columbia River for 30 years, spreads on Puget Sound. In 1896, salmon canneries around the Sound, including Port Angeles and Whatcom County, increase from five to eleven. Most use fish traps, which are more efficient than boats. (Fishermen will later have traps declared illegal.) Anacortes, a busted boomtown that the editor of the *Anacortes American* pronounced "dead" in mid-1895, attracts three canneries, an investment from Oregon and Canada equal to half the assessed value of the town.

As canneries spread, the retail price of a one-pound can of salmon falls to 15 cents. In 1896, the river canneries around Astoria and Ilwaco offer fishermen 4 cents a pound for Chinooks. The Astoria fishermen, most of them immigrant Finns, hold out for the

Salmon Cannery at Point Roberts. *Seattle Post-Intelligencer, 8-2-96*

1895 price: 5 cents. The union calls a strike and undertakes to stop all commercial fishing on the river. Several men who defy the union are killed, and the governors of Oregon and Washington send in the National Guard. The union settles for 4½ cents.

A year later, Columbia River fishermen will be selling Chinooks for 3 cents a pound.[96]

The hard times go on.

In March 1896, Simon Oppenheimer's Spokane ventures in water power, lumber milling, and flour milling collapse. Oppenheimer has skipped town, leaving behind what historian Nelson Durham calls "a tangled mass of books and accounts."

In April 1896, a Philadelphia insurance company forecloses on its mortgage on the Tacoma Hotel and the city's proudest hostelry is placed in receivership. About this time, the steel rolling mill at Lakewood fails, having never produced at a level its promoters promised when they asked for a subsidy.

Still, things are going forward. In 1896, the railroads that fell into receivership in 1893 and 1894 start to come out. In May 1896, the Seattle, Lake Shore & Eastern Railway emerges as the Seattle & International, and its discontinuous Eastern Washington segment as the Spokane & Seattle, each part now independent of the Northern Pacific. In July 1896, the Northern Pacific comes out of receivership with its bondholders forced to accept lower interest rates. Also in July, the Oregon Railway & Navigation Co., owner of the line leased to the Union Pacific between Portland and Spokane, is reborn as an independent road. The Union Pacific will come out of receivership in 1897.

Washington newspapers clamor for a national bankruptcy law. The *Ledger* reports that Pierce County judges have appointed 85 receivers since 1893, and that in most cases "the owners of the property lost everything, and so did their general creditors." The Tacoma paper writes: "Some less expensive method needs to be devised."[97]

The road back to prosperity, says the *Oregonian*, is to "work now upon the natural wealth of the country, instead of speculating on imaginary values." But to revive their prosperity, people need at least *some* belief in those dreams the *Oregonian* dismisses as "imaginary values."

The quickening has begun with gold. In the past two years, the *Seattle P-I* writes: "everywhere, in every quarter of the globe, gold mining has received a wonderful, startling stimulus... The idle money of the world is today looking to this class of investment in greater amount than has ever before been known."

The first of Washington's cities to feel the gold excitement is the stronghold of the silver men: Spokane. If there is a contradiction in this the Spokane papers do not mention it.

In early 1896, Mark Harrington, president of the University of Washington in Seattle, returns from a trip to Eastern Washington, a region stirred by the gold discoveries at Rossland and Trail, British Columbia. He writes: "Spokane is looking prosperous. During the three or four days I was there I did not see any sign of 'to let' on any of the buildings or houses, and there was a general air of activity in the streets." Canadian money is everywhere accepted at par.

Editors of the *Spokane Chronicle* observe that houses that could

The Tacoma Hotel, as it saw itself. *Hotel letterhead courtesy Paul Dorpat*

have been rented for $10 a month are now going for $12 and $15. Noting other signs of prosperity, the paper predicts that by 1900, Spokane will become the largest city in the Pacific Northwest.

The *Chronicle* is aware of another gold play: in Alaska and the Yukon. In March 1896, the paper argues that men have a better chance in the Inland Empire. Spokane's afternoon daily writes: "That's all right, Seattle. Send your spare miners and prospectors to Alaska and let them come home in the autumn more spare than when they went away. Spokane will send hers into the new mining districts of our own state and those just across the border; and we will see which city plays the winning game."

Around Puget Sound, men are roused by thoughts of the North. After the long depression, the *Everett Herald* says, people suffer from a "restive disposition." Miners have left Monte Cristo for Alaska, and have been replaced by men from Wisconsin and Michigan. In March 1896, a miner who earlier brought out $25,000 from the North comes back through Seattle with his pals from Pennsylvania, each to buy 400 pounds of gear: a sled, blankets, clothing, provisions, and for every two men, a tent.

The *Port Townsend Leader* complains that Seattle is taking the Alaska trade while its merchants "sit supinely and let them do it."

The *Tacoma News* quotes these lines in an editorial entitled, "Tacoma Must Wake Up."

The *News's* editors get an earful from Tacoma merchants who say they can't get banks to finance inventory. The paper's next editorial blames the city's bankers. "Seattle merchants have been in the same condition, but the banks over there have come to their relief," the *News* says. "It is such a spirit that builds cities."[98]

On August 31, 1896, Seattle takes a historic step: its first scheduled steamship service to Asia.

Trade with the Orient elicits suspicion. Earlier in the year, *The Blade* of New Whatcom likens the import of products from Japan to an invasion that "must inevitably render competition by the white people impossible..."

In St. Paul, James J. Hill, president of the Great Northern, thinks otherwise. He envisions filling ships with lumber, wheat, and flour for Asia, and importing Asian silk and tea. He considers building a fleet, but Nippon Yusen Kaisha of Japan offers a fleet with a state subsidy that covers the cost of coal and seamen's wages. Hill agrees to fill one ship a month at Seattle.

The Seattle Chamber of Commerce pushes hard for Hill's steamship deal. The town's Chinese merchants also support it, in spite of China's recent defeat in a war with Japan. Says James S. Goldsmith, manager of Schwabacher Brothers & Co., hardware wholesalers: "The leading Chinese merchants of the city are loud in their promises to influence all the freight and passenger traffic they can control in the same direction. Add this to the fact that Tacoma refuses to allow the Chinese to even see what that city is like, and you will see that Seattle will get all this class of business."

The *Everett Herald* publishes a sour-grapes editorial. "A steamer the size of the *Umatilla* or the *Walla Walla*, owned and manned by Japs, will call on Seattle once a month for freight," the *Herald* says. "The line will get very few passengers as the splendid ships from Vancouver and Tacoma are necessarily more attractive than the little Jap boats. A very small shingle mill, for instance, would be of more practical advantage to the city than the once-a-month steamers."

The *Herald* is bad-mouthing the *Miike Maru*, the first Japanese ship, which indeed is 4 percent lighter in tonnage than the *Umatilla*, a local steamer that has been calling on Sound ports for years. But the *Miike Maru* will be replaced by bigger ships soon enough. Its arrival represents a commitment *to Seattle by Japan*—a fact, says the *Seattle Times*, "full of significance."

Seattle people sense the meaning of it. On August 31, 1896, thousands gather on the shoreline and Schwabacher's wharf to greet the Japanese ship. It first appears in outline only, its stack and rigging visible through a swirling fog. Then, reports the *Post-Intelligencer*, "the *Miike Maru* pushed her nose through the fog and returned the screaming whistle of the *Snoqualmie*."

The *Snoqualmie*, Seattle's fireboat, is packed with officials: Thomas Burke, for the Great Northern; Miki Saito, Puget Sound's first Japanese consul, stationed in Tacoma since the previous November; Seattle Mayor William Wood, nine city councilmen, many white businessmen and two Chinese merchants.

Seattle greets the *Miike Maru* with rockets and firecrackers, the tooting and shrieking of steam whistles and full-throated cheers. Within a few days the ship will be loaded with flour, lumber, nails, bicycles, railcar wheels, and animal hoofs and horns—a cargo the *Tacoma Ledger* derides as "insignificant."

Four days later, Seattle has an unusual mixed-race marriage at the Plymouth Congregational Church. Chujiro Matsura, secretary of the Japanese YMCA of Seattle, weds a white woman, Mary Atkinson, who had helped teach him English and Christianity. The bride is from California, where state law forbids marriages between whites and "Mongolians," and will continue to forbid them for the next 52 years.

Such marriages are legal in Washington—Tacoma included, but it's notable that the wedding happens in Seattle.[99]

By mid-1896, Tacoma is carrying more than $1 million in warrant debt, principal and interest— $15 for every dollar of Seattle's.

Tacoma's politicians deny they want to repudiate these warrants but they keep looking for respectable reasons not to pay them.

Already they have argued against paying off bonds the city used to buy the light and water plant, because the city was cheated. Now they argue that because much of the warrant debt was issued above the limit set in the state constitution, they need not repay it. Early in 1896, the Washington Supreme Court undercuts this argument by redefining a higher limit.

With city salaries half a year behind, Tacoma's city council votes to use the cash to pay employees first and warrant holders later. A warrant holder sues the city and wins; the council's decision is overturned. Tacoma merchants stop accepting warrants as cash. City firemen, unpaid for months, announce a strike. Tacoma merchants, faced with a loss of fire-insurance coverage, take up a collection and give firemen one month's pay.

Tacoma's new Democratic mayor, Angelo Fawcett, says the city should pay all "legal debt," which implies that some of it is not. He appoints a Committee of Fifteen to recommend what is and what isn't. They say most of the debt is binding, but that more than $200,000 in city warrants bought at par by former Treasurer George Boggs and deposited in banks have been redeemed and need not be paid.

In August 1896, Tacoma's city council votes to issue bonds to pay off all the warrants except the Boggs warrants. Mayor Fawcett vetoes the ordinance. "What I want to know is that every warrant is legal before it is funded," he says.

In Portland, federal Judge William B. Gilbert rules that Tacoma must pay the Boggs warrants held by the Columbia National Bank. From Seattle, federal judge Cornelius Hanford opines that Tacoma cannot claim the 20 percent dividend on its frozen deposits in the Columbia National and then refuse to pay the warrants that are the basis of its claim.

Judge Hanford, the *Ledger* sarcastically says, "evidently doesn't understand our game of heads I win, tails you lose..."

Tacoma's city council approves a bond sale a second time and Fawcett vetoes it a second time. The council overrides. The Washington Supreme Court rules that Fawcett didn't win the mayoral election, but that incumbent Republican Edward Orr did, and on October 7, 1896, Fawcett is turned out. A warrant holder sues the city, asking that the bond sale be stopped because Orr, the true mayor, never signed the bond ordinance.

Late in the year a record surfaces showing that Boggs bought several times the number of warrants as was supposed. In a warrant holder's lawsuit in Pierce County Superior Court, Judge Stallcup rules that *all* the city's warrants from October 16, 1892, to April 19, 1894—$859,000 of them—are invalid and need never be paid.

The city of Tacoma ends 1896 with its credit in chaos. Its energies are focused inward, in contrast with Seattle.[100]

DECISION (1896)

In November 1896, Americans will decide whether the dollar shall be payable in gold or silver. The uncertainty around that question is what touched off the Panic. It was festering during the Coxey armies and the strikes, and it has prolonged the hard times.

Much of the argument has been about how to explain the generation-long decline in the general level of prices. The supporters of gold say the decline reflects increases in efficiency, and partly they are right. Steel has become cheaper by using the new Bessemer furnaces; railroads have cut transportation costs by replacing iron rails with steel, allowing heavier engines and longer trains; and bread is cheaper as railroads have opened up new areas for growing wheat. In two decades, the cost of transporting a bushel of wheat from the Palouse to Liverpool has fallen by half.

The supporters of silver reply that the prices of goods and services have been falling since 1873, when the United States, joined around that time by other industrial powers, agreed to convert paper money into gold. The scarcity of gold, they say, has driven prices down and made the people poor. Their solution is to monetize silver at $1.29 an ounce, increasing the money supply. They want a silver inflation.

They have been right about a shortage of gold. As more countries have adopted the gold standard, the world supply of the yellow metal has spread thinner. Yet with the help of such cost-cutting innovations as the compressed-air drill and the cyanide process, the world has also been mining more gold. Since 1890, output of gold has nearly doubled—and in the 1890s, gold is not just *worth* money, it *is* money.

In the no-news days before Christmas 1895, an editorial writer at the *Spokane Chronicle* has a subversive thought. Among the bankers and bondholders, he posits, "a new and hideous doubt has arisen." He quotes Wall Street guru Henry Clews, who says: "The

The young W.J. Bryan. *Seattle Post-Intelligencer, 7-11-96*

world is closely verging upon an inflation of its stock of currency."

A gold inflation.

It is a strange idea and the *Chronicle* does not believe it. In the 1896 campaign, Spokane's silver-Democrat paper will declare that there can be no prosperity under the constraints of the gold dollar.

In February 1896, the news seems to confirm it. R.G. Dun & Co. (the company that becomes Dun & Bradstreet) reports: "Prices of commodities as a whole are now at the lowest average ever known."[101]

In June 1896, the Republicans hold their national convention in St. Louis. On the first ballot, delegates nominate for president the man whose name has been in the newspapers for months: Governor William McKinley of Ohio. The party platform calls for a single gold standard until such time as the world can agree on bimetallism. This is a fudge. Really it is an endorsement of the gold standard.

In July, the Democrats hold their national convention in Chicago. The silver men push through a platform calling for free silver—a silver standard at $1.29 an ounce. "As to the candidates," writes the *Post-Intelligencer's* correspondent, "the convention is still groping in the murk."

On July 9, the Democrats hear a former congressman, William Jennings Bryan of Nebraska. At 36, Bryan is known as "the boy orator of the Platte" —in the pre-microphone era, a speaker who can project his voice. When he stands to speak in his sack alpaca suit, the delegates are expecting a performance—and he delivers.

The choice between gold and silver, Bryan declares, is between the "struggling masses" and "the idle holders of idle capital." It is between American independence and kowtowing to international bankers in London. His voice rising, Bryan finishes his oration by deriding the Republican platform's wishy-washy endorsement of gold. "If they dare to come out and in the open defend the gold standard as a good thing, we shall fight them to the utmost," he booms. "Having behind us the commercial interests, the laboring interests, and all the toiling masses, we shall answer their demands for the gold standard by saying to them: 'You shall not press down upon the brow of labor this crown of thorns. *You shall not crucify mankind upon the cross of gold.*'"

The hall erupts. The *Tacoma Ledger* writes, "Cheers swelled to yells, yells became screams. Every chair in the valley of the Coliseum and every chair in the vast wilderness on the hillsides became a dock on which frantic men and women were wildly waving handkerchiefs, hats and umbrellas—anything movable. Some, like men demented, divested themselves of their coats and flung them into the air."

After one of the great speeches of American history, the delegates in Chicago choose Bryan as the Democratic nominee for president.

The *Spokane Chronicle* is delighted. Mimicking Bryan's grandiloquence, the silver-Democrat paper says of him: "He stands for abundant money; for the destruction of classes; for the dethronement of the dictators; for the coining of honest cash with which honest debts may be paid. He stands for the advance of prices, the abolition of panics, the revival of industry, the return of prosperity to the land where the curse of war has not fallen, nor the fear or famine nor the blight of pestilence, yet where strong men kneel before the closed gates of idle factories and beg in vain for one little hour of work—the land where white-faced women and sobbing children are hungering and starving in the very midst of the grandest harvests God ever gave mankind."

The gold-Republican *Post-Intelligencer* reminds its readers that Bryan is a 36-year-old out-of-office congressman whose name "was never spoken of seriously in connection with the nomination until after the convention was actually in session." The *P-I* calls the choice of Bryan "the most erratic nomination ever made, under the most erratic circumstances."

A few weeks later, the People's Party also nominates Bryan,

who is not a member. Bryan becomes the fusion candidate for president.

Bryan is a new sort of Democrat. Since the Civil War, Republicans have favored federal power for railroad subsidies and tariffs, while Democrats, in the words of the *Ledger*, have followed "the teachings of Jefferson, who held, generally, that government should do nothing for the governed that it could reasonably avoid doing."[102]

The fight over gold and silver brings a political realignment.

In Washington state, silver Republicans, including U.S. Senator Watson Squire, split off and endorse Bryan. In Spokane, the silver-Republican *Spokesman-Review* comes out for Bryan. In August 1896, Charles Fishback and Alden Blethen buy the squishy-Republican *Seattle Times* and come out hard for Bryan. In Tacoma, the Populist-leaning *Union* endorses Bryan, as does the Democratic *News*, "heart and soul."

The *Tacoma Ledger*, torn between its Republicanism and silver, stands by its party and endorses McKinley, choosing to believe the platform's talk of bimetallism by international agreement. In Tacoma, lumberman Chauncey Griggs, who was chairman of Washington's delegation to the Democratic convention that nominated Cleveland, announces for McKinley.

Silver Republicans split from the Grand Old Party and join with the Democrats. The People's Party, which in its heart prefers no metallic backing of the dollar, swallows hard and joins the silver men.

Meeting in Ellensburg in August 1896, Washington's Populists, Democrats and silver Republicans agree on a fusion ticket. None of the candidates will be on the ballot as Democrats. All will be on the People's Party's line—a move that allows the gold Republicans to argue that the Democrats have been swallowed up by the Pops. For the fusion ticket, Democrats nominate the candidates for one of the state's two seats in Congress, one of its four presidential electors and a seat on the state supreme court. The silver Republicans nominate the men for attorney general and superintendent of public instruction. The Populists get the rest, including the nominee for governor, state Representative John R. Rogers of Puyallup.

THE DEMOCRATIC PARTY OF THE STATE OF WASHINGTON IS ON THE INSIDE THIS YEAR.

Republican cartoon: Fusion leaves the Democrats swallowed up. *Seattle Post-Intelligencer, 9-23-96*

In 1890, Rogers moved to Washington from Kansas, where he was owner and editor of a Populist paper, the *Kansas Commoner*. Rogers has been a sheep rancher, a real estate agent, the keeper of a general store, and the writer of a radical Populist tract called *The Irrepressible Conflict*. He supports unbacked paper money and has a deep belief in man's right to the land. He assures his party: "I am a Populist from the crown of my head to the toes of my feet, and if I am elected governor of Washington there shall be no vetoes on the will of the people."

Conservatives are horrified by the thought of a Populist governor. In September 1896, the *Post-Intelligencer* twice prints a column that becomes famous: "What's the Matter With Kansas?" by William Allen White of the Kansas-based *Emporia Gazette*. White says that under the regime of the People's Party, Kansas has lost population and wealth. He then mocks the Populist mind:

"We are a people who can hold up our heads. What we need here is less money, less capital, fewer white shirts and brains, fewer men with business judgment, and more of those fellows who boast

John Rogers. *Seattle Post-Intelligencer,*
10-31-97

that they are 'just ordinary old clodhoppers'...

"Whoop it up for the ragged trousers; put the lazy, greasy fizzle, who can't pay his debts, on an altar and bow down and worship him. Let the state ideal be high. What we need is not the respect of our fellow men but the chance to get something for nothing.

"Oh, yes, Kansas is a great state. Here are people fleeing it by the score every day, capital going out of the state by the thousands of dollars, and every industry except farming paralyzed..."

Printing the column about Populism in Kansas is an attack on the Populist running for governor of Washington. Visiting Rogers' Kansas hometown, *Tacoma Ledger* editor Clinton Snowden writes that the man was a sheep farmer, but "then, as now, was more fond of theorizing, talking politics, championing the interests of others than of looking out for his own," and that he lost his farm.

One of Rogers' radical proposals is that farms worth $2,500 or less be made immune to foreclosure. The problem with it, the *Ledger* argues, is that "it will make it impossible for anyone owning or acquiring property of less value than $2,500 to get a loan on it." (This is the same objection German farmers will have in the 1930s to the National Socialist idea of the non-foreclosable farm.)

Gold Democrat Thomas Burke calls Rogers "the worst candidate ever named" for governor of Washington. "It is a terrible thing to think of this state falling into the hands of a man as visionary and harebrained as Rogers," says the Great Northern's Seattle lawyer. "Up to this time the state of Washington has had a good reputation, and shall it now imitate the terrible example of Kansas?"

Rogers' supporters ridicule the comparison to Kansas. The *Chronicle* notes that for two and a half years, Spokane has been "the only city of much size" in the Pacific Northwest with a Populist mayor, Horatio Belt. During that time, Spokane's population has swelled by 25 to 30 percent, the paper says, and the city now has "hardly a vacant storeroom or dwelling." The *Chronicle* makes no attempt to show that Spokane has revived *because* it has a Populist mayor, and no one seriously argues this.

In the *Tacoma Union*, Populist writer Lewis E. Rader says Rogers is no threat. The governor's politics, he writes, amount to "conservative radicalism." Rader writes that the Populist nominee for governor is "one of the most extreme of extremists in theory" but in practice is willing to reform in moderation.

Rader is correct, but the *Post-Intelligencer* doesn't believe it. The *P-I* runs a four-column cartoon on page one showing a bearded old man labeled "Populist" entreating a maiden labeled "Washington." The old man is snuggling up to the maiden on a bench, suggestive of a wicked intent. Behind her a ghostly female figure labeled "Kansas" whispers: *"Beware, little girl. He ruined me."*[103]

Depressed by the cloud of political uncertainty, businessmen spread gloom. In September 1896, the superintendent of the St. Paul and Tacoma mill says the Eastern market for lumber is "almost dead." He blames the talk of free silver. In October, receiver Robert Wingate of the Merchants National Bank of Tacoma writes Comptroller Eckels: "In this City and State, there is almost complete suspension of business, on account of the silver and gold talk."

Not all business is suspended. In late September 1896, Josephine and Edward Nordhoff, who have been in the dry-goods business in Seattle since 1890, have a moving sale. The Nordhoffs are the retailers who introduced the use of pennies in the Queen City, having a few years earlier brought bags of Indian head cents from the East. They are moving their store to bigger quarters at Second and Pike, where it will be for the next 30 years. They call it the Bon Marché, and under the direction of Josephine Nordhoff, after Edward dies, it will become one of Seattle's top department stores.

At Tumwater, south of Olympia, German immigrant Leopold F. Schmidt, who has been a sailor, a prospector, and a brewer, is shown an artesian well. He buys the site of an old tannery and the

The Post-Intelligencer pictures "The Puyallup Philosopher," Populist guberna-
torial nominee John Rogers, haunted by the ghosts of his radical book, "The
Irrepressible Conflict." *Seattle Post-Intelligencer, 10-19-96*

rights to the water. On October 1, 1896, he offers for sale his first
bottles of Olympia beer.

Times are still hard in most of Washington, but there is less
of a sense of social emergency. Carrie Kalloch, executive secretary
of the Benevolent Society of Whatcom, recalls the desperate winter
of 1893-1894, when the society kept open two days a week, dis-
pensing pails of soup and loaves of fresh bread to the unemployed,
as well as clothes, shoes, and sometimes even cash—when possible,
with payment in work.

In September 1896, she announces that the agency is dis-
banding. Whatcom County, she says, no longer has enough demand
for emergency charity.[104]

In the weeks before the November election, Washington's
newspapers foam with propaganda.

The Populist *Ellensburg Localizer* sees the presidential contest

WARNING OF THE GHOST OF KANSAS: "BEWARE, LITTLE GIRL; HE RUINED ME."

Arthur H. Lee, Seattle Post-Intelligencer, 9-27-96

as "the Money Kings of Wall and Lombard Streets vs. the People."

The Republican *Seattle Post-Intelligencer* labels the People's Party as a tribe of deadbeats and losers, "men thrown out of employment by reason of their own shortcomings, the life failures, the briefless lawyers, the farmless farmers, the men who have fallen far short of success in every pursuit." On Election Day the *P-I* runs a six-column headline across the top of page one: "Vote for McKinley, Sound Money, National Honor and Prosperity."

"Vote for humanity," pleads the *Tacoma Union*. "Never before since the dawn of history or the birth of popular government has the broad issue of essential class interest between the poor and the rich been so squarely drawn and presented as in the pending campaign," says the *Union*. It concludes, "At the polls in November we legislate for the universe."

On November 3, 1896, McKinley wins.

Proclaims the *P-I*: "Nation Is Saved!"

The *Oregonian* thanks the Almighty, in Latin: *"Gloria in exelsis deo et in terra pax, homnibus bona voluntas!"*

217

Men pay off their election bets. In Ellensburg, Matt Flynn rides around the block on a donkey. In Hoquiam, reports the *Aberdeen Herald*: "Dr. Cochran parted with half of his mustache, and Mr. Fenelson went home from the barber shop a truly bald-headed man; while Alex Holman wheeled Fritz Bebotzki up Eighth Street in a wheelbarrow and paid for a keg of beer to treat the crowd."

Except for border-state Missouri and silver-state Nevada, McKinley carries all the old Union states. He gets 51.1 percent of the popular vote.

Bryan gets 45.8 percent of the popular vote. He carries 22 states in the South and West—18 of them states that Republican Mitt Romney will carry 116 years later. By 21st century standards, Bryan's electoral pattern is that of a conservative: his best states are Mississippi, 91 percent of the vote; South Carolina, 85 percent; Colorado, 85 percent; Utah, 83 percent; Montana, 80 percent; and Idaho, 78 percent. His worst state is Vermont, 16 percent.

Predictably, the true-blue losers claim they haven't *really* lost. "The principle of bimetallism is not dead," declares the *Spokane Chronicle*. The *Oregonian* disagrees: "The silver vote reached high-water mark yesterday," it says. "The silver vote will dwindle, year by year, from now, till it sinks to nothingness..."

The *Oregonian* is right. This is the high-water mark.

Bryan's defeat leaves unanswered a big question: If America switched to a silver standard, would people who borrowed gold-standard dollars be allowed to repay in silver-standard dollars?

The Dawn, a Populist paper in Ellensburg, argues that if the contract specified gold *dollars*, payment could be in silver dollars because dollars are "the legal unit." The noun counts; the adjectives do not. The silver-Republican *Spokesman-Review* argues that contracts calling for gold dollars would have to be honored with gold dollars.

In 1896, it is an issue to think about. In the 1930s, it will be decided. In 1933, Congress will end the gold standard, declaring all private contracts specifying payment in gold-standard dollars payable in unbacked dollars. In 1939, the U.S. Supreme Court will apply that principle to Dutch investors who hold gold-dollar bonds issued by a U.S. railroad. The Court will order payment in the dollars current at the time.[105]

William Jennings Bryan wins Washington's four electoral votes. His name is not on the ballot. In 1896, citizens vote for the men who will cast the electoral votes. To vote for Bryan requires marking the ballot for the People's Party electors, because the Democratic electors are pledged to support gold Democrats who are not nominees of the Democratic Party. A century later such a ballot would be the subject of lawsuits. In 1896, Washington voters figure it out, and by 55 percent they support Bryan.

William McKinley. *Seattle Post-Intelligencer,* *10-23-96*

To conservative opinion Bryan's capture of Washington is a shocking result. California has gone for McKinley, as has Oregon. Washington, however, "is new, with a large percentage of driftwood in its population, people who have nothing to lose and something possibly to gain by upsetting things," says the *Everett Herald.* "The hard times of the past four years have tried the souls of men."

Viewing its northern neighbor, the *Oregonian* opines that its Populism is a hangover from its time of exuberance: "Investments had been made that did not pay... Debts rested upon unproductive property, and taxes were high. Many who had supposed themselves rich found themselves poor. While this was true, also, to an extent in Oregon, it was much less so than in Washington because Oregon was an older state, and was less affected by new speculation."

The Bryan electors beat the McKinley electors in Spokane County by two to one. Bryan wins 52 and 55 percent, respectively, in Pierce and King counties.

For statewide offices, the ballots' Democratic line is blank. The fusion slate of Populists, Democrats and Silver Republicans is on the People's Party line—and its candidates win every seat. John

John Rogers. *Tacoma Morning Union*,
9-27-96

Rogers of the People's Party is elected governor.

The *Oregonian* offers the Washington its condolences: "She has a Populist legislature; an ignorant and fanatical boor is to be her governor, and she is to start upon a crusade against the principles of economic science and the conditions necessary to business and to prosperity. This frantic fury, beyond doubt, will run its course and exhaust itself; but when, or how long? We are profoundly sorry that Washington has received this backset..." For these comments, the *Tacoma Union* denounces the *Oregonian* as a calamity howler and an enemy of Washington.

The *Post-Intelligencer* sends a reporter to interview the governor-elect. Its reporter tells Rogers that many businessmen fear him.

"They need have no fear," Rogers replies. "I am not entering upon a crusade. I am firmly convinced that this state will be benefited by the measures my party proposes. They will be, however, administered cautiously, so that no hardship shall be inflicted. I know that unless I am backed up by public opinion my administration cannot be a success."

About his book, *The Irrepressible Conflict*, Rogers says, "In my book I was a propagandist... But as governor of the state I have other duties to perform... We shall be sincere, but we shall, I hope, be prudent."

The *Post-Intelligencer* tells the *Oregonian* to take its "mock sympathy" somewhere else.

In Populist-governed Spokane, bankers receive queries from Eastern lenders about the People's Party takeover of Washington. One banker replies: "In some parts of the state where the Populists have gained power, they have reduced expenses one-half, and although they have put some unworthy men into office, on the whole their administration has been homely, old-fashioned, economical, and the right sort."

The banker's message: Don't worry about Washington.[106]

Spokane is out of the hard times already. Just before Christmas, 1896, the *Seattle P-I* runs a Sunday feature on Eastern Washington's principal city.

"A host of the old-timers have fallen never to rise again," writes correspondent P.A. O'Farrell. "But a multitude have recovered and are fast regaining their old place. The mortgage holders, who got possession of the buildings and houses, are surrendering to the old or new owners whom the mines have enriched." Spokane, he says, has become "the most prosperous city of the West."

In the Palouse, the price of wheat is moving up.

At Seattle the *Miike Maru* has been overwhelmed by export cargo, and is due to be replaced by larger ships when the British shipyards deliver them. At Tacoma, investors announce a mill to make woolen suits. At Stevens Pass, the Great Northern is about to start work on its $2 million, 2.5 mile tunnel to cut switchbacks and lower the road's peak elevation by 675 feet. The tunnel will open in 1900 and be used until 1929.

The losers in the election are still "calamity howling." In its New Year's message for 1897, the pro-Bryan *Seattle Times* says the "business disasters" since the election prove "the complete failure of the prophesies made by the advocates of gold monometallism." On the last day of 1896, the Populist Snohomish *Eye* declares that the "epidemic of pauperism... has crushed all hope and ambition from the breasts of millions of earth's noblest men and women."

In December 1896, comes another wave of bank failures in the upper Midwest. Comptroller of the Currency James Eckels tells the nation not to worry: overall, he says, the national banks that have survived the hard times are in good shape. He is right.

Equally important, the national election has removed a huge political and economic uncertainty in all the states, including Washington. Though *The Eye* does not see it, the economic signal is now green.[107]

REVIVAL (1897)

In February 1897, the Chinese celebrate the Year of the Rooster. Newspapers mention these fêtes, often with a mocking tone. The *Ellensburg Localizer* refers to festivals in the "the pigtail kingdom." The *Post-Intelligencer* is more respectful. Its reporter, sent to Seattle's Chinatown, writes of the dinner hosted at the Quong Tuck Co. by the merchant nominated for vice-consul, Chin Gee Hee:

"Seated around four or five large round tables were twenty-five or thirty Chinamen, dressed in the brightest colors. They were eating from a large variety of dishes placed in the middle of the tables, and between mouthfuls talked, laughed and sang."

Cantonese-speaking immigrants greet each other by bowing the head and wishing a prosperous year: *"Gung Hey Fat Choy,"* literally, "Be happy, become rich."

The *Seattle Times* asks banker Jacob Furth to make just such a prediction. Furth recalls that recovery from the hard times of the 1870s began late in the third year—and it has been three years and nine months since the Panic of 1893 began. The *Times* says, "Mr. Furth thinks that the light of prosperity will begin to shine during the year 1897."

He is right.[108]

With the New Year come changes in political power.

In Tacoma, Judge John Stallcup—nominally a Democrat but effectively a Populist—ends his term on the Pierce County Superior Court. Stallcup is the judge who wants Tacoma to repudiate its bond debt. "In the four years he has been on the bench," opines the anti-Populist *Ledger*, "Judge Stallcup has done more than any other one man... to bring the city and the county into disrepute, to injure their credit, to retard progress, to make recovery from the depressed conditions slow and doubtful."

In Olympia, John Rogers becomes Washington's governor.

Senator Squire Reinhart. *Seattle Post-Intelligencer, 1-14-97*

Mary Hobart. *Bellingham Herald, 2-7-1906*

He is a People's Party man, but no socialist. Historian David Griffiths will later write, "An individualist in his social theory, Rogers criticized Edward Bellamy and the socialists for ignoring the importance of private property and individual freedom."

The 1897 House of Representatives in Olympia consists of 44 Populists, 10 Democrats, 11 silver Republicans, and 12 gold Republicans. The Senate, half of which is holdovers, has 12 Populists, five Democrats, 13 gold Republicans and five silver Republicans.

In the Senate, white-bearded Squire D. Reinhart, 70, a Populist from the hamlet of Ten Mile, Whatcom County, remains seated during the first opening prayer. He declares that the Senate needs no "sky pilot." When his colleagues vote for a chaplain anyway, he says, "I am now satisfied that prayers for this house are needed." Later Reinhart votes against a resolution congratulating President McKinley on his inauguration because the resolution refers to the "Almighty."

Half the Populist legislators are radicals. The *Ledger* runs a story about Pops on lunch break who are "steered from one restaurant to another on the ground that the place where they were going was kept by a gold bug." One, wanting a toothbrush, insists on buying it in a Populist-owned drugstore.

In the years before the 17th Amendment, the legislature's first task is to elect a U.S. senator. The hard-core Pops vow to elect a true Populist. One steps forward: Mary E. Hobart of New Whatcom. In 1897, no woman has ever been chosen for the U.S. Senate from Washington or anywhere else. Hobart is not a legislator, but under the law legislators can choose her. In San Francisco, the *Examiner* devotes two-thirds of a page to Hobart, telling its readers this curiosity from up north "has been very prominent in the Populist party and has proved herself a public speaker of force and power." In Olympia, she wins the vote of only one legislator, which the *Tacoma News* notes is the state's first-ever vote for a "senatress." Washington's legislators pass over the chance to make history and choose a silver Republican, George Turner of Spokane.

The legislature of 1897 passes two Populist laws intended to favor small property owners. The first rewrites the law of mortgages, so that on any new mortgage, a lender foreclosing on a property must wait two years to take possession and cannot pursue the borrower for additional amounts. The effect is to make it more costly for lenders to lend and harder for borrowers to borrow. In 1898, in *Dennis v. Moses*, the Washington Supreme Court invalidates much of the law and in 1899, the legislature repeals the whole of it.

The second law exempts the first $500 in personal property and the first $500 of improvements on land from state property tax. This is an attempt to shift the tax burden to the rich. Citing the state constitution, which declares: "All taxes shall be uniform upon the same class of property," the Washington Supreme Court throws this out, too.

The legislature passes a law forbidding contracts that promise payment in gold. The Washington Supreme Court invalidates this. Legislators also put two constitutional amendments on the 1898 ballot. One is a measure to allow a local-option single tax, Henry George's idea to shift the entire tax burden to land. The other is woman suffrage. Voters will reject both of them, the single-tax measure by 2 to 1.

Populist bills to provide for the initiative and referendum, free schoolbooks, low railroad fares, and state inspectors of mines and banks go nowhere. So does the Governor Rogers' dream of the non-foreclosable farm.

The state of Washington suffers no revolution. The Pops are too theoretical and come in too many flavors to get much done. After the session ends, Governor Rogers complains that "each faction or peculiar form of economic belief, whether it be the greenbackers or the old-line Populists, the single taxers or the straight-out silver men, seem more intent on the enforcement of their peculiar ideas" than in reaching agreement. Adds state Senator William H. Plummer, Populist of Spokane: "So soon as a member of the party, by hard work, sacrifice of time, money and patience, shows any ability as a political manager, everybody becomes envious of his success and immediately commences to 'smash the machine.' "

One of the many dead letters of 1897 is Plummer's Senate Bill 46. This would have appropriated $500 to pay the reward former Governor John McGraw promised but never paid to Thomas E. Delaney for finding Charles Gloystein, the anti-Populist farmer who faded into the night in 1894, leaving his bloody hat. The bill is voted down in committee.[109]

Public spending does not drive Washington's recovery, but it does have an effect.

In Snohomish County, the strapping city of Everett wrests the county seat from Snohomish in late 1896. Everett expands. It builds a courthouse; it feels an upturn in private building and a rise in rents. Snohomish shrinks. The *Snohomish County Tribune* drops from three issues a week to one and cuts its page count by half. Early in 1897, the Snohomish National Bank pays off all its depositors and closes. In mid-1897, *The Eye* closes.

In Olympia, the Populist legislature appropriates $500,000 for work on a new capitol, but Governor Rogers vetoes it, and work goes no further than the foundations. (The new capitol will be built in the 1920s.) Rogers also vetoes appropriations for the state normal schools at New Whatcom and Cheney—the future Eastern and Western Washington universities. In the mid-1890s, the state does put up Denny Hall on the new University of Washington campus in Seattle, and in Ellensburg it builds Barge Hall for what is now Central Washington University.

At the national level, a new spending opportunity begins to take form: war. In 1898, America will fight the Spanish-American

The canceled Capitol. *Seattle Post-Intelligencer,* 9-20-96

War. To protect the nation's northwest corner, the Army will build fortifications at Port Townsend, Marrowstone Island, and Whidbey Island at the entrance to Puget Sound. The Navy has already put in a drydock at Port Orchard.

The Army, which in the 1890s is used to curb protesters and strikers rather than fight Native Americans, begins repositioning itself. Spokane attracts an Army post by donating 1,000 acres of land and $15,000 cash, some of it raised through a public raffle. Seattle attracts an Army post on Magnolia Bluff. Walla Walla and Port Townsend lose their Army posts. The economic effects of these moves, however, come mostly after the business recovery is well under way.[110]

In 1897 come the stories of two men accused of financial crimes who leave the state and agree to come back.

The first involves Lewis County banker Frank Hense. In 1889, at 25, Hense moved to Washington from Minnesota. He had worked in a bank there, though he was not educated beyond the eighth grade—common then. In Washington, he helped organize the First National Bank of Centralia, becoming its cashier, vice president, then president.

In early 1894, the First National closes up. Hense, 30, takes it over and tries to make a go of it as the Frank Hense Co., but it fails in September 1894. An angry crowd gathers outside his doors, and his friends spirit him out the back. Depressed, he takes an overdose of the sedative chloral hydrate and almost dies. He soon returns to Minnesota.

In 1897, a borrower alleges that Hense failed to cancel a $1,694 promissory note after she paid it, and that another bank made her pay it again. Hense is indicted for larceny, and the court sends an agent, C.W. Johnsone, to Minnesota to bring him back for trial.

When Johnsone arrests him, Hense weeps. He declares he is ruined. He talks of suicide. He agrees to go back, but for a lawman to take him from Minnesota requires the signature of its Republican governor, lumberman David Clough.

Johnsone and Hense go to Clough's office.

"Don't go with him, Frank," the Minnesota governor says to Hense. "These damned Populists in the state of Washington don't want to prosecute a man, they want to persecute him."

Hense stays in Minnesota. He is never prosecuted on the charge from Washington.

The second case is of Sumner F. Lockwood, 37, the Pacific County treasurer at South Bend from 1893 to 1896. In 1897, Lockwood is discovered to be $5,000 short in his accounts, and is indicted for embezzlement. In jail, he complains to the sheriff that he cannot raise his $2,000 bail from behind bars. The easygoing sheriff lets him out to rustle up bail, and Lockwood flees, walking along the railroad tracks at night toward Chehalis.

A year later, Lockwood gives himself up for trial. In court, he admits to letting the county's money slip through his fingers, including some he entrusted to the Ilwaco bank of the memory-challenged J.R. Morrison. The prosecution cannot prove Lockwood's intent to steal Pacific County's money. Lockwood denies he took any of it. He *lost* it.

Playing on the jury's emotions, Lockwood's attorney describes his client's penurious year on the run and how Mrs. Lockwood toiled as a cook in a lumber camp to send money to him. The jury is reduced to tears. In less than an hour it brings a verdict of not guilty.[111]

By 1897, depositors with money stuck in dead banks are losing hope. In Tacoma, the *Union* takes up their cause. It picks on the receiver of the Commercial Bank, who, it says, "brings no lawsuits for payment, but merely sits and collects rents on the bank's building." The receiver replies that the dead bank's assets are so worthless that it's pointless to offer them for sale.

At the busted Bank of Tacoma, the last batch of assets sells for less than 3 cents on the dollar. The *Ledger* urges the judge to set aside the sale because it is ridiculously low. Receiver Aaron Titlow calls *Ledger* editor Clinton Snowden into court and asks him under oath what he knows of the assets' value. His answer: "Nothing." The judge approves the sale. The bank pays depositors 18.9 cents on the dollar.

Best off among customers of Tacoma's dead banks are depositors at the Traders Bank, closed in 1894. By 1897, the receiver pays them 75 cents on the dollar, and shortly after the turn of the century, owners Chauncey Griggs, Henry Hewitt, George Browne, and Henry Strong will volunteer to bring them up to 100 cents. They and the fugitive J.K. Edmiston of Walla Walla Savings Bank are the only bankers in Washington who do this.

Robert Wingate is the receiver for the Merchants National Bank of Tacoma, the city's first to fail in the Panic. In June 1897, he explains to his boss in Washington, D.C., Comptroller Eckels, why after four years of sitting on the dead bank's assets, he is able to pay depositors only 17.75 cents on the dollar:

"The collapse of values of everything west of the mountains in the state of Washington is the most complete thing of the kind I have seen or heard of... Every year for the past six years things have been finding a lower level of values... A party living in the East where the accumulations of money have been taking place for past hundred years and for past seven years with great rapidity can hardly realize the straits into which we are slowly but surely drifting. There is not the slightest indication of any improvement."[112]

He is wrong. He is holding the wet charcoal of the last boom, not the dry tinder for the next one. The political and economic outlook is better than in years. Land and labor are cheap. For Washing-

Thea Foss. *Collection of Michael Sean Sullivan, Tacoma*

ton entrepreneurs with cash, the time is ripe to invest in new ventures.

William Pigott, who comes to Seattle in late 1895 with his wife and infant son, has been working with a partner to sell rails for logging railroads. The partner gives up on Seattle, leaves the state and wires Pigott to sell out. Pigott stays. He has met a logger who needs steel rails for a narrow-gauge road out of Port Angeles. In payment, Pigott takes the logger's promissory note, and the logger makes good. Pigott's partner returns and in 1898 the two men win the contract to supply rails for the narrow-gauge White Pass and Yukon Route out of Skagway, Alaska. After the turn of the century, Pigott partners with another man, the owner of the rolling mill at Lakewood, now closed, and moves it to Seattle on land reclaimed from the mud flats. In the 21st century, Pigott's mill survives as the Nucor mini-mill, the only steel producer at tidewater on the U.S. Pacific Coast. Pigott will also start a venture to make railcars. It will become Paccar Inc., the producer of Kenworth and Peterbilt heavy trucks.

Recall the suicide in 1893 of Tacoma worker John Fyrk, whose wife, Matilda, takes her children to live with a woman named Thea Foss, who lives with her husband Andrew in a boathouse. In the early 1890s, Thea Foss begins making a living by renting out rowboats. The Fosses expand all through the 1890s depression. They buy larger boats and soon are serving the sawmills on jobs too small for tugboats. Eventually their enterprise becomes the Foss Launch & Tug Co., and a century later Foss Maritime, two of whose big tugs are the *Andrew Foss* and the *Thea Foss*.

George Bartell, who left the family farm in Kansas at 14, has been working 12-hour days mixing medicine at his little pharmacy near Lake Washington. In 1897, he hires a man to run his shop and sets out for the Yukon. During his time in the North he will think up a plan for a more ambitious store. After he returns, an ad begins running on the *Post-Intelligencer's* front page: "The Bartell Drug Co., 506 Second Ave., Near Yesler Way, Open Day and Night." This is the beginning of Washington's largest drugstore chain.

In 1897, Frederick Weyerhaeuser, the white-pine king of the Wisconsin woods, meets privately with Great Northern tycoon James J. Hill at Seattle's Butler Hotel. The meeting makes the "lumber and timber men of the city jump sideways with curiosity," the *P-I* reports, the thought being "that Mr. Hill will interest Mr. Weyerhaeuser in the timber situation on the Pacific coast." Weyerhaeuser is interested; two and a half years later, he will buy 900,000 acres of timberland at $6 an acre. His purchase will endow the Weyerhaeuser Co., which many years later will become the first timber company to farm trees as a crop.

In 1899, Lyman C. Smith of Syracuse, New York, who has made a fortune in typewriters, will look over real estate in San Francisco, Portland, and Tacoma and buy land instead in downtown Seattle. Fifteen years later he will build the Smith Tower, which for 55 years will stand as Seattle's tallest office building.

In 1903, William E. Boeing, 22, having given up his studies at Yale, will intend to make his fortune and take charge of timberland around Grays Harbor inherited from his father. That same year, the Wright Brothers will fly the world's first airplane.[113]

As the depression lifts, such a future begins to be imaginable. Throughout the state, general business is picking up.

In February 1897, James M. Colman begins work on a new office building in Seattle at First Avenue and Marion Street. He orders 300 railcars of stone from a quarry in Tenino that had closed in 1893 for lack of business. Watching the construction of the Colman Building, which includes two 80-foot derricks, a *Times* editor writes: "The great force of men employed reminds one of the 'boom days' before the panic."

In April 1897, the *Post-Intelligencer* reports that merchants still haven't collected many of their old bills, but that new business is up. "Most of the local factories are running full time," the paper says,

Laying the foundations for the Colman Building. *Arthur Lee, Seattle Post-Intelligencer,* 5-23-97

"mills are starting up, mines are being developed, shippers are busy, and the hardware, grocery and general supply merchants have done a very fair trade." Shingle mills put up the price of clears 10 cents per thousand, to $1.20. New Whatcom's shingle mills are experiencing a market the *Blade* says is not yet a boom but "about second cousin to a boom."

In May 1897, the Sailors' Union of the Pacific, which had failed to hold coastwise sailors' pay at $40 a month in 1893, and has since been hammered down to $17.50, puts the wage back up to $25. In Spokane, the carpenters, who took big pay cuts during the hard times, have organized every contractor with the city. They now raise the union scale from 30 cents an hour to 35 cents and cut the workday from nine hours to eight.

In June 1897, Mount Vernon clothing merchant Nelson Moldstad tells the *Seattle Times*: "A year ago, two years ago and even three and four years ago, people coming into town to make their purchases would dig up their money from old, worn-out purses. The money in black, small silver pieces bore evidence of having been long hoarded. It showed that the holders had gotten hold of it and had buried it somewhere in an old tomato can or an old sock... We don't see any more mildewed money; we don't see any more blackened, rusty silver coins. The people now come in and plunk down, in a free-handed, jolly way, $10 and $20 gold pieces."

While the Bryan newspapers are still insisting the recovery isn't real, the McKinley papers perceive that it is. As if to propitiate the gods of commerce, several warn readers not to repeat the frenzy of 1889-90. In April 1897, New Whatcom's *Reveille* tells readers they should be satisfied with "smaller profits, closer calculation, slower accumulation, harder work" and "moderate thrift."

Snowden of the *Tacoma Ledger* disagrees. "The boom," he writes, "is really a condition of progress. It is the active day in which the world's work is done. It does not last always, although we often wish it did. Depression follows it as night follows day, or as winter follows summer. Sometimes the night is long or the winter cold, and the improvident fellow finds his sack of provender running short... but it can't last always. No condition of things ever did or even can... When the long night is over the sun will shine again."

Make hay while the sun shines. That is what people do.[114]

Washington also benefits from the world market.

The wheat that brought farmers 20 cents a bushel in the fall of 1895 because England didn't want it has been offered to a new market: East Asia. By 1896, most of the crop is going across the Pacific. Then Europe wants it again and has to bid for it. In mid-July 1897, Tacoma's most-quoted wheat buyer, Alexander Baillie, says that at the opening of the season, the price at tidewater will be 60 cents.

In the Palouse, farmers have a bumper crop. The wheat harvest fails in Russia, and in Walla Walla the price jumps almost to 80 cents a bushel. Banks report a wave of farmers paying off mortgages.

The Agricultural College at Pullman notes a jump in enrollment as families let their sons leave the farm.

The hogs that farmers bought in 1893 because their grain was wet have fallen in value and many farmers sell them. In April 1897, a Nebraska man is buying cattle cars of live hogs at 2 cents a pound. Horses are worth only a few dollars. In 1897, a Lewiston, Idaho, man is shipping live horses to Japan.[115]

On Puget Sound, the demand is for dogs—to send to the far North, where the *Tacoma Ledger,* quoting an Alaskan source, says a first-class dog is worth "a cool hundred dollars in dust."

The Call of the Wild, Jack London's 1903 novel about a dog sent to the Yukon, begins by saying that the discovery of gold in the North is bad news "for every tide-water dog, strong of muscle and with warm, long hair, from Puget Sound to San Diego."

In February 1897, the *Seattle Post-Intelligencer* writes: "Every man in the city who is the fortunate possessor of a big dog is beginning to look the animal over and to figure how much it is worth to those bound for Alaska... The highest price known to have been paid for a dog this season is $20, and the general prices range between $10 and $20. The dogs wanted are those with long hair, weighing not less than 100 pounds, and not more than two years old."

The *Seattle Times* tells a story: "The other day two men showed up at [police] headquarters with a fine-looking dog. One said he bought it, the other said he raised it from a pup. It was agreed that the dog should be given his liberty and the man that he followed should be declared the owner. Chief [C.S.] Reed took the dog out on the street and set him loose. The two claimants looked longingly at him. The dog sized up the two men and then put his tail between his legs and made a wild rush down the street."

A year later a dog lover from Oregon will write to the *Post-Intelligencer* complaining of "the howls of dogs" bound for Alaska: "I saw dogs and horses taken on board the steamers that are not fit for the work they are expected to do, and will only be taken there to suffer."

In March 1897, the steamer *Al-Ki* leaves Seattle with 245 gold seekers, 30 packhorses, and 90 dogs. On March 26, the steamer

AN EVERY-DAY SCENE IN SEATTLE.

The Steamship Al-Ki Sailed Yesterday for Dyea. During the Day the Wharf Was Crowded With People, Drays Loaded With Merchandise, and Cattle and Horses. When the Al-Ki Pulled Away From the Dock Every Available Space Was Occupied.

Arthur Lee, *Seattle Post-Intelligencer,* 8-4-97

Willapa, bound for Dyea, Alaska, is wrecked in a snowstorm near Bella Bella on the British Columbia coast. The passengers and dogs are saved but much of their cargo is lost. More ships will be wrecked on the Alaska run; busted Ellensburg banker Ben Snipes will lose his son in one such sinking. Men ignore the risk. They will suffer in the Northland, but most of them will come back. Their dogs will be left in the North.[116]

Gold is on people's brains. Prospecting is going on all across northeastern Washington and in the eastern Cascades. On the west side, mines are at work at Monte Cristo in Snohomish County and at Hamilton in Skagit County. A hundred men are prospecting west of Hood Canal, and more on Orcas Island, in Pierce County along the Nisqually River and in Clark County along Canyon Creek.

In May 1897, the *Spokesman-Review* reports on page one that gold-bearing quartz has been discovered a mile and a half from the newspaper's office. In the same month, a man with property along the Tacoma Narrows announces that he has found gold in the beach sand. Within three days the waterfront from Point Defiance to Steilacoom is staked out by gold seekers. Not to be outdone, the *Post-Intelligencer* prints a long report on the gold in eastern King County, around Mount Si.

Suddenly these voices are stilled.

Attention now shifts to the real story. In the first week of July 1897, word comes from the *Alaska Mining Record* of fabulous wealth in the Yukon. The *P-I* runs a story, "Klondyke Is Crazy," but prints it on page 5. The *Seattle Times,* the *Tacoma Union* and the *Tacoma Ledger* give the story similar play, as if their editors do not quite believe it. Then, on July 15, the *P-I* runs a story about the arrival of the steamer *Excelsior* at San Francisco carrying miners and gold. A year ago, one of those miners, T.S. Lippy, was secretary of the Seattle YMCA; he now arrives with $65,000 in gold dust in a sack so heavy he can barely lug it off the boat.

The men on the *Excelsior* say an even greater haul is coming out behind them on the steamer *Portland*, which is due at Seattle. Primed by their own hoopla, the *P-I* editors send reporters out to meet the ship. On July 17, 1897, the paper prints its famous extra, which will be reproduced on shopping bags a century later:
"LATEST NEWS FROM THE KLONDIKE.
9 O'CLOCK EDITION.
Gold! Gold! Gold! Gold!"

The effect is electric. A *Seattle Times* man complains a few days later is that all he hears is Klondike: "The word is almost beginning to be a bugbear. It is impossible to escape it. It is talked in the morning; it is discussed at lunch; it demands attention at the dinner table; it is all one hears during the intervals of his after-dinner smoke, and at night one dreams about mountains of yellow metal with nuggets as big as fire plugs. Men who swear in the morning that the rest of the town is crazy are out hunting a grubstake before dinner."

A quarter of Seattle's police force is reported to be leaving for the North. Seattle mayor William D. Wood asks the city council for an indefinite leave of absence so he can go, too. The council refuses and he goes anyway. Merchants scramble to satisfy the demand for sleds, parkas, camp stoves, bacon, flour, dried fruit, woolen blankets, and a newfangled thing called the sleeping bag. The Moran Bros. Shipyard gears up to build dozens of boats.

Within days, wages on the steamships go up. Wages at the

THIS CROAKER WILL SOON BE OUT OF SIGHT.

Prosperity kills the "croaker" of "hard times." *Tacoma Daily Ledger, 8-1-97*

Everett smelter go up. In the shingle mills of Ballard, knot sawyers working for $2 a day walk out, demanding $2.50. They get $2.25, and will get the rest soon enough.

Seven weeks later an anonymous editorial writer on the *P-I* looks back at the arrival of the *Portland.* "It was a transformation scene as instantaneous as though touched by a magic wand," he writes. "It set the wheels of commerce in motion."

The hard times of 1893-1897 are over. Gold is the exciting

part, but only a part. People have lived through four years of hard times, and have cleaned up enough of the mess to move on. The road ahead is now open. By summer's end 1897, increased demand will push up prices of cotton, wool, iron, steel, copper, and lead, signaling producers to provide more. Gold-standard America will now begin a 2 percent inflation that will last until World War I.[117]

DENOUEMENT

On New Year's Day 1898, the *Tacoma Ledger* looks back. "The dead year 1897 was the last of a series of unusual years—years that will long be memorable for the ruin they witnessed," the paper says. "They are strewn with useless wrecks both of fortune and lives."

The wreckage includes Spokane pioneer Anthony Cannon, who loses his wife Jennie in September 1893, after the failure of his Bank of Spokane Falls. Late in 1893, he scandalously marries a woman half his age in an attempt to revive his life, but in 1895 he dies of heart failure in a New York hotel room. By 1897, Cannon's estate has shriveled to 2 cents on the dollar of what it once was.

Ben Snipes of Ellensburg will also never win back his fortune. Samuel Dusinberre of the Bank of Puyallup, who went to prison in 1893 and is pardoned in 1895, leaves the state in 1896. George W. Boggs, the former Tacoma treasurer, goes to prison in 1897 and is pardoned in 1899. J.K. Edmiston of the Walla Walla Savings Bank remains a fugitive in exile. Lionel Stagge ends his career as a bank receiver and resumes his life as an itinerant con man.

Other figures from those years merely fade away. The state's most colorful Coxeyite, Jumbo Cantwell, never moves back to Tacoma. In 1897, he surfaces in Chicago as the People's Party candidate for alderman. He loses to a Democrat. In 1902, he is caught hiding the principal witness to a burglary, is convicted of conspiracy and obstruction of justice and is fined $100. At his death in 1916, the *Seattle Times* has to explain to its younger readers who Jumbo was.

Populist firebrand Mary E. Hobart, who racked up one vote in the Washington legislature to be a U.S. senator, never achieves public office. She does have three national lecture tours and the national release of her book, *The Secrets of the Rothschilds*. The woman the *Reveille* dismissed as New Whatcom's "prophet of calamity" and "the Western Washington talking machine" dies at 64, on February

7, 1906. Her funeral is at the Christian Science Church in Belling-ham.

Charles Gloystein, the Republican farmer who went miss-ing from Mica, Washington, in 1894, after planting a bloodied hat, lives a quiet life thereafter. His wife, Salina, takes him back, but later they divorce and he remarries. In the mid-1920s, Charles and Anna Gloystein move to suburban Tacoma, where they have a farm. At his death in 1940, the *Tacoma News Tribune* makes no mention of his scandalous and cowardly disappearance in 1894. It tells readers that Gloystein was known in Pierce County for his delicious strawber-ries.[118]

Seattle now cements its dominance on Puget Sound. Seattle and Tacoma both grow but Seattle starts from a higher level and grows more. From 1890 to 1900, Seattle's population swells from 42,837 to 80,676—88 percent. Tacoma's grows from 36,006 to 37,714—5 percent.

This is not a race of equals. Seattle has built up the Alaska trade during the hard times and Tacoma has not. Seattle has also protected its credit and has never turned on its business leaders. An Oregon newspaper editor, writing of Seattle in 1895 says: "There are no mossbacks here."

Tacoma is infected with cynicism. Three months before the *Portland* arrives in Seattle, editor Snowden of the *Ledger* appeals to his Tacoma readers. Seattle is pushing the federal government for an office to assay gold dust. Seattle has pushed the government for an army post and a ship canal. Seattle has pushed for, and got, steam-ship service from Japan. Tacoma is pushing for nothing. The men who formerly pushed on behalf of the Tacoma, writes Snowden, "are not only no longer active, but strangely enough they are no longer popular."

The businessmen who paid Tacoma's bond interest in 1895 and 1896, Snowden writes, "have been sneered at for their self-sacri-fice, and even accused of having some secret intention to rob some-body..." These attacks, he says, have discouraged "everything that could possibly result in the general good."

Two weeks before the arrival of the *Portland* electrifies Seattle, Snowden prints a letter under the title, "What's Wrong With Ta-coma." It is from a small-time salesman who has spent two months knocking on doors in Seattle and three weeks in Tacoma. The man says Seattle people think of their city as a good place to work and live, and that Tacomans bad-mouth theirs. He quotes a woman in Tacoma's south end: "The corporations run the city and the poor man has no show."

In 1899 a new editor—Snowden is gone—will admit there is some truth to that. He diagnoses Tacoma's problem as dependency on two companies, the Tacoma Land Co. and the Northern Pacific Railroad, both of which fell into the hands of receivers in the hard times. A dependent waits to be saved; an independent entity makes its own future.

Tacoma is also in civic turmoil. Its city election in 1896 end-ed with the candidates for mayor two votes apart. The winner was unclear because a bag of ballots had been stolen from city hall. The mayor's office was taken by a Democrat, then a court gave it to a Republican, then a higher court gave it back to the Democrat.

Tacoma's focus is on its own troubles. As Seattle's politicians promote a city pipeline to the Cedar River to secure clean water for the next century, Tacoma's politicians are still trying to get a refund for buying the rotten water system of Charles Wright. And at a time when the Seattle Chamber of Commerce is promoting its city as the gateway to Alaska, the Tacoma Chamber is torn by an abortive effort to oust the executive secretary, Samuel Collyer. He was cashier of the Merchants National Bank, the first bank in Tacoma to fail—and people are still sore about it.

All through the hard times, the editors at the *Tacoma News* and particularly the *Ledger* have been complaining of "croakers" and "calamity howlers" striking notes of negativism. They hear it on the street and read it in the *Tacoma Union*, which in 1897 grum-bles about the "poverty and misery" caused by "the selfish gang of moneychangers and Shylocks in New York." The *Union* even puts a negative spin on the gold rush to the Yukon—that it "illustrates how desperate are the times." Even if men do bring back bags of gold, the *Union* says, the effect will be only "temporary relief" from the chronic shortage of yellow money.

The *Union* is a Populist paper. The Pops are a grumbling gang; they explain the hard times as the result of evil intent, of moneylenders—*foreign* moneylenders—deliberately creating a scarcity of gold to wield power over borrowers. The Pops hate debt. They believe Tacoma's debt was created by thieves, and they feel no obligation to repay it. Morally, they have a case. Financially their search for relief injures their city's future. The Pops also malign bankers. Tacoma is Western Washington's largest Populist stronghold and its largest graveyard of dead banks. Whether it is the Populist grumblers who bring down the banks or the failing banks that raise Populist grumblers may be debated. It's probably both.

Tacoma's Populists also celebrate the expulsion of the immigrant Chinese. Their proud prejudice puts at risk the city's new trade with Asia. For four years, beginning in 1892, Tacoma is Puget Sound's only city to have scheduled cargo service to Far East. It does all of Puget Sound's export business in wheat and flour. By the late 1890s, Seattle takes part of that business. In 1895, Japan places its Washington consulate in Tacoma. In 1901, it will move the consulate to Seattle, where it remains today.

Tacoma will dig itself out of its hole. Its commerce will recover and it will pay its debts. By November 1897, it will be able to pay city employees all past-due wages. And after collecting $125,000 from the estate of Charles Wright, the city will pay off all the embarrassing water bonds.

In 1899, the Washington Supreme Court will order Tacoma to pay all the Boggs warrants, with interest— $1.2 million in 8-percent debt. In June 1900, Tacoma will refinance its warrant debt with an issue of 5 percent, 20-year gold bonds.

"The taint of repudiation, which has hung over the city, arising from these old warrant cases, has now been dissipated," the *Tacoma Ledger* will say. "The defeat of Populism in this city and state at the last election has done much to restore confidence among the people of the East and to show that the people of Washington are honest and willing to pay their debts."

Tacoma will eventually live down its racial past. In 1996, a century after Tacomans voted to ban all Chinese from city jobs, the state will elect America's first Chinese-American governor, Gary

Kamakura Maru loading cotton at Seattle, December 1897. *Arthur Lee, Seattle Post-Intelligencer, 12-31-97*

Locke. He will receive 55 percent of the vote in Tacoma and surrounding Pierce County—and four years later, the same percentage again.

In 2005, Tacoma will begin work on the Tacoma Chinese Garden and Reconciliation Park, as an apology for the actions of 120 years earlier. It will have a new Vietnamese community south of downtown.

Tacoma's 2016 population: 211,277, third-largest in the state, after Spokane, 215,973, and Seattle, 704,352.[119]

Among the grand projects of the 1890s are the development of water power at Spokane Falls and from Snoqualmie Falls, the filling in of mud flats in Seattle and Tacoma, and the completion of the Sunnyside Canal in the Yakima Valley.

Many of the irrigation companies started in the West between 1889 and 1893 are rich-quick ventures focused on the sale of stocks and bonds rather than providing value to farmers. Not the Sunnyside project. Paul Schulze and Walter Granger believe in irrigation and they build a good canal. In 1897, two years after Schulze's suicide and the receivership of the canal company, its receiver cuts the price of irrigated land from $55 an acre to $30. Land sales resume, and just after the turn of the century the project emerges from receivership.

But for the irrigation of the Yakima Valley to expand much more, the Yakima River will have to be managed by storing water at Kachess and Keechelus lakes in the river's headwaters. Really, the entire river needs to be managed, rationing water during times of low runoff, and managing also for salmon spawning and flood control. Managing a river is a prerogative of government which it never delegates to private enterprise.

A new federal law favors public ownership. The Reclamation Act of 1902, signed by President Theodore Roosevelt, creates the Reclamation Service and provides a source of money. Also, the legislature in Olympia passes a law allowing public agencies to take land for reservoirs and canals through eminent domain.

A worry also rises about the shift in America's population to the cities. People fear that the nation could become a net food importer like Great Britain. It is a false argument; farm productivity is also increasing, and within a few decades the federal government will be paying farmers not to grow crops. Still, "food security" becomes a reason for government takeover of irrigation.

There is a deeper motive. Turning the desert green is a demonstration of life. It appeals to people. They want it, whether the nation is going to run short of food or not, and whether the government earns its capital back or not. They also like the way irrigation attracts people and trade. In 1906, when Yakima's population is about 7,000, the *Yakima Herald* says that with government irrigation:

"The city is now practically assured of a population of 50,000." It does reach that number, decades later.

In 1906, the owners of the Sunnyside Canal sell it to the federal government. More than a century later, the canal is the backbone of a cooperative system that waters 99,000 acres. Few remember its origins or the people who created it, though one of the towns in the Yakima Valley is called Granger, after the private company's local manager, Walter Granger. There is no town of Schulze.[120]

Among Washington's coastal boomtowns of the early 1890s that survive, recovery from the hard times is hugely uneven. The 1900 Census finds New Whatcom up 36 percent and Port Townsend down 24 percent.

At Port Townsend, civic promoter James G. Swan makes an appeal for Oregon investors to fund the unfinished railroad from Port Townsend to Olympia. With the completion of the railroad, he says, Portland would have a salt-water port on Puget Sound to "secure the great trade of the North." The Oregon men are not interested. Port Townsend withers away and almost dies. Thirty years later the town will attract a paper mill, and half a century later promoters will turn its 1890s downtown into a tourist attraction. Its 2016 population: 9,527.

At Port Angeles, by 1902 the town has let its warrant debt pile up for so long it can no longer save cash by refinancing 8 percent warrants with 5 percent bonds. Its old bonds are in default. Port Angeles will not dig out of its hole for years but it will grow with the lumber and seafood industries. Its 2016 population: 19,833.

At Bellingham, created by merging New Whatcom and Fairhaven, not until 1908 can Mayor Alfred Black announce that the new city has paid all interest owed on the old cities' bonds. From the Panic of 1893, it takes 15 years to refinance the bonds at lower rates and to redeem at par the warrants that were once worth 65 to 75 cents on the dollar. Bellingham will grow with the wood, paper, seafood, oil-refining, and aluminum industries. Its teacher's college will become Western Washington University. The city's 2016 population: 87,574.

South Bend is overwhelmed by its debts. In 1897, it budgets

four-fifths of its property taxes to debt service, declaring that it will pay the face value of warrants but no interest. Most warrant holders are happy to get what they can. This town, which once dreamed of being "the Baltimore of the Pacific," is today known for its oysters. Its 2016 population: 1,636.[121]

In 1907, the state of Washington will create a banking supervisor, and after 1914 it will ban non-chartered banks like Anthony Cannon's Bank of Spokane Falls and the Frank Hense Co. in Centralia. These acts will not, however, be reforms of the People's Party. By 1901, the Pops will be gone from the governor's office and the legislature. Their victory in 1896 is a sideshow, a historical curiosity.

In 1896, the contest that matters for Washington's economy is the election of President William McKinley. It settles the currency question for the next 37 years. What investors need is neither gold money nor silver money as such, but to know which metal will back the dollar. Had America elected Bryan and replaced gold with silver, no doubt business would have recovered. It will recover after the 1930s, when they elect Franklin Roosevelt, and he replaces gold with paper. In the 1890s it recovers when the gold standard is saved, a development the Populists said was impossible.

The most lasting reform to come out of the Panic of 1893 is Congress's passage in 1898 of the National Bankruptcy Act. It sets up a procedure for viable companies to be reorganized rather than liquidated, and for individuals to wipe the slate clean.

One of the first to use the new law is William Burton Allen, former president of the Bank of Tacoma. Allen owes the dead bank's depositors on a $70,000 loan he took out in 1894. He is one of 23 signers of a surety bond for former Tacoma treasurer George Boggs, each bondsman being fully liable for the $109,000 Boggs still owes Tacoma. Allen owes other creditors more than $50,000. In May 1899, the former president of the Bank of Tacoma is declared to have no assets for creditors and walks away without paying a cent. He has wiped his slate clean.[122]

After the hard times of the 1890s, a new economy rises in the state of Washington. It is a commercial life based on the state's natural resources of timber, coal, farmland, and fish, and the state's geographic position relative to Alaska and Asia. Never again will it be based so heavily on the building of railroads and the booming of town lots.

People in the Puget Sound country will afterward credit the gold rush in the Klondike for ending the hard times. But gold is also booming in Spokane's Inland Empire. And wheat and lumber prices are up. Manufacturing and trade are up across the board.

By 1897, exports from the Puget Sound customs district have doubled from the pre-depression high of 1892, and they will continue to rise. In the old economy, the principal export was wheat for Europe. In the new economy, it is still going there, but wheat and flour are also going to China. Lumber is still going to California and other places by sea, but by depression's end, 75 percent of the region's lumber and shingles are going east by rail. Washington is also sending apples, cherries, peaches, raspberries, strawberries, and canned salmon eastward in ever-growing volumes, providing the income to pay for imports and to attract new capital.

Production for the local market also replaces shipments from out of state. By 1897, Washington is producing its own pork, beef, chickens, eggs, milk, butter, and cheese. In the Kittitas Valley, which had its first small creamery in 1890, there are 16 in 1897, producing one ton of butter per day. Ellensburg businessman P.H.W. Ross writes that dairy farmers there are now earning steady incomes. "For several years past," he writes, "they have as a rule contracted no new indebtedness and have liquidated a large portion of their old obligations."

At the end of hard times brought on by reckless lending and borrowing, people are reminded of the old wisdom about debt. In 1897, the *Seattle Post-Intelligencer* advises its readers: "Get out of debt and keep out of it. The man in debt is a slave to the debtor, and will remain so until his obligation is canceled."

Americans will make plenty of mistakes in the economic boom that opens the 20th century. But the *Oregonian*—the Pacific Northwest's principal newspaper in 1897—will note that most of those who went through the hard times following the Panic of 1893 have a special thing in common: "a horror of debt."

They will, of course, eventually unlearn it.[123]

APPENDIX

Bank Failures in Washington
May 1893 - July 1897

1893

Bank of Puyallup, 5/25/93
Merchants National Bank, Tacoma, 5/31/93
Bank of Spokane Falls, 6/5/93
Washington National Bank, Spokane, 6/6/93
    reopens 7/6/93, closes 7/30/94
Washington Savings Bank, Spokane, 6/6/93
Citizens National Bank, Spokane, 6/6/93
    reopens 12/21/93, closes 11/22/94
First National Bank, Palouse, 6/6/93
    reopens 6/9/93, closes 12/17/94
Ben E. Snipes & Co., Ellensburg, 6/9/93
Bank of Everett, 6/13/93
First National Bank, New Whatcom, 6/22/93
Columbia National Bank, New Whatcom, 6/23/93
First National Bank, Port Angeles, 6/26/93
    reopens 4/26/94, closes 4/17/95
Bank of Sumas, 7/3/93
Puget Sound National Bank, Everett, 7/5/93
    reopens 10/23/93, closes 7/16/95
Bank of Anacortes, 7/17/93
Hoquiam National Bank*, 7/18/93
Traders Bank, Tacoma, 7/21/93
    reopens 1/25/94, closes 5/19/94*
Tacoma National Bank, 7/24/93
    reopens 12/4/93, closes 12/3/94
First National Bank, Spokane, 7/26/93
Spokane Savings Bank, 7/26/93
Ellensburg National Bank, 7/27/93
    reopens 10/23/93, closes 7/10/96
Washington National Bank, Tacoma*, 7/27/93
Puget Sound Loan, Trust & Banking Co., New Whatcom, 7/29/93
    reopens 11/27/94, closes 11/22/95

Bellingham Bay National Bank, New Whatcom, 7/31/93
 reopens 1/9/94, closes 11/4/95
Bank of Colfax, 8/8/93
Port Townsend National Bank, 9/17/93
First National Bank, Slaughter*, 10/25/93
Commercial Bank, Conconully, late fall 1893
 reopens 2/1/94
Buckley State Bank, 11/18/93
Island County Bank, Coupeville, 11/30/93
Walla Walla Savings Bank, 12/9/93
Security Savings Bank, Seattle, 12/9/93

1894

Washington Savings Bank, Seattle, 1/22/94
First National Bank, Centralia*, 2/1/94
 reopens as Frank Hense Co., early 1994, closes 9/25/94
Commercial State Savings Bank, Tekoa, 4/4/94
State Savings Bank, Tacoma, 5/11/94
Edison Savings Bank, Tacoma, 5/12/94
Traders Bank, Tacoma*, 2nd failure, 5/19/94
Washington National Bank, Spokane*, 2nd failure, 7/30/94
First National Bank of Montesano*, 8/28/94
Frank Hense Co., Centralia (was First National Bank, Centralia), 2nd
 failure, 9/25/94
James R. Morrison Co., Ilwaco, 9/94
Blaine National Bank*, 11/5/94; reopens as Blaine State Bank, 2nd
 failure, 9/30/95
Citizens National Bank, Spokane, 2nd failure, 11/22/94
Browne National Bank, Spokane, 11/23/94
Aberdeen Bank, 11/26/94
Tacoma National Bank, 2nd failure, 12/3/94
First National Bank, Palouse*, 2nd failure, 12/17/94
Commercial Savings Bank, Spokane, 12/28/94

1895

First National Bank, Anacortes, 1/17/95
Whatcom County Bank, New Whatcom, 1/28/95
First National Bank, Port Angeles, 2nd failure, 4/17/95
Merchants National Bank, Seattle, 5/21/95
Puget Sound National Bank, Everett, 2nd failure, 7/17/95
Citizens National Bank, Tacoma*, 7/27/95
Wakefield State Bank, Elma, 8/8/95
Bank of Palouse, 8/9/95

APPENDIX

First National Bank, South Bend, 8/12/95
Bank of Tacoma, 8/19/95
Blaine State Bank (was Blaine National Bank), 2nd failure, 9/30/95
First National Bank, Aberdeen*, 10/12/95
Commercial Bank, Tacoma, 10/16/95
German-American Safe Deposit & Savings Bank, Tacoma, 10/22/95
Columbia National Bank, Tacoma, 10/24/95
Bellingham Bay National Bank, New Whatcom, 2nd failure, 11/4/95
Bennett National Bank, New Whatcom, 11/4/95
    reopens 12/20/95, closes 9/14/96
Puget Sound Loan, Trust & Banking Co., New Whatcom,
    2nd failure, 11/22/95

1896

First National Bank of Puyallup*, 1/1/96
Guarantee Loan & Trust Co., Seattle, 5/25/96
Marine Bank, Ballard, 6/20/96
Bank of Cheney, 6/15/96
First National Bank, Cheney, 6/15/96
Seattle Dime Savings Bank, 7/2/96
Commercial State Bank, Chehalis, 7/13/96
Kittitas Valley National Bank (was Ellensburg National), 2nd failure,
    7/10/96
Bank of Auburn, 8/1/96
Bennett National Bank, New Whatcom, 2nd failure, 9/14/96
Bank of Kent, 10/8/96
Fairhaven National Bank*, 10/10/96
First National Bank, Goldendale*, 12/17/96

1897

Seattle Savings Bank, 1/13/97
First National Bank, Olympia, 1/26/97
Farmers' and Traders' Bank, Johnson*, 1/28/97
First National Bank, Oakesdale*, 2/1/97
Snohomish National Bank*, 3/5/97
Union Savings Bank & Trust Co., Tacoma, 6/29/97

Voluntary liquidation

Sources for Bank Failures

1893: Bank of Puyallup: "Bank of Puyallup Closes," *News*, May 26, 1893, p. 7; Merchants National Bank, Tacoma: "The Suspended Bank," *Ledger*, June 1, 1893, pp. 4, 5; Bank of Spokane Falls: "Doors Closed," *Chronicle*, June 5, 1893, p. 1; Washington National Bank, Spokane, Washington Savings Bank, Spokane, Citizens National Bank, Spokane: "They Closed It" and "Citizens Bank Closed," *Chronicle*, June 6, 1893, p. 1, "Putting in Their Coin," *Chronicle*, Dec. 21, 1893, p. 3; First National Bank, Palouse: "Palouse Bank Closed Up," *Chronicle*, June 6, 1893, p. 1, and "The Trouble Is Over," *Chronicle*, June 10, 1893, p. 1; Ben. E. Snipes & Co., Ellensburg: "Snipes & Co. Suspend," *Ellensburgh Capital*, June 15, 1893, p. 3; Bank of Everett: "Bank of Everett Assigns," *Seattle Press-Times*, June 13, 1893, p. 1; First National Bank, New Whatcom: "Note Book and Pencil," *Reveille*, June 23, 1893, p. 2; Columbia National Bank, New Whatcom: "The Columbia Ditto," *Bellingham Bay Express*, June 23, 1893, p. 1; First National Bank, Port Angeles: "Port Angeles Bank Suspends," *P-I*, June 27, 1893, p. 1; Bank of Sumas: "Bank of Sumas," *Oregonian*, July 6, 1893, p. 1; Puget Sound National Bank, Everett: "Temporarily Suspended," *Everett Herald*, July 6, 1893, p.1, "An Everett Bank Resumes," *P-I*, Oct. 24, 1893, p. 5; Washington National Bank, Spokane: "Washington Bank Open" and "The Bank Reopened," *Chronicle*, July 6, 1893, pp. 3, 4; Bank of Anacortes: "The Bank of Anacortes Suspends," *P-I*, July 18, 1893, p. 2; Hoquiam National Bank: *Comptroller's Report*, Vol. 1, 1896, p. 632; Traders Bank, Tacoma: "Traders Bank Closed," *Ledger*, July 22, 1893, p. 5, "The Traders Bank," *News*, July 21, 1893, p. 1; Tacoma National Bank: "Another Bank Closed," *Ledger*, July 25, 1893, p. 5, "The Tacoma National Bank Reopens," *P-I*, Dec. 5, 1893, p. 3; First National Bank, Spokane, and Spokane Savings Bank: "Spokane Banks Suspend," *Ledger*, July 27, 1893, p. 8; Ellensburg National Bank: "Closed Their Doors," *Oregonian*, July 28, 1893, p. 8, and "Closed Its Doors," *Ellensburgh Capital*, Aug. 3, 1893, p. 3, "Good News From Ellensburg," *P-I*, Oct. 22, 1893, p. 1; Washington National Bank, Tacoma: "A Tacoma Bank Case," *P-I*, Aug. 29, 1893, p. 5; Puget Sound Loan, Trust & Banking, New Whatcom: "Wild, Wise nor Witty," *Reveille*, July 29, 1893, p. 1; Bellingham Bay National Bank: "A Silent Quartette," *Reveille*, July 31, 1893, p. 1; Bank of Colfax: "Bank of Colfax Closed," *Review*, Aug. 9, 1893, p. 4; Port Townsend National Bank: "Portland Is Responsible," *Port Townsend Leader*, Sept. 19, 1893, p. 1; First National Bank, Slaughter (Auburn): *Comptroller's Report*, Vol. 1, 1896, p. 633; Commercial Bank, Conconully: Poole, "L.L. Work, Pioneer Banker," *Okanogan County Heritage*, Fall 1988; Buckley State Bank: "Buckley's Bank Closed," *Ledger*, Nov. 23, 1893, p. 5; Island County Bank, Coupeville: "Coupeville Bank Closed," *P-I*, Dec. 2, 1893, p. 1; Walla Walla Savings Bank: "Walla Walla Bank Matter," *Chronicle*, Dec. 13, 1893, p. 1; Security Savings Bank, Seattle: "Seattle's Suspended Bank," *Ledger*, Dec. 12, 1893, p. 5.

APPENDIX

1894: Washington Savings Bank, Seattle: "Another Seattle Bank Fails," *Ledger*, Jan. 23, 1894, p. 1; First National Bank, Centralia: *Comptroller's Report*, 1897, Vol. I, p. 477; State Savings Bank, Tacoma: Commercial State Savings Bank, Tekoa: "Decided in Contempt," *Ledger*, April 5, 1894, p. 3; State Savings Bank, Tacoma: "In the Hands of a Receiver," *Ledger*, May 12, 1894, p. 5; Edison Savings Bank, Tacoma: "Pulled Another One Over," *Ledger*, May 13, 1895, p. 5; Traders Bank, Tacoma: "Traders' Bank, Tacoma, to Liquidate," *P-I*, May 20, 1894, p. 3; Washington National Bank, Spokane: *Comptroller's Report*, 1897, Vol. 1, p. 477; First National Bank of Montesano: *Comptroller's Report*, 1897, Vol. 1, p. 477; Frank Hense Co., Centralia: "Suspended," *Chehalis Nugget*, Sept. 28, 1894, p. 1; James R. Morrison Co., Ilwaco: "Banker Morrison's Flight," *P-I*, Oct. 4, 1894, p. 2; Blaine National Bank: *Comptroller's Report*, 1897, Vol. 1, p. 478; Citizens National Bank, Spokane: "Closed Its Doors," *Chronicle*, Nov. 22, 1894, p. 1; Browne National Bank, Spokane: "Browne National Liquidates," *Chronicle*, Nov. 23, 1894, p. 2; Aberdeen Bank: "Aberdeen Bank Shut," *P-I*, Nov. 27, 1894, p. 1; Tacoma National Bank: "The Tacoma National Bank," *Ledger*, Dec. 4, 1894, p. 4; First National Bank, Palouse: *Comptroller's Report*, 1897, Vol. 1, p. 478; Commercial Savings Bank, Spokane: "Ready for a Receiver," *Spokesman-Review*, Dec. 29, 1894, p. 5.

1895: First National Bank, Anacortes: "Bank Failure at Anacortes," *P-I*, Jan. 18, 1895, p. 2; Whatcom County Bank, New Whatcom: "Whatcom County Bank Closed," *Ledger*, Jan. 29, 1895, p. 1; First National Bank, Port Angeles: "Port Angeles Bank Closed," *P-I*, April 19, 1895, p. 1; Merchants National Bank, Seattle: "Bank Did Not Open," *Seattle Times*, May 21, 1895, p. 1; Puget Sound National Bank, Everett: "An Everett Bank Fails," *P-I*, July 18, 1895, p. 1; Citizens National Bank, Tacoma: *Comptroller's Report*, 1897, Vol. 1, p. 478; Wakefield State Bank, Elma: "Bank Failure at Elma," *P-I*, Aug. 13, 1895, p. 3; Bank of Palouse: "The Bank of Palouse Fails," *P-I*, Aug. 10, 1895, p. 1; First National Bank, South Bend: "South Bend Bank Suspends," *Ledger*, Aug. 13, 1895, p. 1; Bank of Tacoma: "The Bank of Tacoma Assigns," *Ledger*, Aug. 20, 1895, p. 5; Blaine State Bank: "Blaine State Bank Fails," *P-I*, Oct. 1, 1895, p. 1; First National Bank, Aberdeen: *Comptroller's Report*, 1897, Vol. 1, p. 478; Commercial Bank, Tacoma: "Commercial Bank Closes," *Ledger*, Oct. 17, 1895, p. 8; German-American Safe Deposit & Savings Bank, Tacoma: "The Boggs Warrants," *P-I*, Oct. 21, 1895, p. 2; Columbia National Bank, Tacoma: "Columbia Bank Closed," *P-I*, Oct. 25, 1895, p. 1; Bellingham Bay National Bank, New Whatcom: "Two Whatcom Banks," *P-I*, Nov. 5, 1895, p. 2; Bennett National Bank, New Whatcom: "Two Banks Suspend," *Bellingham Bay Reveille*, Nov. 8, 1895, p. 7; Puget Sound Loan, Trust & Banking Co., New Whatcom: "Whatcom's Last Bank Gone," *P-I*, Nov. 23, 1895, p. 2.

1896: First National Bank of Puyallup: *Comptroller's Report,* 1897, Vol. 1, p. 478; Guarantee Loan & Trust Co., Seattle: "Forced to Close," *P-I,* May 26, 1896, p. 3; Marine Bank, Ballard: "Petition for a Receiver," *P-I,* June 22, 1896, p. 2; Bank of Cheney and First National Bank, Cheney: "Doors Closed," *Chronicle,* June 15, 1896, p. 3; Seattle Dime Savings Bank: "Closed Its Doors," *Seattle Times,* July 2, 1896, p. 3; Commercial State Bank, Chehalis: "Two Failures at Chehalis," *Ledger,* July 14, 1896, p. 6; Kittitas Valley National Bank, Ellensburg: "The Bank Closes," *Ellensburg Capital,* July 9, 1896, p. 3; Bank of Auburn: "Auburn Bank Fails," *P-I,* Aug. 2, 1896, p. 5; Bennett National Bank, New Whatcom: "Bennett Bank Closes," *Bellingham Bay Reveille,* Sept. 18, 1896, p. 2; Bank of Kent: "Closed Its Doors," *P-I,* Oct. 9, 1896, p. 5; Fairhaven National Bank, Fairhaven: "Fairhaven National Bank to Liquidate," *P-I,* Aug. 9, 1896, p. 3; First National Bank, Goldendale: *Comptroller's Report,* 1903, Vol. 1, p. 265.

1897: Seattle Savings Bank: "Failed to Open Its Doors," *Seattle Times,* Jan. 13, 1897, p.8; First National Bank, Olympia: "Olympia Bank Goes Down," *P-I,* Jan. 27, 1897, p. 2; Farmers' and Traders' Bank, Johnson: "Into Voluntary Liquidation," *P-I,* Feb. 2, 1897, p. 3; First National Bank of Oakesdale: *Comptroller's Report,* 1903, Vol. 1, p. 265; Snohomish National Bank: *Comptroller's Report,* 1903, Vol. 1, p. 265; Union Savings Bank & Trust Co., Tacoma: "The Union Bank Failure," *Union,* June 30, 1897, p. 4.

APPENDIX

Payouts to Depositors
at all the national banks and some of the others

cents/$

100.00	Aberdeen Bank
100.00	Browne National Bank, Spokane
100.00	Puget Sound National Bank, Everett
100.00	Snohomish National Bank
100.00	Traders Bank, Tacoma*
100.00	Security Savings Bank, Seattle*
100.00	Walla Walla Savings Bank*
97.15	First National Bank, Olympia
84.50	Washington National Bank, Tacoma
82.30	Bennett National Bank, New Whatcom
75.20	Columbia National Bank, Tacoma
75.00	Commercial State Bank, Chehalis
72.00	Port Townsend National Bank
60.00#	Bank of Colfax
58.00	First National Bank, Cheney
55.00	First National Bank, Anacortes
52.00	Merchants National Bank, Seattle
50.00	Frank Hense & Co., Centralia
44.00	Kittitas Valley National Bank, Ellensburg
44.00	First National Bank, Spokane
41.00+	Bank of Puyallup
39.00	Bellingham Bay National Bank, New Whatcom
35.00	First National Bank, South Bend
32.00	First National Bank, Port Angeles
26.26	First National Bank, New Whatcom
21.00	Tacoma National Bank
18.90	Bank of Tacoma
18.24	Columbia National Bank, New Whatcom
17.75	Merchants National Bank, Tacoma
10.00	Citizens National Bank, Spokane
9.72	Ben Snipes & Co., Ellensburg
2.88	State Savings Bank, Tacoma
0.00#	Bank of Spokane Falls

#Approximate
**Includes owners' payments not required by law*
+Paid at least this much

Sources for Payouts to Depositors

For national banks: *Comptroller's Report*, 1904, pp. 350-355; Traders Bank: Chauncey Griggs to Harry Dimmock, Oct. 2, 1898, Griggs letterpress copybooks, *St. Paul & Tacoma Lumber Co. Records*, Univ. of Wash. Libraries; Security Savings Bank of Seattle and Walla Walla Savings Bank: "Edmiston, Former Banker, Wins Governor's Pardon," *Spokesman-Review*, Feb. 1, 1911, p. 1; Commercial State Bank, Chehalis: "Bank's Affairs Wound Up, *P-I*, March 26, 1898, p. 10; Hense: "Centralia Business Troubles," *P-I*, Dec. 11, 1894, p. 2; Bank of Puyallup, *Watterson v. Bank of Puyallup*, File 11747, Pierce County Superior Court, and "Puyallup Receiver's Report," *Ledger*, April 15, 1897, p. 5; Bank of Tacoma: "News of the Court House," *Union*, June 13, 1897, p. 5; Snipes: "Last Snipes Dividend," *Ellensburg Capital*, Sept. 12, 1903, p. 3; State Savings: "Small Dividend Received," *P-I*, Feb. 22, 1898, p. 3; Bank of Colfax and Bank of Spokane Falls: *Preston Papers*, Box 1, File 22, which refer to the Bank of Spokane Falls as "a total loss."

BIBLIOGRAPHY

Books:

Armbruster, Kurt, *Orphan Road*, Washington State University, 1999.

Bagley, Clarence, *History of Seattle from the Earliest Settlement to the Present Time*, S.J. Clarke, 1916.

Baumgart, Howard, *Ellensburg's Tree of Justice*, Sun Lakes, AZ, 2002.

Boyle, O.D., *History of Railroad Strikes*, Brotherhood, 1935.

Bush, John, *The National Bankruptcy Act of 1898*, Banks Law, 1899.

Carlisle, John, *The Free Coinage of Silver*, 1895.

Chin, Art & Doug, *The Chinese in Washington State*, OCA Greater Seattle, 2013.

Clark, Norman, *Mill Town*, University of Washington, 1970.

Daggett, Stuart, *Railroad Reorganization*, Harvard University, 1908.

Dewing, Arthur, *A History of the National Cordage Company*, Harvard University, 1913.

Dougherty, Phil, *The Bartell Story*, Bartell Drug, 2015.

Durham, Nelson, *Spokane and the Inland Empire*, S.J. Clarke, 1912.

Ficken, Robert, *The Forested Land*, University of Washington, 1987.

------------------, *Washington State: The Inaugural Decade 1889-1899*, Washington State University, 2007.

Fraser, Hugh, *Seven Years on the Pacific Slope*, Dodd, Mead, 1914.

Friedman, Milton, *Money Mischief*, Harcourt Brace, 1994.

Funk, Wallie, *Pictures of the Past*, Anacortes Museum, 2015.

Garrett, Garet, *The Driver*, E.P. Dutton, 1922.

Grant, James, *The Forgotten Depression*, Simon & Schuster, 2014.

Groner, Alex, *PACCAR*, Documentary Book Publishers, 1981.

Harvey, Paul, *Tacoma Headlines*, Tacoma News Tribune, 1962.

Harvey, Hope, *Coin's Financial School*, Coin Publishing, 1894.

Henderson, John, ed., *An Illustrated History of Klickitat, Yakima and Kittitas Counties*, Interstate, 1904.

Hines, Neal, *Denny's Knoll*, University of Washington, 1980.

Hobart, Mary, *The Secrets of the Rothschilds*, Charles Kerr, 1898.

Holbrook, Stewart, *Far Corner*, Macmillan, 1952.

Hunt, Herbert, *Tacoma, Its History and Its Builders*, S.J. Clarke, 1916.

Keniston-Longrie, Joy, et al. *Tacoma's Stadium District*, Arcadia, 2010.

Lauck, William, *The Causes of the Panic of 1893*, Houghton, Mifflin, 1907.

Lauridsen, G.M., and A.A. Smith *The Story of Port Angeles*, Lowman & Hanford, 1957.

LeWarne, Charles, *Utopias on Puget Sound 1885-1915*, University of Washington, 1975.

Lockley, Fred, *History of the Columbia River Valley from The Dalles to the Sea*, S.J. Clarke, 1928.

London, Jack, *The Call of the Wild*, Macmillan, 1903.

----------------, *The Road*, Macmillan, 1907.

Lukoff, Benjamin, *Seattle Then and Now*, Thunder Bay, 2010.

Macdonald, George, *Fifty Years of Freethought*, Arno, 1929.

Magden, Ronald, *Furusat: Tacoma-Pierce County Japanese 1888-1977*, Tacoma Japanese Community Service, 1998.

Marple, Elliot and Olson, Bruce H., *The National Bank of Commerce of Seattle, 1889-1969*, Pacific, 1972.

Martin, Albro, *James J. Hill and the Opening of the Northwest*, Minnesota Historical Society Press, 1976.

Martin, Paul, *Port Angeles, Washington*, Peninsula, 1983.

McCurdy, James, *By Juan de Fuca's Strait*, Metropolitan, 1937.

McMurry, Donald, *Coxey's Army*, Little, Brown, 1929.

Meany, Edmond, *History of the State of Washington*, Macmillan, 1909.

Meeker, Ezra, *The Busy Life of Eighty-Five Years*, 1916.

Miles, Charles and Sperlin, O.B., eds., *Building a State*, Washington State Historical Society, 1940.

Morgan, Murray, *The Mill on the Boot*, University of Washington, 1982.

------------------, *Puget's Sound*, University of Washington, 1979.

Nesbit, Robert C., *"He Built Seattle,"* University of Washington, 1961.

Provorse, Barry, *The PeoplesBank Story*, Documentary, 1987.

Roth, Lottie Roeder, *History of Whatcom County*, Pioneer Historical, Chicago, 1926.

Royer, Marie Hamel, *The Saxon Story*, Whatcom County Historical Society, 1982.

Sale, Roger, *Seattle Past to Present*, University of Washington, 1976.

Schwantes, Carlos, *Coxey's Army*, University of Nebraska, 1985.

Sheller, Roscoe, *Ben Snipes*, Binfords & Mort, 1957.

----------------, *Courage and Water*, Binfords & Mort, 1952.

Skalley, Michael, *Foss*, Superior, 1981.

Stratton, ed., *Spokane & the Inland Empire*, Washington State University, 2005.

Tooze, Adam, *The Wages of Destruction*, Viking, 2006.

Van Sycle, Edwin, *The River Pioneers*, Pacific Search, 1982.

Weinstein, Robert, *Grays Harbor 1885-1913*, Viking, 1978.

West, J.B., *Growing Up in the Palouse*, Citizen Journal, 1980.

Whitfield, William, *History of Snohomish County*, Chicago and Seattle, Pioneer Historical, 1926.

Woodhouse, Philip, *Monte Cristo*, The Mountaineers, 1979.

----------------, et al., *The Everett and Monte Cristo Railway*, Oso, 2000.

Zoss, Neel, *McDougall's Great Lakes Whulebucks*, Arcadia, 2007.

BIBLIOGRAPHY

Official Reports:

Compendium of the Eleventh Census: 1890, Part I, Washington, 1892.
Annual Reports of the Comptroller of the Currency for 1893, 1894, 1895, 1896, 1897, 1898, 1901, 1903, 1904 and 1906.
Report of the Controller of the City of Tacoma, 1897.
Revised Ordinances of the City of Seattle, 1893.
Second Report of the Secretary of State, 1892, Olympia, 1893.
Fifth Report of the Secretary of State, 1898, Olympia, 1899.

Booklets and Pamphlets:

"Ocosta!" 1891, Shorey Bookstore, 1967.
Smith, George Venable, "Puget Sound Cooperative Colony," 1887, Shorey Bookstore, 1965.
"Sunnyside Irrigation Canal," Washington Irrigation, Zillah, 1902.
Welsh, William, "A Brief Historical Sketch of Grays Harbor, Washington," Chamber of Commerce, 1942.

Magazines and Journals:

Allen, Doug, "Lewis County to Willapa Bay by Rail," *The Sou'wester,* Pacific County Historical Society, Vol. XLII, Nos. 2 and 3, Summer and Fall 2006.
Beard, Charles, "The Historical Approach to the New Deal," *The American Political Science Review,* Vol. 28, No.1. Feb. 1934.
Bogar, Gerald Dale, "Ocosta-by-the-Sea," *The Pacific Northwest Quarterly,* January 1963.
Coulter, Calvin, "The Victory of National Irrigation in the Yakima Valley, 1902-1906," *The Pacific Northwest Quarterly,* Vol. 42, No. 2. April 1951.
Eckels, James and Pennoyer, Sylvester, "The Financial Situation," *The North American Review,* Vol. 157, Aug. 1893.
Ferris, Joel E., "Early Day Banking in the State of Washington," *Western Banker,* Oct. 1958.
Fisher, Willard, "Coin and His Critics," *Quarterly Journal of Economics,* Vol. 8, No. 4, July 1894.
Fourth Annual Catalogue of the Washington Agricultural College, Experiment Station and School of Science, State of Washington, 1894.
Friedman, Milton, "The Crime of 1873," *Journal of Political Economy,* Vol. 98, No. 6, Dec. 1990.
Gladden, Washington, "Relief Work—Its Principles and Methods," *The Review of Reviews,* Vol. IX, Jan.-June 1894.
Griffiths, David, "Far Western Populist Thought," *Pacific Northwest Quarterly,* Vol. 60, No. 4, Oct. 1969.

259

Hollander, Jacob H., "The Security Holdings of National Banks," *The American Economic Review*, Vol. 3, Dec. 1913, p. 801.

Hynding, Alan, "Eugene Semple's Seattle Canal Scheme," *Pacific Northwest Quarterly*, Vol. 59, No. 2, April 1968.

Macey, Jonathan R., "Double Liability for Bank Shareholders," 27 *Wake Forest Law Review* 31, 1992.

Marquis, Ralph, and Frank Smith, "Double Liability for Bank Stock," *The American Economic Review*, Vol. 27, No. 3, Sept. 1937.

McCausland, Ruth and Joan G. Mann, eds., "The Hotel that Never Opened," *The Sou'wester*, Vol. XXV, No. 4, Winter 1990.

McMurry, Donald L. "The Industrial Armies and the Commonweal," *Mississippi Valley Historical Review*, Dec. 1923.

Merrett, David, "The Australian Bank Crashes of the 1890s Revisited," Discussion Paper 2013-05, April 2013, Centre for Economic History, Australian National University.

Newcomb, Simon, "Has the Standard Gold Dollar Appreciated?" *Journal of Political Economy*, Vol. 1, No. 4, Sept. 1893.

Noyes, Alexander Dana, "The Banks and the Panic of 1893," *Political Science Quarterly*, Vol. 9, No. 1, March 1894.

Pfeifer, Michael, "Midnight Justice: Lynching and Law in the Pacific Northwest," *Pacific Northwest Quarterly*, Vol. 94, No. 2, Spring 2003.

Phillips, John, "Reminiscences of a Newspaper Man," *The Sou'wester*, Vol. VII, No. 4, Winter 1972.

Poole, George, "L.L. Work, Pioneer Banker," *Okanogan County Heritage*, Vol. 26, No. 4, Fall 1988.

Rau, Weldon Willis, "Trail's End and Beyond," *Overland Journal*, Vol. 10, No. 1, Spring 1992.

Ridgeway, Gordon B., "Populism in Washington," *Pacific Northwest Quarterly*, Vol. 39, No. 4, Oct. 1948.

Roberts, George E., "Influence of the New Gold Suppliers," *The Bankers Magazine*, Jan. 1906.

Shaw, Albert, "Relief Measures in American Cities," *The Review of Reviews*, Vol. 9, Jan.-June 1894.

Sherrard, William, "The Kirkland Steel Mill," *Pacific Northwest Quarterly*, Vol. 53, No. 4, Oct. 1962.

Snyder, Carl, "That Flood of Gold!" *The Review of Reviews*, Vol. 13, No. 2, Feb. 1896, pp. 167-173.

Stevens, Albert Clark, "An Analysis of the Phenomena of the Panic in the United States in 1893," *Quarterly Journal of Economics*, Vol. 8, No. 2, Jan. 1894.

Taussig, F.W., "The Crisis in the United States and the Repeal of Silver Purchase," *The Economic Journal*, Vol. 3, No. 12, Dec. 1893.

Voeltz, Herman C., "Coxey's Army in Oregon, 1894," *Oregon Historical Quarterly*, Vol. 65, No. 3, Sept. 1964.

BIBLIOGRAPHY

Volpp, Leti, "American Mestizo: Filipinos and Antimiscegenation Laws in California," 33 *U.C. Davis L. Rev.* 795 (1999).

White, Eugene Nelson, "State-Sponsored Insurance of Bank Deposits in the United States, 1907-1929," *Journal of Economic History*, Vol. XLI, No. 3, Sept. 1981.

Winston, A.P., "The Significance of the Pullman Strike," *Journal of Political Economy*, Vol. 9, No. 4, Sept. 1901.

Wooddy, Carroll, "Populism in Washington," *The Washington Historical Quarterly*, Vol. XXI, No. 2, April 1930.

Dissertations:

Arntzen, Katherine, "Ocosta-by-the-Sea," M.A. Social Sciences, University of Denver, Aug. 2009.

Dembo, Jonathan, "A History of the Washington State Labor Movement, 1885-1935," University of Washington, 1978.

Freece, David, "A History of the First Railway Systems of Vancouver, Washington, 1889-1926," M.A. History, Portland State University, 1984.

Papers and Records:

Ames, Edwin, papers. Allen Library, University of Washington.

Baker family papers, Penrose Library, Whitman College.

Census of the United States, 1900, Census Reports Volume III.

Comptroller of the Currency, National Bank Receivership Records, 1865-1927. Records Group 101, NARA College Park, MD.

Edmiston, J.K., pardon and correspondence, Pardons and Pardon Applications, Washington State Archives, Olympia.

Jewett Home Sanitarium for Electronic Treatment and Other Modalities, articles of incorporation, Washington State Archives, Ellensburg.

McGraw, Gov. John, papers, Washington State Archives, Olympia.

Morse Hardware Records, Washington State Archives, Bellingham.

Preston, Howard, papers, Allen Library, University of Washington.

Schulze, Paul, papers. Allen Library, University of Washington.

Seattle Chamber of Commerce, Records of the Minutes of Meetings, 1893 and 1896, Seattle Public Library.

Thompson, Walter, papers. Washington State Historical Society, Tacoma.

Walla Walla Savings Bank papers, Washington State University.

Court Cases:

Allen, in Re William B., Case 207, U.S. District Court, Tacoma (1899), RG 21, Box
    15, NARA Seattle.
Bardsley v. Sternberg, 18 Wash. 612, 1897 and 1898.
Barto v. Dusinberre, File 11721, Pierce County Superior Court, 1894.
Barto v. Nix, 15 Wash. 563, 1896.
Barton v. Hopkins, 14 Wash. 59, 1896.
Blanchard v. Commercial Bank of Tacoma, Ninth Circuit, June 8, 1896.
Cannon v. Snipes, Washington State Archives, Ellensburg.
Eidemiller v. City of Tacoma, 14 Wash. 376, 1896.
Fong Yue Ting v. United States, 149 U.S. 698, 1893.
Guaranty Trust Co. v. Henwood, 307 U.S. 247, 1939.
Hewitt v. Traders Bank, File 11673, Pierce County Superior Court, 1900.
Howarth v. Angle, 162 N.Y. 179, 1900.
Last Chance Mining Co. v. Tyler Mining Co., 157 U.S. 683, 1895.
Muhlenberg v. City of Tacoma, 21 Wash. 306, 1899.
Roberts v. Hense, Minn. Sup. Ct., 1916.
Stallcup v. City of Tacoma, 13 Wash. 141, 165 U.S. 719.
State, Ex Rel, Chamberlin v. Daniel, 17 Wash. 111 (1897).
State v. Halbert, 14 Wash. 306 (1896).
State of Idaho v. Michael H. Leitch, 1893, Tape 33, Criminal #49.000.0 to
    #93.228.0, Latah County Court, Moscow, Idaho.
State of Washington v. J.K. Edmiston, 1894, Case No. 1331, Walla Walla Superior
    Court, Walla Walla; files 374, 375, 376, 377, 390, 391, 438 and 448,
    Washington State Archives, Ellensburg.
State of Washington v. Raz Lewis, 1893, criminal No. 1632, Kittitas County
    Superior Court, Roslyn robbery case files, Key 221, Box 1, Kittitas
    County records, Washington State Archives, Ellensburg.
Tedford v. People, 219 Ill. 23, 1905.
Titlow v. Allen, File 16703, Pierce County Superior Court (1897).
United States v. Hattie Stratton, 1894, and presidential pardon. U.S. District Courts,
    Western District of Washington. RG-21, Box 33, 666-687, NARA
    Seattle.
Washington National Bank of Tacoma v. Eckels, 57 Fed. Rep. 870, 1893.
Watterson v. Bank of Puyallup, File 11747, Pierce County Superior Court, 1895.

ENDNOTES

Note: *"P-I"* means *Seattle Post-Intelligencer,* *"Telegraph,"* the *Seattle Telegraph, "News,"* the *Tacoma Daily News, "Union"* the *Tacoma Morning Union, "Chronicle"* the *Spokane Chronicle, "Review"* the *Spokane Review,* and *"Reveille"* the daily *New Whatcom Reveille. "Comptroller's Report"* means *Annual Report of the Comptroller of the Currency. "National Bank Receivership Records"* means Records Group 101, Office of the Comptroller of the Currency, Division of Insolvent National Banks, 1865-1945, National Bank Receivership Records, 1865-1927, National Archives and Records Administration, College Mark, Md.

1   Holbrook, *Far Corner,* pp. 129-130; Garrett, "Looking in the Ditch," *Saturday Evening Post,* March 14, 1931, p. 4; Hunt, *Tacoma,* Vol. II, p. 112.

2   Editorial, *Seattle Times,* June 11, 1895, p. 4.

3   "Hello to Spokane," *P-I,* Oct. 17, 1893, p. 8; "Death in Cold Water," *Telegraph,* Dec. 3, 1893, p. 8; "Schools of King County," *Telegraph,* Aug. 26, 1894, p. 2; *Compendium of the Eleventh Census, 1890,* Part I, p. xxxviii; "Women Can Vote," *Ledger,* Jan. 14, 1896, p. 4; "Lucky Washington," *Chronicle,* Dec. 12, 1894, p. 2; "Three Millmen Hurt," *Telegraph,* June 14, 1893, p. 2; "Torn to Pieces," *Chronicle,* Aug. 19, 1893, p. 1; "Human Driftwood," *Oregonian,* Oct. 8, 1894, p. 4; on "embarrassment" in "A Palouse Bank Suspends," *P-I,* June 7, 1893, p. 1; concerning "the economy," see Grant, *The Forgotten Depression,* p. 67; on "a job" vs. "work," see Garrett, "The Youth Document," *Saturday Evening Post,* Nov. 7, 1936; on the use of "homeless," see "Homeless, Starving," *Review,* Oct. 7, 1893, p. 1 and "A Worthy Object: To Discuss the Cause of Homeless and Indigent Children," *Oregonian,* Nov. 11, 1894, p. 2.

4   "The Monterey," *South Bend Journal,* July 7, 1893, p. 1; "On the Water Front," and "The Eagle's Scream," *Telegraph,* July 5, 1893, pp. 3, 5; "The Great Northern," *P-I,* March 30, 1893, p. 4; "The City of Destiny," *Ledger,* Jan. 6, 1893, p. 2; "Tacoma and the Wheat Crop," *Ledger,* Sept. 4, 1893, p. 4; "The Shippers Unite," *P-I,* Dec. 28, 1894, p. 2; "The Great Northern," *Telegraph,* Jan. 1, 1893, p. 9; Bagley, *History of Seattle,* Vol. I, pp. 257-258; "The Forty-Cent Rate" and "Hill's Promise Kept," *Aberdeen Herald,* Feb. 16, 1893, p. 2.

5   "The Western Town," *P-I,* Feb. 9, 1896, p. 4; "Across the Boundary," *Victoria Colonist,* Sept. 5, 1896, p. 3; "The City Is Growing," *Telegraph,* Aug. 27, 1893, p. 3; "New Commercial Waterway," *Telegraph,* June 10, 1893, p. 5; "A Commercial Center: Seattle as a Port," *P-I,* Jan. 3, 1897, p. 22; Holbrook, *Far Corner,* p. 116; "Tacoma Still Grows," *Ledger,* Oct. 31, 1893, p. 5; "Roys Committee Reports," *Ledger,* Dec. 11, 1895, p. 1; "Tacoma Is Prospering," *Pacific Banker and Investor,* Vol. I, No. 1, March 1893, p. 34; "How We Grow," *Weekly Ledger,* March 31, 1893, p. 4; editorial, *Pacific Banker and Investor,* April 1893, p. 11; "The Year's Brick Building," *Weekly Ledger,* Jan. 6, 1893, p. 11; "In New Quarters," *Ledger,* April 30, 1893, p. 4; "The Wreckers Answered," *Ledger,* Nov. 30, 1895, p. 4; "Seattle's Change in Policy Toward Tacoma," *News,* Nov. 21, 1893, p. 2; "Portland's Waning Wheat Trade," *Ledger,* Oct. 9, 1893, p. 4; "Seattle's Fifty Wheat Ships," *Ledger,* Oct. 19, 1893, p. 4; Durham, *Spokane,* Vol. I, p. 449; "Many Manufactories," *Chronicle,* Dec. 20, 1893, p. 4; "As Others See Us," *Chronicle,* Nov. 6, 1894, p. 4; "Good Government —Prosperity," *Chronicle,* March 16, 1895, p. 2.

6   Weinstein, *Grays Harbor,* p. 19; Welsh, "A Brief Sketch of Grays Harbor, Washington"; Ade Fredericksen, "Grays Harbor City: Boom and Bust," *Aberdeen Daily World, Harbor Country* magazine, March 2, 1975, p. 3; editorial, *Aberdeen Herald,* May 28, 1891, p. 4; "A Harbor View," *Aberdeen Herald,* June 25, 1891, p. 4; "A Matter of History," *Aberdeen Herald,* Aug. 6, 1891, p. 4; "A Sample Town Lot Trap," *Ledger,* Aug. 22, 1891, p. 4; "Aberdeen and Railroads," *Aberdeen Herald,* Nov. 5, 1891, p. 4; "Twas a Boom Town," *Oregonian,* Oct. 23, 1893, p. 4; "Hunt Asks Damages," *Ledger,* Feb. 21, 1894, p. 1.

7   Ad from Benham & Smith, *News,* Sept. 10, 1890, p. 2; "Commerce Addition," *South Bend Journal,* March 10, 1897, p. 8; "Last Rail Laid," *South Bend Journal,* Dec. 23, 1892, p. 3; "Its History," *South Bend Journal,* Dec. 30, 1892, p. 1; "An Old Bill," *South Bend Journal,* Nov. 23, 1894, p. 1; Phillips, "Reminiscences of a Newspaper Man," *The Sou'wester,* Winter 1972, p. 67; McCausland, "The Hotel that Never Opened," *The Sou'wester,* Winter 1990, p. 82; Allen, "Lewis County to Willapa Bay by Rail," *The Sou'wester,* Summer & Fall 2006, pp. 29-30; Armbruster, *Orphan Road,* p. 20; McCurdy, *By Juan de Fuca's Strait,* pp. 289-304; "Port Townsend," *Townsend Leader,* April 23, 1893, p. 3; "Oregon Improvement," *Review,* Nov. 25, 1890, p. 2; "Must Do Business," *Weekly Townsend Leader,* March 18, 1897, p. 1; "Just a Plain Talk," *Townsend Leader,* June 13, 1893, p. 2; "Key City Is Prosperous," *P-I,* Feb. 23, 1898, p. 12; "Lying About Us," *Anacortes Progress,* March 8, 1890, p. 1; "To Be or Not To Be," *Anacortes Progress,* April 10, 1890, p. 2; "The City at the Straits," *Anacortes Progress,* April 17, 1890, p. 2; "Wonderful," *Anacortes Progress,* April 23, 1890, p. 1; "Marvelous" and "Self Reliance," *Anacortes Progress,* April 24, 1890, p. 1-2; "The Venice of America, Part II," *Anacortes Progress,* May 29, 1890, p. 1; "The Electric Motor Line," "Completed in Time," and "The Electric Cars," *Anacortes Progress,* April 3, 1891, pp. 1-2; "Why Parker Paid It Back," *P-I,* Feb. 22, 1898,

p. 2; "Everett Incorporation," *Weekly Ledger,* Feb. 24, 1893, p. 3; "Everett's New Buildings," *P-I,* Nov. 16, 1892, p. 2; Walker to Pope & Talbot, July 11, 1892, and to Will Talbot, July 19, 1892, pp. 56, 65-66, Puget Mill Co. letterbooks, Box 131A, *Ames Papers.*

8   "Washington Leads All," *Weekly Ledger,* Jan. 6, 1893, p. 10; "Railway Construction in Washington," *Telegraph,* Oct. 11, 1893, p. 4; "The Bank of Venice," *Reveille,* June 13, 1894, p. 2; "Editorial Expressions," *Telegraph,* Oct. 2, 1894, p. 4; "Progress of the State," *News,* Sept. 14, 1896, p. 4; Hunt, *Tacoma,* pp. 498-499; editorial, *Reveille,* June 24, 1893, p. 2; "Justices of the Peace," *Chronicle,* Dec. 18, 1894, p. 2; "Lost Capital," *Oregonian,* Dec. 8, 1893, p. 4; a similar explanation is offered by Paul Mohr, "Sources of Wealth," *P-I, July* 7, 1895, p. 6; "Interest on Public Debts," *Weekly Ledger,* Jan. 20, 1893, p. 3; "Looking Forward," *Review,* Jan. 1, 1893, p. 6; "Hail Ninety-Three," *Ledger,* Jan. 1, 1893, p. 4.

9   "Not Exchangeable for Gold," *Seattle Times,* Aug. 4, 1896, p. 4; "The Issue Plainly Stated," *Review,* July 7, 1893, p. 4; "The Sherman Law," *Chronicle,* July 18, 1893, p. 4; "Debts are Payable In Gold," *P-I,* July 10, 1896, p. 4; "Wrong Reasoning," *Press-Times,* May 10, 1893, p. 4; Speech at Memphis, May 23, 1895, in *Carlisle, The Free Coinage of Silver,* p. 33; "They Want the Smelter," *Chronicle,* March 3, 1893, p. 7; "Bank Closed Its Doors," *Chronicle,* April 7, 1893, p. 3; "Think the Money Is Safe," *Chronicle,* April 8, 1893, p. 3; "Banks Cannot Pay Up," *Chronicle,* April 17, 1893, p. 3; "Big Bank Failure," *Chronicle,* April 4, 1893, p. 1; "Great Bank Failure," *Chronicle,* April 13, 1893, p. 1; "A Financial Crisis," *Chronicle,* April 19, 1893, p. 1; Henry Clews, "Affairs on Wall Street," *Chronicle, April* 21, 1893, p. 3; "No Danger of Panic," *Chronicle,* April 24, 1893, p. 1; "The President Speaks," *Chronicle,* April 24, 1893, p. 2; "The Australian Crash," *News,* May 1, 1893, p. 4; "A Great Day," *Chronicle,* May 1, 1893, p. 1; "Big Idaho Failure," *P-I,* April 25, 1894, p. 3; "Big Moscow Failure," *Review,* April 25, 1893, p. 1; "Kansas Sores Paraded," *Ledger,* April 26, 1893, p. 1.

10   "A Stock Panic," *Chronicle,* May 4, 1893, p. 1; Dewing, *A History of the National Cordage Company,* pp. 11-30; "A Day That Tried Men's Souls," *Chronicle,* May 5, 1893, p. 1; "Brighter Prospects," *P-I,* May 14, 1893, p. 4; editorial, *News,* May 6, 1893, p. 4; "The Business Situation," *Ledger,* May 13, 1893, p. 4; "Bank Failure," *Chronicle,* May 9, 1893, p. 1; "Columbia Fails," "Mixed Up With the Chemical," and "California Bank Fails," *Chronicle,* May 11, 1893, p. 1; "A Bad Day for Banks," *Telegraph,* May 12, 1893, p. 1; "Banks All Right," *Chronicle,* May 13, 1893, p. 1; "A Bad Day for Banks," *P-I,* May 13, 1893, p. 2; "Heavy Run on Bank," *P-I,* May 14, 1893, p. 7; "That Tired Feeling," *Ledger,* May 14, 1893, p. 1; "A Milwaukee Crash," *P-I,* June 2, 1893, p. 3; "There Is No Panic," *Telegraph,* May 14, 1893, p. 4; "Heavy Run on Bank," *P-I,* May 14, 1893, p. 7.

11 "Could Not Sell," *Chronicle*, June 3, 1893, p. 1; "Headquarters at the Fair," *P-I*, Aug. 8, 1892, p. 5; "S.A. Wheelwright Dead," *Ledger*, May 28, 1893, p. 1; "Failure Drove Him to Despair," *P-I*, May 29, 1893, p. 8; "Death His Relief," *News*, May 29, 1893, p.1; "Wheelwright's Suicide," *P-I*, May 30, 1893, p. 2; "Heard at the Hotels," *Ledger*, May 31, 1893, p. 3; "Wheelwright's Last Request," *P-I*, June 4, 1893, p. 8; "A Horrible Sight," *News*, May 27, 1893, p. 1; "Suicide in a Saloon," *Weekly Ledger*, June 2, 1893, p. 7; "He Shot the Banker," *Review*, June 20, 1893, p. 2; "Mikey Mint's Gun," *Pullman Herald*, June 23, 1893, p. 1; "Mike Leitch Bound Over," *Pullman Herald*, June 30, 1893, p. 1; *State v. Leitch*, Tape 33, Criminal #49.000.0 to #93.228.0, Latah County files.

12 "Bank of Puyallup Closes," *News*, May 26, 1893, p. 7; "His Life Threatened," *Ledger*, Sept. 7, 1893, p. 5; *Barto v. Nix*, 15 Wash. 563, Nov. 18, 1896; complaint of Fred D. Barto, Jan. 29, 1894, *Barto v. Dusinberre*, File 11721, Pierce County Superior Court; depositions of Willis Boatman, March 27 and Oct. 10, 1895, *Watterson v. Bank of Puyallup*, file 11747, Pierce County Superior Court; Rau, "Trail's End and Beyond," *Overland Journal*, Spring 1992, pp. 2-13; *Proceedings of the Twentieth Annual Convention of the American Bankers' Association, 1894*, p. 132; Hunt, *Tacoma*, Vol. I, pp. 307, 314, 462, 471, 494, 495; "Bennett Takes Hold," *News*, May 22, 1893, p. 1; "The Financial Situation," *Ledger*, May 31, 1893, p. 4; "Nelson Bennett," *Ledger*, March 29, 1896, p. 4; "The Financial Situation" and "The Suspended Bank," *Ledger*, June 1, 1893, pp. 4, 5; "Temporary Suspension," *News*, June 1, 1893, p. 1; "Confidence Restored" and "The Sun Comes Out," *News*, June 2, 1893, pp. 1, 4; "Now! All together! Pull!" *News*, June 6, 1893, p. 4; "The Anxiety Is Ended," *Ledger*, June 3, 1893, p. 8; "Reassured" and "The Merchants and the Chase," *Ledger*, June 3, 1893, pp. 4, 8; "Mr. Cannon and Boom Towns," *Ledger*, June 5, 1893, p. 4; "An Enemy of the West," *Ledger*, June 11, 1893, p. 4. Bennett's agreement with the Merchants National, May 30, 1893; Clary to Eckels, June 2, 1893; Kimball to Eckels, June 2, 1893; Bennett to Eckels, June 8, 1893; Wingate to Eckels, July 14, 1893; Chase National Bank's Proof of Claim filed against Merchants National Bank, Nov. 21, 1893; all from Merchants National Bank, File 209, *National Bank Receivership Records*.

13 Connor, "Chroniscope," *Chronicle*, July 23 & 27, 1964, pp. 19, 8; Fahey, "Requiem for a High Roller," *Spokane Magazine*, Oct. 1979; "Hon. A.M. Cannon's New Railway," *News*, Oct. 17, 1891, p. 7; "A.M. Cannon Dead," *Weekly Spokesman-Review*, April 11, 1895, p. 1; "A.M. Cannon Is Dead," *P-I*, April 7, 1895, p. 1; Durham, *Spokane*, pp. 449-450; Glover, "Borrowed Coin Started First Bank in Spokane," *Chronicle*, April 3, 1917, p. 13; "Have a Clearing House," *Chronicle*, May 20, 1893, p. 3; "Doors Closed" and "All Are United," *Chronicle*, June 5, 1893, pp. 1,4; "They Closed It," "Citizens Bank Closed" and "Use Common Sense," *Chronicle*, June 6, 1893, pp. 1, 4; "Dollar for Dollar" and "Banks Stood the Run," *Review*, June 6, 1893, pp. 1, 4; "Retrench" and "The Bank of Spokane," *Walla*

Walla Statesman, June 6, 1893, pp. 2, 3; "What Is There to Lose?" *Spokane Review,* June 7, 1893, p. 4; "The Financial Situation," *Chronicle,* June 10, 1893, p. 4; "Use Common Sense," *Chronicle,* June 6, 1893, p. 4; "A.M. Cannon Is Dead," *P-I,* April 7, 1895, p. 1; "Bank of Spokane Falls," *Chronicle,* June 7, 1895, p. 4; Fahey, "Requiem for a High Roller," *Spokane Magazine,* Oct. 1979, pp. 34-35, 73-78; Preston, "Liquidation of State Banks in Washington," *Preston Papers,* Univ. of Wash., Box 1, File 22.

14   Fraser, *Seven Years on the Pacific Slope,* p. 226; Henderson, *An Illustrated History,* pp. 255-261; "End of Roslyn Case," *Weekly Ledger,* March 31, 1893, p. 2; "Betrayed by a Woman," *Ellensburgh Capital,* April 20, 1893, p. 3; *State v. Raz Lewis,* Roslyn Bank Robbery Case Files, Criminal No. 1632, Key 221, Box 1, Kittitas County records, Washington State Archives, Ellensburg; "Snipes & Co. Suspend," *Ellensburgh Capital,* June 15, 1893, p. 3; "Snipes' Bank Secure," *Ledger,* June 15, 1893, p. 1; "Snipes Bank to Resume," *Ellensburgh Localizer,* June 17, 1893, p. 4; "Snipes' Bank All Right," *Ledger,* June 30, 1893, p. 8; "Snipes' Indebtedness," *Ellensburgh Capital,* Aug. 10, 1893, p. 3; "Trustees Named," *Ellensburgh Capital,* Aug. 24, 1893, p. 3; "North Yakima and Vicinity," *Yakima Herald,* July 19, 1900, p. 4; "Cheering Outlook," *Everett Herald,* June 8, 1893, p. 1; Granger to Schulze, June, 14, 1893, *Schulze Papers,* Box 1; "Note Book and Pencil," *Reveille,* June 23, 1893, p. 2; "The Bank Suspensions" and untitled editorial, *Reveille,* June 24, 1893, pp.1,2; "Too Much Freedom," *Bellingham Bay Express,* June 6, 1893, p. 2; Lauck, *The Causes of the Panic of 1893,* p. 103; "Port Angeles Bank Suspends," *P-I,* June 27, 1893, p. 1; "Bank of Sumas," *Oregonian,* July 6, 1893, p. 1; "Temporarily Suspended," *Everett Herald,* July 6, 1893, p. 1.

15   "The Sun Comes Out," *News,* June 2, 1893, p. 4; "No Time for Grumbling," *Ledger,* June 22, 1893, p. 6; "Washington Bank Open" and "The Bank Reopened," *Chronicle,* July 6, 1893, pp. 3, 4; "Keep the Money Moving," "Spokane's Great Victory," and "Our Friends in Need," *Chronicle,* June 8, 1893, p. 4; "Clearing House Certificates at Issue," *P-I,* June 16, 1893, p. 1; "Silver Is Falling," *P-I,* June 27, 1893, p. 2; "Not Demonetization," *Victoria Colonist,* July 8, 1893, p. 4; "Call Loans Way Up," *Chronicle,* June 29, 1893, p. 1; "Had No Effect," *Chronicle,* June 30, 1893, p. 1; "The Bank of Anacortes Suspends," *P-I,* July 18, 1893, p. 2; "All Denver Excited," *Oregonian,* July 19, 1893, p. 2; "Many More Banks," *Oregonian,* July 20, 1893, p. 2; "Traders Bank Closed," *Ledger,* July 22, 1893, p. 5; "The Traders Bank," *News,* July 21, 1893, p. 1; "Another Bank Closed," *Ledger,* July 25, 1893, p. 5; "The News of Tacoma," *Telegraph,* July 25, 1893, p. 3; "How Panics Start," *News,* July 25, 1893, p. 1; Lauck, *The Causes of the Panic of 1893,* p. 103; "Close to a Panic," *Oregonian,* July 27, 1893, p. 1; "Spokane Banks Suspend," *Ledger,* July 27, 1893, p. 8; "Closed Their Doors" and editorial, *Oregonian,* July 28, 1893, pp. 4, 8; "Closed Its Doors," *Ellensburgh Capital,* Aug. 3, 1893, p. 3; Henderson, *An Illustrated History,* p. 262; "A Tacoma Bank Case," *P-I,*

Aug. 29, 1893, p. 5; "Eckels Was Right," *P-I*, Aug. 30, 1893, p. 6; *Washington National Bank of Tacoma v. Eckels*, 57 Fed. Rep. 870; "Wild, Wise, nor Witty," *Bellingham Bay Express*, July 29, 1893, p. 1; "A Silent Quartette," *Bellingham Bay Express*, July 29, 1893, p. 1; "Bank Temporarily Closed," *Reveille*, July 30, 1893, p. 1; "Another Bank Suspends," *Reveille*, Aug. 1, 1893, p. 1; Roth, *History of Whatcom County*, Vol. I, p. 454; editorial, *Reveille*, Aug. 2, 1893, p. 2; *Comptroller's Report*, 1893, Vol. I, p. 175.

16   *Comptroller's Report*, 1897, Vol. I, pp. XXII, 477; Eckels, "The Financial Situation," *North American Review*, Vol. I57, Aug. 1893; *Comptroller's Report*, 1893, pp. 12, 15, 127, 128; "The Old Stocking," *Oregonian*, Aug. 27, 1893, p 4; "Bank of Colfax Closed," *Review*, Aug. 9, 1893, p. 4; Poole, "L.L. Work, Pioneer Banker," *Okanogan County Heritage*, Fall 1988; Martin, *Port Angeles*, p. 71; Lauridsen and Smith, *The Story of Port Angeles*, p. 197; Roth, *History of Whatcom County*, Vol. I, pp. 457-459.

17   "Murdered for Money," *Telegraph*, Sept. 5, 1893, p. 2; "Three Suspects Held," *Telegraph*, Sept. 6, 1893, p. 5; "Working Up Other Clues," *Telegraph*, Sept. 7, 1893, p. 5; "The Mystery of Two Cities," *Telegraph*, Nov. 20, 1893, p. 3; "Charged With Murder," *Telegraph*, Nov. 25, 1893, p. 1; "The Fetting Mystery," *P-I*, Nov. 24, 1893, p. 1; "He Gets the Limit," *P-I*, March 29, 1894, p. 5; "One Juror Was Not Qualified," *P-I*, March 23, 1895, p. 5; "Wilcox Not Guilty," *P-I*, May 25, 1895, p. 8; "Brief News," *P-I*, Feb. 21, 1895, p. 1; "The Moral of a Crime," *Telegraph*, Sept. 8, 1893, p. 4; "Tacoma Man's Queer Actions," *Telegraph*, Dec. 29, 1893, p. 3; "Sturdevant Is Insane," *Telegraph*, Dec. 30, 1893, p. 3.

18   "The Monterey," *South Bend Journal*, July 28, 1893, p. 1; "The Battleship," *South Bend Journal*, Aug. 4, 1893, p. 1; "Excursion to South Bend," *Chehalis Nugget*, Aug. 4, 1893, p. 1; "After the Ball," *South Bend Journal*, Aug. 11, 1893, p. 1; McCausland, "The Hotel That Never Opened," *The Sou'wester*, Winter 1990, p. 82; Allen, "Lewis County to Willapa Bay by Rail," *The Sou'wester*, Summer and Fall 2006, p. 30.

19   Nesbit, *He Built Seattle*, pp. 105-106, 159; "Demand a Receiver," *P-I*, March 25, 1893, p. 8; "A Receiver Named," *P-I*, June 27, 1893, p. 8; "Mr. Brown's Road," *P-I*, July 1, 1893, p. 6; "The N.P. Says 'Check'," *P-I*, July 14, 1893, p. 8; "The Lake Shore Bonds," *P-I*, July 18, 1893, p. 8; Sherrard, "The Kirkland Steel Mill," *Pacific Northwest Quarterly*, Vol. 53, No. 4, October 1962, p. 136; "A Big Road," *Yakima Herald*, March 23, 1893, p. 2; "The Northern Pacific," *Yakima Herald*, June 7, 1894, p. 1; "Can't Pay Expenses," *P-I*, Aug. 16, 1893, p. 6; "Is Short of Funds," *Telegraph*, Aug. 16, 1893, p. 1; "In Receivers' Hands," *Ledger*, Aug. 16, 1893, p. 1; "Northern Pacific Receivership," *Press-Times*, Aug. 16, 1893, p. 2; "Union Pacific Fails," *Oregonian*, Oct. 14, 1893, p. 1; "A Strike on the Great Northern," *P-I*, Aug. 2, 1893, p. 2.

20   Ficken, *The Forested Land*, p. 59; "All Centering on Puget Sound," *Everett Herald*, March 9, 1893, p. 3; "Washington Lumber and Shingles," *Aberdeen Herald*, April 13, 1893, p. 4; "Lumber for Cars," *Seattle Times*, Dec. 12, 1895, p. 5; "The Lumber Industry Reviewed," *Puget Sound Lumberman*, January 1893, pp. 9-16; "The Shingle Trade," *Puget Sound Lumberman*, April 1893, p. 13; "Views on Shingles," *Press-Times*, April 17, 1893, p. 8; "Our Lumbermen's Opportunity," *Ledger*, April 20, 1893, p. 4; "A Go-As-You-Please," *Seattle Post-Intelligencer*, April 12, 1893, p. 8; "A Shingle Trust," *P-I*, May 4, 1893, p. 8; "The Shingle Men Growl," *Ledger*, May 9, 1893, p. 4; "Shingle Men Meet," *Press-Times*, May 9, 1893, p. 5; "Shingles to Go Up," *P-I*, May 10, 1893, p. 3; "Shingle Forfeits" and "The Shingle Market," *Press-Times*, May 11, 1893, p. 8; "The Shinglemen's War," *P-I*, May 13, 1893, p. 1; "How to Combine," *P-I*, May 17, 1893, p. 6; "Shingle Makers Bolt," *Ledger*, May 17, 1893, p. 5; "Lumbermen's Meeting," *Ledger*, May 25, 1893, p. 5; "The Lumber Situation," *Ledger*, May 29, 1893, p. 5; "Shingles Going Down," *Ledger*, June 19, 1893, p. 2; "Shinglemen in Session," *Press-Times*, June 20, 1893, p. 1; "Prices Up, Wages Down," *P-I*, June 21, 1893, p. 3; "The Shingle Combine," *Press-Times*, June 29, 1893, p. 1; "The Shingle Trade," *Press-Times*, July 19, 1893, p. 4; "Among the Mills," *Press-Times*, Sept. 26, 1894, p. 4; "The Shingle Combine," *P-I*, Jan. 28, 1894, p. 4; "The Shingle Fight," *P-I*, March 26, 1894, p. 5; "Shingle Combine Off," *P-I*, May 13, 1894, p. 8.

21   "Prices Up, Wages Down," *P-I*, June 21, 1893, p. 3; "Shingle Weavers Firm," *Press-Times*, June 22, 1893, p. 4; "Mills at Ballard," *Press-Times*, July 17, 1893, p. 5; "Shingle-Weavers," *Press-Times*, July 18, 1893, p. 1; "Strike in the Mills," *P-I*, July 18, 1893, p. 7; "Strike at Ballard," *Puget Sound Lumberman*, July 1893, p. 15; "Labor and Wages," *P-I*, July 24, 1893, p. 1; "The Ballard Mill Troubles," *Press-Times*, July 24, 1893, p. 1; "Renewing the Fight," *P-I*, July 25, 1893, p. 8; "No Trouble at Ballard," *Press-Times*, Aug. 5, 1893, p. 1; "No Cut in Wages," *P-I*, Aug. 11, 1893, p. 6; "Unaccepted Shingle," *P-I*, Aug. 29, 1893, p. 8; "The Shingle Scale," *P-I*, Oct. 2, 1893, p. 8; "The Scrip Scheme at Mount Vernon," *Puget Sound Lumberman*, July 1893, p. 11; "Blaine's Shingle Mills," *Reveille*, Nov. 23, 1893, p. 1; "Shinglemen Try to Collect Wages," *P-I*, Dec. 8, 1893, p. 2; editorial, *Reveille*, Dec. 28, 1893, p. 2.

22   "Abolish the Evil," *Aberdeen Herald*, Feb. 18, 1892, p. 4; "Dead Comrades Honored," *Review*, July 12, 1893, p. 6; Ficken, *Washington State*, pp. 65-68; "The Gilman Strike," *Review*, July 5, 1893, p. 4; "Wages Cut at Gilman," *Telegraph*, July 7, 1893, p. 1; "Strangers Led the Strike," *Review*, July 10, 1893, p. 5; "Ferocious," *News*, Nov. 6, 1893, p. 1; "Must Have Been a Cannibal," *Telegraph*, Nov. 7, 1893, p. 2.

23   "Sailors Are Assaulted," *Ledger*, July 1, 1893, p. 5; "Sailors Found Guilty," *Ledger*, July 2, 1893, p. 4; "Sailors Beaten," *News*, Aug. 5, 1893, p. 1; "Sailors Were On Deck," *Ledger*, Sept. 13, 1893, p. 3; "Sailors Found Guilty," *Ledger*, Sept. 14, 1893, p. 5; "News," *Telegraph*, Sept. 14, 1893, p. 2; "The News of Tacoma," *Telegraph*, Sept. 20, 1893, p. 2; "Bullets Sped Like Hail," *Townsend Leader*, Aug. 12, 1893, p. 1; "Bloody Marine Riot," *Bellingham Bay Express*, Aug. 12, 1893, p. 1; "In a State of Siege," *Ledger*, Aug. 13, 1893, p. 1; "Coast Seamen's Pay," *P-I*, Sept. 7, 1893, p. 1; "To Reduce Seamen's Wages," *Ledger*, Sept. 13, 1893, p. 5; "Sailors Union Fight," *P-I*, Sept. 15, 1893, p. 5; "Killed by Dynamite," *P-I*, Sept. 24, 1893, p. 1; "The Union to Blame," *P-I*, Sept. 26, 1893, p. 2; "Note Book and Pencil," *Reveille*, Sept. 27, 1893, p. 2; "Ear on the Sailors' Union," *Ledger*, Oct. 12, 1893, p. 2; "Ruined by Dynamite," *P-I*, Oct. 13, 1893, p. 2; "Throws in the Sponge," *P-I*, Oct. 18, 1893, p. 8; "Strike of Coast Seamen," *P-I*, March 20, 1895, p. 1; "Old Men Shut Out," *P-I*, Jan. 14, 1894, p. 7.

24   Harvey, *Tacoma Headlines*, p. 35; "The News," *P-I*, June 14, 1893, p. 2; "The Press-Times Fails," *Ledger*, Oct. 19, 1893, p. 8; "Rats for the Ledger," *P-I*, Nov. 20, 1893, p. 1; handbill, *Ledger*, Nov. 21, 1893; "Union Printers' Address to the People of Tacoma," *Union*, Nov. 21, 1893, p. 1; "Rats," *News*, Nov. 21, 1893, p. 1; "War Upon Free Labor," *P-I*, Nov. 21, 1893, p. 1; "The Tacoma Lockout," *P-I*, Nov. 22, 1893, p. 2; "Ready for Business" and "Notes and Comments," *Union*, Nov. 23, 1893, pp. 2, 4. "To the Rescue," *Union*, Nov. 24, 1893, p. 1; "The Ledger Crippled," *Telegraph*, Nov. 24, 1893, p. 3; "What's in a Name?" and "Sale of the Press-Times," *Union*, Nov. 25, 1893, pp. 2,4; "Press-Times Receivership," *P-I*, Dec. 10, 1893, p. 5; "The Ledger and Printers," *Ledger*, Nov. 26, 1893, p. 1; "For Fair Play to All," *Ledger*, Dec. 1, 1893, p. 1; "State Press Opinion," *P-I*, Dec.1, 1893, p. 4; "The Ledger," *Ledger*, May 16, 1897, p. 4; "The Ledger Changes Hands," *P-I*, July 17, 1897, p. 2; "Loses the City Printing," *Ledger*, July 23, 1897, p. 1; "Ousted the Rats," *Union*, July 26, 1897, p. 2; "Announcement," *Union*, July 31, 1897, p. 2.

25   "The Taxpayers Kick," *P-I*, March 27, 1893, p. 2; "A Corporation's Grip," *P-I*, April 8, 1893, p. 1; "A Tacoma Protest," *P-I*, April 11, 1893, p. 2; "Tacoma Bond Vote," *P-I*, April 12, 1893, p. 2; "Brief Tacoma News," *P-I*, June 24, 1893, p. 1; "Tacoma's Water Steal," *P-I*, Dec. 3, 1893, p. 2; "Report of the Controller," *Ledger*, March 29, 1896, p. 11; "Bond Sale Approved," *P-I*, Oct. 31, 1893, p. 5; "The City Bonds," *P-I*, Nov. 17, 1893, p. 5, quoting *The Commercial Bulletin*, Boston, Nov. 11, 1893; "Bonded Debt of Seattle" etc., *P-I*, Oct. 14, 1898, p. 7; "To Wash the Tramps," *Ledger*, Oct. 8, 1893, p. 2; "City Scrip for Money," *P-I*, Aug. 23, 1893, p. 6; "Will Issue Warrants," *Chronicle*, Aug. 12, 1893, p. 3; "City School Matters," *Ledger*, Sept. 30, 1893, p. 5; "Teachers Made Happy," *Ledger*, Oct. 2, 1893, p. 5; "About the City," *Review*, Sept. 26, 1894, p. 4; "Editorial Notes," *Reveille*, Aug. 17, 1893, p 1; "Our Huge County Debt," *Reveille*, Oct. 19, 1894, p. 1; "Fuel for Schools," *P-I*, Aug. 31, 1893, p. 1; "To Do Without Light," *P-I*, Aug. 31, 1893, p. 5; "Can't Pass City Scrip," *Ledger*, Sept. 14, 1893, p. 7; "Arc Lights Must

Go," *Ledger*, Oct. 4, 1893, p. 2; "Bond Election," *South Bend Journal*, Sept. 29, 1893, p. 1; "Lights Out," *South Bend Journal*, Oct. 13, 1893, p. 1; "City Officers Without Salaries," *P-I*, Oct 17, 1895, p. 1; "Has Reached the Limit," *Telegraph*, Oct. 31, 1893, p. 3; "Ballard's Mayor Goes to Work," *Ledger*, Sept. 12, 1893, p. 8; *Seattle City Directory*, 1893, pp. 971, 1007; "Ten Patrolmen Gone," *Ledger*, May 26, 1893, p. 5; "Big Cut in Salaries," *P-I*, July 23, 1893, p. 7; "Down Go the Salaries," *Review*, Aug. 23, 1893, p. 3; "Salaries for Justices," *Telegraph*, July 14, 1893, p. 8; "They Want the Salary," *Chronicle*, Sept. 9, 1893, p. 3; "He Is After the Dogs," *Chronicle*, July 31, 1893, p. 4; "Jerry Is Out of a Job," *Chronicle*, Sept. 23, 1893, p. 4.

26   "Head and Thresher," *P-I*, Aug. 31, 1893, p. 8; Stine to Macintosh, May 27, 1893, Box 2, Letterbook 3, p. 960, *Walla Walla Savings Bank Papers;* "The Price of Wheat," *P-I*, Aug. 7, 1893, p. 4; "The Crop Enormous," *P-I*, Aug. 9, 1893, p. 3; "In the Wheat Fields," *Chronicle*, Aug. 10, 1893, p. 4; "Rain in the Palouse Country," *Chronicle*, Sept. 14, 1893, p. 4; "Damage to Wheat Crop," *Chronicle*, Oct. 7, 1893, p. 4; "They Want Sunshine," *Chronicle*, Oct. 9, 1893, p. 3; "Cannot Cut the Grain," *Chronicle*, Oct. 11, 1893, p. 1; "The Damaged Crops," *Pullman Herald*, Oct. 13, 1893, p. 1; "Half the Wheat Crop Lost," *P-I*, Oct. 14, 1893, p. 8; "Hard on the Farmers," *Chronicle*, Oct. 18, 1893, p. 3; West, *Growing Up in the Palouse*, p. 56-58; "The Wheat Fields," *Pullman Herald*, Nov. 3, 1893, p. 1; "News of the City," *Pullman Herald*, Nov. 10, 1893, p. 1; "Will Try Stock Raising," *Chronicle*, Nov. 18, 1893, p. 4; "It Was a Wet Year," *Pullman Herald*, Jan. 19, 1894, p. 1; "The Palouse Farmers," *P-I*, Jan. 6, 1894, p. 2; "From the Palouse," *P-I*, July 24, 1896, p. 7; "What the Census Shows," *Ledger*, Oct. 9, 1894, p. 2; "Shipped Four Million Bushels," *Ledger*, April 4, 1894, p. 2; "Facts About Wheat," *Pullman Herald*, April 20, 1894, p. 1; "Closes Its Doors," *Walla Walla Statesman*, Dec. 11, 1893, p. 2.

27   LeWarne, *Utopias on Puget Sound*, pp. 48-54; Smith, *Puget Sound Cooperative Colony*, pp. 2-21; "Port Angeles Colony," *P-I*, Nov. 28, 1893, p. 1; "How to Take Stock," *P-I*, Dec. 4, 1893, p. 2; "Scramble in Port Angeles," *Union*, Dec. 4, 1893, p. 1.

28   "Message," *Chronicle*, Aug. 8, 1893, p. 1; "Is Legislation the Remedy?" *Telegraph*, June 10, 1893, p. 4; "Work Hard for Silver," *Chronicle*, July 7, 1893, p. 4; "A Question of Finance," *P-I*, June 17, 1893, p. 4; "A Plain Statement of Facts," *P-I*, June 30, 1893, p. 4; "Against Free Silver," *P-I*, July 12, 1893, p. 8; "Sherman Silver Law," *Press-Times*, July 5, 1893, p. 1; "Railroaded Through" and "The Chamber of Commerce Resolutions," *News*, Aug. 2, 1893, pp. 1, 2; "Silver Men on Top," *Ledger*, Aug. 2, 1893, p. 5; "Chamber of Commerce," *News*, Aug. 3, 1893, p. 1; "No Snap Judgment," *Ledger*, Aug. 3, 1893, p. 4; "All-Round Advice," *Ledger*, Aug. 7, 1893, p. 4; "Free Silver Endorsed," *Ledger*, Aug. 4, 1893, p. 5; "Clews Is a Big Gold Bug," *Chronicle*, Nov. 3, 1893, p. 3; editorial, *Chronicle*, Nov. 2, 1893, p. 2.

29   "The 'Wild Men' Kick" and "A Courageous Clergyman," *News*, Aug. 8, 1893, pp. 1, 2; " 'Wild Men' Answer 'Wise Men'," *News*, Aug. 9, 1893, p. 8; "Is Mr. Hallock a Martyr?" " 'Wild Men' Answer 'Wise Men' " and "Mr. Hallock's Defense," *News*, Aug. 10, 1893, pp. 2, 8; "Mr. Hallock's Double Ender," *News*, Aug. 11, 1893, p. 2; "Eckels on Finance," *Ledger*, July 19, 1893, p. 1; "Champagne Froth," *Review*, July 20, 1893, p. 4; "Mr. Eckels Meant It," *Review*, July 22, 1893, p. 1; "Men You've Heard Of," *News*, Oct. 5, 1893, p. 8; "A Relic Comes to Light," *Townsend Leader*, Jan. 13, 1894, p. 1; Clary to Eckels, Oct. 12, 1893, *Port Townsend National Bank*, File 250, Box 491, *National Bank Receivership Records*; *Blanchard v. Commercial Bank of Tacoma*, U.S. Court of Appeals, Ninth Circuit, June 8, 1896, in *The Bankers' Magazine*, Vol. 53, July-Dec. 1896, p. 526; Blanchard to Eckels, Feb. 1, 1894, and Oct. 17, 1893, *First National Bank of Whatcom*, File 211, Box 426; Jennings to Eckels, Aug. 23, 1893, *First National Bank of Spokane*, File 257, Box 506; Wingate to Eckels, Feb. 3, 1894, *Merchants National Bank of Tacoma*, File 209, all from *National Bank Receivership Records*; "By the Way," *Press-Times*, Aug. 25, 1893, p. 2; Keniston-Longrie, *Tacoma's Stadium District*, p. 36; unsigned 4-page letter to Eckels, undated, Item #34, *Puget Sound National Bank of Everett*, File 221, Box 442, *National Bank Receivership Records*.

30   "Krug a Defaulter," *P-I*, Sept. 13, 1893, p. 8; "The Krug Shortage," *P-I*, Sept. 14, 1893, p. 8; "The Treasury Looted," *P-I*, Sept. 15, 1893, p. 2; "Krug an Idiotic Dupe," *Ledger*, Sept. 15, 1893, p. 1; "Chase After Krug," *P-I*, Sept. 17, 1893, p. 8; "Krug Is Caught," *P-I*, Sept. 19, 1893, p. 1; "Bled by Friends," *P-I*, Sept. 21, 1893, p. 5; "Krug's Bondsmen Put Up," *Ledger*, Oct. 19, 1893, p. 8; "The Isensee Deficit," *P-I*, Nov. 5, 1893, p. 7; "Isensee Runs Away," *P-I*, Nov. 17, 1893, p. 2; "Boodler Isensee Indicted," *P-I*, Nov. 19, 1893, p. 2; "Isensee's Admissions," *Reveille*, March 2, 1894, p. 1; "A Very Peculiar Plea," *Reveille*, March 3, 1894, p. 1; "Isensee's Testimony," *Reveille*, March 4, 1894, p. 1; "Isensee Found Guilty," *Reveille*, March 9, 1894, p. 1; "Whatcom a Heavy Loser," *P-I*, Feb. 9, 1897, p. 3; "How Clump Escaped," *Seattle P-I*, Feb. 9, 1895, p. 3; "Clump Is Captured," *Port Angeles Democrat-Leader*, July 12, 1895, p. 1; "The Officers Return," *Port Angeles Democrat-Leader*, July 19, 1895, p. 1; "Six Years for Clump," *P-I*, Nov. 15, 1895, p. 1; "On Boodle Charges," *Review*, Aug. 30, 1893, p. 1; "The Bribery Cases," *Review*, Sept. 6, 1893, p. 1; "Mr. Graham Goes Out," *Review*, Oct. 3, 1893, p. 1; "Jury Acquits Graham," *Review*, Nov. 4, 1893, p. 3; Weir, *Second Report of the Secretary of State, 1892*, pp. 15, 286-287; "Affairs in Bad Shape," *Review*, Oct. 2, 1893, p. 1; "Everybody Took a Grab," *Review*, Oct. 3, 1893, p. 3; "Manager Hopkins Arrested," *Review*, Oct. 4, 1893, p. 3; "Charged With Larceny," *Chronicle*, Oct. 4, 1893, p. 3; "Kept the Notes," *Chronicle*, Oct. 7, 1893, p. 1; "Insurance Men on Trial," *Review*, Oct. 8, 1893, p. 3; "Held Them for Trial," *Chronicle*, Oct. 10, 1893, p. 1; "Farmers Insurance Company," *Review*, Nov. 11, 1893, p. 1; "Hopkins on Trial," *Review*, June 22, 1894, p. 3; "Hopkins Found Guilty," *Review*, June 24, 1894, p. 3; "Buckley Bank Closed," *Ledger*, Nov. 23, 1893, p. 5; "Buckley's Bunco

Bankers," *P-I*, Nov. 23, 1893, p. 2; "Bankers Skip for Japan," *Pullman Herald*, Nov. 24, 1893, p. 4; "Absconder Hart," *News*, Nov. 25, 1893; "A Woman in the Case," *Ledger*, Nov. 26, 1893, p. 1; "No Reward for Hart," *Ledger*, Nov. 28, 1893, p. 8; "Was Hart a Mormon," *Ledger*, Dec. 4, 1893, p. 8; "Buckley Bank Robbers," *Telegraph*, Dec. 4, 1893, p. 1; "His Many Schemes," *Ledger*, Dec. 6, 1893, p. 1; "His Buckley Record," *Ledger*, Dec. 8, 1893, p. 3; "Miscellaneous. $1,000 Reward," *Police Gazette of Western Australia*, Jan. 3, 1894, p. 23; "Why Absconder Hart Is Free," *Ledger*, Oct. 11, 1894, p. 2; "Lived Very High," *Ledger*, Dec. 5, 1893, p. 5; "The Bank Was Left," *Ledger*, Dec. 8, 1893, p. 5; "Loved Women and Wine," *Union*, June 19, 1894, p. 3; "The Flight of Beals," *P-I*, June 20, 1894, p. 1; "Local Small Shot," *Townsend Leader*, Sept. 13, 1894, p. 4; "S.B. Dusinberre," *News*, July 15, 1893, p. 1; "Information Filed," *News*, Aug. 11, 1893, p. 1; "Dusinberre Guilty," *News*, Sept. 21, 1893, p. 1; "Dusinberre Sentenced," *Ledger*, Sept. 24, 1893, p. 3; "Dusinberre's Statement," News, Sept. 25, 1893, pp. 1,2; "Is Sam Dusinberre a Convict?" *P-I*, Dec. 20, 1894, p. 4; "His Life Threatened," *Ledger*, Sept. 7, 1893, p. 5; "No Proof Against Him," *Ledger*, Sept. 9, 1893, p. 2; editorial, *Chronicle*, Jan. 5, 1894, p. 2; "Court at Moscow," *Review*, Dec. 9, 1893, p. 1; no headline, *Pullman Herald*, Dec. 1, 1893, p. 1; "News of the City," *Pullman Herald*, Dec. 8, 1893, p. 1; "News of the City," *Pullman Herald*, Dec. 15, 1893, p. 1; *State v. Leitch*, Tape 33, Criminal #49.000.0 to #93.228.0.

31   "The Stability of Seattle," *P-I*, July 20, 1893, p. 4; Marple and Olson, *The National Bank of Commerce of Seattle*, p. 47; book of loans: "National Banks of Washington," *P-I*, Feb. 7, 1898, p. 2; Bagley, *History of Seattle*, Vol. II, pp. 732-738; Stevens, "An Analysis of the Phenomena of the Panic in the United States in 1893," *Quarterly Journal of Economics*, Vol. 8, No. 2, Jan. 1894, p. 148; "Seattle's Sound Sense," *Press-Times*, July 31, 1893, p. 4; "Seattle's Unity," *Yakima Herald*, Aug. 3, 1893, p. 2; "Seattle's Secret," *News*, Aug. 9, 1893, p. 1; "The Northwestern Banks," *Oregonian*, Nov. 7, 1893, p. 4; "Glass Expert Here," *Ledger*, Oct. 3, 1893, p. 5.

32   "Hard and Good Times," *Chronicle*, June 13, 1893, p. 4; "Have Good Times Arrived?" *Ledger*, June 17, 1893, p. 4; "How to Be Happy," *Ledger*, June 18, 1893, pp. 4, 12; Boynton to Thompson, Sept. 24, 1893, Box 2, Folder 11, *Walter J. Thompson Papers*; "Marnie" is Mary E., born 1877 in Milwaukee, U.S. Census, 1880; "Our Darkest Hour," *Ellensburgh Capital*, Aug. 3, 1893, p. 2; "Advice to Unemployed," *Ledger*, Aug. 21, 1893, p. 4; "Wait on No One," *Telegraph*, Aug. 5, 1893, p. 4; "Of Local Interest," *Walla Walla Statesman*, Aug. 12, 1893, p. 3; "Glad to Return," *Review*, Sept. 2, 1893, p. 2; "Hunting for Work," *Ledger*, July 11, 1893, p. 4; "The Popular Protest," *Everett Herald*, Dec. 28, 1893, p. 2; "A Lesson in Economy," *Telegraph*, Jan. 24, 1894, p. 4; "The Good Side of Hard Times," *Review*, Dec. 22, 1893, p. 2.

33   "Incendiary Speeches in New York," *P-I,* Aug. 19, 1893, p. 2; "Rioting in Chicago," *P-I,* Aug. 27, 1893, p. 3; "Foreigners Rioting at Chicago," *P-I,* Aug. 31, 1893, p. 2; "A Murderer Lynched," *Ledger,* July 27, 1893, p. 1; "Situation Is Serious," *Ledger,* July 28, 1893, p. 8; "Denver Is Alarmed," *P-I,* July 28, 1893, p. 1; "Feeding Denver's Unemployed," *Ledger,* July 29, 1893, p. 8; "Denver's Idle Poor," *P-I,* July 30, 1893, p. 2; "Denver's Unemployed," *Ledger,* July 30, 1893, p. 1; "The Army of the Unemployed," *Telegraph,* Aug. 13, 1893, p. 4.

34   "Need for Action," *Everett Herald,* Oct. 12, 1893, p. 2; Clark, *Mill Town,* p. 30; "The Employed and the Unemployed," *Ledger,* July 24, 1893, p. 4; "The Demand of Demagogues," *Ledger,* July 25, 1893, p. 4; Shaw, "Relief Measures in American Cities," *Review of Reviews,* Vol. IX, Jan.-June 1894, p. 189; "Chance for Married Men," *Telegraph,* July 13, 1893, p. 2; "No Bride So He Loses a Job," *Telegraph,* Jan. 11, 1894, p. 8; "Married Women as School Teachers," *Oregonian,* Feb. 11, 1894, p. 4; "They're Restrained," *Review,* Nov. 21, 1893, p. 1; "Day of Excitement," *Review,* Nov. 24, 1893, p. 1; "An Awful Groan," *Chronicle,* Nov. 23, 1893, p. 1; "To Talk It Over," *Chronicle,* Nov. 24, 1893, p. 1; "Water Works Begin," *Review,* Jan. 17, 1894, p. 3; "Doing the Best He Can," *Chronicle,* Jan. 24, 1894, p. 4.

35   "Hop Picker Migration," *Telegraph,* Aug. 25, 1893, p. 8; editorial, *Reveille,* Aug. 11, 1893, p. 2; "A Six Weeks' Picnic," *Ledger,* Aug. 15, 1893, p. 5; "Will Employ White People," *Ledger,* Sept. 12, 1893, p. 4; "Almost a Battle," *News,* Sept. 13, 1893, p. 1; "The News of Puyallup," *News,* Sept. 14, 1893, p. 1.

36   "The Japs Must Go," *Ledger,* Sept. 12, 1893, p. 4; "In the Hop Fields," *Press-Times,* Sept. 5, 1893, p. 4; "Piquant Is Pennoyer," *Ledger,* May 4, 1893, p. 1; *Fong Yue Ting v. U.S.,* 149 U.S. 698, May 15, 1893; "The Chinese Case," *P-I,* May 17, 1893, p. 2; "The Chinese Went," *Oregonian,* Sept. 5, 1893, p. 1; editorial, *Oregonian,* Sept. 6, 1893, p. 4; "The Hobo a Failure," *Yakima Herald,* Sept. 21, 1893, p. 5; "More Chinese Evicted," *The Dalles Daily Chronicle,* Sept. 27, 1893, p. 1; "Chinese Leave La Grande," *Review,* Sept. 26, 1893, p. 4; "Chinese Evicted Near La Grande," *Oregonian,* Sept. 27, 1893, p. 2; "Anti-Chinese Raids," *Review,* Sept. 27, 1893, p. 1; "Anti-Chinese Citizens Indicted," *Review,* Nov. 2, 1893, p. 1; Chin, *The Chinese in Washington State,* pp. 67-75; editorial, *Union,* Feb. 21, 1894, p. 2; "An Inevitable Conflict," *Telegraph,* Sept. 10, 1893, p. 4; "Restrict Immigration," *P-I,* May 5, 1894, p. 4.

37   "They Were Starving," *News,* July 22, 1893, p. 1; "An Appeal for the Poor," *Ledger,* Dec. 10, 1893, p. 2; "Only One Destitute Family," *Ledger,* Jan. 2, 1894, p. 5; "Mother Sent Us a-Begging," *Telegraph,* Nov. 14, 1893, p. 8; "Children Sent Out to Beg," *P-I,* Nov. 14, 1893, p. 8; "The Sick and the Poor," *P-I,* Sept. 10, 1893, p. 8; "Care of the Poor," *P-I,* Sept. 12, 1893, p. 8; "Who Must Care for the Sick," *P-I,* Sept. 13, 1893, p. 4, "May Die of Red Tape," *P-I,* Sept. 24, 1893,

ENDNOTES

p. 8; "Hit With a Coupling Pin," *Telegraph*, Sept. 24, 1893, p. 5; "The Injured Improving," *Telegraph*, Sept. 27, 1893, p. 5; "Stood Off the Sick," *P-I*, Nov. 9, 1893, p. 8; "The Care of the Poor," *P-I*, Nov. 13, 1893, p. 5; Letter from F.S. Palmer, health officer, in *Annual Report for 1894*, Seattle Board of Health.

38   "Spokane Sparks," *Chronicle*, Sept. 17, 1894, p. 3; "A Word to Snohomish People," *Snohomish County Tribune*, April 16, 1897, p. 4; editorial, *Oregonian*, Nov. 26, 1893, p. 4; "Practical Charity," *Telegraph*, Sept. 2, 1893, p. 4; Gladden, "Relief Work, Its Principles and Methods," *Review of Reviews*, Vol. IX, Jan.-June 1894, pp. 38-40; "No One Need Suffer," *News*, Sept. 26, 1893, p. 1; "The Poor in the City," *P-I*, Nov. 12, 1894, p. 5; Shaw, "Relief Measures in American Cities," *Review of Reviews*, Vol. IX, Jan.-June 1894, p. 189; "Food and Home for the Poor," *P-I*, Dec. 1, 1893, p. 8; "Works of Charity," *Ledger*, Jan. 22, 1894, p. 8; "Associated Charities Meeting," *Ledger*, Sept. 12, 1893, p. 5; "Charity Covers a Multitude of Sins," *Union*, Jan. 22, 1894, p. 2; "Are Feeding the Poor," *Chronicle*, Dec. 5, 1893, p. 4; "Need a Better Plan," *Chronicle*, April 12, 1894, p. 3; "Tramps Are Scarce Now," *Chronicle*, Oct. 4, 1894, p. 4; "Delay Is Expensive," *Chronicle*, Oct. 17, 1894, p. 4; "From All Professions," *Chronicle*, Nov. 16, 1893, p. 3; "This Is the Last Day," *Chronicle*, March 15, 1895, p. 3; "He Likes the System," *Chronicle*, Nov. 22, 1893, p. 3; "From All Professions," *Chronicle*, Nov. 16, 1893, p. 3; "Caring for the Needy," *Review*, Nov. 11, 1893, p. 3; "Charity and Business," *Review*, Jan. 8, 1894, p. 3.

39   "Life Has No Charms," *Ledger*, Aug. 1, 1893, p. 5; "Signs of a Suicide," *P-I*, Sept. 23, 1893, p. 8; "Ruined Merchant Suicides," *Ledger*, Oct. 31, 1893, p. 1; "Could Not Find Work," *Ledger*, Nov. 28, 1893, p. 1; "Drank from a Poison Cup," *Telegraph*, Nov. 28, 1893, p. 3; "Took Carbolic Acid," *P-I*, Nov. 28, 1893, p. 8; "Took Carbolic Acid," *Union*, Nov. 28, 1893, p. 1; "Increase of Crime," *P-I*, Feb. 7, 1895, p. 2; 1900 Census, *Census Reports Vol. III, Vital Statistics, Part 1*, Sect. 4, "Causes of Death," p. cxl.

40   "Thieves," *News*, Nov. 15, 1893, p. 1; "Arrests During 1893," *Review*, Jan. 6, 1894, p. 3; "He Wanted Food and Shelter," *P-I*, Oct. 24, 1893, p. 5; "Hungry Cripple Gets a Job," *P-I*, Oct. 25, 1893, p. 5; "Was an Absolute Untruth," *Ledger*, Aug. 22, 1893, p. 4; "Learned's Pretty Prize," *Townsend Leader*, Aug. 30, 1893, p. 1; "A Female Opium Smuggler Caught," *P-I*, Aug. 31, 1893, p. 2; "Female Smuggler Out on Bail," *P-I*, Sept. 1, 1893, p. 2; "Reason She Smuggled," *Port Angeles Democrat-Leader*, Sept. 1, 1893, p. 1; "Hattie Hastings Gone," *P-I*, Sept. 25, 1893, p. 2; "A Brief Review of the Career of Miss Hattie Hastings," *Port Angeles Democrat-Leader*, Sept. 8, 1893, p. 4; "New Suits Filed," *P-I*, Dec. 21, 1893, p. 3; "The Blotter," *P-I*, Dec. 23, 1893, p. 5; "Pardon of Miss Hastings," *Port Angeles Democrat-Leader*, April 13, 1894, p. 1. *U.S. v. Hattie Stratton*, U.S District Court, Seattle, 1894, NARA Seattle. Newspapers use "Hastings;" legal records use "Stratton." "Imports of Opium," *P-I*, Jan. 4, 1895, p. 2; "The Passing Throng," *P-I*, Feb. 26, 1899, p. 6.

41   "The Rights of Tramps," *Oregonian,* April 11, 1894, p. 4; "The Heritage of Self-Respect," *Oregonian,* Feb. 10, 1895, p. 4; "The Tramp Question," *Ledger,* Oct. 26, 1893, p. 4; "Chinese in Bad Luck," *Chronicle,* June 8, 1894, p. 4; the first Chinese vagrant: "Hune Bou Is a Vag," *Chronicle,* June 10, 1895, p. 1; "Spokane Sparks," *Chronicle,* Oct. 23, 1893, p. 3; "Brevities," *P-I,* Nov. 23, 1893, p. 8; "Our Policy Toward Vagrants," *News,* Dec. 7, 1893, p. 2; London, *The Road,* pp. 74-121; "Is He a Vagrant?" *P-I,* Nov. 3, 1893, p. 4; "Help for the Respectable Poor," *P-I,* Nov. *19, 1893, p. 4;* "Charitable Work," *P-I,* Nov. 25, 1892, p. 4; "The Agents' Story," *P-I,* Aug. 8, 1894, p. 5; "New Vagrancy Law," *Spokesman-Review,* Jan. 15, 1897, p. 5.

42   Wheeler, "Shack Life on Puget Sound," *Union,* Dec. 24, 1895, p. 14, from New York *Sun;* "A Tramp Killed," *P-I,* June 3, 1893, p. 5; London, *The Road,* pp. 29-43; "A Tramp Killed by the Cars," *Review,* June 25, 1894, p. 4; "A Demagogue's Manifesto," *Oregonian,* Dec. 13, 1893, p. 4; "A Sad Accident," *Ellensburgh Capital,* April 6, 1893, p. 3; "From Colfax," *Review,* Oct. 1, 1893, p. 5; "In Search of Employment," *Yakima Herald,* Aug. 17, 1893, p. 2; London, *Ibid.,* pp. 1-8; Royer, *The Saxon Story,* Vol. 2, p. 257.

43   "A Word About the Tramp," *Yakima Herald,* Aug. 10, 1893, p. 3; "Devilment of Tramps," *Ellensburgh Capital,* Aug. 17, 1893, p. 3; "Whipping Hobos," *News,* Sept. 19, 1893, p. 1; "To Wash the Tramps," *Ledger,* Oct. 8, 1893, p. 2; "Our Bath for Tramps," *Ledger,* Jan. 10, 1894, p. 4.

44   "Red's Eastern Trip," *P-I,* Nov. 6, 1893, p. 3; "Jimmy Egan's Trip," *P-I,* Dec. 21, 1893, p. 3; "Jimmy Egan's Walk," *Oregonian,* Oct. 31, 1893, p. 3; "Reddy's Round Trip," *Telegraph,* Nov. 13, 1894, p. 8; "Two Youthful Tramps," *Press-Times,* Sept. 5, 1893, p. 2; "The Youthful Tramps Again," *Press-Times,* Sept. 6, 1893, p. 1.

45   "The White Metal," *Chronicle,* Aug. 1, 1893, p. 1; Schwantes, *Coxey's Army,* pp. 25, 37-40; Garrett, *The Driver,* pp. 3-4; "General Coxey's Views," *Yakima Herald,* May 3, 1894, p. 4.

46   "Are These Populists?" *Union,* March 11, 1894, p. 1; "To Washington!" *Chronicle,* March 13, 1894, p. 1; "On to Washington," *Review,* March 14, 1894, p. 1; "March of the 'Unemployed,' " *P-I,* March 16, 1894, p. 5; "Gen. Fry's Army Breaks Ranks," *Ledger,* March 18, 1894, p. 6; "The Tramp Armies," *P-I,* March 21, 1894, p. 2; "Army of Unemployed," *Chronicle,* March 21, 1894, p. 2; editorial, *Chronicle,* March 22, 1894, p. 2; "Recruits for Coxey," *Review,* March 25, 1894, p. 1; "Not a Laughing Matter," *Union,* March 26, 1894, p. 1; "Coxey's Army Moves," *Review,* March 26, 1894, p. 1; "The Industrial Armies," *Aberdeen Herald,* April 26, 1894, p. 2; "What Labor Wants," *Union,* April 2, 1894, p. 1; editorial, *Oregonian,* April 21, 1894, p. 4; "The Anti-Workers," *Oregonian,* April 27, 1894,

ENDNOTES

p. 8; "Governor M'Graw and the Army of Industriless Industrials," *Townsend Leader*, May 6, 1894, p. 2; "The Battalion of Bums," *Chronicle*, April 10, 1894, p. 1; editorial, *Everett Times*, May 16, 1894, p. 2; editorial, *Ledger*, May 1, 1894, p. 4; "Industrial Army Parade," *P-I*, April 19, 1894, p. 2; "Coxey's Industrial Army," *P-I*, March 27, 1894, p. 4; London, *The Road*, p. 178; "An Unfortunate Misnomer," *Everett Herald*, June 14, 1894, p. 2; "The Danger of Industrialism," *Telegraph*, April 24, 1894, p. 4; "The Industrial Army," *Telegraph*, April 26, 1894, p. 4; Meeker, "In Fruitful Yakima Valley," *Ledger*, May 18, 1894, p. 2; "The Coxey Crusade and Its Significance," *News*, April 14, 1894, p. 1.

47   "Coxey's Army Formed," *P-I*, April 8, 1894, p. 8; "They Number Two Hundred," *Telegraph*, April 9, 1894, p. 8; "Industrial Army Growing," *Telegraph*, April 10, 1894, p. 2; "Commonwealers to March," *Telegraph*, April 25, 1894, p. 9; "Industrial Army Parade," *P-I* April 19, 1894, p. 2; "Harry Morgan's Estate," *P-I*, Feb. 25, 1892, p. 1; "Jumbo Threatens Morgan's Widow," *P-I*, Jan. 7, 1893, p. 2; "Tribulations of Tacoma Police," *P-I*, April 15, 1893, p. 2; "Mrs. Jumbo Cantwell's Ancient Lover," *P-I*, Nov. 23, 1893, p. 2; "Good for Jumbo," *News*, April 2, 1894, p. 1; "Who Jumbo Is," *News*, April 20, 1894, p. 4; "My Point of View," *News*, April 3, 1897, p. 4; "As We Go Marching On," *Union*, April 16, 1894, p. 4; "Puyallup," *News*, April 30, 1894, p. 4; "Are Not Hobos," *News*, April 25, 1894, p. 4; "Displays His Strength," *Union*, April 20, 1894, p. 4; "The Commonweal," *Union*, April 24, 1894, p. 2; "Army on the March," *P-I*, April 26, 1894, p. 1; "The Industrial Army," *Telegraph*, April 26, 1894, p. 4; "On the March," *News*, April 28, 1894, p. 1; "Forward Fours March," *Union*, April 29, 1894, p. 1; "The Army Has Gone," *Ledger*, April 29, 1894, p. 5; "An Army Mostly of Tramps," *Telegraph*, April 23, 1894, p. 5; "Two Regiments at Puyallup," *P-I*, April 29, 1894, p. 1; "In Camp at Puyallup," *P-I*, April 30, 1894, p. 1; "They Will Plead," *News*, May 1, 1894, p. 3; Hartman, "The Coxey Army Invasion of Puyallup," in Miles and Sperlin, eds., *Building a State*, p. 544; Petition to McGraw, *McGraw Papers*, Box 5; "Jumbo and John," *News*, May 3, 1894, p. 4; "Two Regiments at Puyallup," *P-I*, April 29, 1894, p. 1.

48   "Butte Excited," *Chronicle*, April 24, 1894, p. 1; "Ran Off With a Train," *P-I*, April 25, 1894, p. 1; "Blood Spilled" and "Uncle Sam's Aid Is Sought," *Chronicle*, April 25, 1894, p. 1; "Taken by Surprise," *Chronicle*, April 26, 1894, p. 1; "Coxey Train Caught," *P-I*, April 26, 1894, p. 1; "The Train Stealers," *P-I*, April 27, 1894, p. 1; "The Portland Industrials," *P-I*, April 26, 1894, p. 2; "The Portland Regiment," *P-I*, April 27, 1894, p. 2; "Portland Regiment Left," *P-I*, April 28, 1894, p. 1; "Federal Troops Out," *P-I*, April 29, 1894, p. 1; Schwantes, *Coxey's Army*, pp. 197-199; Voeltz, "Coxey's Army in Oregon, 1894," *Oregon Historical Quarterly*, Sept. 1964, pp. 277-289 (The spelling "Shreffler" rather than "Scheffler" is from Voeltz, and is verified by two city directories); "In Camp at Puyallup," *P-I*, April 30, 1894, p. 1; "Puyallup," *News*, April 30, 1894, p. 1; "Boarded a Freight Train,"

277

Ledger, May 4, 1894, p. 1; "Jumbo Gets Away," *Union*, May 4, 1894, p. 1; "The Army Going East," *P-I*, May 5, 1894, p. 1; "Scattered Along the Track," *Ledger*, May 5, 1894, p. 2; "Call Off the Marshals," *News*, May 5, 1894, p. 2; "Are Still Moving On," *Telegraph*, May 6, 1894, p. 1; "Those Brave Deputies," *Union*, May 6, 1894, p. 1; "Jumbo's Men," *News*, May 7, 1894, p. 1; "Oddities of the Genus Tramp," *Ledger*, May 21, 1894, p. 6.

49   "Moses Jeffries to the Fore," *Telegraph*, May 4, 1894, p. 2; "Woes of the Wealers," *Ellensburgh Capital*, May 10, 1894, p. 3; "A Real Pleasure Trip," *P-I*, May 7, 1894, p. 1; "Good Bye Wealers," *Ellensburgh Capital*, May 17, 1894, p. 3; "Away They Go," *News*, May 10, 1894, p. 1; "Some Walk, Some Ride," *P-I*, May 11, 1894, p. 1; "Coxeys and Deputies," *Telegraph*, May 12, 1894, p. 8; "Four Men Drowned," *P-I*, May 13, 1894, p. 1; "They Went for Blood," *Yakima Herald*, May 10, 1894, p. 3; "The Battle at Yakima," *P-I*, May 11, 1894, p. 1; "Who Shot Jack Jolly?" *Yakima Herald*, May 17, 1894, p. 1; "Tacoma Man Is Hung in Alaska," *Ledger*, Jan. 6, 1899, p. 2; "On the Verge of a Riot," *Review*, May 13, 1894, p. 3; "Why the Troops Are Here," *P-I*, May 14, 1894, p. 4; "The Vindication of Law and Order," *P-I*, May 23, 1894, p. 4; "More Found Guilty," *P-I*, May 26, 1894, p. 8; "Off to McNeil's Island," *P-I*, May 28, 1894, p. 2; "It's Any Way to Go Away," *Chronicle*, May 15, 1894, p. 3; "Going to See Grover," *Chronicle*, May 22, 1894, p. 3.

50   "Gen. Coxey's Circus," *P-I*, May 2, 1894, p. 1; "Coxeyites Convicted," *Telegraph*, May 9, 1894, p. 1; Schwantes, *Coxey's Army*, pp. 207-208; "They Stole an Engine," *Telegraph*, May 18, 1894, p. 1; "Is Jumbo a Lothario?" *Review*, May 25, 1894, p. 3; "Jumbo's Winning Ways," *Review*, May 26, 1894, p. 4; "Jumbo a Philanthropist," *Review*, May 29, 1894, p. 4; editorial, *Ledger*, June 9, 1894, p. 4; "Give Them a Real Welcome," *Chronicle*, June 29, 1896, p. 2; "Waiting for Mrs. Jumbo," *P-I*, July 27, 1894, p. 4, reprinted from *Washington Post*, July 16; "Commonwealers Return," *Telegraph*, Oct. 7, 1894, p. 9; "Jumbo's Wife Sued," *Seattle Times*, June 11, 1895, p. 2; "A Coxey Leader," *Seattle Times*, July 22, 1895, p. 8; "Ruler of Coxeyites," *Chronicle*, Sept. 10, 1894, p. 4; "Jeffries' Roast," *Chronicle*, Sept. 11, 1894, p. 4.

51   "The Duty of Democracy," *Telegraph*, July 11, 1894, p. 4; "The Shotgun League," *Review*, March 4, 1894, p. 2; "Patriot Army," *Telegraph*, May 14, 1894, p. 8; "Minute Men Almost in Arms," *Telegraph*, May 15, 1894, p. 8; "More Titles Made," *P-I*, May 15, 1894, p. 8; "The Patriot Army," *Telegraph*, May 18, 1894, p. 4; "Raiding the Chinese," *Oregonian*, May 15, 1894, p. 8; "Anti-Chinese Society," *Oregonian*, June 6, 1894, p. 4; "The A.P.A. Platform," *Ledger*, May 7, 1894, p. 4; "Principles of the A.P.A.," *Review*, May 6, 1894, p. 2; "Work of the A.P.A.," *Ledger*, Feb. 17, 1894, p. 5; "A.P.A. Ticket Elected," *Telegraph*, June 15, 1894, p. 1; "A Ballard Sensation," *Telegraph*, June 18, 1894, p. 1; "A Hotbed of Vice," *P-I*, March 21, 1894, p. 8; "Cairns and the A.P.A.," *Telegraph*, June 19, 1894, p. 2; "No Sign

of Scandal," *P-I*, June 19, 1894, p. 8; "Not to Be Justified," *P-I*, June 20, 1894, p. 4; "The Attack on Miss Johnson," *Telegraph*, June 21, 1894, p. 4; "A.P.A. Properly Squelched," *Telegraph*, June 23, 1894, p. 2; "Proper Action," *P-I*, June 23, 1894, p. 4; "It Was a Surprise," *P-I*, Nov. 4, 1895, p. 5; "The A.P.A. in Tacoma," *P-I*, July 27, 1894, p. 1; "Hemp Wins," *Chronicle*, June 2, 1894, p. 1; "The Colfax Lynching," *Telegraph*, June 5, 1894, p. 4.

52   "Fight Over the Negro," *Chronicle*, June 18, 1894, p. 1; "Negroes Rejected," *Chronicle*, June 19, 1894, p. 1; "Railroad Men Unite," *Chronicle*, Nov. 18, 1893, p. 1; "It Is a Strong Society," *Chronicle*, Nov. 22, 1893, p. 3; "In One Great Union," *P-I*, Nov. 24, 1893, p. 8; "Railway Employees," *Union*, Nov. 27, 1894, p. 1; "Where Law Means Justice" and "Want Wages Restored," *Chronicle*, April 7, 1894, pp. 2, 3; "Employees All Go Out," *Telegraph*, April 14, 1894, p. 1; "The Law of Strikes," *P-I*, April 24, 1894, p. 4; "The Great Northern Strike," *Telegraph*, April 16, 1894, p. 4; "Individualism vs. Socialism," *Telegraph*, June 17, 1894, p. 4; Boyle, *History of Railroad Strikes*, p. 51; Martin, *James J. Hill and the Opening of the Northwest*, p. 416; "The Strike Is Off," *Review*, May 2, 1894, p. 1.

53   "Pullman Will Not Arbitrate," *Ledger*, June 16, 1894, p. 4; "They Will Fight," *Chronicle*, June 26, 1894, p. 1; "Pullman's Protest," *Chronicle*, July 14, 1894, p. 3; "Character of Pullman" and "Cause of the Strikers," *Spokesman-Review*, July 22, 1894, p. 7; "The Facts," *P-I*, July 7, 1894, p. 4; "Pullman's Written Statement," *Telegraph*, July 11, 1894, p. 1; "Pullman a Witness," *P-I*, Aug. 28, 1894, p. 1; "The Town of Pullman," *Oregonian*, July 19, 1894, p. 3; "Pullman Roasted by Pastor," *Ledger*, July 30, 1894, p. 2; "The Condition of the Laboring Man at Pullman," cartoon, *Socialist News-Paper Union*, St. Louis.

54   "Bloody Polish Riot," *P-I*, April 20, 1894, p. 1; "Nine Men Shot Dead," *P-I*, April 5, 1894, p. 3; "The Strike at Roslyn," *P-I*, May 2, 1894, p. 2; "On Strike at Roslyn," *P-I*, May 3, 1894, p. 2; "Ask for $3.50 Each," *Review*, May 15, 1894, p.1; "They Make It General," *Chronicle*, June 26, 1894, p. 3; "May Blow Over," *Chronicle*, June 28, 1894, p. 4; "Foul Murder at the Gem," *Spokesman-Review*, July 4, 1894, p. 1; "The Situation at Gem," *Spokesman-Review*, July 5, 1894, p. 1; "No Lawlessness Here," *Chronicle*, July 5, 1894, p. 2; "The Situation at Gem" and "Anarchy at Gem," *Spokesman-Review*, June 5, 1894, pp. 1, 2; "The Murder of Kneebone," *Spokesman-Review*, July 8, 1894, p. 1; "The Coeur d'Alene Outrages," *P-I*, July 9, 1894, p. 1.

55   "Has Nothing to Arbitrate," *P-I*, June 16, 1894, p. 1; "Boycott Getting Serious," *Union*, June 28, 1894, p. 4; "A United Stand," *Union*, June 29, 1894, p. 1; "Big Battle Begun," *Telegraph*, June 29, 1894, p. 1; "The Boycott," *Ledger*, June 29, 1894, p. 4; "Justice to Debs," *P-I*, July 12, 1894, p. 4; "The Eye Would Like to See," *The Eye*, July 19, 1894, p. 2; "President Debs' Statement," *Spokesman-Review*,

July 3, 1894, p. 4; "A Struggle for Life," *Oregonian*, July 4, 1894, p. 4; "Rioting at Chicago," *P-I*, July 7, 1894, p. 1; "The Chicago Mob," "Words and Acts," and "The Facts," *P-I*, July 7, 1894, pp. 1,4; "A Charge by Militia," *P-I*, July 8, 1894, p. 1.

56   "Choked Up With Shingles," *Ledger,* June 29, 1894, p. 2; "The Deputies Were Stoned," *Ledger,* July 2, 1894, p. 5; "Was Assaulted by Strikers," *Ledger,* July 6, 1894, p. 4; "A.B. Todd Beaten by Strikers," *Ledger,* July 7, 1894, p. 5; "First Serious Trouble," *Union,* July 10, 1894, p. 4; "Violence Should Not Be Tolerated," *News,* July 7, 1894, p. 2; "Ran the Train like Wealers," *Ledger,* July 17, 1894, p. 3; "First Shots Fired," *Chronicle,* July 6, 1894, p. 1; "One Man Was Shot," "Rioting at Night" and "Enforce the Law," *Spokesman-Review,* July 6, 1894, pp. 1, 2.

57   "Militiamen on Strike," *P-I,* July 9, 1894, p. 1; "Company G Comes Home" and "Insurrection in the Ranks," *Spokesman-Review,* July 10, 1894, p. 1; "The Mutiny of Company G," *P-I,* July 18, 1894, p. 4; "M'Carthy's Case," *Chronicle,* Aug. 17, 1894, p. 1; "Gen. Curry's Story," *P-I,* July 31, 1894, p. 8; "The Soldiers' Trip," *P-I,* Aug. 5, 1894, p. 6; "May be Court-Martialed," *Spokesman-Review,* July 12, 1894, p. 3; "Met With Baby Carriages," *Union,* July 15, 1894, p. 1; editorial, *Spokesman-Review,* July 10, 1894, p. 2; "Disband Company G," *Spokesman-Review,* Sept. 16, 1894, p. 1; "Good-bye to Company G," *Chronicle,* Oct. 10, 1894, p. 3; "Will Try to Re-Enlist," *Spokesman-Review,* Oct. 19, 1894, p. 1; "Mob at Wardner," *Chronicle,* July 7, 1894, p. 1; "Two Large Bridges Burned," *Ledger,* July 11, 1894, p. 5; "Strikers Wreck a Train," *Ledger,* July 10, 1894, p. 1; "What Caused the Wreck," *Union,* July 11, 1894, p. 4; "As a Military Road," *P-I,* July 8, 1894, p. 8; "Strike Is Waning," *P-I,* July 10, 1894, p. 1; "Is a City of Soldiers," *Chronicle,* July 10, 1894, p. 3; "More Troops Wanted," *P-I,* Dec. 1, 1894, p. 3; "A General Strike Ordered," *P-I,* July 11, 1894, p. 2; "Strike Nearly Ended," *P-I,* July 12, 1894, p. 1; "Boycott," *Chronicle,* July 21, 1894, p. 1; "Lawlessness Does Not Pay," *P-I,* Aug. 1, 1894, p. 4; "Faults of Spokane," *P-I,* July 31, 1894, p. 5; "They Ask for Work," *P-I,* Aug. 11, 1894, p. 4; "On the Waiting List," *P-I,* Aug. 12, 1894, p. 8; "A Chance to Return," *P-I,* July 14, 1894, p. 8; "The Strike's Effect," *Oregonian,* July 30, 1894, p. 7; "Two Railroad Men Injured," *Ledger,* July 25, 1894, p. 3; "A Crash of Engines," *Telegraph,* Aug. 15, 1894, p. 2; "Northern Pacific Train Wreck," *P-I,* July 29, 1894, p. 2; "A Serious Train Wreck," *Union,* July 29, 1894, p. 1; "The News of Tacoma," *Telegraph,* July 23, 1894, p. 3.

58   "Coal Company Threat," *Union,* July 19, 1894, p. 1; "Idle Roslyn Miners," *Ledger,* July 25, 1894, p. 8; "Negroes for Roslyn," *P-I,* July 27, 1894, p. 1; "The Negro Miners," *P-I,* July 28, 1894, p. 2; "Colored Contract Laborers," *Union,* Aug. 28, 1894, p. 3, quoting *Kittitas County Courier* and *Roslyn News,* Aug. 25, 1894; Boyle, *History of Railroad Strikes,* p. 46.

59 "Labor Day," *P-I*, Sept. 4, 1888, p. 3; "Labor Day," *P-I*, Aug. 31, 1890, p. 4; "Trade Unionism's Holiday," *Ledger*, Sept. 3, 1894, p. 4; "Labor's Grand Jubilee," *Chronicle*, Sept. 3, 1894, p. 3; "Labor Takes a Holiday," *Spokesman-Review*, Sept. 3, 1894, p. 1; "Spokane Labor in Line," *Spokesman-Review*, Sept. 4, 1894, p. 3; "Progress of the Colored Race," *Ledger*, Sept. 23, 1894, p. 8.

60 Young, H.C., "Words of Warning: The Battle Is On, No Compromise with the Gold Bug Plutocracy," *The Champion*, Sept. 2, 1893, p. 1; "A Wild Goose Chase," *The Eye*, May 17, 1894, p. 4; "The West and Silver," *P-I*, July 25, 1895, p. 4, from *United States Investor;* Beard, "The Historical Approach to the New Deal," p. 13; "The Populists," *Victoria Colonist*, Aug. 12, 1896, p. 4; "The Busted Community," *Weekly Bellingham Bay Express*, Oct. 7, 1893, p. 2; editorial, *News*, April 6, 1897, p. 2; "Visscher Scores Republicans," *Telegraph*, Nov. 2, 1894, p. 3; editorial, *The Eye*, Sept. 27, 1894, p. 4; "Mrs. Hobart and 'Unemployed'," *Ledger*, Aug. 7, 1893, p. 5; "The Duty of the Hour," *Seattle Times*, Nov. 23, 1895, p. 4; "Blaineites Burn Bonds," *Ledger*, Feb. 21, 1894, p. 1; "Taking All in Sight," *P-I*, Jan. 13, 1896, p. 2; People's Party, Omaha Platform, 1892, financial plank, item 2; "Not a National Party," *Chronicle*, Oct. 12, 1894, p. 2; "The Judgment Day," *Union*, Jan. 18, 1894, p. 4; "Present Issues," *Reveille*, Sept. 1, 1893, p. 2; "The Doctrines of Populism," *Union*, May 11, 1894 p. 2; editorial, *Yakima Herald*, May 25, 1893, p. 2; "There Must Be a Standard," *Telegraph*, Aug. 5, 1893, p. 4.

61 "True Americanism," *Seattle Times*, Jan. 10, 1896, p. 4; "Pennoyer Opens the Campaign," *P-I*, April 29, 1894, p. 4; "Should Be Impeached," *Ledger*, May 19, 1893, p. 1; "Pennoyer's Consistency," *Ledger*, July 25, 1893, p. 4; "Oregon's Surprising Governor," *Ledger*, July 26, 1893, p. 4; "Inflexible Pennoyer," *Ledger*, Oct. 10, 1893, p. 2; "Pennoyer Is Pilloried," *Ledger*, Nov. 6, 1893, p. 1; "The Pennoyer of Illinois," *P-I*, June 28, 1893, p. 4; "Turmoil in Denver," *P-I*, March 16, 1894, p. 1; "The Mistake of Gov. Waite," *P-I*, March 17, 1894, p. 4; "A Bitter Lesson," *P-I*, March 22, 1894, p. 4; "The Everett Election," *P-I*, April 29, 1893, p. 1; "The Populists Carry Port Angeles," *P-I*, Dec. 7, 1893, p. 2; "Who Is Orr-r-r-r-r," *Union*, April 4, 1894, p. 1; "Belt Is Mayor," *Chronicle*, May 2, 1894, p. 1; "A Striking Result," *Oregonian*, June 6, 1894, p. 4; "The Issue Was Pennoyer," *Oregonian*, June 9, 1894, p. 4.

62 "Kidnapped," *Chronicle*, July 30, 1894, p. 1; "Kidnapped and Murdered," *Spokesman-Review*, July 31, 1894, p. 1; "May Be Alive," "Each Blow Drew Blood," "He Had Bitter Enemies" and "The Gloystein Outrage," *Chronicle*, July 31, 1894, pp. 1, 2; "The Gloystein Mystery" and "Reward of $1,000 Offered," *Spokesman-Review*, Aug. 1, 1894, pp. 2, 3; "Is Gloystein in Hiding" and "Cut Down the Reward," *Chronicle*, Aug. 4, 1894, p. 3; "Remember Your Oath," *Spokesman-Review*, Aug. 11, 1894, p. 3; "Did Populists Do It?" *P-I*, July 31, 1894, p. 1; "The Populist Ku Klux," *P-I*, Aug. 6, 1894, p. 1; "The Silver Ku-Klux," *P-I*, Aug. 8, 1894, p.

1; "The Gloystein Murder," *P-I*, Aug. 11, 1894, p. 1; "The Populist Ku Klux," *P-I*, Aug. 3, 1894, p. 4; "Editorial Expressions," *Telegraph*, Sept. 7, 1894, p. 4, quoting the *Colfax Advocate;* "The Gloystein Mystery," *P-I*, Aug. 13, 1894, p. 4, quoting *Ballard Searchlight;* "Editorial Expressions," *Telegraph*, Aug. 25, 1894, p. 4, quoting *Vancouver Register;* "Populism Leads to Anarchy," *P-I*, Aug. 11, 1894, p. 4; "Gloystein Is Not Dead," *Spokesman-Review*, Sept. 24, 1894, p. 1; "Gloystein Was Scared," *Chronicle*, Sept. 24, 1894, p. 3; "Gloystein's Story," *Spokesman-Review*, Dec. 23, 1894, p. 1; "Hark, From the Tomb!" *Telegraph*, Sept. 24, 1894, p. 1; "We Told You So," *The Eye*, Sept. 27, 1894, p. 2; "Gloystein Not Dead," *P-I*, Sept. 24, 1894, p. 3.

63   "Enough of Populism," *Everett Herald*, Oct. 25, 1894, p. 2; "The Fruits of Populism," *Spokesman-Review*, Nov. 3, 1894, p. 1; "Silver at 16 to One," *Spokesman-Review*, Sept. 20, 1894, p. 1; "In the State of Washington," *Oregonian*, Oct. 13, 1894, p. 4; editorial, *Reveille*, Nov. 9, 1894, p. 2; "The New Legislature," *Post-Intelligencer*, Nov. 22, 1894, p. 4; "Look Over the List," *Weekly Spokesman-Review*, Jan. 17, 1895, p. 8; "A Blank Cartridge," *Ledger*, Aug. 26, 1894, p. 4; "How Taylor Flayed Rogers," *Ledger*, Oct. 18, 1894, p. 2; "Local Politics," *Ledger*, Oct. 15, 1894, p. 5.

64   "Why Old Town Is Not Tacoma," *Ledger*, March 3, 1895, p. 9; "C.P. Ferry Gives Advice," *Ledger*, March 30, 1895, p. 2; "The Seattle Idea," *Ledger*, April 15, 1895, p. 4; "Pulling Together," *Ledger*, April 5, 1895, p. 4; "They Hate to Pay," *P-I*, Aug. 5, 1895, p. 4.

65   "Bank Receiver Sale," *News*, July 21, 1897, p. 4; Clary to Eckels, Oct. 12, 1893, *Port Townsend National Bank*, File 250, Box 491, *National Bank Receivership Records;* "Cadwell Tells His Story," *Ledger*, May 14, 1894, p. 5; "Peculiar Banking Methods," *Ledger*, May 18, 1894, p. 2; Blanchard to Eckels, Feb. 1, 1894, *First National Bank of Whatcom*, File 211, Box 426, *National Bank Receivership Records;* "A Relic Come to Light," *Townsend Leader*, Jan. 13, 1894, p. 1; "Bank Officers Acquitted," *Ledger*, Aug. 17, 1894, p. 4; "Now He Pleads Guilty," *Ledger*, Sept. 22, 1893, p. 3; "Dusinberre Sentenced," *Ledger*, Sept. 24, 1893, p. 3; "Warden Coblentz's Life," *Reveille*, weekly ed., Dec. 14, 1894, p. 2; Cameron to McGraw, Dec. 13, 1894; Parker to McGraw, April 22, 1895; Reynolds to McGraw, May 14, 1895; Morton to McGraw, May 23, 1895, and Pardon of Samuel Dusinberre, June 13, 1895, all in File 175, *McGraw Papers;* "Snap Shots at Yakima," *Yakima Herald*, May 28, 1896, p. 3; *Proceedings of Engineers Society of Western Pennsylvania*, Vol. 18, No. 5, June 1902; "Samuel B. Dusinberre," *Automobile Trade Journal*, Vol. 23, No. 11, May 1, 1919, p. 213.

66   Tate, "Columbia City — Thumbnail History," *www.historylink.org*, essay 3327; "A Wildcat Scheme," *P-I*, March 30, 1895, p. 5; "Cloud on the Title," *P-I*, Feb. 17, 1895, p. 5; "Report by the Expert," *Walla Walla Statesman*, Sept. 1, 1894, p. *1;* Stine to Edmiston, March 15, 1893, Box 2, Letterbook 3, and Mills to Edmiston, Aug. 29, 1893, Box 5, Letterbook 14, *Walla Walla Savings Bank Papers*; "Receiver for Security Savings," *Telegraph*, Dec. 12, 1893, p. 5; "Closes Its Doors," *Walla Walla Statesman*, Dec. 11, 1893, p. 2; "A Big Overdraft," *Ledger*, Jan. 16, 1894, p. 8; "The Edmiston Overdraft," *P-I*, Feb. 25, 1894, p. 7; "Edmiston to Be Tried," *P-I, Feb. 22, 1894, p. 1;* "Notes of the Trial," *Walla Walla Statesman*, April 16, 1894, p. 3; "Non-Suit Denied," *Walla Walla Statesman*, April 17, 1894, p. 3; declaration of J.L. Sharpstein, case file 375, Washington State Archives, Ellensburg; death notice, *Walla Walla Statesman*, April 14, 1894, p. 3; "Edmiston in Peril," *Walla Walla Statesman*, April 23, 1894, p. 3; "The Edmiston Shooting," *Walla Walla Statesman*, April 24, 1894, p. 3; "Five Erring Shots," *Walla Walla Union*, undated, from Edmiston file, State Archives, Ellensburg; "The Line Is Drawn," *Walla Walla Statesman*, April 24, 1894, p. 3; "Mr. Tobin in Tacoma," *P-I*, May 4, 1894, p. 3; "In the Toils of Law," *Yakima Herald*, Feb. 14, 1895, p. 3; "The Edmiston Trial," *P-I*, Feb. 14, 1895, p. 2; "The Edmiston Trial," *P-I*, Feb. 15, 1895, p.1; "Half a Victory," *Chronicle*, Feb. 16, 1895, p. 1; "Close of the Edmiston Bank Cases" and editorial, *Yakima Herald*, Feb. 21, 1895, p. 2; "Edmiston Convicted," *P-I*, June 9, 1895, p. 1; "Edmiston Surprised," *Yakima Herald*, June 13, 1895, p. 2; affidavit of H.J. Snively, June 12, 1895, case file 376, and complaint, *State v. Edmiston*, July 8, 1896, case file 438, State Archives, Ellensburg; Smith to Hay, April 25, Sept. 19, Oct. 14 and Nov. 4, 1910, and Feb. 1, 1911; Tobin to Hay, Feb. 14, 1911; and pardon of Edmiston, Jan. 28, 1911; all in Pardon 940, *Governor's Office, Clemency and Pardon Case Files*, Vol. 61.5 c.f., Washington State Archives, Olympia. "Edmiston, Former Banker, Wins Governor's Pardon," *Spokesman-Review*, Feb. 1, 1911, p. 1.

67   The cashiers charged under the law forbidding a failing bank from taking deposits were A.F. Peters of the Bank of Everett, Charles Atkins of the First National Bank of Whatcom, E.H. Wheeler of the Blaine State Bank, Horace Cutter of the First National Bank of Spokane, Earnest Bickford of Frank Hense Co., Centralia, and A.L. Denio of the First National Bank of South Bend. The bank presidents were J.K. Edmiston of Walla Walla Savings Bank, Frank Hense of Frank Hense Co., Centralia, and W.L. Thompson of the Bank of Sumner. Sources for this section: "Merchants Bank Frauds," *Union*, March 2, 1894, p. 1; "Wasted Sympathy," *Union*, Jan. 28, 1894, p. 2; "Won't Get a Cent," *Union*, Jan. 14, 1894, p. 1; "Unloaded Real Estate," *Union*, Feb. 4, 1894, p. 1; "Four Are Indicted," *Ledger*, March 2, 1894, p. 5; "Bank Officers Acquitted," *Ledger*, Aug. 16, 1894, p. 3; "Bank Officers Free," *Union*, Aug. 16, 1894, p. 2; "An Information Filed," *Everett Times*, May 9, 1894, p. 4; "Peninsular Points," *Everett Herald*, June 21, 1894, p. 1; "Trying Cashier Atkins," *P-I*, Dec. 13, 1894, p. 5; "Atkins Goes Free," *P-I*, Dec. 22, 1894, p. 5; "He Has Skipped," *Chronicle*, July 12, 1894, p. 1; "Why He Crossed the Line,"

Spokesman-Review, July 13, 1894, p. 1; "Hogan After Cutter," *Spokesman-Review*, July 26, 1894, p. 3; "The Cloud Lifted," *Spokesman-Review*, Nov. 13, 1894, p. 1; "County Books to Be Experted," *South Bend Journal*, Aug. 6, 1897, p. 1; "The Reason Why," *South Bend Journal*, Dec. 17, 1897, p. 4; "Two Bankers Arrested," *Ledger*, Sept. 30, 1894, p. 1; "Hense Dismissed," *Oregonian*, Oct. 6, 1894, p. 3; "Non-Suit in Wheeler Case," *P-I*, May 30, 1896, p. 2; "Banker Thompson's Trial," *P-I*, Oct. 11, 1898, p. 3; "W.L. Thompson Not Guilty," *P-I*, Oct. 19, 1898, p. 3; "City Brevities," *South Bend Journal*, July 21, 1893, p. 3; "Pacific County Republicans," *P-I*, Sept. 4, 1894, p. 4; "Populists Pop," *South Bend Journal*, Sept. 14, 1894, p. 3; "A Missing Banker," *Sacramento Record-Union*, Sept. 26, 1894, p. 6; "A New Call," *South Bend Journal*, Oct. 5, 1894, p. 1; "Morrison Again," *South Bend Journal*, Oct. 12, 1894, p. 1; "Banker Morrison's Flight," *P-I*, Oct. 4, 1894, p. 2; "Banker Morrison Returning," *P-I*, Oct. 9, 1894, p. 2; "Morrison Coming Home," *Oregonian*, Oct. 10, 1894, p. 3; "Morrison Turns Up," *P-I*, Oct. 13, 1894, p. 1; "In Pacific County," *Oregonian*, Oct. 13, 1896, p. 3; "City Brevities," *South Bend Journal*, Dec. 7, 1894, p. 3.

68   "Snipes & Co. Suspend," *Ellensburgh Capital*, June 15, 1893, p. 3; "Snipes' Indebtedness," *Ellensburgh Capital*, Aug. 10, 1893, p. 3; "Trustees Named," *Ellensburgh Capital*, Aug. 24, 1893, p. 3; "Snipes' Deed of Trust," *Ellensburgh Capital*, Sept. 28, 1893, p. 3; "Ben E. Snipes' Affairs," *P-I*, Nov. 20, 1893, p. 1; "The Roslyn Bank Failure," *P-I*, Nov. 21, 1893, p. 1; "Snipes Affair," *Ellensburgh Capital*, Nov. 23, 1893, p. 3; "Suit Against Ben E. Snipes," *P-I*, Nov. 30, 1893, p. 2; "Dr. Power Appointed Receiver," *Ellensburgh Capital*, Dec. 14, 1893, p. 3; "The Affairs of Snipes," *Ellensburgh Capital*, March 22, 1894, p. 3; "Last Snipes Dividend," *Ellensburg Capital*, Sept. 12, 1903, p. 3, though Henderson, *An Illustrated History*, p. 261, has 9.55 cents; editorial and "Closed Their Doors," *Oregonian*, July 28, 1893, pp. 4, 8; "Talk of the State," *Weekly Spokesman-Review*, July 4, 1895, p. 4; "Oregon National," *Oregonian*, Sept. 10, 1893, p. 12; "They Are Indicted" and "Care of Public Money," *Oregonian*, Dec. 9, 1893, pp. 1, 4; *Comptroller's Report, 1904*, Vol. 1, p. 353.

69   Stagge to Eckels, Nov. 27, 1893, *First National Bank of Spokane*, File 257, Box 506, *National Bank Receivership Records*; "Five Republicans, Two Democrats," *Townsend Leader*, Oct. 6, 1893, p. 1; "Republican Bank Receiver," *Telegraph*, Nov. 26, 1893, p. 1; "Makes Eckels Sick," *P-I*, Dec. 18, 1893, p. 2; "Served at Salem," *Oregonian*, Jan. 12, 1894, p. 8; "Led a Dual Life," *Ledger*, Jan. 12, 1894, p. 1; "In the Northwest: Career of Lionel Stagge Gets Further Ventilation" and "The Case of Lionel Stagge," *Review*, Jan. 13, 1894, pp. 1, 2; "Lionel Stagge," *News*, Jan. 12, 1894, p. 2; "Mr. Eckels' Personal Selection" and "Stagge Has Friends," *Ledger*, Jan. 13, 1894, pp. 4, 8; "Had Many Aliases" and "The Case of Lionel Stagge," *Ledger*, Jan. 15, 1894, pp. 1, 4; 1880 Census, Oxford Precinct, Oneida County, Idaho, Page 49, Supervisor's Dist. 1, Enumeration Dist. 25, from *heritagequest.com*; "Wednesday, Dec. 16," *Eugene City Guard*, Dec. 16, 1891, p. 5; "Tuesday, Dec. 22," *Eugene City Guard*, Dec. 26, 1891, p. 5; "Music Department Recital," *Eugene City*

ENDNOTES

Guard, Jan. 18, 1890, p. 5; "State University," *Eugene City Guard,* March 1, 1890, p. 5; "Commencement Week," *Eugene City Guard,* June 20, 1891, p. 1; "The Most Popular," *Eugene City Guard,* Jan. 3, 1891, p. 5; Mitchell to Eckels, April 5, 1894, *Oregon National Bank,* File 259, Box 513, Item 79, *National Bank Receivership Records;* "The Case of Stagge," *Oregonian,* Jan. 21, 1894, p. 1; "Stagge-Waterhouse," *Eugene City Guard,* Jan. 20, 1894, p. 6; "A Referee in Oregon," *Oregonian,* March 13, 1894, p. 1; "Why Mr. Stagge Was Removed," *P-I,* April 16, 1894, p. 1; "Too Much Hard Luck," *Washington Post,* March 16, 1903, p. 2; "Lionel Stagge in Jail," *Oregonian,* March 17, 1903, p. 14; "Oregon at the Capital," *Oregonian,* March 19, 1903, p. 2; "Tries New Scheme," *Oregonian,* Dec. 15, 1906, p. 4; "Lionel Stagge Is Again in Trouble," *Eugene Register-Guard,* Jan. 2, 1907, p. 3; "Fuller Is Selling Stock Again," *Financial World,* June 3, 1916, p. 33; "Bogus Lord Held Here as Swindler of Prominent Men," *Philadelphia Inquirer,* Feb. 23, 1922, p. 1; "Police Say Stagg Is One of Big Gang," *Philadelphia Inquirer,* Feb. 24, 1922, p. 3; " 'Sir' Lionel Will Die Without Drug, He Says," *Philadelphia Inquirer,* Feb. 26, 1922, p. 1; "Swindler Trapped in Banker's Office," *New York Times,* June 23, 1933, p. 7; "Swindler Gets Three Years," *New York Times,* July 6, 1933, p. 8.

70   "Washington Bank Open," *Chronicle,* July 6, 1893, p. 3; "Bank Resumes," *Everett Herald,* Oct. 26, 1893, p. 1; "Tacoma National Bank's Resumption," *P-I,* Dec. 1, 1893, p. 2; "The Tacoma National Bank Reopens," *P-I,* Dec. 5, 1893, p. 3; "A Plan to Resume," *Port Angeles Democrat-Leader,* Aug. 11, 1893, p. 8; "Depositors' Meeting," *Port Angeles Democrat-Leader,* Dec. 22, 1893, p. 1; Eldredge to Eckels, March 28, 1894, Item 32; Eldredge to Eckels, Aug. 7, 1894, Item 66; and petition of depositors to Eckels, Item 77, *Columbia National Bank,* File 212, Box 427, *National Bank Receivership Records;* "The Columbia National Bank," *P-I,* May 18, 1894, p. 3; *Comptroller's Report, 1904,* Vol. 1, p. 351; editorial, *Reveille,* Nov. 28, 1894, p. 2; "The Directors Got the Money," *P-I,* Dec. 22, 1893, p. 1; "The Port Angeles Bank," *P-I,* Dec. 24, 1893, p. 1; "Red Letter Day," *Port Angeles Democrat-Leader,* April 27, 1894, p. 1; "Traders Bank Open," *Ledger,* Jan. 25, 1894, p. 1; "Traders Bank Open Again," *Ledger,* Jan. 26, 1894, p. 5; "There's Only One Closed," *Telegraph,* Jan. 26, 1894, p. 1; "Traders Bank is Liquidated," *Pacific Banker and Investor,* Vol. 2, No. 3, May 1894; *Comptroller's Report, 1904,* Vol. I, pp. 336, 338.

71   Marquis and Smith, "Double Liability for Bank Stock," *The American Economic Review,* Vol. 27, No. 3, Sept. 1937, pp. 497, 499, 500; *Comptroller's Report, 1904,* Vol. 1, pp. 350-355; "Whatcom's Bank Troubles," *P-I,* May 19, 1895, p. 1; "Bank Receiver Sale," *News,* July 21, 1897, p. 4; *Comptroller's Report, 1904,* Vol. 1, p. 349; Blanchard to Eckels, June 21, 1894, *First National Bank of Whatcom,* File 211, Box 426; Eldredge to Eckels, March 5, 1894, Wingate to Eckels, June 20, 1894, *Merchants National Bank of Tacoma,* File 209, *National Bank Receivership Records;* "Last Chance Mine," *Weekly Spokesman-Review,* Sept. 12, 1895, p. 2; "F. Lewis Clark, Spokane Millionaire," *Spokesman-Review,* Jan. 18, 1914, p. 1; *Comptroller's Report, 1903,* Vol. I, p. 351.

285

72   Harrison to Burke, July 17, 1894, and Burke's undated reply, Box 7/48, Burke to Sawyer, Oct. 10, 1894, Box 21/11, all from *Burke Papers*, Acc. 143-002, Special Collections, University of Washington; Nesbit, *'He Built Seattle,'* pp. 251-266. *En Arcadie* was bought by the French government and now hangs in the Musée d'Orsay in Paris.

73   Cole to Morse, Jan. 16, 1894, File 3; Williams to Morse, Jan. 23, 1894, File 9; Paden to Morse, Jan. 8, 1894, File 9; Langdon to Morse, March 6, 1894, File 7; Hutchcroft to Morse, April 21, 1894, File 6; Cline to Morse, May 12, 1894, File 3; Branin to Morse, June 18, 1894, File 2, all in *Letters to R.I Morse*, Box 2, *Morse Hardware Co. Papers*, Washington State Archives, Bellingham.

74   Baker to Grube, Dec. 28, 1892, p. 37; Baker to Grube, June 15, 1893, p. 99; Baker to Freygang, Aug. 29, 1893, p. 125; Baker to Grube, Aug. 29, 1893, p. 126; Baker to Freygang, Dec. 26, 1893, p. 159; Baker to Orchard, Oct. 14, 1893, p. 137; Baker to Orchard, Dec. 27, 1893, p. 162; Baker to Freygang, Dec. 27, 1893, p. 163; Baker to Freygang, June 25, 1894, p. 205; Baker to Freygang, Oct 19, 1895, p. 382, all from Letterbook 3, Box 50, *Baker Family Papers*, Whitman College, Walla Walla; L. Walker, "The Manufacturing Idea," *Union*, Sept. 16, 1894, p. 3.

75   "Receiver in Charge," *Ledger*, March 7, 1894, p. 6; "A Big Boomer Fails," *P-I*, March 7, 1894, p. 8; "Another Report," *News*, May 24, 1894, p. 3; "The Gilman Miners," *P-I*, March 18, 1894, p. 5; "A Heavy Mortgage," *P-I*, June 13, 1894, p. 5; "For the Hunt Lines," *P-I*, Aug. 25, 1894, p. 5; "Shelton's Railroad in Trouble," *Ledger*, April 21, 1894, p. 3; "C.B. Hurley Is Now Receiver," *Ledger*, May 8, 1894, p. 5; "Seizing the Stock," *P-I*, Sept. 1, 1894, p. 1; "Going Out of Business," *Ledger*, Oct. 9, 1894, p. 5; "Result of the Shingle War," *P-I*, Nov. 18, 1894, p. 1; "Receiver for the Tacoma Roads," *P-I*, Dec. 25, 1894, p. 1; "Request for a Receiver," *Telegraph*, Aug. 25, 1894, p. 8; "A Receiver Refused," *P-I*, Dec. 9, 1894, p. 5; "The Appointment of Receivers," *Ledger*, July 21, 1894, p. 2.

76   "A Funeral for 90 Cents," *Review*, Feb. 16, 1894, p. 4; "Beneficial to Portland," *Oregonian*, Nov. 19, 1893, p. 12; "Butchers," *News*, Nov. 27, 1893, p. 1; "Flour Is Cheap," *Chronicle*, Jan. 2, 1894, p. 1; "Local Brevities," *Review*, Jan. 29, 1894, p. 2; "Will Double Its Capacity," *Chronicle*, Jan. 29, 1894, p. 3; "Food at the Cost of Air," *Review*, Feb. 12, 1894, p. 8; no headline, *Shelton Weekly Tribune*, April 7, 1894, p. 3; "Tacoma Impurity," *News*, Dec. 7, 1894, p. 1.

77   "A Reign of Folly," *Ledger*, July 3, 1894, p. 4; "Basis of a New Prosperity," *Oregonian*, Feb. 8, 1894, p. 4; "We Can, After All," *Oregonian*, Aug. 28, 1894, p. 4; Cow Butter Store ads in the *Chronicle*, Nov. 7, 1893, p. 1, the *Everett Herald*, Oct. 11, 1894, p. 3 and the *News*, April 13, 1894, p. 3; "Killing the Poor Cows," *Chronicle*, March 7, 1894, p. 4; editorial, *Everett Herald*, Aug. 23, 1894, p. 2; "Our

Future Butter Supply," *Oregonian*, April 16, 1894, p. 2, quoting *West Coast Trade*; editorial, *Everett Herald*, Aug. 23, 1894, p. 2; "Butter Production Increase," *P-I*, Oct. 21, 1895, p. 1; "Feed the Wheat to Hogs," *Chronicle*, Oct. 15, 1894, p. 4; "Keeps Right Ahead," *Ledger*, April 19, 1894, p. 3; "To Make Glass in Tacoma," *Ledger*, Aug. 12, 1894, p. 2; "Will Build Here," *News*, Dec. 26, 1894, p. 1; "Fresh Fish for the East," *Reveille*, Jan. 3, 1894, p. 1; "Shipping Fresh Fish," *Everett Herald*, April 26, 1894, p. 1; "Our Fruit to the Front," *Spokesman-Review*, Sept. 3, 1894, p. 3; "He Has the Last Laugh," *Chronicle*, Aug. 27, 1894, p. 3; editorial, *Chronicle*, Oct. 25, 1894, p. 2; "Spokane Flour to China," *Review*, May 17, 1894, p. 3; "Spokane as a Milling Center," *Chronicle*, Aug 11, 1894, p. 2; "Shingle Mills Hum Again," *P-I*, Aug. 3, 1894, p. 3; "Heavy Shipments Continue," *Ledger*, Aug. 29, 1894, p. 3; "The Lumber and Shingle Trade," *P-I*, Nov. 15, 1894, p. 8; "Demand for Lumber," *P-I*, Sept. 22, 1894, p. 2; "Lumber for Honolulu," *Port Angeles Democrat-Leader*, July 30, 1894, p. 1; "New Industrial Epoch," *Port Angeles Democrat-Leader*, Nov. 9, 1894, p. 1; "Sending Red Cedar Abroad," *P-I*, Nov. 14, 1894, p. 1, quoting *Puget Sound Lumberman*; "Rolling Mill Looming Up," *Ledger*, Oct. 27, 1894, p. 3; "Rolling Mill Starts Up," *Ledger*, April 25, 1895, p. 3; "A New Alaska Line," *P-I*, Nov. 16, 1894, p. 4; "Satisfactory Work," *Everett Times*, Oct. 3, 1894, p. 1; Zoss, *McDougall's Great Lakes Whalebacks*, pp. 8-9; "God Speed the 'City of Everett'," *Everett Herald*, Oct. 25, 1894, p. 1; editorial, "Greatest Day in Our History" and "Everett's Record," *Everett Times*, Oct. 24, 1894, pp. 1, 2.

78　　　　"Business Is Improving," *Ledger*, Sept. 14, 1894, p. 4; "Editorial Expressions," *Telegraph*, Aug. 28, 1894, p. 4, quoting the *Blaine Journal*; "Signs of Good Times," *Chronicle*, Aug. 31, 1894, p. 2; "Our Irrigation Bonds Sold," *Ellensburgh Capital*, June 7, 1894, p. 3; "Now For Better Times" and "The Ditch," *Ellensburg* (new spelling) *Capital*, Aug. 23, 1894, pp. 2, 3; "The Ditch Matter," *Ellensburg Capital*, Nov. 15, 1894, p. 3; "Both Sides of the Story," *Wenatchee Advance*, Nov. 17, 1894, p. 1; "Libeling the State," *Ledger*, Nov. 21, 1894, p. 4; "The Ditchmen's Distress," *P-I*, Nov. 26, 1894, p. 4; "On to Olympia," *Oregonian*, Dec. 4, 1894, p. 3; "General News," *Ellensburg Dawn*, Dec. 8, 1894, p. 2; "Still They Come," *News*, Dec. 14, 1894, p. 4; "Horses Dirt Cheap," *P-I*, Nov. 8, 1894, p. 8, quoting the *Oregonian*; "Hop Pickers' Wages," *P-I*, Aug. 12, 1894, p. 7; "Getting Ready to Pick Hops," *Ledger*, Aug. 23, 1894, p. 3; "Hops and Hop Pickers," *Ledger*, Sept. 16, 1894, p. 6; "Indians as Hop Pickers," *Ledger*, Oct. 28, 1894, p. 9; "How Grain Is Grown," *P-I*, Jan. 3, 1895, p. 7; "Wheat 19 Cents," *P-I*, Oct. 8, 1894, p. 4, quoting the *Garfield Enterprise*, Sept. 28, 1894; "The Street Light Question," *P-I*, Oct. 17, 1894, p. 5; "The Contract Let," *P-I*, Nov. 9, 1894, p. 8; "The Future of Whatcom," *P-I*, Jan. 3, 1895, p. 3; "Populists Don't Want School," *P-I*, Aug. 29, 1894, p. 8; "The News," *P-I*, June 14, 1894, p. 2; "The City's New Official Paper," *Ledger*, Oct. 5, 1894, p. 5; "Receiver for the Union," *Ledger*, Oct. 20, 1894, p. 2; "Woes of the 'Onion' Related," *Ledger*, Oct. 24, 1894, p. 3; "Bellingham Bay News," *P-I*, Aug. 5, 1894, p. 2; "An Important Transfer," *P-I*, Dec. 8, 1894, p. 4; editorial, *News*, Dec.

13, 1894, p. 2; "Press of the State," *Seattle Times*, Aug. 7, 1895, p. 2; E.L. Reber, "How a Newspaper Died," *P-I*, Nov. 28, 1897, p. 4; "Goes the Liquidation," *P-I*, Jan. 23, 1894, p. 5; "In the Hands of a Receiver," *Ledger*, May 12, 1894, p. 5; "Pulled Another One Over," *Ledger*, May 13, 1894, p. 5; "Two Bankers Arrested," *Ledger*, Sept. 30, 1894, p. 1; "News From Centralia," *Ledger*, Oct. 1, 1894, p. 3; "Closed Its Doors," *Chronicle*, Nov. 22, 1894, p. 1; "Browne National Liquidates," *Chronicle*, Nov. 23, 1894, p. 2; "Commercial Bank Closed," *Chronicle*, Dec. 28, 1894, p. 1; "Aberdeen Bank Shut," *P-I*, Nov. 27, 1894, p. 1; "The Tacoma National Bank," *Ledger*, Dec. 4, 1894, p. 4; "The Tacoma Bank Failure," *P-I*, Dec. 5, 1894, p. 4; "Wright's Reason," *News*, Dec. 19, 1894, p. 1; "President Blackwell Home," *Ledger*, Dec. 20, 1894, p. 4; "Water Bonds Not Good," *P-I*, Dec. 25, 1894, p. 1; Morgan, *Puget's Sound*, p. 277.

79   "Nearly 5,000 Received Aid," *P-I*, Jan. 23, 1895, p. 5; "The Old and New Years," *Ledger*, Jan. 1, 1895, p. 4.

80   "Land of Corn and Wine," *Chronicle*, Feb. 12, 1894, p. 4; "Arcadia of the Pacific," *Chronicle*, Feb. 20, 1894, p. 4; Lockley, *History of the Columbia River Valley*, Vol. II, pp. 246-247; "New Co-operative Scheme," *Oregonian*, March 4, 1894, p. 2; "Big Co-operative Company," *Chronicle*, March 14, 1894, p. 1; "Trying the Bellamy Plan," *Chronicle*, March 28, 1894, p. 4; surname spelled "Hunsecker" in *Chronicle* stories, "Hunsicker" in "White Salmon," *Hood River Glacier*, obituary, June 22, 1921, p. 5; "Hunsucker" in 1900 Census (Timber Valley, Klickitat, Wash.; Roll 1746; Page 4B; Enumeration District 0114), and "Hunsacker" in 1910 Census (Fruit Valley, Klickitat, Wash., Roll T624 1656; Page 14B; Enumeration District 0108), and on Daniel and Marietta's tombstone at West Klickitat District 01 Cemetery (found at www.findagrave.com); "All Are Like Brothers," *Chronicle*, May 19, 1894, p. 4; "This Town Needs a Name," *Chronicle*, June 13, 1894, p. 4; "Can't Pool Farms," *Chronicle*, June 27, 1894, p. 4; "One Gave It Up," *Chronicle*, July 16, 1894, p. 4; "It Broke Up the Colony," *Chronicle*, Aug. 28, 1894, p. 4; "Socialists and Co-ops," *Chronicle*, Dec. 7, 1894, p. 4; Henderson, *An Illustrated History*, pp. 146-147, 517-518; "Summer Resorts," *Klickitat Heritage*, Klickitat County Historical Society, May 1975, pp. 1-2; *Jewett Home Sanitarium for Electronic Treatment and Other Modalities*, articles of incorporation, Washington State Archives, Ellensburg.

81   Arntzen, "Ocosta-by-the-Sea"; ad for Ocosta Land Co., *Ledger*, May 1, 1891, p. 2; "The City of Ocosta," *Oregonian*, Jan. 2, 1893, p. 4; "Very High Tides," *Oregonian*, Jan. 15, 1895, p. 3; Lukoff, *Seattle Then and Now*, photograph, p. 50; Weinstein, *Grays Harbor*, p. 24; Macdonald, *Fifty Years of Freethought*, p. 29; editorial, *Aberdeen Herald*, Dec. 17, 1891, p. 4; editorial, *Aberdeen Herald*, Nov. 5, 1891, p. 4; "Ocosta-in-the-Sea," *Aberdeen Herald*, Dec. 10, 1891, p. 4; "What Has the Moon Got to Do With It?" *Aberdeen Herald*, Sept. 24, 1891, p. 8; "Must Operate Trains," *Seattle Times*, Feb. 10, 1911, p. 2; Bogar, "Ocosta-by-the Sea," *The Pacific Northwest*

ENDNOTES

Quarterly, January 1963; "The Railroad Situation," *Aberdeen Herald,* Sept. 24, 1891, p. 4; "Facts for Conclusions," *Aberdeen Herald,* Dec. 3, 1891, p. 4; "Meeting Saturday Night," *Aberdeen Herald,* April 28, 1892, p. 1; "The Railroad Again," *Aberdeen Herald,* Sept. 8, 1892, p. 2; editorial and "Railroad Meeting," *Aberdeen Herald,* Feb. 9, 1893, pp. 2, 3; "Railroad Meeting," *Aberdeen Herald,* July 6, 1893, p. 3; "A Story of the Times," *Oregonian,* July 11, 1893, p. 8; "Another Opportunity," *Aberdeen Herald,* July 5, 1894, p. 1; Van Sycle, *The River Pioneers,* p. 210; "Mass Meeting Tonight," *Aberdeen Herald,* Sept. 6, 1894, p. 3; "At Work on the Road," *Aberdeen Herald,* Sept. 13, 1894, p. 2; "Railroad, Railroad!" *Aberdeen Herald,* Nov. 15, 1894, p. 3; "The Railroad," *Aberdeen Herald,* Nov. 29, 1894, p. 3; "Aberdeen's New Railroad," *Ledger,* Dec. 31, 1894, p. 3; "The First Train at Aberdeen," *P-I,* April 3, 1895, p. 1; "The First Train," *Aberdeen Herald,* April 4, 1895, p. 2; "The Abercorn's Rails," *P-I,* Sept. 14, 1895, p. 3; "Some Railroad Reminiscences," *Aberdeen Herald,* Oct. 19, 1911, p. 8; "Brief Mention, *Aberdeen Herald,* June 20, 1895, p. 2; "Big Hotel Adrift," *Aberdeen Herald,* Jan. 11, 1904, p. 1; Bogar, "Ocosta-by-the Sea," *The Pacific Northwest Quarterly,* January 1963.

82   Woodhouse, *Monte Cristo,* pp. 1-97, 151-152, 163-206; "Wayside Notes," *The Blade,* May 27, 1897, p. 2; "Monte Cristo Mines," *Everett Times,* Feb. 19, 1896, p. 1; "Growth of Everett," *Everett Times,* May 9, 1894, p. 1; "Clear the Road," *Everett Herald,* Dec. 28, 1893, p. 1; "Pushing Mines," *Everett Herald,* March 8, 1894, p. 1; "Silver Outlook," *Everett Herald,* May 17, 1894, p. 1; "Repairing Tram," *Everett Herald,* June 28, 1894, p. 1; "Steady Stream of Wealth," *Everett Times,* Dec. 5, 1894, p. 2, quoting the *P-I;* "Started for Home," *Everett Times,* Sept. 26, 1894, p. 1; "Everett Industries All Running," *P-I,* June 27, 1895, p. 5; "Rockefeller's Loss $1,500,000," *New York Sun,* Feb. 3, 1895, p. 8; "Monte Cristo All Right," *Everett Herald,* Feb. 21, 1895, p. 2; "A Liar at Large," *Everett Times,* Feb. 13, 1895, p. 1; "Another Mill," *Everett Herald,* March 14, 1895, p. 1; "The Concentrator," *Everett Herald,* April 11, 1895, p. 1; "Monte Cristo Road to Be Abandoned," *P-I,* Dec. 12, 1897, p. 1; "Damage to the Monte Cristo," *P-I,* Nov. 23, 1892, p. 1; "Abandoning Monte Cristo," *Ledger,* Dec. 13, 1897, p. 4; Woodhouse, *The Everett and Monte Cristo Railway,* pp. 72-73.

83   Smalley, "Memories of Schulze," *P-I,* Feb. 1, 1899, p. 5; Hunt, *Tacoma, Vol. II,* pp. 174-175; "Irrigation is King," *Ledger,* May 8, 1893, p. 3; "Tacoma Is Prospering," *Pacific Banker and Investor,* Vol. I, No. 1, March 1893, p. 34; Coulter, "The Victory of National Irrigation in the Yakima Valley, 1902-1906," *The Pacific Northwest Quarterly,* Vol. 42, No. 2, April 1951, pp. 99-102; "Thought Himself Ruined," *Ledger,* April 20, 1895, p. 2; editorial, *Yakima Herald,* April 18, 1895, p. 2; Charles Woodbury, "Social Life at Zillah," *Yakima Herald,* Feb. 16, 1893, p. 4, from *New York Evening Post;* "Career of Paul Schulze," *Ledger,* March 8, 1896, p. 9; Anderson to Schulze, April 3, 1893; McElroy to Schulze, July 5, 1893, Folder 2-20; Cowley to Schulze, Sept. 5, 1893, Folder 2-96; Foster to Schulze, July 24, 1893,

Folder 2-95; Thayer to Schulze, Feb. 21, March 2 and March 5, 1894, Folder 2-37, all in *Schulze Papers*, Vo244d; "Big Sale of Irrigation Bonds," *Yakima Herald*, June 22, 1893, p. 1, quoting the *News*; Allyn to Walker, Nov. 8, 1893, Box 55, and Allyn to Walker, June 13, 1894, Box 56, in *Ames Papers*; "Sunnyside Canal Bonds," *Yakima Herald*, June 14, 1894, p. 3; "The Local Maelstrom," *Yakima Herald*, July 19, 1894, p. 3; Allyn to Walker, Aug. 20, 1894, Box 56, *Ames Papers*; Shaubut to Schulze, Sept. 6, 1894, Folder 2-66, *Schulze Papers;* "Sub-Head Storyettes," *Yakima Herald*, Nov. 22, 1894, p. 3; "Shaubut in London," *P-I*, Jan. 21, 1895, p. 8; Booth to Schulze, Sept. 5, 1893, April 6, 1894, Aug. 31, 1894 and Sept. 4, 1894, Folder 1-26, and Brown to Schulze, Dec. 11, 1894, *Schulze Papers;* "Crushed by Its Debt," *P-I*, Jan. 3, 1895, p. 1; Hunt, *Tacoma*, pp. 174-175; "Schulze Studied Suicide," *Ledger*, April 14, 1895, p. 1; "Paul Schulze Is No More," *Yakima Herald*, April 18, 1895, p. 3; "Shortage Exceeds $100,000," *Ledger*, April 22, 1895, p. 3; "Will Auction His Effects," *Ledger*, May 15, 1895, p. 3; "Schulze's Personal Property," *P-I*, May 15, 1895, p. 2; "The Paul Schulze Defalcation," *Weekly Spokesman-Review*, May 23, 1895, p. 8; "Robbed a Blind Man," *P-I*, July 30, 1895, p. 1; "Paul F. Mohr's Wine," *P-I*, July 28, 1895, p. 1; "Paul Schulze's Bogus Drafts," *P-I*, March 26, 1896, p. 3.

84   "The Kirkland Ditch," *Review*, Aug. 26, 1892, p. 6; editorial, *Review*, Aug. 18, 1892, p. 6; "The Ditch," *Review*, Aug. 20, 1892, p. 6; "The Truth About That Canal," *Aberdeen Herald*, Sept. 8, 1892, p. 2; "A Mutual Dose," *Review*, Aug. 28, 1892, p. 6; "The Semple Scheme," *Telegraph*, July 21, 1893, p. 1; "Canal at the South," *P-I*, June 24, 1894, p. 7; map, *P-I*, July 12, 1894, p. 3; "The Semple Waterway," *Telegraph*, Aug. 8, 1894, p. 5; "The Money Ready," *P-I*, Oct. 29, 1894, p. 8; "Papers Are Signed," *P-I*, Jan. 10, 1895, p. 8; "The Ideal Harbor," *P-I*, Feb. 3, 1895, p. 8; "The South Canal Enterprise," *P-I*, Feb. 9, 1895, p. 4; "Encouraging Indications," *P-I*, March 18, 1895, p. 4; "All Are Of One Mind," *P-I*, March 26, 1895, p. 8; "The Old Spirit," *P-I*, March 29, 1895, p. 1; "The Goal Reached," *P-I*, May 10, 1895, p. 1; "Land for the Canal," *P-I*, Dec. 1, 1894, p. 8; Hynding, "Eugene Semple's Seattle Canal Scheme," *Pacific Northwest Quarterly*, Vol. 59, No. 2, April 1968, pp. 78-87.

85   When Times Will Improve," *Ledger*, Jan. 17, 1895, p. 4; "A Receiver Appointed," *Port Angeles Democrat-Leader*, Feb. 1, 1895, p. 1; "Whaleback Wins," *Everett Herald*, July 11, 1895, p. 1; Fahey, "When the Dutch Owned Spokane," in Stratton, *Spokane and the Inland Empire*, pp. 195-196, 202; "Happy New Year!" *News*, Jan. 1, 1895, p. 2.

86   Noyes, *Forty Years of American Finance*, pp. 234-242; Editorial, *Snohomish County Tribune*, March 1, 1895, p. 4; "Populists Carry Port Angeles," *P-I*, Dec. 7, 1893, p. 2; "Faithful Public Service," *Port Angeles Democrat-Leader*, Nov. 1, 1895, p. 2; "Our City Finances," *Everett Times*, May 23, 1894, p. 2; editorial, *Everett Herald*, March 28, 1895, p. 2; "The Mayor's Message," *Anacortes American*, Jan. 11, 1894,

p. 1; *State and City Supplement of the Commercial and Financial Chronicle,* April 11, 1896, p. 155; "Spokane's Cash Box," *Chronicle,* March 25, 1895, p. 3; "Tacoma's Giant Debt," *P-I,* July 25, 1895, p. 1; *Report of the Controller of the City of Tacoma,* 1897, p. 9; "What Populist Rule Does," *Townsend Leader,* Oct. 23, 1894, p. 1; "The Whatcom Warrant Case," *P-I,* March 22, 1895, p. 3; "The Fouts Warrant Case," editorial, and "Fouts and Attorney," *Bellingham Bay Reveille,* Feb. 22, 1895, pp. 1, 2; March 21, 1895, p. 1; "The Whatcom Warrant Case," *P-I,* March 22, 1895, p. 3; "Whatcom County Warrants," *P-I,* April 18, 1895, p. 1; "The Treasury Opened," *Bellingham Bay Reveille,* April 19, 1895, p. 7; "The Bonds Defeated," *P-I,* Feb. 11, 1894, p. 7; "The Debt Ratified," *P-I,* April 28, 1895, p. 8; "A Bid for Ballard Bonds," *P-I,* May 2, 1895, p. 8; "Pay Her Obligations!" *Everett Times,* June 18, 1895, p. 1; "Port Townsend Validates," *P-I,* June 24, 1895, p. 1; "Vancouver Will Pay," *Vancouver Independent,* Aug. 8, 1895, p. 2; "No Invalid Claims Paid," *Ledger,* Jan. 15, 1896, p. 5; "A Judge's Plain Talk," *Union,* May 22, 1895, p. 4; "No Repudiation," *Ledger,* Nov. 16, 1894, p. 4; "The Validation Questions," *Union,* June 9, 1895, p. 7; "One Proposition Carries," *Ledger,* June 27, 1895, p 3; "The East Looking Westward," *Ledger,* Aug. 1, 1895, p. 4; "Pierce County Sells Bonds," *P-I,* Aug. 16, 1895, p. 3; "The Union Bank Failure" and "The Suspended Bank," *Union,* June 30, 1897, pp. 2, 4; "The Union Savings Bank," *Union,* July 15, 1897, p. 4; *Bardsley v. Sternberg,* 18 Wash. 612.

87   State law is H.B. 297, described in "The Finished Work," *P-I,* March 15, 1895, p. 2; "Financial Record," *P-I,* Jan. 1, 1895, p. 38; Charles H. Baker to Eckels, Aug. 7 and Aug. 27, 1895, and Miller to Eckels, Sept. 13, 1895, in File 303, Box 607, Merchants National Bank, *National Bank Receivership Records;* "Had Deposit to Pay the Note," *P-I,* Oct. 5, 1895, p. 5; Miller's title is in *Annual Report for 1895,* Seattle Board of Health; "A Bank Quits Business," *P-I,* May 22, 1895, p. 2; "Merchants' National Bank," *P-I,* June 25, 1895, p. 5; "Officers in Danger," *P-I,* July 17, 1895, p. 5; "Merchants' National Bank," *P-I,* Sept. 13, 1895, p. 3; Baker to Eckels, May 28 and Nov. 18, 1896, and Feb. 13, 1897, in *National Bank Receivership Records;* "Merchants' National Bank," *P-I,* March 11, 1898, p. 8; "Baker After Mackintosh," *P-I,* April 1, 1898, p. 11; "Macintosh a Final Winner," *P-I,* July 25, 1899, p. 12; "An Old Sore" and "Into An Assassin's Hands," *Union,* Aug. 20, 1895, pp. 2, 4; "The City's Funds," *News,* Aug. 20, 1895, p. 2; "News of the Courthouse," *Union,* Aug. 23, 1895, p. 4; "The Busted Bunco Bank," *Union,* Sept. 8, 1895, p. 8; "A.R. Titlow Is Receiver," *Union,* Sept. 14, 1895, p. 4; "Debtors of the Tacoma Bank," *Ledger,* Sept. 15, 1895, p. 5; "Where the City Money Went," *Ledger,* Sept. 17, 1895, p. 3; "To Cancel Accounts," *News,* Oct. 15, 1895, p. 3; "The Oatmeal Mortgage," *P-I,* Feb. 29, 1896, p. 1; "Round Them Up," *Union,* Oct. 29, 1895, p. 2; "Boggs' Big Heart," *News,* Oct. 31, 1895, p. 2; "Boggs May Go Free," *Ledger,* April 23, 1897, p. 1; "He Knew Nothing of It," *Union,* Jan. 5, 1897, p. 2; "Three Banks Won't Pay," *Union,* Oct. 17, 1895, p. 4; "The Boggs Warrants," *P-I,* Oct. 21, 1895, p. 2; "The Bottom Is in Sight," *Union,* Oct. 26, 1895, p. 1; "Geo. W.

Boggs Is Acquitted," *Ledger*, Dec. 19, 1894, p. 3; "The Warrant Juggle," *P-I*, Oct. 16, 1895, p. 1; "A Tacoma Bank Fails" and "The Warrants Boggs Deposited," *P-I*, Oct. 17, 1895, p. 1; "The Banks of Tacoma," *P-I*, Oct. 18, 1895, p. 1; "Receiver in Charge," *News*, Oct. 22, 1895, p. 1; "A Receiver in Charge," *P-I*, Oct. 23, 1895, p. 1; "No Cash for Deposits," *Ledger*, Nov. 15, 1897, p. 3; "Columbia Bank Closed," *P-I*, Oct. 25, 1895, p. 1; "The Iron Is Hot. Strike!" *Union*, Oct. 26, 1895, p. 2; "Subscribers to Interest Fund" and "The Wreckers Answered," *Ledger*, Nov. 30, 1895, pp. 1, 4; "Tacoma's Credit Sustained," *Ledger*, Nov. 28, 1895, p. 1; "How Tacoma Loses Money," *Ledger*, Sept. 3, 1896, p. 5; "Allen Freed From Guilt," *Ledger*, May 8, 1896, p. 3; "Charges Dismissed," *News*, Jan. 9, 1897, p. 2; "George W. Boggs Sentenced," *Ledger*, Dec. 24, 1895, p. 3; "To Serve Sentence," *News*, Dec. 11, 1896, p. 4; "What Is to Be Done?" *News*, Oct. 22, 1895, p. 2.

88 Henderson, *An Illustrated History*, pp. 263-265; Baumgart, *Ellensburg's Tree of Justice*, p. 45; "Lynched by a Mob," *P-I*, Aug. 14, 1895, p. 1; "Double Murder, Double Lynching," *Ellensburg Capital*, Aug. 15, 1895, p. 3; "A Double Murder and a Double Lynching," *Ellensburg Localizer*, Aug. 17, 1895, p. 1; "Brutality of the Lynchers," *Ledger*, Aug. 19, 1895, p. 5; "Outside Opinion," *Ellensburg Capital*, Aug. 22, 1895, p. 2; "The Horrible Judge," *P-I*, Aug. 15, 1895, p. 4; "That Lynching," *Seattle Times*, Aug. 15, 1895, p. 4; editorial, *Yakima Herald*, Aug. 22, 1895, p. 3; "Judge Lynch's Mission," *Everett Herald*, Sept. 19, 1895, p. 2; "The Great Trial Ends," *Ellensburg Capital*, Sept. 26, 1895, p. 1. Surname is spelled "Kohlepp" by the *Capital*, the *P-I* and Baumgart. I spell it "Kohlhepp" following the *Localizer*, Henderson and a warranty deed for property Kohlhepp purchased Jan. 29, 1889.

89 "United for Charity," *P-I*, Nov. 27, 1895, p. 7; "Back to the Land," *P-I*, April 10, 1895, p. 3; "Pingree Plan for the Poor," *P-I*, April 13, 1895, p. 8; "Self-Help Succeeds," *P-I*, Sept. 12, 1895, p. 3; "Local Pingree People," *P-I*, Jan. 4, 1898, p. 3.

90 "Proofs of Better Times," *Weekly Spokesman-Review*, April 18, 1895, p. 4; "New Company Incorporates," *Ledger*, Feb. 1, 1895, p. 2; "Cutting Rates to Alaska," *P-I*, Aug. 11, 1895, p. 5; "Alaska Rate Way Down," *P-I*, Sept. 11, 1895, p. 3; "Greater Spokane," *Chronicle*, May 13, 1895, p. 4; Durham, *Spokane, Vol. I*, p. 473; "Biggest in the West," *Ledger*, July 14, 1895, p. 12; "Ship Owners' Combination," *Ledger*, May 6, 1895, p. 2; "Three New Ships Secured" and "Our Growing Commerce," *Ledger*, May 1, 1895, pp. 3, 4; "To Resume Work," *Weekly Spokesman-Review*, June 20, 1895, p. 1; "Bunker Hill Mine," *Weekly Spokesman-Review*, June 27, 1895, p. 1; "Hums All Day Long," *Seattle Times*, Aug. 19, 1895, p. 3; "Lumber Trade Here," *Seattle Times*, Jan. 16, 1896, p. 2; "Better Time for Tacoma," *Ledger*, June 2, 1895, p. 4; Hollander, "The Security Holdings of National Banks," p. 801; Freece, "A History of the Street Railway Systems of Vancouver," pp. 15-21, 35-30, 44;

rails to Shelton: *Anacortes American,* Aug. 22, 1895, p. 3; rails to Montana: *Anacortes American,* Dec. 5, 1895, p. 3; "Drove Away the Guards," *P-I,* Aug. 18, 1895, p. 1, reprinted from *Colfax Gazette,* Aug. 8; "To Resist the Law," *Weekly Spokesman-Review,* Aug. 22, 1895, p. 7; "Receiver for Crops," *P-I,* Sept. 8, 1895, p. 3; "A Curse on the Hops," *P-I,* Sept. 6, 1895, p. 8; "The Curse on the Hop," *P-I,* Sept. 8, 1895, p. 4; "That 'Hop Louse' Incident, *P-I,* Sept. 12, 1895, p. 2; "The O.I. Gives Up," *P-I,* Oct. 5, 1895, p. 8; "Business Reviewed," *Seattle Times,* June 13, 1896, p. 1; "City Lights Will Continue to Burn," *Townsend Daily Leader,* Oct. 31, 1895, p. 3; "Lights That Will Stay," *Townsend Weekly Leader,* Nov. 14, 1895, p. 6; "Amusements," *P-I,* Nov. 1, 1895, p. 5, and Nov. 5, 1895, p. 8; "Two Banks Suspended," *Bellingham Bay Reveille,* Nov. 8, 1895, p. 7; "Whatcom County Doesn't Trust Banks," *P-I,* Nov. 19, 1895, p. 2.

91   "Chinese Domestics," *News,* Dec. 15, 1895, p. 3; "Tacoma Much Stirred," *P-I,* Dec. 6, 1895, p. 1; "The Early Chinese Exit," *Union,* Dec. 9, 1895, p. 1; "Chinese Domestics," *Union,* Dec. 6, 1895, p. 2; "Are They Necessary for Our Happiness?" *News,* Dec. 6, 1895, p. 2; "Keep Them Out," *Union,* Dec. 9, 1895, p. 2; "Celebrate November 3," *Union,* Dec. 30, 1895, p. 2; editorial, *Ledger,* Dec. 9, 1895, p. 4; "The Chinese Labor Question," *Union,* Dec. 14, 1895, p. 2; "Mr. Riggs and His Servants," *Ledger,* Dec. 16, 1895, p. 4; "The Old Spirit Lives," *P-I,* Dec. 15, 1895, p. 1; on Bulger: "Now Seeking Fusion," *P-I,* March 30, 1896, p. 2, and "An Old Timer Talks," *Seattle Times,* July 20, 1896, p. 5; Hunt, *Tacoma,* Vol. I, pp. 364, 365, 372, 381, and Vol. II, p. 173; "Anti-Chinese Meeting," *Ledger,* Dec. 15, 1895, p. 8; "The People's Voice," *News,* Dec. 16, 1895, p. 4; "Chinese Needn't Go," *P-I,* Dec. 20, 1895, p. 1; "Another Flop," *Union,* Dec. 20, 1895, p. 2; "The Chinese Are Gone," *P-I,* Jan. 3, 1896, p. 1; "Anti-Chinese," *Union,* March 4, 1896, p. 2; "Adopt Amendments," *News,* Feb. 5, 1896, p. 1; "Legal Notice," *Ledger,* March 17, 1896, p. 7; "Fawcett by Two Votes," *Ledger,* April 15, 1896, p. 1; "First Vice Consul," *P-I,* Oct. 29, 1896, p. 3; editorial, *The Blade,* March 3, 1896, p. 2; editorial, *Seattle Times,* March 5, 1896, p. 4; "Li May Land," *Union,* March 24, 1896, p. 2; "For Seattle's Good," *P-I,* Sept. 24, 1896, p. 5; "Chamber of Commerce," *P-I,* Oct. 1, 1896, p. 5; minutes, Sept. 23 and 30, 1896, Seattle Chamber of Commerce archives; *Articles of Incorporation of the Seattle Chamber of Commerce,* 1890.

92   "The Mining Outlook," *P-I,* June 4, 1895, p. 4; "Back from the Mining Camps," *Ledger,* June 3, 1895, p. 5; "The Methow Mines," *P-I,* May 26, 1895, p. 8; "The Outlook Bright," *Chronicle,* May 22, 1895, p. 2; "Home from Yukon Placers," *Telegraph,* Oct. 21, 1893, p. 8; "3,000 Miles Down the Yukon," *P-I,* Aug. 20, 1894, p. 1; "Many Want to Go," *Seattle Times,* June 5, 1895, p. 5; "Land of Disappointment," *P-I,* Aug. 28, 1895, p. 8; "A Letter from the Yukon,' *Shelton Weekly Tribune,* Nov. 9, 1895, p. 2.

93   "Big Mortgage Sale," *P-I*, Jan. 21, 1898, p. 3; Seeley to Eckels, Oct. 13, 1896, *First National Bank of South Bend*, File 308, Box 621; A.D. Lynch to Eckels, Dec. 19, 1895, *Port Townsend National Bank*, File 248, Box 492, Item 121; Seeley to Eckels, Sept. 27, 1896, Item 39, *First National Bank of Anacortes*, File 291, Box 583, all in *National Bank Receivership Records;* "New Whatcom as Pasture," *Bellingham Bay Reveille*, March 20, 1896, p. 8.

94   "Editors in Council," *Everett Times*, July 15, 1896, p. 1; "No Special Rights," *Chronicle*, Dec. 23, 1895, p. 4; "Must Pay Interest," *Chronicle*, Dec. 24, 1895, p. 3; "Nice Row This," *Chronicle*, Dec. 26, 1895, p. 1; "No End of the Row," *Chronicle*, Dec. 27, 1895, p. 3; "Writ Denied," *Chronicle*, Dec. 31, 1895, p. 1; "Spokane Treasurer," *P-I*, Oct. 6, 1896, p. 2; Puget Sound Cooperative Colony letterhead, Malony to Washington Mill Co., May 5, 1894, Bert Kellogg Photograph Collection, Port Angeles Public Library, call No. WRIT-005; "Port Angeles Pops Out for Lynching," *Weekly Townsend Leader*, May 7, 1896, p. 7; "City Warrant Matter," *Port Angeles Democrat-Leader*, May 8, 1896, p. 1; "Mr. Rupert Was Not Long in Court," *Weekly Townsend Leader*, Feb. 6, 1896, p. 4; "County Dodging Bills These Days," *Weekly Townsend Leader*, Jan. 9, 1896, p. 8; "City Auditor's Statement," *Bellingham Bay Reveille*, Dec. 14, 1894, p. 2; "The New Council Here," *Bellingham Bay Reveille*, Jan. 10, 1896, p. 6; "Policemen's Salaries," *Bellingham Bay Reveille*, March 27, 1896, p. 2; "Policemen's Salaries," *Bellingham Bay Reveille*, April 3, 1896, p. 7; "The Council in Action," *Bellingham Bay Reveille*, Feb. 28, 1896, p. 2; "City Dads Speechify," *Bellingham Bay Reveille*, March 6, 1896, p. 7; "Trying to Cut Down Interest," *P-I*, Jan. 19, 1898, p. 3; editorial, *Anacortes American*, May 28, 1896, p. 2; editorial, *Anacortes American*, March 26, 1896, p. 2; editorial, *Anacortes American*, May 16, 1895, p. 2; editorial, *Anacortes American*, Aug. 22, 1895, p. 2; editorial, *Anacortes American*, Aug. 29, 1895, p. 2; editorial, *Anacortes American*, March 26, 1896, p. 2; "Our City Schools," *Anacortes American*, June 25, 1896, p. 2; "Anacortes News," *P-I*, March 28, 1896, p. 3; "Many Disappointed," *News*, Dec. 21, 1895, p. 3; "City's Tax Levy," *Spokesman-Review*, April 11, 1897, p. 8; "Shall We Have More School?" *Snohomish County Tribune*, March 11, 1896, p. 2; editorial, *Snohomish County Tribune*, March 26, 1896, p. 2; "Extension of School Term," *Snohomish County Tribune*, March 28, 1896, p. 1; "Inaugural Address," *Everett Times*, Jan. 15, 1896, p. 1; "Retrenchment the Word," *Everett Herald*, May 7, 1896, p. 1; "Count the Cost," *Everett Times*, March 7, 1894, p. 2; *Vancouver Register*, Feb. 20, 1896.

95   "The Dawn Is Coming," *Ledger*, Jan. 3, 1896, p. 4; "City of Destiny," *Ledger*, Jan. 1, 1894, p. 5; "To Overthrow the Light and Water Purchase," *News*, Dec. 24, 1894, p. 2; "Stallcup Suit Scotched," *Ledger*, Nov. 30, 1895, p. 2; "The City the Winner," *P-I*, Aug. 26, 1897, p. 8; "The Argument for Default," *Ledger*, May 25, 1896, p. 4; "Reasoning With Wreckers" and "Mr. Sternberg's Letter," *Ledger*, May 21, 1896, pp. 2, 4; "How to Maintain the City's Credit," *News*, May 16, 1896, p. 2; "The June Interest," *Union*, May 26, 1896, p. 2; "The June Interest

ENDNOTES

Paid," *Ledger*, May 31, 1896, p. 5; "Tacoma Pays the Interest," *P-I*, June 3, 1896, p. 2; "The City Finances," *Ledger*, Jan. 10, 1896, p. 4; "Finances Taken Up Again," *Union*, April 26, 1896, p. 8; "The Debt of Two Cities," *Ledger*, May 1, 1896, p. 4; "The City in a Dilemma," *Union*, April 10, 1896, p. 4.

96   "A New Lumber Trust," *P-I*, Aug. 6, 1895, p. 1; "The Combine Grows," *P-I*, Dec. 7, 1895, p. 8; "An Enormous Trust," *P-I*, Feb. 3, 1896, p. 1; "Not in the Combine," *Seattle Times*, Feb. 13, 1896, p. 5; "The Lumber Combine," *P-I*, Feb. 28, 1896, p. 5; "The Lumber Trust a Fact," *Ledger*, March 13, 1896, p. 1; "Prices Go Up," *P-I*, March 14, 1896, p. 8; "The New Price List," *P-I*, March 22, 1896, p. 8; "Passing of the Lumber Trust," *P-I*, Dec. 2, 1896, p. 2; "Down With a Crash," *P-I*, Jan. 5, 1897, p. 8; "Refused to Pay Up," *P-I*, April 16, 1897, p. 8; Ficken, *The Forested Land*, pp. 82-84; "Many New Canneries," *P-I*, Feb. 17, 1896, p. 9; "The Fisheries Question," *P-I*, Feb. 19, 1897, p. 4; editorial, *The Blade*, Dec. 15, 1896, p. 2; "The Anacortes Salmon Canneries," *P-I*, Feb. 18, 1896, p. 8; editorial, *Anacortes American*, Aug. 22, 1895, p. 2; "Two Salmon Canneries" and "Big Cannery," *Anacortes American*, Feb. 13, 1896, pp. 2, 3; "City's Business Affairs," *Anacortes American*, Sept. 12, 1895, p. 3; "Finn Fishermen Firm," *Weekly Ledger*, April 21, 1893, p. 8; "Cannerymen are Organized," *Astorian*, April 2, 1896, p. 4; "The Death of Searcy," *Oregonian*, May 23, 1896, p. 12; "Acts of Lawlessness," *Oregonian*, May 25, 1896, p. 1; "Murdered at Smith's Point, *Astorian*, May 31, 1896, p. 4; "Exciting Fishermen," *Oregonian*, June 4, 1896, p. 3; "Both Were Drowned," *Oregonian*, June 10, 1896, p. 3; "Striking Fishermen Very Ugly," *P-I*, June 14, 1896, p. 1; "Militia Called Out," *Oregonian*, June 16, 1896, p. 1; editorial, *Astorian*, June 18, 1896, p. 2; "Canneries Packing Fish," *Ledger*, June 17, 1896, p. 1; "Salmon Strike Lost," *P-I*, June 18, 1896, p. 3; "Fishermen's Strike Broken," *Ledger*, June 20, 1896, p. 4; "Columbia Strike Ended" and "The War on the Columbia," *Ledger*, June 21, 1896, pp. 3, 8; "Price of Fish Down," *Oregonian*, July 15, 1897, p. 3; "Will Be No Strike," *Oregonian*, July 17, 1897, p. 3.

97   "Heavy Failure at Spokane," *P-I*, March 17, 1896, p. 3; "That Mill of Simon," *Spokesman-Review*, Aug. 14, 1896, p. 3; "Former Spokane Man Leaves Fortune in Mexico," *Chronicle*, May 30, 1930, p. 3; Durham, *Spokane*, Vol. I, pp. 473-474; Morgan, *Puget's Sound*, p. 253; "The Tacoma Hotel," *News*, May 1, 1896, p. 3; "Refuse to Pay the Subsidy," *Ledger*, May 19, 1896, p. 3; Daggett, *Railroad Reorganization*, p. v; "Sale of SLS&E," *P-I*, May 8, 1896, p. 8; "Sold for $1,000,000," *P-I*, May 17, 1896, p. 8; "An Enormous Capitalization," *P-I*, April 2, 1896, p. 4; Daggett, *Ibid.*, pp. 373-386; "Bid in by Winter," *Spokesman-Review*, July 26, 1896, p. 1; "The O.R. & N. Sold," *Seattle Times*, July 17, 1896, p. 5; "M'Neil at Its Head," *Oregonian*, July 18, 1896, p. 10; "The Wrecks of Three Years," *Ledger*, Oct. 11, 1896, p. 4.

98   "Our Outlook Today," *Oregonian*, Jan. 1, 1896, p. 30; "Washington's Interest in Gold," *P-I*, June 18, 1896, p. 4; "Prosperous Spokane," *P-I*, March 8, 1896, p. 8; editorial, *Chronicle*, March 9, 1896, p. 2; "All Money at Par," *Spokesman-Review*, Sept. 3, 1896, p. 3; "Dwellings Are Scarce," *Chronicle*, April 6, 1896, p. 3; "Spokane the Chief City of the Northwest," *Chronicle*, March 7, 1896, p. 2; editorial, *Chronicle*, March 10, 1896, p. 2; editorial, *Everett Herald*, March 19, 1896, p. 2; "From Monte Cristo," *Seattle Times*, April 22, 1896, p. 1; "For the Gold Fields," *P-I*, March 9, 1896, p. 8; "After Alaska Gold," *P-I*, March 13, 1896, p. 5; "Board of Trade," *Weekly Townsend Leader*, Feb. 20, 1896, p. 6; "Tacoma Must Wake Up," *News*, Feb. 18, 1896, p. 2; "A Word to the Banks," *News*, March 10, 1896, p. 2.

99   "The Rising Industrialists," *The Blade*, Feb. 27, 1896, p. 2; "Trade of the Orient, *P-I*, April 9, 1897, p. 1; "Work of the Chamber of Commerce in 1896," *P-I*, Feb. 7, 1897, p. 16; "Seattle Scores Again," *P-I*, July 18, 1896, p. 8; "The New Steamship Line," *Seattle Times*, Aug. 29, 1896, p. 4; "Unity of the Orient and the Occident," *Seattle Times*, Aug. 31, 1896, p. 1; "Thousands of Throats Give Voice to the Welcome," *P-I*, Sept. 1, 1896, p. 1; editorial, *Everett Herald*, July 23, 1896, p. 2; "Shipping," *Everett Herald*, July 30, 1896, p. 3; "Seventy-Three Thousand," *Ledger*, July 22, 1896, p. 3; editorial, *Ledger*, Sept. 4, 1896, p. 4; "A Japanese Husband," *P-I*, Aug. 27, 1896, p. 5; "Japan and America," *P-I*, Sept. 5, 1896, p. 5; California Civil Code of 1880, Chapter 41, Section 1; Volpp, "American Mestizo: Filipinos and Antimiscegenation Laws in California," *U.C. Davis Law Rev. 795* (1999).

100   "The Debt of Two Cities," *Ledger*, May 1, 1896, p. 4; "Tacoma's Floating Debt," *P-I*, April 17, 1896, p. 2; "Fawcett's Opportunity," *Ledger*, April 18, 1896, p. 4; "The Committee's Report," *News*, June 26, 1896, p. 2; "Tacoma's Debt Dilemma," *P-I*, June 6, 1896, p. 1; "To Pay Accruing Bills," *Ledger*, June 6, 1896, p. 5; "Boggs Paid the Warrants," *P-I*, June 11, 1896, p. 2; *Eidemiller v. City of Tacoma*, 14 Wash. 376; "City Treasurer Restrained," *Ledger*, June 16, 1896, p. 3; "Her Credit Used Up" and "Tacoma Firemen Protest," *P-I*, June 20, 1896, p. 3; "Tacoma's Hands Tied," *P-I*, June 27, 1896, p. 1; "Exhaustive Exposition of the City's Condition," *Union*, June 28, 1896, p. 6; "That Gove Injunction," *News*, July 1, 1896, p. 2; "Business Men Help Again" and "Government By Private Subscription," *Ledger*, July 1, 1896, pp. 3, 4; "City Must Pay Warrants," *Ledger*, Sept. 25, 1896, p. 8; "Staggered Judge Hanford," *Ledger*, Nov. 26, 1896, p. 5; "Judge Hanford's Reproof," *Ledger*, Nov. 27, 1896, p. 4; "Bonds for Warrants," *News*, Aug. 20, 1896, p. 4; "Result of Fawcett's Veto," "Funding Ordinance Is Dead," and "Why the Mayor Objected," *Ledger*, Aug. 23, 1896, pp. 2, 5, 8; "Tacoma Not to Refund," *P-I*, Aug. 23, 1896, p. 1; "How Tacoma Loses Money," *Ledger*, Sept. 3, 1896, p. 5; "To Raise the Money," *P-I*, Sept. 13, 1896, p. 3; "Passed the Second Time," *Ledger*, Sept. 13, 1896, p. 8; "Ten Pages of Red Ink," *Ledger*, Sept. 16, 1896, p. 5; "Mayor's Veto on Record," *Ledger*, Sept. 18, 1896, p. 5; "The Mayor's Vetoes," *Ledger*, Sept. 19, 1896, p. 4; "Funding Ordinance Is Law," *Ledger*, Sept. 20, 1896, p. 6; "Orr Was

ENDNOTES

Re-Elected," *P-I,* Aug. 7, 1896, p. 2; "Exit Fawcett's Regime," *Union,* Oct. 7, 1896, p. 4; "Injunction Suit Begun," *Ledger,* Oct. 13, 1896, p. 4; "The Murry Suit," *Ledger,* Oct. 14, 1896, p. 4; "Paid," *Seattle Times,* Nov. 11, 1896, p. 1; "Is Against the City," *News,* Dec. 5, 1896, p. 1; "The Money Is Still Tied Up," *Union,* Dec. 13, 1896, p. 8; "News From Tacoma," *P-I,* Dec. 16, 1896, p. 2.

101   "Prices of Farm Products," *P-I,* Sept. 23, 1896, p. 4; Eckels and Pennoyer, "The Financial Situation," *North American Review,* Vol. 157, August 1893, pp. 133-144; Newcomb, "Has the Standard Gold Dollar Appreciated?" *Journal of Political Economy,* Sept. 1893, pp. 503-512; Friedman, "The Crime of 1873," *Journal of Political Economy,* Dec. 1990, pp. 1159-1194; Mackenzie, "Gold Has Risen," *Spokesman-Review,* Aug. 4, 1896, p. 2; Snyder, "That Flood of Gold," *The Review of Reviews,* February 1896, pp. 167-172; "Wall Street's New Nightmare," *Chronicle,* Dec. 20, 1895, p. 2; "Business to Improve," *P-I,* Feb. 22, 1896, p. 1, quoting *Dun's Review of Trade.*

102   "W.J. Bryan's Speech," *P-I,* July 10, 1896, p. 3; "The Banner of Silver Planted on the Ramparts of Democracy," *Ledger,* July 10, 1896, p. 1; "Choose Your Flag," *Chronicle,* July 14, 1896, p. 2; "Fit Head for a Fit Body," *Oregonian,* July 11, 1896, p. 4; "A Spectacular Nomination," *P-I,* July 11, 1896, p. 4; "The Difference," *Ledger,* July 10, 1896, p. 4.

103   "Squire Is a Bolter," *P-I,* Aug. 6, 1896, p. 8; "How to Vote for Bryan," *Spokesman-Review,* Oct. 29, 1896, p. 4; "To the Public," *Seattle Times,* Aug. 10, 1896, p. 4; editorial, *Seattle Times,* Aug. 17, 1896, p. 5; "Our Candidate," *Chronicle,* July 11, 1896, p. 2; "The People Aroused," *Union,* Aug. 10, 1896, p. 2; "The Men the News Would Nominate," *News,* Aug. 11, 1896, p. 2; editorial note, *Ledger,* Aug. 6, 1896, p. 4; "Hugh C. Wallace Has Resigned," *Union,* Aug. 6, 1896, p. 1; Hunt, *Tacoma, Vol. III,* p. 15; "Lumbermen Alarmed," *P-I,* Aug. 11, 1896, p. 2; "Fusion Finally Carried," *Ledger,* Aug. 15, 1896, p. 1; Ridgeway, "Populism in Washington," pp. 302-303; "John R. Rogers," *Chronicle,* Aug. 15, 1896, p. 1; William Allen White, "What's Wrong With Kansas?" *P-I,* Sept. 4, 1896, p. 4, reprinted as "What's the Matter With Kansas," Sept. 27, 1896, p. 8; Snowden, "The Trouble With Kansas," *Ledger,* Sept. 14, 1896, p. 8; "The Gold Men's Scarecrow," *Chronicle,* Oct. 8, 1896, p. 2; "To Defeat 16 to 1," *P-I,* Sept. 10, 1896, p. 8; Griffiths, "Far Western Populist Thought," *Pacific Northwest Quarterly,* October 1969, p. 184; Tooze, *The Wages of Destruction,* p. 182; "Gov. Rogers' Free Land Idea," *Ledger,* Dec. 15, 1896, p. 4; "John R. Rogers," *Union,* Sept. 27, 1896, p. 3.

104   "Agitation Hurts Business," *Ledger,* Sept. 2, 1896, p. 5; Wingate to Eckels, Oct. 3, 1896, *Merchants National Bank of Tacoma,* File 209, Box 420, *National Bank Receivership Records;* Display ad, *P-I,* Sept. 27, 1896, p. 9; "Bon Marché Will Have Birthday," *Times,* April 26, 1931, p. 24; "History of the Olympia Brewing Co."

THE PANIC OF 1893

and "Leopold Schmidt: Brewer," brewerygems.com; editorial, *The Blade*, Aug. 20, 1896, p. 2; "Friends of the Needy," *Bellingham Bay Reveille*, Sept. 4, 1896, p. 2.

105   "Plutocracy vs. People," *Ellensburg Localizer*, Oct. 31, 1896, p. 4; "What Is the People's Party?" *P-I*, Oct. 14, 1896, p. 4; "Vote for McKinley, Sound Money, National Honor and Prosperity," *P-I*, Nov. 3, 1896, p. 1; editorial, *Union*, Oct. 19, 1896; "For All Mankind," *Union*, Oct. 16, 1896, p. 2; "Nation Is Saved!" *P-I*, Nov. 4, 1896, p. 1; editorial, *Oregonian*, Nov. 4, 1896, p. 4; "County Items," *Aberdeen Herald*, Nov. 19, 1896, p. 1; "Make Ready for 1900," *Chronicle*, Nov. 7, 1896, p. 2; "High-Water Mark," *Oregonian*, Nov. 4, 1896, p. 4; "Gold Contracts," *Dawn*, Jan. 2, 1897, p. 1; "Real Cause of Distrust," *Spokesman-Review*, Aug. 10, 1896, p. 4; *Guaranty Trust Co. v. Henwood*, 307 U.S. 247 (1939).

106   "Anti-Bryan Trick," *Weekly Spokesman-Review*, Oct. 26, 1896, p. 5; "How to Vote for Bryan," *Weekly Spokesman-Review*, Oct. 29, 1896, p. 4; "Populistic Washington," *Everett Herald*, Nov. 5, 1896, p. 2; "Unfortunate Washington," *Oregonian*, Nov. 6, 1896, p. 4; "Abstract of Votes Polled," 1896, Washington Secretary of State; "Calamity Howling," *Union*, Nov. 5, 1896, p. 2; "Enemies of Washington," *Union*, Nov. 7, 1896, p. 2; "Misplaced Sympathy," *P-I*, Nov. 15, 1896, p. 4; "The Governor-Elect," *P-I*, Nov. 8, 1896, p. 1; "They Want to Know," *Weekly Spokesman-Review*, Nov. 12, 1896, p. 1.

107   "The Spokane of Today," *P-I*, Dec. 20, 1896, p. 23; "Nearing the Dollar Mark," *Ledger*, Nov. 11, 1896, p. 2; "Our Trade With Japan," *P-I*, Dec. 27, 1896, p. 3; "Another Tacoma Industry," *Ledger*, Dec. 18, 1896, p. 6; "The Cascade Tunnel," *Seattle Times*, Nov. 24, 1896, p. 3; "First Contract Let," *P-I*, Dec. 28, 1896, p. 8; "1897: What Shall It Bring Forth?" *Seattle Times*, Jan. 2, 1897, p. 4; "The Old Year and the New," *The Eye*, Dec. 31, 1896, p. 2; "Failures in Chicago," *P-I*, Dec. 22, 1896, p. 1; "Bank Runs Checked," *P-I*, Dec. 23, 1896, p. 1; "Banks in Good Shape," *P-I*, Dec. 29, 1896, p. 1.

108   "Chinese New Year," *Ellensburg Localizer*, Feb. 6, 1897, p. 1; "Annual Chinese Banquet," *P-I*, Feb. 5, 1897, p. 5; Editorial, *Seattle Times*, Jan. 5, 1897, p. 4.

109   "Vale Stallcup," *Ledger*, Jan. 12, 1897, p. 4; Griffiths, "Far Western Populist Thought," *Pacific Northwest Quarterly*, October 1969, pp. 184-186; table, *Seattle Times*, Dec. 2, 1896, p. 4; "Plummer Gets In," *Spokesman-Review*, Jan. 12, 1897, p. 1; "Religious Controversy Again," *Spokesman-Review*, Jan. 18, 1897, p. 2; "Nearing the Windup," *The Blade*, March 6, 1897, p. 1; "Week's Events At Olympia," *Ledger*, Jan. 17, 1897, pp. 1-2; "What I Would Do if Elected United States Senator," *San Francisco Examiner*, Jan. 17, 1897, p. 29; "Mrs. Mary E. Hobart," *The Blade*, Jan. 28, 1897, p. 2; editorial, *News*, Jan. 21, 1897, p. 2; "Mischievous Legislation," *P-I*,

ENDNOTES

Feb. 17, 1898, p. 4; "Good Commercial Laws," *P-I*, March 16, 1899, p. 4; *Dennis v. Moses*, 18 Wash. 537, Feb. 15, 1898; *State, Ex Rel. Chamberlin v. Daniel*, 17 Wash. 111, May 28, 1897; "Only a Few Bills Pass," *Bellingham Bay Reveille*, March 5, 1897, p. 4; "To the Extremists," *Spokesman-Review*, May 23, 1897, p. 1; Wooddy, "Populism in Washington," *The Washington Historical Quarterly*, Vol. XXI, No. 2, April 1930, pp. 113-116; Ridgeway, "Populism in Washington," *Pacific Northwest Quarterly*, Oct. 1948, p. 310; *Rader*, "Legislative Reflection," *Union*, April 4, 1897, p. 6; "Will Let Taxes Go," *P-I*, May 22, 1897, p. 2; "Are Not Lawful," *P-I*, May 30, 1897, p. 2; Plummer, "The Populist Party Is Dead," *P-I*, Dec. 5, 1898, p. 4; "Senate Proceedings," *Ledger*, Feb. 11, 1897, p. 2; "The Legislature," *Washington Standard*, Feb. 19, 1897, p. 1.

110   Whitfield, *History of Snohomish County*, Vol. I, p. 139; "Everett Is Again Prosperous," *Seattle Times*, Feb. 16, 1897, p. 5; editorial, *Snohomish County Tribune*, Jan. 29, 1897, p. 2; editorial, *Snohomish County Tribune*, Jan. 8, 1897, p. 4; "News of Snohomish," *Seattle Times*, March 2, 1897, p. 3; "Snohomish National Going Out of Business," *Snohomish County Tribune*, Feb. 19, 1897, p. 2; "Announcement," *The Eye*, June 10, 1897, p. 2; "Barefoot Bill Passed," *P-I*, March 9, 1895, p. 1; "The New University," *P-I*, Dec. 16, 1894, p. 16; "Temple of Learning," *P-I*, June 9, 1895, p. 16; "The State Normal School," *P-I*, Sept. 21, 1894, p. 2; "The New Normal School Opened," *P-I*, Sept. 4, 1894, p. 8; "A Very Wise Move," *Union*, April 9, 1897, p. 2; "Spokane Must Have It," *Chronicle*, July 21, 1894, p. 4; "Sold 5568 Tickets," *Spokesman-Review*, Jan. 1, 1895, p. 1; "The Army Post," *Spokesman-Review*, Jan. 9, 1895, p. 4; "Now Let the Sun Shine," *Chronicle*, Jan 21, 1895, p. 3; "The Post Is Ours," *Spokesman-Review*, Feb. 7, 1895, p. 4; "A Memorable Achievement," *Spokesman-Review*, March 7, 1895, p. 4; "The Site Accepted," *Spokesman-Review*, Oct. 24, 1895, p. 8; "Spokane Army Post," *P-I*, April 2, 1896, p. 1; Perry, "How Spokane Won the Army Post," in Durham, *Spokane*, Vol. I, p. 465; "At Magnolia Bluffs," *P-I*, Jan. 9, 1896, p. 8; "For the Army Post," *P-I*, Feb. 11, 1896, p. 3; "The Site Approved," *P-I*, March 4, 1896, p. 1; "Fort Townsend Abandoned," *Ledger*, March 7, 1895, p. 2; "A Reserve No Longer," *P-I*, May 4, 1895, p. 8; "When the Fort Is Abandoned," *P-I*, Feb. 11, 1896, p. 1.

111   1940 U.S. Census entry, Frank Hense, supervisor's district 10, enumeration district 1-2A, sheet 5, April 12, 1940, *Ancestry.com;* Social Security Application for Hense, SSN 470-16-0978, 1938, *Ancestry.com;* "Centralia Bank Closed," *Oregonian*, Sept. 26, 1894, p. 2; "Two Bankers Arrested," *Ledger*, Sept. 30, 1894, p. 1; "Frank Hense's Luck," *News*, April 16, 1897, p. 1; "News from Centralia," *Ledger*, Oct. 1, 1894, p. 3; "Hense Dismissed," *Oregonian*, Oct. 6, 1894, p. 3; "Hense's Bank Is Attached," *Chehalis Nugget*, Nov. 9, 1894, p. 2; "Centralia Business Troubles," *P-I*, Dec. 11, 1894, p. 2; "Frank Hense Arrested," *P-I*, Dec. 22, 1894, p. 5; "The Centralia Banker Bound Over," *Oregonian*, Jan. 10, 1895, p. 3; *In re Hense*, 13 Wash. 614, Feb. 7, 1896; "Hense to Be Tried," *Chehalis Nugget*, April 2, 1897, p.

1; "Gone After Banker Hense," *Chehalis Bee*, April 2, 1897, p. 1; "Struck a Snag," *Chehalis Bee*, April 9, 1897, p. 8; "Clough Saves Him," *St. Paul Globe*, April 13, 1897, p. 8; "Hense Will Not Come," *P-I*, April 21, 1897, p. 1; "Frank Hense's Case," *Chehalis Nugget*, April 23, 1897, p. 1; "Couldn't Get Hense," *Chehalis Bee*, April 23, 1897, p. 1; for spelling of "Johnsone," see display ad, *Chehalis Bee*, June 11, 1897, p. 8; *Roberts v. Hense*, Minn. Sup. Ct., Dec. 8, 1916, *The Northwestern Reporter*, Vol. 160, p. 198; Minnesota Death Index, record# 897239, June 25, 1942, *Ancestry.com*; "Lockwood Skips," *South Bend Journal*, Sept. 3, 1897, p. 1; "Lockwood's Shortage $4,798," *South Bend Journal*, Nov. 5, 1897, p. 1; "The Reason Why," *South Bend Journal*, Dec. 17, 1897, p. 4; "Lockwood Comes Back for Trial," *P-I*, Oct. 15, 1898, p. 1; "Verdict of Not Guilty for Lockwood," *P-I*, Nov. 2, 1898, p. 8.

112   "The High Art of Receiving," *Union*, April 9, 1897, p. 4; "News of the Court House," *Union*, June 13, 1897, p. 5; "Bank Assets, Etc.," *Union*, May 11, 1897, p. 2; "Forty Thousand Dollars," *Union*, June 25, 1897, p. 4; *Howarth v. Angle*, 162 N.Y. 179, Feb. 27, 1900; Marple and Olson, *The National Bank of Commerce of Seattle*, p. 46; Wingate to Eckels, June 9, 1897, *Merchants National Bank*, File 209, Box 421, *National Bank Receivership Records*.

113   Groner, *Paccar*, pp. 9-15; "Alaska Railroad to Be Constructed," *P-I*, May 21, 1898, p. 10; "Alaska's New Railroad," *P-I*, May 24, 1898, p. 10; "Real Estate Transfers," *P-I*, Jan. 2 & 13, 1900, pp.10, 11; Morgan, *Puget's Sound*, pp. 261-262; Dougherty, *The Bartell Story*, pp. 12-15; Bartell ads, *P-I*, Jan. 23, 26, 28 and 29, 1899, p. 1; "Hill, the Enigma," *P-I*, July 10, 1897, p. 8; "Prize Secured by Seattle," *P-I*, Feb. 15, 1899, p. 5.

114   "Big New Building," *P-I*, Feb. 17, 1897, p. 8; "Bucoda News," *P-I*, March 3, 1897, p. 5; "State News," *Snohomish County Tribune*, Aug. 31, 1893, p. 1; "Two Monster Derricks," *Seattle Times*, April 21, 1897, p. 8; "The Colman Improvement," *Seattle Times*, May 7, 1897, p. 4; "The Hard Times," *P-I*, April 10, 1897, p. 4; "Shingles Going Up," *Snohomish County Tribune*, April 16, 1897, p. 4; editorial, *The Blade*, May 15, 1897, p. 2; "Union in Control," *P-I*, May 9, 1897, p. 2; "Among the Unions," *Chronicle*, April 22, 1896, p. 4; "Carpenters Win," *Chronicle*, Dec. 21, 1896, p. 3; "For Higher Wages," *Spokesman-Review*, April 29, 1897, p. 2; "Good Times in Skagit County," *Seattle Times*, June 6, 1897, p. 5; "Failures for Three Years," *Seattle Times*, June 13, 1897, p. 4; "Condition of Trade," *Union*, May 6, 1897, p. 2; "Good Times," *Bellingham Bay Reveille*, April 9, 1897, p. 2; "Booms," *Ledger*, May 27, 1897, p. 4.

115   "Trade of the Orient," *P-I*, April 9, 1897, p. 1; "The Passing Throng," *P-I*, July 11, 1897, p. 5; "Cheering Bulls in New York" and "Dollar Wheat," *P-I*, Aug. 21, 1897, pp. 1, 4; Walla Walla prices from "Portland Wheat Market," *P-I*, runs every day, p. 7; "The Passing Throng," *P-I*, Sept. 12, 1897, p. 5; "Prosperous

Farmers," *Ledger*, Oct. 30, 1897, p. 4; "Paying Off Their Debts," *P-I*, March 12, 1898, p. 3; "No Money in Hogs," *Spokesman-Review*, March 30, 1897, p. 3; "Big Profit in Hogs," *Spokesman-Review*, April 11, 1897, p. 16; "Wants Our Horses," *Ellensburg Capital*, Oct. 22, 1896, p. 1; "American Horses for Japan," *P-I*, April 26, 1897, p. 2; "Fifty-Cent Horses," *P-I*, April 27, 1897, p. 4.

116   "Alaska's Favorite Animal," *Ledger*, March 17, 1897, p. 8; "Dogs For Alaska," *P-I*, Feb. 23, 1897, p. 8; "Will Go to the Yukon," *Seattle Times*, March 24, 1897, p. 5; "Dogs and Alaska Traffic," *P-I*, March 26, 1898, p. 4; "On the Way to Alaska," *Aberdeen Herald*, March 18, 1897, p. 3; "Details of the Willapa Wreck," *Ledger*, March 28, 1897, p. 8; "Drawn to Death Beneath the Waves of the Pacific," *P-I*, June 2, 1898, p. 1.

117   "Lifts Up Her Head," *Spokesman-Review*, July 9, 1897, p. 8; "Skamania's Mines," *Oregonian*, April 30, 1897, p. 7; "Mines and Mining," *Ledger*, April 19, 1897, p. 6; "Prospectors Starting Out," *Ledger*, April 22, 1897, p. 6; "Slate Creek News," *Snohomish County Tribune*, Feb. 19, 1897, p. 2; "Mines of Hamilton," *P-I*, May 7, 1897, p. 8; "High Mountain of Ore," *Seattle Times*, April 27, 1897, p. 5; "Prospecting the Olympics," *P-I*, May 25, 1897, p. 2; "Rich Placers Discovered," *Ledger*, May 1, 1897, p. 6; "Mines of Clarke County," *Ledger*, June 2, 1897, p. 6; "Gold in Spokane," *Spokesman-Review*, biweekly ed., May 24, 1897, p. 1; "Gold in Prospect," *P-I*, May 25, 1897, p. 2; "Mines of Snoqualmie," *P-I*, July 12, 1897, p. 16; "Klondyke Is Crazy," *P-I*, July 5, 1897, p. 5; "From the Yukon," *Union*, July 5, 1897, p. 4; "Golden Tales from Alaska," *Ledger*, July 7, 1897, p. 6; "Riches of the Clondyke," *Seattle Times*, July 8, 1897, p. 5; "On the Klondike," *P-I*, July 12, 1897, p. 5; "From St. Michaels," *P-I*, July 15, 1897, p. 1; "Millions in Sight," *P-I*, July 16, 1897, p. 1; "Fairy Tale," *Seattle Times*, July 16, 1897, p. 1; "Latest News From the Klondike," *P-I*, July 17, 1897, p. 1; "All Is Now Excitement," *Seattle Times*, July 29, 1897, p. 8; "Klondike and the Policemen" and "Sound and Inland," *Seattle Times*, July 23, 1897, pp. 2, 3; "He Will Not Resign," *P-I*, Aug. 15, 1897, p. 5; sleeping bag: "News Notes Gleaned," *The Blade*, April 1, 1897, p. 1; "Prosperous Days in the Ship Yards," *P-I*, Jan. 16, 1898, pp. 1-2; "Strike Is Ended," *P-I*, July 24, 1897, p. 8; "Wages Up, Laborers Scarce," *P-I*, July 31, 1897, p. 3; "Increase in Wages," *P-I*, Aug. 3, 1897, p. 2; "It Was Gold," *P-I*, Sept. 5, 1897, p. 4; Roberts, "Influence of the New Gold Supplies," *The Bankers' Magazine*, Jan. 1906, p. 22; "The Advance in Prices," *P-I*, Sept. 3, 1897, p. 4; Friedman, *Money Mischief*, p. 78.

118   "A Golden Year," *Ledger*, Jan. 1, 1898, p. 4; Prager, Mike, "Pioneer A.M. Cannon Honored in Many Ways," *Spokesman-Review*, Feb. 13, 1997, p. S-2; "Refuses to Pay," *Chronicle*, April 23, 1897, p. 3; "Ben E. Snipes Passes Away," *Ellensburg Capital*, Dec. 19, 1906, p. 3; "He Goes to Prison Today," *Ledger*, June 4, 1897, p. 5; "Council by Sixteen," *Chicago Tribune*, April 7, 1897, p. 1; "Jailed in Chicago," *News*, Jan. 25, 1897, p. 4; *Tedford v. People*, 219 Ill. 23, Supreme Court of Illinois,

Dec. 20, 1905; "Oldtime Character in This Section, 'Jumbo' Cantwell, Dies in East," *Seattle Times,* Feb. 9, 1916, p. 4; "Farmer Populists," *Reveille,* May 15, 1894, p. 2; editorial, *Bellingham Bay Reveille,* Feb. 26, 1897, p. 4; "Mrs. M. Hobart Died Yesterday," *Reveille,* Feb. 8, 1906, p. 5; "The Finding of Gloystein," *Spokesman-Review,* Sept. 24, 1894, p. 2; *Spokane City Directory* 1895, R.L. Polk & Co., p. 245, and 1896, p. 273; Marriage record, Snoshone County, Idaho, Aug. 17, 1918; 1920 Census, Twin Falls, Idaho, Enumeration District 253, Sheet 6, Jan. 7-8; *Tacoma City Directory,* R.L. Polk & Co., 1928, p. 318; "Death Takes Strawberry Expert Here," *News Tribune,* July 13, 1940, p. 11.

119   *Compendium of the Eleventh Census, 1890,* Part I, p. 523; "A Eulogy For Seattle," *Seattle Times,* Oct. 1, 1895, p. 8, quoting *The Dalles' Times-Mountaineer;* "A Contrast," *Ledger,* April 23, 1897, p. 4; "A Question for Today," *Ledger,* April 25, 1897, p. 4; "The Day of Better Things," *Ledger,* April 28, 1897, p. 4; "What's Wrong With Tacoma," *Ledger,* July 3, 1897, p. 4; "A Good Start," *Ledger,* Jan. 4, 1899, p. 4; "Weary of Collyer," *P-I,* Oct. 7, 1897, p. 2; "The Anxiety Is Ended," *Ledger,* June 3, 1893, p. 8; "Now! All together! Pull!" *News,* June 6, 1893, p. 4; "Not Just at Present," *Union,* March 31, 1897, p. 2; editorial, *Union,* April 4, 1897, p. 4; "Cold Comfort," *Union,* April 5, 1897, p. 2; "Work of the Wreckers," *Union,* April 12, 1897, p. 2; "The Lesson from the Clondyke Excitement," *Union,* July 26, 1897, p. 2; "No Room For Chinese," *News,* Oct. 26, 1893, p. 2; editorial, *Union,* Feb. 21, 1894, p. 2; Japan consulate: www.seattle.us.emb-japan.go.jp; "Salaries Up to Date," *Ledger,* Nov. 17, 1897, p. 1; Hunt, *Tacoma,* Vol. II, p. 151; *Stallcup v. Tacoma,* 13 Wash. 141 and 165 U.S. 719; *Bardsley v. Sternberg,* 18 Wash. 612; *Muhlenberg v. Tacoma,* 21 Wash. 306; Morgan, *Puget's Sound,* p. 319; "Warrant Cases Decided," *(Guaranty Trust) P-I,* Jan. 6, 1899, p. 3; "Another Warrant Case," *(Muhlenberg) P-I,* Feb. 5, 1899, p. 10; "City of Tacoma Must Pay $1,200,000 of Obligations," *Ledger,* June 28, 1899, p. 1; "Tacoma Funding Bonds," *P-I,* May 1, 1900, p. 3; "Tacoma's Outstanding Warrants," *P-I,* June 26, 1900, p. 7; Ad for gold bonds, Seymour Bros. & Co., N.Y., New York *Sun,* July 15, 1900, p. 28; "Cheap Money for Warrants," *Ledger,* June 29, 1899, p. 4. Gary Locke results from Washington Secretary of State: www.sos.wa.gov.

120   "Capital Is Afraid," *P-I,* Sept. 30, 1897, p. 2; "Will Cut the Price," *P-I,* June 16, 1897, p. 5; "Bought the Canal," *Dawn,* July 26, 1906, p. 1; F. Walden, "Irrigation and the Sunnyside Canal," *The Ranch,* Jan. 15, 1905, pp. 1-2; Coulter, "The Victory of National Irrigation in the Yakima Valley, 1902-1906," *The Pacific Northwest Quarterly,* April 1951, p. 102; "Investigating Irrigation," *Walla Walla Evening Statesman,* June 27, 1905, p. 3; Coulter, pp. 102-106; Garrett, "The Tale of Uncle Sam's Voyage in an Irrigating Ditch," *Saturday Evening Post,* January 17, 1925; "Tietan Project Is Approved," *Yakima Herald,* March 28, 1906, p. 1.

ENDNOTES

121   Ficken, *Washington State*, p. 10; "Business Is Here for the Railroad," *Weekly Townsend Leader*, June 25, 1896, p. 1; "Will Aid Portland," *Oregonian*, June 22, 1896, p. 3; "Portland's Help," *Weekly Townsend Leader*, July 29, 1897, p. 1; "Financial Statement," *Port Angeles Democrat-Leader*, Feb. 7, 1902, p. 1; "The City Debt," *Port Angeles Democrat-Leader*, Feb. 21, 1902, p. 2; "Note Book and Pencil," *Reveille*, Feb. 7, 1894, p. 2; "The New Council Here," *Bellingham Bay Reveille*, Jan. 10, 1896, p. 6; "That City Tax Case," *The Blade*, Dec. 11, 1901, p. 4; "Municipal Administration Makes a Good Record," *Reveille*, Jan. 7, 1908, p. 1; "County Books to Be Experted" and "Pay Their Face," *South Bend Journal*, Aug. 6, 1897, pp. 1, 4; "Taxes Reduced," *South Bend Journal*, Oct. 1, 1897, p.1; "The City Debt," *Port Angeles Democrat-Leader*, Feb. 7, 1902, p. 1; "Financial Statement," Port *Angeles Democrat-Leader*, Feb. 27, 1903, p. 2.

122   *Fifth Report of the Secretary of State*, 1898, pp. 13-15; Preston, "Banking Development in Washington," *Preston papers*, 1867-84-30, File 1-32, p. 1; Bush, *The National Bankruptcy Act of 1898*, pp. 16-18; *In Re William B. Allen*, Case 207, U.S. District Court, Tacoma, Jan. 9, 1899, RG 21, Box 15, NARA Seattle; Complaint of A.R. Titlow, *Titlow v. Allen*, Case 14217, Pierce County Superior Court, 1897.

123   "Puget Sound's Great Promise in the Orient," *P-I*, Jan. 1, 1899, p. 28; "The Passing Throng," *P-I*, Dec. 7, 1898, p. 6; "Other Parts of the State," *Ledger*, May 23, 1897, p. 2; "Small Fruits Thrive Here," *Ledger*, July 13, 1897, p. 6; "Dairying in the Kittitas Valley," *Spokesman-Review*, June 26, 1897, p. 6; "The State of Washington," *Seattle Times*, May 8, 1897, p. 4; "City and County of Spokane," *Spokesman-Review*, May 6, 1897, p. 7; "Slaves to Debt," *P-I*, Sept. 12, 1897, p. 4; "Old Times and New," *Oregonian*, June 28, 1897, p. 4.

INDEX OF BANKS

INDEX OF PEOPLE

Costello, Peter 162
Cox, William C. 199
Coxey, Jacob 97-98, 108-109, 136
Coxey, Legal Tender 98, 108
Crooker, J.B. 173
Curry, A.P. 121
Dazey, Charles Turner 141, 191
Dean, Carroll 87
Debs, Eugene V. 113-114, 117-119, 123
Deckebach, Frank 168-170
Delaney, Thomas E. 135, 226
Denny, David T. 189
Dinsmore, Frank A. 66
Dolan, James 88
Dorman, John W. 47
Drum, Henry 63, 143
Dumas, Alexandre 171
Dunlap, Robert E. 112
Durham, Nelson 34, 202
Dusinberre, Samuel & Agnes 29, 67, 139-140, 239
Eckels, James 62, 145-150, 184, 186, 215, 221, 229
Edmiston, James K. 140-144, 229, 239
Egan, Jimmy, John J. 94-95
Eldredge, Zoeth 149
Emery, Sarah E.V. 128
Eugene, Mary 81
Everette, Willis E. 173
Fahey, John 181
Fawcett, Angelo V. 207
Ferry, Clinton P. 136-137
Ferry, Elisha 48
Fetting, Charlotte & Ernest 40-41
Fishback, Charles 212
Flannigan, Edward 102
Flynn, Matt 218
Fogg, Charles Sumner 157
Foss, Thea & Andrew 28, 230
Fraser, Hugh 35
Fry, Lewis 99

Furth, Jacob 68-69, 223
Fyrk, John & Matilda 27-28, 87, 230
Garrett, David C. 189
Garrett, Garet 5
Gasch, Fred 81, 189
George, Henry 225
Gilbert, William B. 207
Gilman, Daniel 43, 153
Gladden, Washington 83
Glasgow, Joseph M. 90
Gleason, John 94-95
Glover, James 33, 34, 63
Gloystein, Anna 240
Gloystein, Charles 133-135, 226, 240
Gloystein, Salina 134-135, 240
Goldman, Emma 72
Goldsmith, James S. 205
Grady, H.C. 105
Graham, Peter 65
Granger, Walter 36, 174, 244, 245
Graves, Edward O. 179
Griffiths, David 224
Griggs, Chauncey 212, 229
Grube, Aaron 155-156
Hackett, George H. 159
Hallock, Leavitt 61
Hanford, Cornelius 108, 123, 156, 191, 207
Hanson, Andrew J. 191
Harrington, Mark 203
Harrison, Alexander 153-154
Harrison, Benjamin 23, 78, 131
Harrison, Carter H. 97-98
Hart, Samuel & Nellie 66
Harvey, William Hope 128
Hay, Marion 143
Hense, Frank 227-228
Hewitt, Henry 21, 149, 171, 229
Hill, Ed 112
Hill, James J. 13-15, 21, 114, 154, 171, 205, 231
Hobart, Mary E. 128, 224-225, 239-240

INDEX OF PEOPLE

Temple, W.G.H. 189
Thompson, Amaryllis 71
Thompson, Walter J. 29-30, 63, 71, 143
Thorne, Chester 69
Tingle, A.K. 89
Titlow, Aaron 229
Tobin, Henry 142-143
Todd, Alexander B. 120
Todd, Charles 49
Trumbull, L.G. 79
Turner, George 225
Valjean, Jean 147, 148
Vernon, James 197
Vinson, Sam, Charles 187-188
Visscher, William 100, 103, 127
Vivian, Thomas J. 120
Wainwright, Marie 177
Waite, Davis H. 73, 132, 136
Walker, Cyrus 21, 176
Wall, F.R. 168
Walling, Norton D. 161
Waterhouse, A.L. 146
Weatherwax, Clyde 170
Weatherwax, John 170
Weaver, James B. 131
West, Arnold J. 169
Westcott, George 129
Weyerhaeuser, Frederick 231
Wheatley, James 87
Wheeler, Jas. Cooper 90
Wheelwright, Samuel 27
White, Albert 95
White, Thomas 90
White, William Allen 213
Whitney, Mrs. C.L. 142
Wilcox, W.A. 139
Williams, A. 154
Williams, F.M. 92
Williams, H.B. 197
Williams, James 45
Willis, Gertie 66
Wilson, Charles R. 170

Wilson, Henry 146
Wilson, John L. 146
Wingate, Robert 63, 150, 215, 229
Wood, William D. 206, 236
Woods, Nina 166
Wright, Charles B. 52-53, 186, 199, 241-242
Wright, Orville, Wilbur 231

GENERAL INDEX

CPSIA information can be obtained
at www.ICGtesting.com
Printed in the USA
FSHW02n1017110618
49093FS